Philosophical Siblings

Philosophical Siblings

Varieties of Playful Experience in Alice, William, and Henry James

Jane F. Thrailkill

PENN

UNIVERSITY OF PENNSYLVANIA PRESS

PHILADELPHIA

Published by
University of Pennsylvania Press
Philadelphia, Pennsylvania 19104-4112
www.upenn.edu/pennpress

Printed in the United States of America on acid-free paper
10 9 8 7 6 5 4 3 2 1

Library of Congress Cataloging-in-Publication Data
Names: Thrailkill, Jane F., author.
Title: Philosophical siblings : varieties of playful experience in Alice, William, and Henry James / Jane F. Thrailkill.
Description: Philadelphia : University of Pennsylvania Press, [2022] | Includes bibliographical references and index.
Identifiers: LCCN 2021015361 |
ISBN 978-0-8122-5332-0 (hardcover)
Subjects: LCSH: James, Alice, 1848–1892. | James, William, 1842–1910. | James, Henry, 1843–1916. | Play (Philosophy) | Play in literature. | Consciousness in literature.
Classification: LCC CT275.J278 T47
2022 | DDC 973.092—dc23
LC record available at https://lccn.loc.gov/2021015361

For Cathy Kerr, my brilliant friend
(1964–2016)

CONTENTS

Introduction

"Daring to Go Lightly amid the Solemnities"

> And what are all men and women but children placed in a world of phenomena to learn, as in a vast kindergarten, in ways adapted to their sensuous and feeble apprehension?
>
> —Frank Sewall, *The Angel of the State* (1896)

Alice James: an exemplary nineteenth-century neurasthenic. William James: a foundational figure for American psychology and philosophy. Henry James: a prominent author and literary critic. These iconic figures of nineteenth-century American culture and letters are close relations, children of the storied James family, but the three siblings' writings have rarely been considered together, on an even playing field. The diarist, the psychologist, and the novelist have appeared to occupy distinct realms of cultural authority and to speak to different audiences (or, in the case of AJ's Diary, to no audience at all).[1]

This book instead reads their writings collectively, as manifesting a shared project based in play. Their writings, I argue, constitute a long-term, slow-motion conversation, deploying the vocabulary of post-Darwinian science alongside the teasing, playful idiom they cultivated as members of an eccentric and close-knit family. What WJ (only half-jokingly) said of HJ, that "He's really [. . .] a native of the James family, and knows no other country," indicates the siblings' sense of their own tight collectivism, accompanied by a sense of their quirky exceptionalism.[2] AJ, however, nuances her brother's assertion of a particular "James-ness." AJ sensuously described "the exquisite *family* perfume of the days gone by" as being "made up of the allusions, the memories and the point of view in common."[3] The

James family in fact occupied a cultural orbit with other intellectuals and artists, whose work in turn shaped their worldviews—thinkers like Herbert Spencer, Charles Darwin, Charles Sanders Peirce, G. Stanley Hall, Henri Bergson, and John Dewey. The Jameses give expression to the ways that human beings came to navigate, understand, and flourish in the contingent world of the late nineteenth century, a vibrant environment newly described by evolutionary theory and mapped by fresh work in the fields of psychology, neurology, and education.

Philosophical Siblings examines the Jameses' literary productions as complementary investigations into the phenomenology of consciousness via the embodied nature of play. Thinking, for the James trio, takes place not just within but, importantly, *outside* the mind: they play with ideas materially, through textual performance; formally, through different genres; and relationally, with significant people, places, and things. In approaching these writers through play, *Philosophical Siblings* takes seriously the kinetic and sensory aspects of what the siblings variously called "mental pirouettes" (AJ), "intellectual larking" (HJ), and simply "keeping the ball rolling" (WJ).[4] As Ross Posnock observes in his study of the two eldest of the four James brothers' complementary intellectual styles, their distinctive capacity for wide-ranging curiosity is "closely related to the aptitude for play."[5] This intellectual playfulness is manifested in an expressive style that exploits incongruity, lights up absurdities, and sometimes, teasingly, inflicts the sting of critique.

Genre, in its varieties, proves central to the Jameses' shared undertaking, for the siblings played with the conventions of their chosen literary modes, setting into motion the play of their own ideas and inviting readers to play along. AJ used the literary form of the diary, to which she brought edgy affection and disruptive humor, to convey the complex interaction of an elastic wit and an invalid's recalcitrant, aching body. WJ, trained in medicine, philosophy, and the natural sciences, used the form of the lecture—later adapted into published texts—to recruit his audiences into active, embedded mind play. HJ, best known as a novelist of psychological realism, used his more fantastic, playful works—particularly those novels and novellas focusing on children—to toy with the divergent ways that human minds envision and concretize past experiences. Youth provides a proxy for playfulness, though for the Jameses chronological age does not preclude a ludic openness to what is happening. AJ is past forty as "childish impressions of light and color" continue to saturate her senses (*Diary*, 34); an aging bachelor in HJ's *The Ambassadors* learns, finally, to "toddle alone" through the stimulating streets of Paris.[6] While the siblings arrived at different modes of writing-as-play, they are unified, I argue, in exploring the embodied, embedded, and relational aspects of consciousness—and in using their writings to bring readers into the game.

In other words, AJ, WJ, and HJ put into practice the ludic spirit. The term "ludic," derived from the Latin noun *ludus*, "refers to a whole range of fun things—stage shows, games, sports, even jokes."[7] I use the term in its capaciousness throughout the chapters that follow, which examine how the Jameses' literary works emphasize dynamic practices such as joking, teasing, and toying as resonant investigations into human experience. As the Jameses seem to know, play leads us to the nature of perception; it straddles the disciplines of aesthetics, science, and philosophy, taking up the question of agency and free choice while also attending to human beings in their sociality. Play brings ideas out from the individual into a mutual world to be messed with (the way that children learn math and spatial reasoning through counting actual manipulatives and blocks). As Johan Huizinga wrote in *Homo Ludens: The Play-Element in Culture* (1938), "In play we may move below the level of the serious, as the child does; but we can also move above it—in the realm of the beautiful and sacred."[8] To attend to the spirit of play is to foreground amusement, experimentation, and transformation as dynamic elements of literary artifacts—and as foundational to the human experience.[9]

The James siblings insist that we take seriously not the instrumental but the autotelic aspect of reading, writing, and interacting—an insistence on pleasure for its own sake. This demand runs counter to recent trends in cognitive and evolutionary literary theory, which argue for art's utility and instrumentalism.[10] Cognitive literary criticism tends to see literature as a kind of training regime for developing social skills and knowledge, and evolutionary literary critics (as Nancy Easterlin has shown) emphasize the species-level utility of making art or engaging in play.[11] For instance, Brian Boyd in *On the Origin of Stories: Evolution, Cognition, and Fiction* (2009) argues that art (like play, from which it is derived) "offers tangible advantages for human survival and reproduction."[12] For Darwin-inspired literary critics, the aesthetic part of existence hones skills and affects that promote the endurance of *Homo sapiens*: for these critics, one plays to live.

But the Jameses ask: What if we live to play? Maybe, they posit, the experience of engaged vitality reminds us *to want* to survive, and to wish for the survival of our vexatious species, which can easily think its way—individually and jointly—into a suicidal posture (what WJ called "world-sickness").[13] Indeed, for me, the sine qua non of the James siblings' contributions is AJ's refusal of suicide—her active decision *not* to die but to laugh in the face of self-annihilating misery. WJ echoes her exhilaration for facing life's contests in an essay entitled "What Makes a Life Significant," where he describes the "pathological anæsthesia" of those who are indifferent to the zest of agonistic mutuality (861). He pokes and prods and argues for the value of encounters that make us feel alive—encounters where, through intense and playful sparring, we "realize each other in this intense, pathetic, and important way."[14] HJ, too, sees (as Strether realizes in *The Ambassadors*) that the only way to lose is not to play: "Holding off could be but a losing game" (177). Taken together, these diverse states of being offer a central insight about play: like sex, play is "a pleasure for its own sake, but its genetic gift is perhaps the sense that life, temporarily at least, is worth living."[15]

This convergence of writing, play, and intimate connection between people illuminates a particularly American nineteenth-century epistemology: the way that thought and ideas can be played with in their material and embodied manifestations in the world, tossed like a ball between playful participants. Against the background hum of what WJ called "the big outside worldly wilderness with all its sins and sufferings" (863)—the revolution in nineteenth-century thought about evolution, cognition, and shared subjectivity—the following chapters unfold how the three writers approached their respective projects with *serious lightness*, an affective state that captures the central paradox of play.

"Diction and Tricks"

The Jameses were busy and productive people, and their family relationships were often conducted and sustained via letter (particularly after AJ moved her household to England and became increasingly homebound). These letters show their affectionate connectedness.[16] Indeed, such was their intimacy that a letter to one might as well be a letter to all. In a missive from WJ to HJ dated 20 August 1891, WJ assumes that his sister will also read it. He declares that AJ is "certainly the most remarkable member of the family" (*WHJ*, 257), then acknowledges "the risk of flattering" her "in view of the probability that this letter will meet her eyes!" (*WHJ*, 257).

In many ways, this particular letter is exemplary, for it condenses the Jameses' relationship. The circumstances in which the letter was written indicate the literary productivity of all three siblings in the early 1890s. WJ penned it during a vacation in Asheville, North Carolina, which was intended to help him recover from a long stint of intense work. He had recently published his highly anticipated, two-volume text *The Principles of Psychology* (1890) and had just finished trimming this magnum opus into *Psychology: Briefer Course* (1892) for general use in college classrooms. (WJ's students called the larger work "James," and the condensed work "Jimmy"—catching the Jamesian spirit of playfulness with ideas and with one another.) Completing both projects had left WJ "elaborately tired on his insides," he told his brother (*WHJ*, 256). HJ, for his part, had just published his short story "The Pupil" and was preparing a dramatic adaptation of his popular novel *The American* for the London stage. AJ, the youngest James and the only sister, was living in England and working on her Diary, a literary project known to the women of her household but not to her brothers. But although her brothers did not know of this project, they knew well her talent and wit. In a comment that now seems prescient, in this same letter WJ affirmed, "I am as sure as I am of anything that her life has been bearing its fruit, fruit not only for her, I mean, but for life at large" (*WHJ*, 257).

The letter demonstrates both the teasing banter between the siblings and their fierce loyalty—loyalty that, here, is expressed in support of WJ's writing style. In the letter, WJ revels in his siblings' outrage over a recent negative review of the *Psychology* published in the *Nation*, which homed in on the text's startling prose style. "I am much amused at your and Alice's indignation over the Nation's review," WJ writes, "which was simply an eccentric production, probably read by no one" (*WHJ*, 258). The review of *Psychology* (which, by WJ's account, had otherwise met with "great success so-far," *WHJ*, 258) disparaged it on a number of counts, but the reviewer made particular mention of "Prof. James's . . . extraordinarily racy and forcible style," which "wrest[ed] words and phrases of exact import to unauthorized and unsuitable uses."[17] The anonymous reviewer traced WJ's objectionable writing style back to the entire iconoclastic James family, an attribution that clearly tickled all three siblings: in *Psychology*, the review notes, WJ "indulges himself with idiosyncrasies of diction and tricks of language that usually spring up in households of great talent" (15). (Unbeknownst to the siblings, the reviewer was Peirce, WJ's eccentric philosopher friend whom he generously supported as Peirce tried and repeatedly failed to achieve a university position and financial solvency—not to mention a lucid, publishable prose style.)

In a Diary entry written a few days after the *Nation* review was published, AJ characterized WJ's "racy and forcible" writing style in terms of its playfulness and its lightness: "One day, talking about some good reviews of William's *Psychology*, which reprobate his mental pirouettes and squirm at his daring to go lightly amid the solemnities, H.[enry] said, 'Yes; they can't understand intellectual larking'" (*Diary*, 217). The siblings, far from disputing the "reprobation," applaud WJ's intellectual flair. The phrases that tumble forth—"mental pirouettes," "daring to go lightly," "intellectual larking"—make AJ and HJ stylistic accessories after the fact, happy to celebrate their brother's "diction and tricks" as very much a family affair. Indeed, the quoted passage continues with AJ saying, "I remember the *Spectator* once describing some of Father's flights from the Commonplace as 'coarse'" (*Diary*, 217). "Father" was Henry James Sr., a philosopher, raconteur, and writer whose style was, in the apt words of F. O. Matthiessen, "racily colloquial, satiric, stinging, and tender, in robust and ardent sequence."[18]

The terms in which AJ characterizes both WJ's and their father's writing draw on the notions of play and enjoyment ("pirouettes," "larking," "flights"), which Bergson argues occur within a circle of intimates (such as families). In *Laughter: An Essay on the Meaning of the Comic* (1900), Bergson notes that amusement defines a coterie of insiders playing off one another, bandying jokes among themselves: "Laughter," he writes, "appears to stand in need of an echo"; it "would fain be prolonged by reverberating from one to another" and "can travel within as wide a circle as you please: the circle remains, none the less, a closed one."[19] This type of amusement seems to be a James family affair, for the household indeed shared these peculiar "larky" modes of thought and expression. Thus "daring to go lightly amid the solemnities" offers a keynote for this study, which explores, explicates, and plays along with the siblings' texts as a way of lighting up the ludic aspects of their thought and practice.

A key element of the Jamesian style that this book traces is a shift from substantive nouns to transitive verbs, from static states of being to lively, embodied action. The Jameses' compositional gymnastics include gerunds such as laughing, teasing, challenging, joking, testing, provoking, flirting, probing, gossiping, and toying, which I have gathered into the subtitle, *Varieties of Playful Experience*. These verbals designate an intense sense of participation and propulsion that emerges from a desire not just to convey ideas or understand things but also to *make things happen*. Readers familiar with WJ's work will perhaps hear in the phrase "make things happen" a restatement of the method of pragmatism: the notion that "truth *happens* to an idea."[20] Louis Menand helpfully describes pragmatism as "an account of the way people think—the way they come up with ideas, form beliefs, and reach decisions."[21] Like pragmatism, play can also be seen as a method of inquiry, for both entail practical engagement and physical action: what Menand calls "getting a handle" (351) on a situation. Mary Reilly, in *Play as Exploratory Learning: Studies of Curiosity Behavior* (1974), frames play as a form of investigation: "Play, as an appreciative construct, is conceptualized as a curiosity-based phenomenon that explores outer reality through playful interaction with the environment and, in this process, the rules or the tools of mastery are fashioned."[22] As we shall see in Chapter 3, a play-based approach gives a ludic spin to HJ's turgid honorific, "The Master"—the title of Leon Edel's last volume of his five-volume biography; also, the title of Colm Tóibín's novel about HJ).[23]

But play and pragmatism are not identical. In my account, play involves five key elements, some of which it shares with pragmatism and some of which it does not. While play (like pragmatism) is social, situated, and embodied, it is also (unlike pragmatism) importantly spontaneous: artless, unmethodical, surprising. Most significant of all is that play is autotelic, done for its own sake; this is in direct opposition to pragmatism's instrumental attitude. Play is an "oxymoronous approach to puzzling reality" (Reilly 15) that is done not for profit but "for fun."[24]

These are the five core aspects of play that inform the rest of this book:

1. *Social*: play transpires in relation to other involved parties and properties.
2. *Situated*: play takes place within certain specifiable coordinates, which may involve space, rules, and implied contexts.
3. *Embodied*: play involves some element of bodily effort, reorientation, and transformation.
4. *Spontaneous*: play is free, extemporaneous, and entails acts of imagination in excess of preset or deterministic rules.
5. *Autotelic*: play is engaged in for the experience and carries powerful affective tones and textures (in shorthand, *fun*) that often, but not always, involve pleasure.

With these elements in mind, we can recognize that "mental pirouettes"—the twirling, spinning, jesting ideas that each of the James siblings sets in literary motion—are playful. They are social, characterized by an invitation (implied or explicit) to join in. They are situated, for jokes require context. They kindle responsive activity such as laughter or the synaptic sparks required to iterate and to offer ripostes. And they require spontaneity: the freedom to accept the invitation and play along—just for the fun of it.

Troping Devices: Reading Texts Under the Aspect of Play

The playful nature of the Jameses' embodied, collaborative revolving of ideas is perhaps best figured in WJ's preferred image, the child's game of playing with tops. When spinning a top, the play is situated: it "fits" in a variety of venues—a floor or an alleyway, say—and emphatically *not* in other places, such as a chapel, a bed, or table set with china. Some of the constraints on the play context are social (for example, the traditional reverence displayed in church), some are physical (the softness of the mattress), and some are a little of both (a cluttered dining table). Top spinning is embodied: children set their tops in motion using their hands, and expert top spinners may goad the toy along by a few calculated prods with a stick. One can play alone, but the spinning top presupposes the possibility, indeed, the hope, that another person will join in and increase the play's already existing spontaneity (and thereby its fun). One player may bow out and another arrive; someone's top may rebound off a wall or careen into someone else's toy. These contingencies (literally, spin-offs) change the encounter and transform the field of play in random, kaleidoscopic ways.

Like any game, playing with tops has some basic imperatives: as Dewey writes, "No rules, then no game; different rules, then a different game."[25] For instance, within the game a top must spin, not be rolled, bounced, or thrown. The play is autotelic, because it isn't done for work, to learn a useful skill, or for improvement; it is done merely for enjoyment. This social, situated, embodied, spontaneous, autotelic practice carries an implicit invitation to take part, to enter into the activity, which will necessarily (and not by premeditated design) include the possibility of caroming off of others' tops in distinctive, surprising ways.

Accordingly, AJ's idea of the "mental pirouettes," WJ's metaphor of the spinning top, and HJ's suggestive phrase "the turn of the screw" offer both an analogy and a method that I take up in the following pages. *Philosophical Siblings* investigates the narrative performances of the three published children of Mary and Henry James Sr. as "turnings," with the texts themselves as *troping devices*. I argue that their literary works are designed to do three things: to set minds in motion, to call attention to the mental motion so generated, and to enable a ludic form of deconstruction. That is, the narrative "devices" work and at the same time draw attention to their workings—they ask to be taken apart to reveal *how* they produce their turnings. Indeed, many of the siblings' literary productions (notably *The Turn of the Screw*) come equipped with what I am calling operating instructions: fairly explicit directions that encourage particular forms of engagement on the part of the reader. These troping devices, like the spinning top, afford both the activity of playing *and* the ability to pause the spinning in order to investigate the apparatus.

As is probably becoming clear, my book treats play very differently from New Historicist approaches such as Bill Brown's *The Material Unconscious: American Amusement, Stephen Crane, and the Economics of Play* (1996) and

William Gleason's *The Leisure Ethic: Work and Play in American Literature, 1840–1940* (1999). These works examine play not playfully but critically; they examine play as a cultural phenomenon aligned with consumerism, industrialization, and the entrenchment of corporate-style capitalism. The "pleasure industry" of nickelodeons and amusement parks "infiltrated human consciousness," Brown writes, by tethering thrill-seeking consumers to machines that "transform novelty into homogeneity, seriality, and boredom."[26] Literature, by his account, absorbs this cultural logic into a "material unconscious" that encrypts the truth of amusement's deceptions. The critic's task is to bring to bear "a certain kind of attention, concentration, or inhabitation" (14)—to take over the text and find the "cracks" that signal the workings of ideology: "While ideology perpetuates a fantasy of coherence, the fissures in the literary text expose the fantasy for what it is" (14). In other words, these previous studies discount the autotelic dimension of play; they insist we in a sense "break" the text to reveal its (now stilled) turnings. Play in these accounts is of interest for its (somewhat nefarious) cultural work.

Yet the purely critical attitude, says WJ, is a mistake, and the game of spinning the top can show us the pitfalls of not-playing—the problems with the unduly serious attempt of sedulous researchers to explicate an experience as it is transpiring. "The attempt at introspective analysis in these cases is in fact like seizing a spinning top to catch its motion" (*Psychology*, 160), WJ writes, a self-defeating effort that is a kind of vivisection. The idea that one can stop the play of thought to examine it, WJ urges, leads to the mistaken notion that there is a separation between our ideas and the things of the world, which they mysteriously "copy." Instead, ideas and things (like play and criticism) are all part of the same game: "Simple substantive 'ideas,' sensations and their copies, [are] juxtaposed like dominoes in a game," he writes (161). As any nineteenth-century child could advise, the best way to understand the spinning top is to play with it—to follow its course as it wobbles, receives pokes from a stick, and bumps into constraints and other spinning tops. For sustained play, sometimes careful investigation is called for. Why is the top listing to the left? Is the top's pivot dulled or bent? Is the ground uneven? But this sort of query is neither abstract nor disinterested: carried out, say, as a study in physics (arguably, another sort of game). The point of such play-oriented investigations is, of course, to get more and better playtime.

This is not the investigative attitude of previous literary critics of play (or the figure of the child) in the nineteenth-century United States.[27] *We are not amused* might be the critical mantra. This disavows any frivolous desire for fun while at the same time asserting the refusal to be duped, for as the etymology of *amuse* shows, it can also mean "to deceive" or "to stupefy." In contrast, *Philosophical Siblings* actively enlists "musement," which Peirce (who was a tough-minded logician) described as the free play of ideas that doesn't presuppose an outcome. Musement, Peirce approvingly writes, "has no purpose, unless recreation."[28] Recreation in Peirce's sense is more than a break from the serious business of life; it is literally *re-creation*: an active freshening, refurbishment, and enlivening of awareness.

What happens when we approach the Jameses' literary works under the aspect of play? For one thing, the purely analytical approaches that seek to "expose a cultural illogic" (Brown 171), compelling as they are, start to look like a spoilsport move. As Reilly describes it, "The spoilsport shatters the play world itself. . . . He robs play of its illusion, a word which literally means 'in play.'"[29] Rita Felski in *The Limits of Critique* (2015) speaks in terms similar to Reilly, when she refers to literary critics' "misguided desire to nail down a final or ultimate meaning."[30] The spoilsport move is not wrong, exactly. It's just that seeking to nail down an interpretation risks ending the spinning, stopping the fun.

Accepting the invitation to enter the play frame of a text, by contrast, allows for what Reilly calls "spinoffs." These are quite lovely: Reilly lists "reduc[ing] discouragement," "strengthening courage," and of course "fun, pleasure, and enjoyment" as "the great spinoffs" (60).[31] For each of the James siblings, the spinoffs are generative for themselves and, I argue, for readers. As the Jameses turn out narrative tools—to shift the idiom slightly, we might say narrative *toys*—for setting minds in motion, they are also generating new, different experiences. As Felski has eloquently argued, resonant texts encase delights and difficulties of new, surprising ways of thinking—all the while inviting the reader to do the same.[32] The siblings' ideas sometimes carom off one other or their intimate interlocutors, spinning off new possibilities. For example, in his work on HJ and neuroscience, Paul Armstrong describes the complex winding together of pleasure and instruction in HJ's novels using WJ's game-of-tops metaphor. Asserting the difficulty of capturing the "life of the mind" for "direct observation," Armstrong argues that the alternation between play and investigation-in-the-service-of-more-play helps explain "the joys and frustrations, the pleasures and instruction, that his [HJ's] works provide."[33] The spinoffs for the reader are myriad. Surprise becomes a possibility: a diary might set in relief the absurd structure of the human organism puffed up with a sense of potency; a psychology textbook might entice students to look cross-eyed at a figure on the page to make the dots meld together; a novel might afford ground-level insights into do's and don'ts of child-rearing.[34]

How We Think About the Jameses

Although the James family's distinctive intellectual style as a "household of great talent" (as noted in Peirce's review) has been observed by many previous scholars, fewer of these scholars have focused on the way that their literary works play off of each other. Paul Fisher examines the family culture in his *House of Wits: An Intimate Portrait of the James Family* (2008). But as Fisher himself notes, his interest lies centrally in the Jameses as a group portrait of American eccentricity: "Somewhere between the Alcotts and the Royal Tenenbaums, the Jameses come into the American story and add much to our perception of it. In their ambitions, ambiguities, and affectations, the Jameses can strike us as curiously contemporary—the forerunners of today's Prozac-loving, depressed or bipolar, self-conscious, narcissistic, fame-seeking, self-dramatized, hard-to-mate-or-to-marry Americans."[35] A half century earlier, Matthiessen offered a less neurosis-centric, more scholarly perspective in *The James Family* (1947). But while Matthiessen includes a small excerpt from AJ's *Diary* and correspondence, and quotes from a few letters written by Bob and Wilky James, *The James Family* primarily traces the intellectual effects of the father on the two eldest sons, WJ and HJ. Matthiessen's method, however, reflects his astute sense of the affectionate, performance-oriented quality of the James family writings. Describing his approach as editor, Matthiessen writes, "My own role has been something like that of the director of a play," staging the excerpts so that the family writings "were dovetailed together" with a minimum of commentary, after which he "sat back and enjoyed the performance" (v). These two biographical works on the James family, along with the truly dazzling individual biographies written by Jean Strouse (on AJ), Robert Richardson (on WJ), and Leon Edel (on HJ), have offered crucial insights for *Philosophical Siblings* about the playful and cerebral aspirations the James siblings had for their distinct yet overlapping intellectual projects.[36]

Other excellent book-length analyses have examined WJ and HJ as an intellectual dyad whose works influenced each other's thinking. For example, in his landmark 1991 study, Posnock has brilliantly argued for the brothers' cerebral compatibility and yet distinctive literary styles in their complementary investigations of selfhood, conducted through the open-eyed medium of curiosity.[37] Joan Richardson and Steven Meyer, in their respective works, pick up the experiential (and experimental) thread that extends from Ralph Waldo Emerson through WJ's radical empiricism to (HJ's) literary modernism.[38] More recently, Paul Grimstad and Kate Stanley have expanded on the James brothers' philosophical debts to an Emersonian account of experience.[39] With different emphases and beautifully meticulous readings, these critical endeavors give powerful accounts of the cognitive and affective processes enlisted by works of literature written under the banner of a Henry-and-William-Jamesian understanding of experience.

My addition to these studies begins with a deceptively small step. I take seriously AJ as a full contributor to the James family intellectual project, which aims to light up, record, and above all experience the recursive motions of human minds immersed in worlds that are, and are not, of their making. The inclusion of AJ brings along a set of elements that prove both vexing and illuminating. For one thing, attending to the writings of a nineteenth-century woman brings the slight stutter in the prior sentence—"not, of their making"—to the fore. WJ's keynote for thinking about experience could be summed up in the term "plasticity" and HJ's in the term "experimentation"—both nouns that imply agency and suggest a world susceptible to being shaped, tested, and rearranged. But AJ's rendering of experience sounds a set of minor (though not weaker) notes: disruption, resistance, concussion, endurance, obstruction. Even more than her brothers, AJ emphasizes the affective and bodily components of thinking; her edgy humor and dependence on others even to pen her Diary entries and correspondence unsettle conceptions of agency, autonomy, and selfhood. The world is not infinitely plastic, this nineteenth-century woman attests; her "Life is simply a huge joke!" (*Diary*, 56) flies in the face of Progressive Era optimism, instead tuning into the dark undercurrents of human folly and absurdity. As AJ herself said, it was her brothers who eventually "caught up" to her, not the other way around.[40] As the youngest sibling, a woman, writing a Diary in a milieu that valued the public art and science of talented men, AJ in her incarnate style and durable resistance in fact provides a linchpin for this book.

The work of AJ—her Diary, letters, and a single published work—adds an essential ingredient to critical accounts of literary pragmatism, which have examined only the complementary philosophical projects of the James men (principally WJ and HJ, although some include Henry James Sr.). AJ's work more thoroughly grounds the epistemological investigations of her brothers in the body: she examines the ways that corporeality sutures the human animal uncomfortably to the world of objects and persons and at the same time provides the basis for a shared sensibility, expressed in laughter, cringes, flushes, and the "getting" of another's surprising tics and quirks. Indeed, AJ poses a striking rebuttal to two accounts of pain: one based in connection (the sympathetic premise that pain is sharable by virtue of the mind's imaginative capacities), the other based in isolation (the materialist premise that pain is unsharable by virtue of the body's sequestered neurology). The latter is at the core of Elaine Scarry's *The Body in Pain: The Making and Unmaking of the World* (1987).[41] I concur with Cynthia J. Davis that for AJ (and for HJ), suffering has a very different telos, not separating but "tethering the imagination to the material world."[42] In her Diary, AJ delves into a ludic zone of experience, mustering what Bergson calls "the comic spirit" to open up channels for shared affection and the affirmation of a fractured (even absurd) selfhood in the face of existential threats.[43]

Between Self and Other: Plasticity in Practice

The James children, as we have seen, were themselves aware of the unusual closeness and the unique tenor of the family's intellectual interplay, and they theorized how this interchange between minds had developed. HJ, in *A Small Boy and Others* (1913), a work that blurs the line between memoir and biography, seeks to give an account of what it was like to "spring up" (to use Peirce's phrase) within the eccentric James family. A tribute to his recently deceased older brother, WJ, the book intends to "present him in his setting, his immediate native and domestic air"; yet the singular pronouns smudge into plurals: "I retrace our steps," HJ writes, "feeling our small feet plant themselves afresh."[44] In fact, the question of where one James sibling leaves off and another begins serves as a theme for the text as a whole: "We were, to my sense, the blest [*sic*] group of us, such a company of characters and such a picture of difference, and withal so fused and united and interlocked, that each of us, to that fond fancy, pleads for preservation" (5–6). The recipients of an intermittent education, the James children moved from school to school and witnessed a procession of tutors and nurses as the family traveled through Europe at their father's whim. HJ spoke of "our small vague spasms of school" (108); WJ later noted that they grew up "zig-zag";[45] AJ recalled the atmosphere of family life as loving yet fickle, with a "definite portion of friction and serenity" (*Diary*, 78). HJ praises the "felicities of destitution" caused by the constant uprooting and erratic schooling, "which kept us, collectively, so genially interested

Figure 1. A portrait of the James family ("this heavenly group") sketched by William James and included in a letter home: (from left to right) sister Alice, mother Mary, father Henry Sr., brother Wilkie (Garth Wilkinson), Aunt Kate (Catharine Walsh), and brother Bob (Robertson). By permission of the Houghton Library, Harvard University: MS Am 1092.9 (2501).

in almost nothing but each other and which come over me now as one of the famous blessings in disguise" (40). The cultural and intellectual centers of New York and then Newport, Rhode Island, along with the sights and spectacles of Europe, provided the perceptual playground for what HJ dubs "our small opening minds" (40).

The question that preoccupied HJ—how the "unschooled" James children nonetheless came to know the world and its inhabitants—had a deceptively simple answer. The adult siblings agreed that they learned through experience, by appreciating, digesting, adapting to, and embedding themselves in the world into which they were thrown. *A Small Boy and Others* is thus a "tale of assimilations, small and fine" (182), along with "some easy accommodations" (128). Encapsulated in the concept of experience is a radical insight, one that is implied in the promiscuous pronoun swapping of the text: that "others" are central to self, that there is an irreducibly outward dimension to human life. What may look like individual happenings and individual selves are embedded—and indeed conjoined—in a common world inhabited by other persons, other bodyminds.[46] For small children, *assimilation* of novel objects and events into their understanding and the reciprocal *accommodation* to the stubborn intransigence of the world's qualia (hot stoves, adults' authority) happens not in solitude but within the context of an "us." This relational rhythm of push-me-pull-you, rough-and-tumble, assimilation accommodation can be seen as an organic version of the game of tops: though here the toys (human beings) are equipped with neural plasticity, a penchant for kinship, the capacity for pain and pleasure, and feelings of autonomy.

As children, the James siblings' "small opening minds" were directed toward each other and the world, an imbrication articulated by twenty-first-century philosopher Alva Noë in his *Out of Our Heads* (2009). "The child," Noë writes, "is always already in a context in which shared feeling and mutual responsiveness are a given": "Young children take for granted that they and others share a common world and also common interest in that world, and [. . .] this assumption leads them to be unable to fathom that the attention-grabbing pull of the chocolate itself won't be experienced by others as it is experienced by them. But far from showing that they have no conception of the minds of others, this shows that they have no conception of the minds of others as private and unobservable. And in a way they are right about this."[47] It is this interconnection of James minds that is so visible in their work. Sharon Cameron, in her important book *Thinking in Henry James* (1991), has noted that in the novelist's late fiction what we expect to be internal and subjective transpires *between* characters.[48] Rather than "she thinks," it is more apposite to say "thinking happens."[49] Yet these three James siblings do more than provide a biographical case study of a strange mode of interpersonal attunement; all of them actively theorize through their work the ways that minds—which, crucially, are embedded in sentient bodies—meet in the world.

The Jameses' explorations of interconnected consciousness were taking place during a period in which child minds—and human consciousness more broadly—were objects of research for thinkers in the fields of education, child development, and psychology; these explorations, in turn, drew on Darwinian ideas of environmental adaptation. For example, Dewey's investigations into how human beings learn were based not in assumptions about atomized agents and inert objects (a child and lesson, say) but in the unfolding experiences that transpire in particular situations and in relation to the object world. In *Experience and Education* (1938) Dewey affirms, "An experience is always what it is because of a transaction taking place between an individual and what, at the time, constitutes his environment, whether the latter consists of a person with whom he is talking about some topic or event, the subject talked about being also a part of the situation; or the toys with which he is playing; the book he is reading (in which the environing conditions at the time may be England or ancient Greece or an imaginary region); or the materials of an experiment he is performing" (44). Dewey's studies in child learning index the intellectual shift after 1859, when Charles Darwin's *On the Origin of Species by Means of Natural Selection* was published, which made human childhood a vital object of scientific investigation. (Indeed, Darwin himself inaugurated the field of child study with his article "A Biographical Sketch of an Infant," published in the journal *Mind* in 1877.)

Nineteenth-century researchers investigating the peculiarly human brain and nervous system identified an unprecedented adaptive advantage: the fact that, as WJ wrote, "organic matter, especially nervous tissue, seems endowed with a very extraordinary degree of plasticity."[50] Plasticity means the ability to take an impression, to be shaped by external forces, to sustain the new form, and even to design environments and devices that help cultivate transformation. Neural plasticity allows humans (especially children, whose brains are far more plastic than those of adults) to adapt to and learn from the people, events, and things around them. Child's play interlocked with this new understanding of biology and came to be seen as modeling a receptivity essential for developing the cultural capacities—language, learning, and love—that allow human beings to flourish in a volatile, demanding world. Karen Sanchez-Eppler makes an important point about the modern view of childhood, which is also peculiarly Jamesian: "One of the transformations wrought by the study of childhood is the reevaluation of conceptions of autonomy, power, and agency," which has led to an emphasis on "interdependence or partial dependence" and on "the precarious power of the partial subject."[51] For thinkers of the late nineteenth century, children modeled the curiosity, experimentation, and cognitive intimacy central to the serious cultural pursuits of philosophical inquiry, scientific research, and literary arts.

Raised and (erratically) educated in this intellectual climate, by a childish philosopher father and a self-sacrificing mother, the James siblings' lifelong intimacy and conversational sparring cultivated their adaptive capacities and put the notion of plasticity into practice: "Teasing," Strouse writes, "was a favorite form of social exchange in the James household."[52] More important, I argue, for AJ, WJ, and HJ, biography meets biology: as the young Jameses were coming of age, the dispositions and activities associated with immaturity—such as making jokes, playing games, manipulating toys and tools, fabricating stories, wrestling with persons and ideas—were newly understood as adaptive survival strategies. Evolutionary theories provided a new lens on everyday experience, lending significance to even the most homely gestures.

Between Self and World: Affordances and Genre

In their work, the Jameses actively theorize how plastic minds (crucially embedded in sentient material bodies) meet in the world. Indeed, their investigations laid the conceptual groundwork for a range of twentieth- and twenty-first-century fields of study, including cognitive neuroscience, play studies, affect theory, and ecological psychology, which investigates human perception as it is situated in particular environments. For example, the modern concept of *affordances* (common in fields ranging from various subdisciplines of psychology to technical fields studying user-computer interactions) is based in this contextual view of human minds as embedded in their circumstances. In Anthony Chemero's definition, affordances describe "relations between the abilities of an animal and some feature of a situation."[53] James J. Gibson, credited with originating the idea, describes the concept of affordance as liminal: "An affordance is neither an objective property nor a subjective property; or it is both if you like. An affordance cuts across the dichotomy of subjective–objective and helps us to understand its inadequacy. It is equally a fact of the environment and a fact of behavior. It is both physical and psychical, yet neither. An affordance points both ways, to the environment and to the observer."[54] This definition should remind us of WJ's assertion that the things of the world are not separate from our ideas about them but instead are parts of the same game: "Simple substantive 'ideas,' sensations and their copies, [are] juxtaposed like dominoes in a game" (*Psychology* 161). An affordance has a twinned existence "in" the world and somehow "in" another entity—a betwixt-and-between state that removes its "ontological respectab[ility]" (183), according to Chemero.

When we think in terms of affordances, things in the environment become invitations to *do* something—implicit, material calls to (inter)act. Works of fiction are precisely invitations of this sort. Terence Cave and Caroline Levine have made the case for thinking about fiction in terms of affordances: as Levine puts it, "The idea of affordances is valuable for understanding the aesthetic object as imposing its order among a vast array of designed things, from prison cells to doorknobs."[55] The affordance reminds us that we can kinetically connect with aspects of the environment—for example, Dewey's toys, books, and test tubes, or WJ's printed dots inviting undergraduates to cross their eyes—to serve a variety of needs. Embedded in the world are potentialities that we can spin off into improvisations of our own. As Cave argues, this is as true of literary genres (which, like the Jameses' troping devices, use forms and conventions to coax particular readerly acts) as it is of "tools, instruments, and devices of all kinds" (49). And when the responsive improvisation tips away from practical effects and toward autotelic affects—when it spins off into sheer mental and emotional play—the behavior becomes aesthetic: the zone of art, of pure human vitality.[56]

The idea of a resourceful organism positioned in a resonant environment filled with opportunities and dangers was a defining concept for nineteenth-century thinkers after Darwin. Indeed, during the decades on either side of 1900, philosophers, scientists, and artists developed, without explicitly naming, the idea of affordances. Evolutionary psychologists and play theorists pointed out the importance of toys and other persons for scaffolding thinking, entities that we must append to Cave's list of tools, instruments, and devices. As WJ observed, for any human being, "the most important part of my environment is my fellow-man."[57] Affordances can also be thought of in terms of genre. A diary, a series of lectures, a work of fiction: each of these, as we shall see, call out certain kinds of perceptual behaviors while cutting off others.

Narrative is a natural fit for the study of minds at work. Indeed, science and literature, once seen as opposed, in the twenty-first century are finding shared fields of play. As literary scholars increasingly turn to the sciences and philosophy of mind to understand how readers engage with and respond to texts, scientists are turning to literature to see how minds work, for literary works, as a "special expression of mind and culture," *represent* thinking as well as constitute it.[58] *Philosophical Siblings* is thus poised at the intersection of literary studies, the history of science, and cognitive theory. It describes the James siblings' overlapping projects, all of which sought to understand and express how human beings adapt, persist, and resist in order to navigate changeable cultural and physical milieus. The three Jameses initiated complementary investigations into the phenomenology of consciousness—the lived textures of, say, carrying on a conversation while propped up by cushions, or teaching students to dissect a brain, or toddling around Paris in late middle age.[59] As Jonathan Kramnick has said of contemporary works by Ian McEwan and Marilynne Robinson, the James siblings' literary productions are "written with attention to the science and philosophy happening around them, but with a mind to contribute via the unique properties of their medium."[60]

The siblings are unified, I argue, in exploring the embodied, embedded, and relational aspects of consciousness—a preoccupation that reflects their engagement with ideas circulating "around them" as well as between and indeed through them. These explorations have left a lasting impression on modern studies of consciousness and cognition: Chemero has argued that "radical embodied cognitive science is a direct descendant of the pragmatism of American naturalists William James and John Dewey."[61] In this book, I therefore put the Jameses in conversation with theories about human cognition being developed today by their intellectual descendants who are working across disciplines to investigate the complexities of human consciousness in action. As the book argues, AJ, WJ, and HJ, in their philosophically playful, action-oriented writings, light up the ways that thinking takes place: not just inside skulls but through written expression; not just cerebrally but through acts of movement, gesture, and projection; and not just in isolation but through intimacy with other minds. The Jameses' thinking about consciousness itself arises communally, affectively, and iteratively. As my book shows, they do not merely present a theory of mind; they dramatize it in their writings as a practice, they *play it out*. I accept the invitation to mindful play that the texts extend.

What to Expect

As noted earlier, I take my subtitle from what is perhaps WJ's most popular and enduring book: *The Varieties of Religious Experience* (1902), which originated in talks that he delivered in Edinburgh for the prestigious Gifford Lectures in natural theology. In this work, he proposes to "play fair" with hard-to-pinpoint, spiritual-feeling experiences of "immediate luminousness": not to root out their "hysterical" sources or to reduce them to the firings of neurons, but to explore their significance and felt meaningfulness (25). WJ investigates these experiences phenomenologically, "following the purely empirical method of demonstration" (53). He sought to specify the many manifestations of the religious in people's lives though case studies, by attending to the "*feelings, acts, and experiences of individual men in their solitude, so far as they apprehend themselves to stand in relation to whatever they may consider the divine*" (36, emphasis in original).

This same empirical and phenomenological (rather than purely critical) spirit animates the ensuing chapters, which, following WJ's example, also serve as case studies. I focus each chapter on a sibling, showing how each manifests a different aspect of play, which, again following WJ, I see as the feelings, acts, and experiences of persons in their sociality, so far as they apprehend themselves to be freely engaged in an autotelic activity they consider beyond the seriousness of everyday life. There is a paradox in play, just as there is in religious experience, insofar as both designate what Huizinga calls "a sacred space, a temporarily real world of its own," which often feels more saturated with significance than the "real world" it rises above—or sinks below.[62]

Each of the book's author-centered chapters picks up a particular story line—disruption, plasticity, experimentation—that unsettles the deterministic and functionalist narratives associated with nineteenth-century biological science. But these are not simply themes that I have abstracted from the texts; each story line is set in motion by a practice—joking for AJ, teaching for WJ, and toying for HJ—that is artful, enlists affect, entails performance, and depends upon reciprocity. In turn, each chapter enters into and sets in motion the playful practice it describes. These practices have both textual and "real-world" expressions: indeed, they call attention to the act of making palpable and invite instantiation of ideas through action. In this sense, these practices serve not just as representations but as *manifestations.*

The chapters weave together philosophical, scientific, and literary sources as they trace a commitment to the serious playfulness shared by these remarkable siblings. Their writings take up questions of intimacy, of collaborative thinking, of contact, of transformation: of what it means to come into correspondence with one's self, other human beings, and the world beyond the flesh. AJ, WJ, and HJ had common intellectual roots and influences; despite the divergence of their life trajectories, they sustained lifelong affection and overlapped in how they sought to express lived experience in written form. The literary projects of all three investigate, as well as invite, body-based expressive practices; they publicly manifest, at the level of style, what transpires within what Huizinga calls "the play-ground of the mind" (119). Taken together, the writings of these related turn-of-the-century thinkers provide multifaceted case studies in the phenomenology of literary encounters—what the subtitle refers to as "varieties of playful experience."

Studying the James siblings jointly affirms a productive kinship among fields of study. While literary scholars think primarily about works of written expression, we have something to learn from work being done—both now and a hundred years ago—in cognitive science and evolutionary biology. The reverse is also true: psychologists and biologists can learn from literary study. Arts of mind such as playing, joking, imagining, and toying are illuminating as well as enticing: as Alison Gopnik observes, "[Because we] can learn about our environment, we can imagine different environments, and we can turn those imagined environments into reality."[63] (In an apt spin-off, Gopnik cites HJ's preface to *The Ambassadors* as shedding light on children's psychology: "Many authors describe their fictional imaginings in much the same terms as children do [their imaginary companions], as if they were independent people who just happened to be nonexistent" [63]). Fiction, seen from this perspective, is a fertile blend of the child's capacity for confabulation and the adult's technical expertise, animated by curiosity and provoking new perceptions. Resonant literary texts manifest human beings' natural capacity for culture; harking backward and spinning us forward, they are the collective result of centuries of artful minds at work and at play.

CHAPTER 1

Alice's Bite

Body-Based Humor in *The Diary of Alice James*

> Our laughter is always the laughter of a group.
>
> —Henri Bergson, *Laughter* (1900)

For just under three years, while Henry James worked to adapt his novel *The American* for the London stage and William James put the finishing touches on his textbook *The Principles of Psychology*, Alice James kept a diary. She composed the first entry in the spring of 1889 and dictated her last entry from her deathbed, in early March 1892. Her friend, caregiver, and amanuensis Katharine Peabody Loring added a final entry in the diary, before having the whole text printed and delivered to AJ's surviving brothers in 1894. Loring's appended note begins, "All through Saturday the 5th and even in the night, Alice was making sentences. One of the last things she said to me was to make a correction in the sentence of March 4th 'moral discords and nervous horrors.'"[1]

Astonishingly, even as AJ was "being ground slowly on the grim grindstone of physical pain," she was revising the passage that recorded her anguish—while also praising her friend's "rhythmic hand" that inscribed the entry and kept her suffering at bay through massage (232). The final pages of the diary are expressive of great intimacy and care. Yet the last sentence of AJ's entry nonetheless musters a small joke about her companion's multitasking: "Katharine can't help it, she's made that way, a simple embodiment of Health as [Dr.] Baldwin called her, 'The

New England Professor of doing things'" (232). Mere hours before she died, AJ was editing passages and teasing the woman who committed them to paper.

This chapter analyzes how AJ's Diary, composed as it is of many tones, accents, and concussive expostulations, constitutes a form of kinship, bodying forth a strikingly literal form of what Mikhail M. Bakhtin calls *heteroglossia*.[2] AJ's multivocal Diary is written in a conversational, disjointed style and gives expression to a cacophony of voices, from friends and family to neighbors, staff, authors and public figures. The Diary incorporates, in Bakhtinian fashion, bits and pieces from other genres, such as the newspaper, letters, parliamentary proceedings, poems, memoirs, philosophical tomes, and jokes. In these moments "the heteroglossia of the clown sound[s] forth" (273) as different linguistic registers—that of rural England, elite America, official theology, governmental commissions, lyric poetry, and parlor humor—jar against each other. Some of the voices and dramatic scenarios are supplied by HJ and other visitors to AJ's English households, primarily a boardinghouse in Leamington Spa and—during the final year of her life—in Kensington, a close suburb of London. Others come from members of AJ's immediate domestic circle or float in through thin walls that permit close if impersonal acquaintance with the private lives of other boarders. The Diary from start to finish filters and incorporates the perspectives of both intimate and far-flung others—sometimes offered unwittingly, as in the case of her brothers WJ and HJ. At times, the influence of intimates is expressed directly on the pages of the Diary, when a prostrate AJ dictated entries that were inscribed in the hand of Emily Ann Bradfield (referred to as "Nurse" in the Diary) or Katharine Peabody Loring. The pages are riddled with AJ's sense of life's daily absurdities, her frustrations with her troublesome maladies and ineffectual physicians, and her self-deprecating amusement at her own prostration and egoism. She herself is the most frequent butt of her jokes.

Yet AJ, I argue in this chapter, has the last laugh; in her hands, the diary form becomes a device for manifesting and managing the incongruities of daily existence. She develops and deploys her own comic sense, one that innovates on the traditional modes elucidated by theorists of humor to become a form of philosophical play. Joking, as mobilized by AJ in her letters and in her Diary, is an existential practice that stages the conflict between autonomy and dependence, between isolation and intimacy, and between embodiment and transcendence. For AJ, this practice becomes a way of translating sequestered, frequently painful human subjectivity into shared and thus manageable experience—as well as a way to pull back and assert fractured but potent selfhood. The personal diary offers a forum to dramatize a self struggling to make sense of its own mortality, to express intensities of affection and filial belonging, and to engage questions that include, but extend beyond, what we commonly think of as the subjective or psychological. Indeed, humor for AJ offers an indispensable way of making sense of material existence in a species endowed (and afflicted) with the capacity for self-reflection. Like a fun-house mirror, AJ's Diary magnifies the tiny and shrinks the grand. In this way the Diary serves as a troping device that tampers with the conventional calibrations of a staid society and troubles the pat diagnoses of medical culture.

AJ's corporeal experience is essential to the Diary, though not in the way biographers and critics have traditionally understood it to be. Leon Edel begins his preface to the 1964 publication of AJ's Diary by emphasizing her poor health and the slightness of her literary productivity: "The Diary of Alice James, invalid sister of the psychologist William and the novelist Henry, represents her modest claim on posterity beside the works of her famous brothers. She kept the record of her sickroom world in two closely-written scribblers during the final months of her abbreviated life."[3] This perspective, centering invalidism, has set the tone for James critics following Edel, though scholars of nineteenth-century American women's writing have offered illuminating readings of her Diary in light of disability studies, her manipulation of the diary as a genre, and her struggle to assert herself intellectually within the family.[4] Recently, Cynthia Davis has powerfully argued that AJ's experience of bodily pain helped to shape her exquisite consciousness, a rarified sensibility that distilled from material woes an almost vaporous perceptiveness.[5]

Whereas WJ praised her wit, and HJ wrote that her "rich irony and humor" marked the Diary as constituting a "new claim for the family renown," even perspicacious critics have largely sidelined the humor of AJ's writings.[6] Biographical details have no doubt played a part. AJ did not begin writing her Diary until the age of thirty-nine, and she died in 1892 at forty-two of breast cancer. She had been living in England since 1884, cared for intermittently by Loring and a small staff. And it is true that in her final years AJ ventured outside infrequently, often propped up by cushions in a Victorian wheelchair operated by an attendant. Many days she was unable to rise from her bed. In a life so familiar with suffering and disability, focusing on humor could seem strange, even unethical.

Yet Bakhtin provides terms for understanding AJ's turn to the comic as a complex form of existential inquiry: "Laughter demolishes fear and piety before an object, before a world, making of it an object of familiar contact and thus clearing the ground for an absolutely free investigation of it. Laughter is a vital factor in laying down that prerequisite for fearlessness without which it would be impossible to approach the world realistically. As it draws an object to itself and makes it familiar, laughter delivers the object into the fearless hands of investigative experiment—both scientific and artistic—and into the hands of free experimental fantasy" (23). Fearless experimentation, as we shall see, is an apt phrase for AJ's Diary, with its comedic anecdotes, amusing gossip, ironic asides, off-beat vignettes, self-deprecating reflections, puns, quips, jibes, and black humor. AJ, operating on what Bakhtin calls "the plane of laughter," is able to "disrespectfully walk around . . . the back and rear portion of an object (and also its innards, not normally accessible for viewing)" (23). The "object" for AJ is frequently her own person, hence Edel's accusation of egotism. She positions herself, however, as a "member," of a household, a family, a nation, and ultimately the human comedy writ large.

The Diary's unsettling effects redound on the beloved brothers whose perspectives it also incorporates. In a letter to WJ, AJ wrote, "When I am gone, pray don't think of me simply as a creature who might have been something else, had neurotic science been born. Notwithstanding the poverty of my outside experience, *I have always had a significance for myself*."[7] One can hear the echo of AJ's admonition to WJ in his essay-lecture entitled "On a Certain Blindness in Human Beings," published in 1899, five years after Loring gave him a printed copy of the Diary. WJ affirms that, despite the obtuseness of onlookers, even those in "prisons and sick-rooms" possess a "higher vision of an inner significance" and harbor profound feelings of "conscious, burning, willful life."[8] This chapter reads AJ's Diary with her explicit instructions in mind, seeing it not as the record of a thwarted life but as a formally innovative, ticklish work of body-based philosophy rooted in everyday lived experience.

AJ's correspondence—often overlooked in discussions of her Diary—is the focus of the next section. In her letters, AJ experiments with the teasing colloquies and wry, body-based perceptions that predate—and in some cases, were written in parallel to—her Diary. Letters provide a vehicle for the siblings' networked affection and shared humor, while also calling attention to the physical body and its tendency to obstruct connections. I then examine AJ's humor in relation to other theorists. Biographer Norman Malcolm writes, "It is worth noting that [Ludwig] Wittgenstein once said that a serious and good philosophical work could be written that would consist entirely of *jokes* (without being facetious)."[9] AJ in her writing proleptically takes up this challenge: in theorizing the comic, she actively *makes* jokes, recruiting literary modes that seek to record and elucidate life's absurdities.

Next I discuss the Diary as contact sport. AJ's biographer Jean Strouse has emphasized the Diary's privacy, noting that "the only people who were aware of the Diary while Alice was alive were Katharine Loring and Alice's nurse."[10] Edel, in his preface to AJ's Diary, notes its role as an "anodyne against loneliness and desolation," a feature he attributes to spinsterhood that is never remedied since "no Robert Browning came to carry off Alice to some Italy of her own" (8). These accounts, however, underplay the extent to which intimates within and beyond her household play significant roles in constituting the Diary. Within, they were themselves instruments and catalysts of its production; without, they appeared as foils for AJ's banter and, not infrequently, as the target of her jokes.[11] In AJ's hands, joking packs a punch.

I then make the case for the "minorness" of the Diary, reframing this notion to emphasize—as AJ herself does—the peculiar potency of the small. Gilles Deleuze and Félix Guattari's conception of a minor literature helps to explicate the Diary's stylistic and thematic experimentation, which plays out in relation to children, expatriation, and Irish home-rule politics. In a section entitled "The Cosmic Joke" I follow AJ into what she calls her "mortuary moment" (218), where she addresses what it means to live by choice, to abjure suicide and face mortality. The concluding section urges that the Diary, ultimately, presents a koan, a philosophical puzzle rooted in paradox. As such, the Diary itself—which, when her brothers held printed copies in their hands, delighted and dismayed them—constitutes the most influential joke of AJ's career.

The emotional, sensory, and philosophical impact of the Diary, this book argues, reverberates in key writings of WJ and HJ. AJ activates interruption, jolting surprise born of incongruity, and dark humor throughout her writings, giving readers a homeopathic dose of contingency and unpredictability as she wrestles to bring life and death into the realm of human agency.

Epistolary Affection and Bodily Travails

Letters carry with them the back-and-forth element of conversation—albeit a conversation with days- or weeks-long gaps between reply or riposte. Within the James family, letters were common property, frequently passed from hand to hand, and AJ's in particular—at the beginning and the end of her life—were occasionally written in different hands. Handwritten missives, many of which crossed the Atlantic Ocean by boat, modeled for AJ a mode of expression that was simultaneously intimate and public. Letters marked separation but conveyed poignant presentness; they embodied beloved familiarity through texture, tone, and style. "The rich robustness of Father's texture is simply overpowering," a middle-aged AJ wrote to her sister-in-law Alice Howe Gibbens James in 1890, after receiving a cache of old letters from her (then deceased) parents: "This has been brought home to me by the arrival of the dear old Davenport about a fortnight ago, in it were father's & mother's old letters. I fell upon them and wallowed for two days in the strangest & most vivid experience. I had to tear myself away for pathologic causes & I do not dare return yet, but they are perpetually soliciting me; like living things sucking me back into the succulent past of this anomalous death in life—an existence as juicy as that of a dried cod-fish! They both *exist* so in their letters!" (188–89). These penned missives carried material and existential potency, conjuring deep affective ties with an immediacy that made the middling dailiness of adult life pale in comparison. AJ transforms this rush of feeling into "spinster-like" advice for her sister-in-law's children: "Bend all your energies to instil in them the most conservative habits with regard to their family letters, *their own*, as well as the rest, they will have priceless value in time" (188). Engaging in correspondence, casting identity into the textual clasp of a letter to a loved one, is the stuff not just of adulthood but also of childhood.

Happily, much of AJ's correspondence has survived and been collected.[12] And whereas Ruth Bernard Yeazell has called AJ's youthful correspondence "girlish and naïve, conventionally mild in their sentiments" (8), even her early letters reveal an ear for mockery and a penchant for irony. As a child, AJ writes a letter to her father describing WJ's "extraordinary state of mind, composing odes to all the family," including a mock-heroic poem to their Aunt Kate (Catherine Walsh, Mary James's sister). "We have all come to the conclusions that he is fit to go to the lunatic asylum," she writes, "so make haste home before such an unhappy event takes place" (49). At the bottom of the letter, in her brother Bob's hand, is the addendum, "All Alice's *own composition* except the first sentence. She wanted to be started" (53). Keeping in touch was a collective priority, and these missives scaffolded AJ's emerging sense of sibling identity.

Passing along humorous tales of each other's goings-on was a staple of the family correspondence. Strouse has written perceptively about the young WJ's proclivity for writing mock-romantic letters to or about his sister.[13] The letters AJ herself composed as a teenager reflect her awareness that James family humor often devolved on women, who were cast in the role of "straight man" to male wit. When WJ was studying in Europe, young AJ gave him a full report on a comical dinner table conversation at the family home in Cambridge:

> I will recount to you some jokelettes of the Harriette which will probably bore you, but which at the time they were perpetrated amused this innocent family very much. The scene is laid in the dining-room, time, dinner.
>
> Harry to the mother. "May I have some of those brown-rolls that were left this morning at breakfast."
>
> M. "Yes, certainly, but do you wish to eat them with your soup." H. "You can't certainly expect me to minutely explain what I intend to do with them." Laughter from the family & pause. H. "I was coming over the bridge this afternoon and stopped a run-away horse." You may easily imagine the shouts of the family at this. A.K. [Aunt Kate]. "I hope you did not try and stop him by the bridle." H. "Would you prefer to have me take hold of his legs." A.K. "But you should not run after horses and stop them." H. "Would you have me run before them." You must let your imagination supply the manner of this Harry, a good deal of eyebrow nostril and shoulder affectation. (52)

AJ continues the letter in this vein, quoting a joke that she'd shared with Mary James and adding to the humor by appending their mother's absent-minded reply: "I read to mother the other day . . . that there was a paper printed in Paris on some sort of material that could be eaten after read, consequently the contents would be well digested, whereupon mother remarks in her charming way, why that's very true, isn't it?" (56). This tiny vignette shows AJ at a young age testing out the family humor—laughing with WJ at the expense of their mother—and picking up on "digestion" as a flexible term that brought the brain and the gut into incongruous correspondence.

Diagnosing Alice

Biographers have noted the Jameses' tendency to dwell on their bodily ailments. WJ's son would later itemize his father's youthful afflictions: "Insomnia, digestive disorders, eye-troubles, weakness of the back, and sometimes deep depression of spirits followed each other or afflicted him simultaneously."[14] Uncomfortable and fluctuating, Jamesian complaints largely skirted the pathos that would attend major or mortal illness. Henri Bergson's *Laughter: An Essay on the Meaning of the Comic* (1900) provides a lens for thinking about the "paltry" yet frustrating presence of the body. For Bergson, "When we see only gracefulness and suppleness in the living body, it is because we disregard in it the elements of weight, of resistance, and, in a word, of matter; we forget its materiality" (25). The impression of the comic, by contrast, appears when "we are shown the soul TANTALISED by the needs of the body: on the one hand, the moral personality with its intelligently varied energy, and, on the other, the stupidly monotonous body, perpetually obstructing everything with its machine-like obstinacy. The more paltry and uniformly repeated these claims of the body, the more striking will be the result" (25). Bergson's terms—resistance, obstruction, obstinacy—are put into play in AJ's correspondence. Because of his own neurasthenic tendencies, WJ recommended the salutary effects of time spent walking in nature, and early in his married life he purchased a bucolic retreat in Chocorua, New Hampshire. AJ's letters home from rustic travels push back against WJ as purveyor of medical advice and offer AJ's own spin on the fleshy discomforts of what Bergson calls the "stupidly monotonous body."

AJ held her own when writing letters about the vexations of the body—and WJ. She writes to her friend Sara Darwin (who had recently married the son of Charles Darwin), "I made a bold push and started off with Katharine Loring for the Adirondacks to try William's panacea for all earthly ills" (80). Contra her brother, AJ describes their woodsy abode as a "shanty" that "lacks nothing in the way of discomfort," including "little crawlers" who looked upon her "as a delectable and succulent . . . feast" (81). The corporeal irritations are myriad: "We perched ourselves on the sharpest stones we could find and religiously spent endless hours in listening to the babbling water, the gentle hum of the mosquito, giving joy untold to the sportive midge who found me quite the loveliest production civilization had as yet sent to him" (81). She rejects WJ's enthusiastic, masculine embrace of time spent roughing it at Putnam Farm, in the wilds of New York State, joking to her friend, "I assure you that for purposes of cutaneous refreshment a tub in the hand is worth fifty brooks in the bush" (85). Sigmund Freud, three decades later on his only trip to the United States, would separately affirm AJ's assessment of Putnam Camp's discomforts: biographer George Prochnik writes that "after returning to Europe Freud insisted for the rest of his life on referring to his 'American Colitis,'" having "blamed the New World for ruining his digestion."[15]

Digestion and the indignities of the belly become fodder for letters. To her friend Frances Rollings Morse, AJ writes in 1884, "I came to the conclusion that I was the lowest of organism with absolutely no insides but a stomach" (89). Were her digestion "in order," she imagines her indominable good spirits and physical vigor: "The universe might crumble and I should be found dancing a jig on top of the heap" (89). Regarding her health, AJ chaffingly claims authority over others' points of view—including that of her two oldest brothers. "The excellent Henry's pathological apprehension is as vague as his financial & both a direct inheritance from Father," she writes to WJ, "so that any account of his of my insides, or rather what may have been said about them, . . . could hardly have much scientific accuracy" (117). AJ overwrites HJ and lists for WJ the latest diagnoses—"a gouty diathesis," an "abnormally sensitive nervous organization," and "legs neurosis"—along with the startling symptom of "hav[ing] had sixteen periods the last year" (118). This is surely a rare instance in correspondence of a sister informing her brother of the oddities of her menstrual cycle.

For psychoanalysis, the hysterical body is an open book of symptoms, rewarding the diagnostic gaze. AJ in her letters reverses the trajectory of the gaze. She documents the physicians who come and go in her life, casting them as a series of comedic characters who are invariably ineffectual. Of one Dr. Garrod, AJ writes to her sister-in-law Alice Howe Gibbens James, "On Saturday afternoon . . . a round, genial ball of seventy rolled into the room with whom I passed the most affable hour of my life, an old fellow all rounded & smoothed by tradition, with all the graces of the mendacious Slave & the honesty of the angular Oliver" (97). She concludes that "they ought to have a lot of lesser men, like tenders to do their dirty-work for them, curing their patients etc." (100). In a postscript she praises HJ, who "show[s] no outward sign of impatience at having an old man of the Sea [AJ] indefinitely launched upon him"; and she envisions herself as his appendage: "I am afraid that he will find me attached to his coat-tails for the rest of my mortal career" (100). AJ makes explicit the target of her mordant wit: "These details, medical, are for William's delectation" (97).

The network of edgy affection is on display in another letter that AJ sent to her sister-in-law. She dictated the letter, which was penned by her nurse, and the text of the letter creates a composite speaker as everyone in her South Kensington household watches breathlessly for reviews of WJ's recently published *Principles of Psychology* (1890) and the opening of HJ's play *The American*: "I am going to ask of you a sisterly favour, that you should tell us of any *favourable* notices there may be of William's book, as we are quite out of the way of getting any here. Our absorbing interest just now is of course Harry's dramatic debut at the end of next month. . . . How Harry, Katharine & I are to live through the first night I have no idea" (184, 185). A later letter to WJ, dictated to Loring, begins self-reflexively with a joke about her amanuensis: "A thousand thanks for your beautiful & fraternal letter, which came, I know not when, owing to Katharine's iron despotism" (185). The joshing rubs up against the purpose of the correspondence, which is to respond to—and remonstrate with—her brother's sympathetic note upon hearing his sister had breast cancer. Referring obliquely to her Diary, an accomplishment as yet unknown to WJ, AJ affirms what she calls "my task," which, she writes, "[I] could carry about in my pocket & work away upon . . . in complete security from the grotesque obstructions supposed to be *life*, which have, indeed, only strengthened the sinews to whatever imperfect accomplishment I may have attained" (187). Here AJ hints that what looks like an obstructed life provides, in her case, the resistance necessary for creative expression. Part of the "grotesque obstructions supposed to be *life*," for AJ, were the pitying perceptions that her sympathetic correspondents had of her.

In the give-and-take of epistolary exchange, in other words, AJ frequently found herself playing defense. When WJ tries to sympathize with her residence in England, hinting that the cloudy days and dim winter light might engender spiritual gloom, AJ offers resistance in the form of a laugh: "I was much amused and entertained by your description of the 'aureate darkness'" (98). When WJ urges her to place herself in the hands of a physician, she portrays her reluctance not as passivity but as the wise course of a weary warrior: "It may seem supine to you that I don't descend into the medical arena, but I must confess my spirit quails before any more gladiatorial encounters. It requires the strength of a horse to survive the fatigue of waiting hour after hour for the great man & then the fierce struggle to recover one's self-respect" (107). These letters from AJ, studded with prickly humor, serve as instruments precisely to recover her self-respect with respect to WJ.

The Brothers' Constipation Letters

AJ wrote openly about "that omnivorous Organ of mine"—her stomach—detailing in a letter addressed to "Dear Aunt, brothers & sister" how she was "rent by perpetual & violent indigestion" during a passage across the Atlantic (98). Her brothers, however, were not always as forthcoming. In the fall of 1869, WJ and HJ began an intense correspondence about their disrupted digestion. "I blush to say that detailed bulletins of your bowels, stomach &c as well as back are of the most enthralling interest to me," the older brother writes to HJ: "A good plan is for you to write such on separate slips of paper marked private, so that I may then give freely the rest of the letter to [sister] Alice to carry about & re-read and wear in her bosom as she is wont to. If you put it in the midst of other matter it prevents the whole letter from circulation."[16] At the time they corresponded about the ill health of their backs and bowels, neither brother had formalized his life's work: HJ's travels in Europe were intended to jump-start his writing career, and WJ was at loose ends himself, living with his parents and sister while studying medicine (a pursuit he would soon drop). HJ writes to his older brother, "Mother . . . gives me your message—that you want awfully to write, but that you've so much to say you don't *dare* to begin. . . . I was extremely interested, as you may suppose, in her mention of Dr. Wilkinson's diagnosis & prescription for you. I *palpitate* to hear more" (50). Blocked bowels, the letters suggest, are somehow involved in writer's block. The missives HJ sends to WJ during this period are a bizarre blend of the impressions he is harvesting from his European sightseeing, his desire to shape his writing into publishable form, and the meticulous depiction of what WJ calls his "dorsal insanity" (45)—that is, constipation.

AJ, as well as her parents, are exempted from what WJ referred to as their "constipation letter[s]," letters that become an elaborate, riffing conversation on the links between literary expression and defecation (54). The inability to have a bowel movement becomes intertwined with HJ's difficulty focusing on his writing projects: "My condition affects alike my mind & my body," he writes, punning on his inability to "get a daily passage" (49). "*I can't get a passage*," he reiterates, with emphasis (49) and, nine days later, "my bowels horribly stuffed and my head infernal" (45).[17] WJ writes encouragingly about dietary remedies—figs, aloe, rhubarb—as well as his brother's literary prospects. "I can't help hoping that . . . there will be a distinct *precipitate* from your experience" (58; emphasis added), again blurring the lines between creative and digestive output. HJ describes his diet while traveling as heavy on roasts and boiled beef. WJ replies, "It doeth my very gizzard good to think of you being able to lay all those *meaty experiences* to your soul" (62, emphasis added)—punning on the dietary and the cultural sustenance from other lands.[18]

Over the course of the fall of 1869 the brothers played with the topic of obstruction, bemoaning the lack of "passages" yet frankly producing a voluminous correspondence in the meantime. Bergson's body-based theory of humor provides a gloss on the odd productivity and off-beat humor of WJ and HJ's digestive concerns. For Bergson, the "claims of the body" override the mind's impulses (25). For the prolific letter writers, the hand—that part of the body that casts the mind's creativity into visible form—gives way to the potency of the gut. WJ is emphatic that HJ must place himself "in the hands of a Doctor" (4). Mind over matter is the explicit goal as HJ seeks relief from the "fatal grasp" of his bowels (*HJ Selected Letters*, 47). Unfortunately HJ's "little squirt"—a self-applied enema—hasn't worked: "Somehow or other I *must* take the thing in hand" (*WHJ Selected Letters,* 49). The doctor HJ sees "to keep me in hand," as he puts it, found "no palpable obstruction"—a non-diagnosis achieved "by the insertion of a finger (horrid tale!)" (*HJ Selected Letters,* 45).

WJ had recommended a system for keeping HJ's letters out of the hands of twenty-one-year-old AJ, casting her as a sentimental girl who tucked family letters next to her heart. AJ, on the other hand, perceives herself as fiercely, ironically, potent. "To have a tornado going on within one, whilst one is chained to a sofa, is no joke," she darkly jokes in a letter to WJ (109–10). Whereas the brothers kept their digestive trials (somewhat) private, AJ calls out a character that plays an active role in family conversations: "that dissipated organ known in the family as 'Alice's tum'."[19]

Inside Jokes and Interwoven Selves

AJ's personal documents—letters sent and received, and later her Diary—were shared openly and often composed with intimates; these latter created a play frame for small inside jokes. In a letter she sent to her Aunt Kate in December of 1888, for instance, AJ enlisted the help of her nurse, dictating not just her thanks to her aunt for enclosing a monetary gift for the holiday but also a tease for "Nurse," her amanuensis Bradfield, about her appetite. Flush with the sudden influx of cash, AJ dictates: "I shall invest it in some luxury, otherwise unattainable. I feel very rich, of course, at not having to pay the tax, and have abandoned trying to devise means of reducing Nurse's food, so as to make two ends meet" (156). Emphasizing Bradfield's financial dependence, AJ in the next line calls attention to her dependence on the young woman: "I am sorry not to be able to write myself," she says, before going on to describe how another tenant in her boarding house had recently given birth (156). The "battle" had "raged" for a day and ended with the death of the infant. Her amanuensis makes a heroic appearance in the tale: "After Nurse had towed my heart back to its moorings by Digitalis & poured a sufficient amount of Bromide upon my gunpowder nerves, I returned to my ordinary passivity, although not serenity" (156).

Through the act of writing AJ communicates with Nurse as well as her aunt and offers further instructions for handing the letter along the James network of affection: "You might send this [letter] to Cambridge"—where WJ and his wife were living—"as I shan't be able to write them for some time" (157). The epistolary collaboration continues, in a postscript written in HJ's hand, which explains some messy editorial corrections inked onto the prior pages: "Alice sends this because of her recent troubles; she has improved the 'Liege's' letter before she sends it off—At first I could hardly understand it. I don't want this back. But send me back the one which Alice sent me" (157). Apparently, HJ had tucked into the envelope yet *another* letter for Aunt Kate to read (and pass along), written by AJ to HJ on a prior occasion. This collaboratively composed and circulated missive creates a literary arena for the expression of James intimacy.

Letters that reflect on—and frequently ridicule—the manners and mores of the English further tighten the circle. To Aunt Kate, AJ derides British culture as "fetid with scandal & the voice of the evil tongued" (112). She jokes in her letters about English ladies' "*au pied de la lettre* [literal-minded] nature," which "rather arrests the flow of analytical & rhetorical gymnastics" (112). Ludwig Wittgenstein described shared humor as a form of play. The reverse is also true: an inability to share a laugh can mark a chasm that is at once cognitive and affective. "What is it like for people not to have the same sense of humor? They do not react properly to each other. It's as though there were a custom among certain people for one person to throw another a ball that he is supposed to catch and throw back; but some people instead of throwing it back, put it in their pocket."[20] AJ recounts in the letter how "the other day I said something to one of them about things being more or less chaotic at home," only to have her English guest—apparently thinking of Boston's revolutionary history—reply, "'Why I thought there was very little that was *wild* about Boston *now*'" (112). As Strouse writes in her biography of AJ, "Her letters during this period [London, 1886] show her honing her wit and literary skills."[21]

In these jesting micro-narratives AJ reaffirms a shared sensibility with a selected audience. Indeed, these jokes quite explicitly index this function. She laughs at her English visitors' inability to find *her* amusing: "I *simmer* with a Goethian like sense of my own superiority. A few virtuous matrons have come to *nibble* at me but no one worth recording, they all seem like the tamest of tame Boston, Boston minus the capacity for understanding one's jokes or one's misguided flights of rhetoric" (107, emphasis added). This letter to WJ portrays lofty intelligence and a sense of grandeur diminished to a light meal, adding a mild metaphorical flavor of cannibalism for pure amusement. In *On Humour*, Simon Critchley argues that "joking is a specific and meaningful practice that the audience and the joke-teller recognize as such. There is a tacit social contract at work here, namely some agreement about the social world" (157–58).[22] The letter establishes a horizontal field for sibling relations, and it references, obliquely, the omnipresence of AJ's bodily exigencies—which are indexed "on" the text by Nurse's handwriting and "in" the text by the onomatopoetic metaphors of simmering and nibbling. Taking aim at her visitors, AJ invites the laughing complicity of her brother (and others) back in Massachusetts.

The circulation of letters, with tidbits of news, brisk retorts to prior missives, and ongoing inside jokes, constitutes a form of play. Like fencing, or a domesticated Greek chorus, there is parry and riposte, stroph and antistrophe. Metaphor, of course, can be defined as a play on words. Johan Huizinga observes that poetry is the literary form that best expresses the flights and rhythms of play, writing that the figurative use of language is "a product of the age-old game of attraction and repulsion played by young men and girls in a spirit of badinage," or, in other words, that playful banter is a part of courtship.[23] AJ pushes against this heteronormative understanding, suggesting that sibling behavior may be more primal than courtship—though of course that construal begs the chicken-egg question of whether siblinghood predates mating relations. Elizabeth Duquette, writing of AJ's Diary, describes it as a bid for establishing her cerebral standing in the family: "The result is a text that explicitly strives to establish Alice's credentials as a thinker, but, more importantly, as a James."[24] I would refine this point to say that AJ's letters—especially those written from England in the 1880s—do not seek to elevate her as a thinker so much as to create a shared field of play. The world they create is both intellectual and affective, in which to be a James *intime* is to be amused by and thus to "get" each other.

Even in her correspondence, we begin to see that joking in AJ has another valence, one that expands her practice to include the empirical and philosophical alongside the affective and personal. Her late letters, written at the same time she is composing her Diary, use dark humor to point up the effortful task of sheer existence. In January 1889, after "having rolled over in my bed with laughter" at WJ's praise of her letters' sharp observations and literary flair, AJ writes to him about her slow improvement over the new year: "Fate decreed that I shd. begin the year from the very bottom of my little hill & now Sisyphus-like I have begun the climb again. Henry was like an angel & watched beside my couch for a week, but a whirring heart & panting breath are such child's play compared to what might be" (159). She describes her physical incapacitation as an "aesthetic incongruity" but resolves to persevere because "there are a good many jokes left still, and that's the main thing after all" (185). Her literal-minded physician, she jokes, prefers her in sickness rather than (relative) health: "As my symptoms decline & my conversation revives I sicken him more & more" (160). When AJ tried to explain to him her morbid fixation with her neighbors—"My mind is simply *cramped* upon those people upstairs!"—the doctor's face was blank: "As H[enry] said, 'He knew there was no dose for it at the chemist's'" (160).

Unable to catch AJ's humor, the physician occupied the same room but not the same worldview. By appending HJ's quip to serve as a satisfying punchline, AJ enlists WJ's amusement, closing the circle of reverberative mirth. Behind the humorous tales of baffled physicians is that entity that is pervasive in all of AJ's writings even when—or as we shall see, *especially* when—she is not describing it directly: her body.

The Limits of the Letter

In her letters AJ gives friends and family oblique glimpses into the material disruptions that characterize her quotidian existence. Her jokes, anti-aesthetic anecdotes, and bouts of laughter offer little "explosions" that simultaneously draw on and dislodge shared assumptions about social life and women's everyday experience in the nineteenth century. The circulation of letters among family members and occasionally friends gives her a medium for recasting her bodily pains, diagnoses, and indignities into amusing anecdotes. Still, the epistolary genre has its limitations. For one, the sending of letters depends on reciprocity, which constrains to some extent the nature and content of replies. As with many families, letters among the Jameses were frequently used to convey information about money matters and information about the wider family and circle of friends, especially key events such as marriages and births. Moreover, as demonstrated by the brothers' constipation letters, the very fact of their circulation conditioned the nature of what was expressed—especially before the deaths of the elder generation.

AJ does test out taking the epistolary genre to the next level of circulation. A short letter penned by AJ appeared in the *Nation* in 1890, which she wryly signed with the pseudonym "INVALID."[25] Dated the fourth of July, the letter offers AJ's version of American girlhood, a whirling dervish of energy and amusement: "Although so far from home, every now and then a transatlantic blast, pure and undefiled, fans to a white heat the fervor of my patriotism" (139). Quoting the published letter in its entirety in her Diary, she goes on to recount how an American lady and her daughter, seeking lodging in AJ's boardinghouse, were warned that "there was an invalid in the house; whereupon the lady exclaimed, 'In that case perhaps it is just as well that you cannot take us in; for my little girl, who is thirteen, likes to have plenty of liberty and to *scream* through the house'" (139). Spared the cacophonous experience of an unruly teenager, AJ takes pleasure in aligning herself with the "white heat" of tumultuous American femininity—only revealing in the signature line that she is in fact the "invalid" who could not tolerate the ruckus.

Writing about this publication in her Diary, AJ tries to explain the point of her joke. In the process she makes a wry commentary on both the letter and the English newspaper's amusingly stilted translation of it. As if in response to critics like Edel who point to her scanty literary productivity, she jokes about her truncated experience of anonymous authorship, casting herself as a competitor to her brothers: "A *European Reputation* at the first go off! How fortunate for the male babes that I am physically so debile!" (139). She pushes the joke further:

> In comparing notes with H.[enry], I find that had I brought forth *The Tragic Muse*, I could not have gone through with more *author-processes.* As so often happens in a work of genius I had to leave out the chief points, fearing length and editorial veto: which was that Miss C.'s [her landlady's] passive manner of relating the tale illustrated very well the absence of reaction in the British masses against the accidents of life, making an instructive contrast of type to that of the aggressive infant from beyond sea and the inability of the American Mother to imagine a momentary suppression of the screams in favour of the Invalid; but Shakespeare may have felt Othello commonplace! (139–40)

AJ uses the Diary as a troping device that "turns" the original publication, presenting a different viewpoint. The static invalid is no longer the narrator (as she is in the published letter) but a character, as AJ-as-narrator-of-the-Diary kicks the diegetic level up a notch. The Diary entry brings together invalid and girl, her authorship and Shakespeare's, into a playful assemblage, thus reasserting and indeed ramping up authorial agency. In this way the "clumsy body"—the invalid, the tiny publication—crackles with energy born of incongruity and audacity. Changing the back-and-forth rhythm of letters, this entry instead resembles a dynamo that generates excess energy from a series of turnings.

The Diary: A New Literary Play Space

Though she does not give up letter writing, by embarking on the Diary in 1889 AJ creates a new field of play: one in which she will (as she puts it in the first entry) "have it all my own way" (25). Strouse interprets this as a move from publicity to privacy, to a zone of safety outside the masculine sphere, because a diary makes "no claim as a work of art or an intellectual argument."[26] I would suggest that, as a forum for creativity, AJ has taken the epistolary genre as far as she could. She moves from early exploration (as when Bob helps her "get started"), to imitation (of family wit), to outright competition (with WJ, especially). Shifting genres, she enters a realm where she can innovate and test the affordances of a diurnal, nonreciprocating literary form.

Christina Sjödblad has argued that the private diary as a genre emphasizes interiority, offering a space where women in particular could explore and "confront their inward life, ask questions, and develop their identities outside the roles that society offered them."[27] Yet AJ, in an early entry discussing the private writings of George Eliot, embarked on a cutting critique of the British novelist's emphasis on interiority, rumination, and self-conscious probings into her private experience: "Read the third volume of George Eliot's Letters and Journals at last. I'm glad I made myself do so for there is a faint spark of life and an occasional, remotely humorous touch in the last half. But what a monument of ponderous dreariness is the book! What a lifeless, diseased, self-conscious being she must have been! Not one burst of joy, not one ray of humour, not one living breath in one of her letters or journals" (40–41). AJ continues with ad hominem descriptions that liken the introspective elements of Eliot's journals to blobby organisms that thrive in airless caverns: "Whether it is that her dank, moaning features haunt and pursue one thro' the book, or not, but she makes upon me the impression, morally and physically, of mildew, or some morbid growth—a fungus of a pendulous shape, or as of something damp to the touch" (41). Eliot's novels, in AJ's estimation, transmute life's absurdities and sorrows into the sublime ("compact of wisdom, humour, and the richest humanity" [41]). The least (or perhaps the most) that her journals could do is give voice not to "futile whining" but rather to the comic element of human existence (42). The want of humor in Eliot's personal writings makes them merely "the *vehicule* for a moan" (42, emphasis added).

What, then, do we make of AJ's own decision to keep a diary? The very fact that AJ uses the "vehicule" of the diary to attack a celebrated writer is an enticing paradox, though it becomes apparent that her beef is not with Eliot the writer (she adored *The Mill on the Floss*) but with a literary form keyed to solipsistic subjectivity. She deplored the pursuit of inwardness for its own sake. Most introspection, she suspects, is unexamined self-worship masquerading as a quest for self-knowledge. AJ writes of Marie Bashkirtseff, a Russian woman known for keeping one of the most intimate and yet widely publicized journals of the nineteenth century, "What a sense of superiority it gives one to escape reading some book which every one else is reading . . . and so far I have not succumbed to Marie [Bashkirtseff's] *Journal*. I imagine her the perverse of the perverse and what so dreary to read of, or what part so easy to act as we walk across our little stage lighted up by our little self-conscious footlights?" (125). Keeping the spotlight on the self being staged ("surrendering . . . to a Colossal Vanity" [120]) and broadcasting "all the cowardices, follies and self-love" (120) through the medium of publication are at odds with her own project: seeking the meeting of minds in a shared world.

AJ shifts away from Bashkirtseff to a home-grown writer—Emily Dickinson—committed to exploring the existential realms of experience. In a Diary entry dated 6 January 1892, AJ comes close to stating explicitly her own project: to use her own "purely innocuous" self as a medium for exploring what it means to live a human life in a fallible human body—which includes *deflating* the inevitable human penchant for self-inflation, rather than merely exemplifying it: "It is reassuring to hear the English pronouncement that Emily Dickinson is fifth-rate, they have such a capacity for missing quality . . . what tomes of philosophy *resumes* the cheap farce or expresses the highest point of view of the aspiring soul more completely than the following—'How dreary to be somebody / How public, like a frog / To tell your name the livelong day / To an admiring bog!'" (227). The mode for expressing human truths must be comedic rather than bathetic or tragic. The earnest portrayal of the grinding nature of routine existence (like the merely personal journal) or abstract philosophizing that eschews contact with frogs and bogs misses the interplay of the material and the spiritual, the domestic and the cosmic. Human existence, AJ hints, transpires in an in-between zone and follows a ludic rhythm of self-aggrandizement and self-abasement—which depends on the puncturing perspective of intimate others. Dickinson's wit inheres in the capacity to voice the inflated perspective of the "aspiring soul" while humorously personifying it (really, "amphibianizing") with the image of a frog swelling his gullet with air to emit a croak. The key is to catch the motion and the tension, not just the "dreary" matter. The Diary as AJ reimagines it is an elastic form that can, like an instrument, be played, and thus sound "its own rhythm, its own style, its own timing, its own value," as Jennifer Sinor has written.[28]

Humor and the Diary

With its short entries, the Diary supports a staccato syntax, with sudden changes of tone, mood, or subject. An entry can shrivel to portray "wretched little demolishing trifles" or swell to encompass the "Masters of the world" (113).

Comedic contraction and expansion in the Diary operate like an accordion: inflation is essential, but deflation is what actually expresses the sound. AJ plays with the figure of a bellows in describing her mind at play, using her Diary to capture "those exquisite moments of mental flatulence which every now and then inflate the cerebral vacuum" (66). On the one hand, she diminishes herself as empty-headed; on the other, she aggrandizes herself as infused with the potency born of pressure. She refers to herself as a "feeble reed" (66)—calling to mind the free-reed, bellows-blown instruments like the melodeon, harmonica, and concertina. As musicians know, the tones of these vary depending on the player's wind and the instrument's shape. (WJ, hearing of AJ's death, wrote to HJ: "What a life! I can't believe that that imperious will and piercing judgment are snuffed out with the breath.")[29] Breath and body: an apt figure for the Diary's presentation of AJ as both narrator and character. The intensity born of (frequent) incongruity and (occasional) rupture echoes through the writing, as the little sister riffs with, complains to, amuses, unsettles, and in the end jolts her accomplished brothers. The Diary becomes both instrument of and figure for her peculiar and potent body-based expression.

The very first entry of her Diary displays AJ's twinned attraction and resistance to the genre, while also giving a sly tutorial in its ludic style of hermeneutic play. The first line begins audaciously with an echo of René Descartes—"I think"—a beginning that places the emphasis on the erect singular pronoun, with its implication of an authorial ego backed by a reasoning mind. This self-assertive start falters almost immediately and lapses into the conditional tense, dropping the hope of clarity and concreteness, instead entering a terrain characterized by uncertainty: "I think that if I get into the habit of writing a bit about what happens, or rather doesn't happen, I may lose a little of the sense of loneliness and desolation which abides with me" (25). The assertive beginning belies the smallness of the aspiration at hand; the language of getting *into the habit,* of writing *a bit,* expresses routine rather than grand endeavor. Yet the end of the sentence enters new, existential territory characterized by *abiding loneliness and desolation.*

The voice in the Diary emerges from and speaks to a void; the invocation of human anguish, however, marks the connection to the material world. Doubt for Descartes is a hypothesized state, a mere tool for thinking; AJ, by acknowledging anguish at the outset, gives a hint of its phenomenology, what it *feels like,* to cast off on "a turbulent sea of doubt upon which one is tossed without pilot or compass" (202). Descartes doesn't acknowledge seasickness, stomach churning, or gnawing uncertainty. Despite acknowledging the real potential for wreckage, the voice in the Diary is eager, anticipatory—even mischievous. For, of course, uncharted waters offer an occasion for discovery and adventure. AJ's first entry all but replicates in its final clause the playful performative *ready, set, go!*—"So here goes, my first Journal!" (25). In AJ's phrasing, the Diary becomes less a noun than a verb: something that, presumably, one might "do"—and keep doing. While AJ often tips toward despair, at other moments she acknowledges the potential for rapture as long as one allows for the sensory to inflect one's philosophy. "When," she queries in a later entry, "will men pass from the illusion of the intellectual, limited to sapless reason, and bow to the intelligent, juicy with the succulent science of life" (225)?

Recording What Doesn't Happen

AJ in her first entry sets herself a version of the riddle of the Sphinx: she will fill the Diary with "what happens"—a nonspecific, stretchable clause that could encompass precisely everything—then appends a corrective, "or rather, what doesn't happen," an even broader, paradoxically infinite category. It is possible, of course, to read the object of the Diary—writing "what happens, or rather what doesn't happen"—as mild, self-deprecating humor. Read in this vein, the demurral calls attention to the daily (non)experience of the invalid, a person whose circumscribed life lacks the absorbing events generally associated with middle-class womanly life in the 1880s: keeping house, being a helpmeet to a husband, raising a family, attending church, making the social rounds, and so on. But it is also possible to read this first sentence of AJ's Diary as meaning almost the exact opposite, that only in the privileged space of lack (including the lack of paid work afforded by a small but comfortable annual income) could a certain kind of existential truth be discovered and tested out.

To support this reading, one can harken back to one of the most quoted statements from HJ at the time AJ was writing: his famous account of the absent things in American life. In his early work of criticism on Nathaniel Hawthorne, HJ expands on the "ludicrous" number of "items of high civilization" that the United States lacks, "until it should become a wonder to know what was left."[30] HJ's negating catalogue is longer than Hawthorne's—"No sovereign, no court, no personal loyalty, no church, no clergy, no army, no diplomatic service, no country gentlemen, no palaces, no castles . . ."—and culminates with this affirmation of cultural desolation: "The natural remark, in the almost lurid light of such an indictment, would be that if these things are left out, everything is left out. The American knows that a good deal remains; what it is that remains—that is his secret, his joke, as one might say" (43). HJ's list, written at a youthful age, may describe a land where "everything is left out," but affectively it sustains the urbane, cultivated tone of a cosmopolitan at home in the world. HJ is unflustered by the "negative side of the American social situation," and he casually points to "our author's Diaries" (that is, Hawthorne's) to discover "the minuteness of the things that attract his attention and that he deems worthy of being commemorated" (43). Unlike AJ's account of Eliot's inward-focused journal, HJ describes Hawthorne's diaries as rich with outwardly focused observations about "walks in the country, drives in stage-coaches, [talks with] people he met in taverns" (43).

The "joke" for HJ is that an American writer can find his material in simple wayside places and persons, such as the dusty archives of the Custom House (for example, *The Scarlet Letter*) or an upscale watering place in Switzerland (for example, *Daisy Miller*). AJ, a single woman transplanted to an English boarding house, is neither Hester Prynne nor an innocent abroad; she does, however, take a page from HJ and Hawthorne in identifying the Diary as a likely aesthetic response to the apparent paucities of living under constraint. Early Diary entries, especially, are devoted, Hawthorne-like, to her observations of the landscape in and around her rented quarters in Leamington Spa. Yet even in this regard AJ registers her edgy sensibility: "If I make this a receptacle for feeble ejaculations over the scenery, what a terror it will be" (37). AJ is the complicated, uncomfortable, intellectually dazzling author of her own experience, registering her own sharp opinions. Her list of *present* things in English life is powered by a combination of biting satire and moral outrage:

> A monarchy to which they bow down in its tinsel capacity only, denying to it a manly movement of any sort; a boneless Church broadening itself out, up to date; the hysterical legislation over a dog with a broken leg whilst Society is engaged making bags of 4,000 pheasants, etc. etc., or gloating over foxes torn to pieces by a pack of hounds; the docility with which the classes enslave themselves to respectability or non-respectability as the "good-form" of the moment may be; the "sense of their betters" in the masses; the passivity with which the working man allows himself to be patted and legislated out of all independence; thus the profound ineradicables in the bone and sinew conviction that outlying regions are their preserves, that they alone of human races massacre savages out of pure virtue. (88)

She registers the brutal incongruities that reflect, to her mind, "the absolute want of humour in the Briton at large" (30). And, as we shall see, AJ is the perpetrator of her own jokes, thereby using the episodic affordance of the diary to develop an anti-aesthetic method of surprise, interruption, and disjuncture.

To return to the opening sentence of her Diary: AJ's terse commitment to writing "what happens"—with its expanding/negating appositive, "what doesn't happen"—compresses HJ's capacious list, even as it inflates her brother's cry, "no Oxford, nor Eton" (43), to include the more minor notes of existence, including human existential distress. AJ continues the brief entry with the following: "My circumstances allowing of nothing," she writes, "but the ejaculation of one-syllabled reflections, a written monologue by that most interesting being, *myself*, may have its yet to be discovered consolations. I shall at least have it all my own way and it may bring relief as an outlet to that geyser of emotions, sensations, speculations, and reflections which ferments perpetually within my poor old carcass for its sins . . . !" (25). Having suggested she is a person without a life—"my circumstances allowing of nothing"—AJ marshals irony in claiming the title of "most interesting being" even as she demotes herself from the subjective pronoun *I* to the objective possessive, *myself*, and then to "my poor old carcass." Yet "hav[ing] it all my own way" pushes back against passivity and stasis. In sum, the very first entry swells and deflates in a most remarkable manner.

Testing the Relief Theory of Humor

A number of critics have read AJ's first Diary entry in therapeutic terms, and indeed to twenty-first-century minds there would appear to be a self-help element at play. Taken in conjunction with AJ's writing about Eliot's journals, however, this first entry in fact points us toward the Diary's philosophical aspirations. First, we know from AJ's response that she resists the equation of the diary as a genre with psychological interiority, insofar as it shifts the focus inward toward a subjectivity understood as private. Instead, AJ's explicit and richly worded disgust at the merely ego-centric, and her wish for Eliot's diary to exude a "living breath" or "ray of humour" (41) savors of Friedrich Nietzsche in *The Birth of Tragedy* (1872), for whom the "repulsive thoughts about the terrible or absurd nature of existence" can only be redeemed through the representations of "the sublime, whereby the terrible is tamed by artistic means, and the comical, whereby disgust at absurdity is discharged by artistic means."[31] Second, the Diary entry's explicit reference to relief invokes not a psychoanalytic writing cure but rather Herbert Spencer's physiological psychology and his relief theory of humor. And even that invocation is ambivalently handled: AJ does not simply affirm Spencer's theory but herself makes a joke out of it.

In his essay *The Physiology of Humor* (1860), Herbert Spencer poses the question: "Why do we smile when a child puts on a man's hat? Or what induces us to laugh on reading that the corpulent Gibbon was unable to rise from his knees after making a tender declaration?"[32] The answer, for Spencer, lies in the hydraulics of human perception. An unfolding event generates a quantity of "mental excitement" (401). If something incongruous or disproportionate transpires, the energy from the original "mental strain" comes out in a "gush of agreeable feeling" (399). The analogy is with a balloon, swollen with air, suddenly released in a whoosh. But not just any disproportion between expectation and outcome produces mirth. Spencer mentions the despair and pity evoked by "five loaves and two fishes among a multitude" and a "decrepit man under a heavy burden" (400). To be ludic, the shift of scale must go downward. "Laughter," Spencer concludes, "naturally results only when consciousness is unawares transferred from great things to small—only when there is what we may call a *descending* incongruity" (400). Arthur Schopenhauer similarly emphasizes the centrality of scale incongruity to humor, pointing out that laughter is catalyzed when the particular outstrips the general, what he calls the "incongruity of sensuous and abstract knowledge."[33] The two theories, relief and incongruity, help to explain the aptness of Thomas Huxley's famed joke about his scientific rival Spencer, a thinker whom WJ came to disparage for his unduly abstract synthetic philosophy. Spencer's idea of a tragedy, Huxley quips, was "a beautiful *theory* destroyed by a nasty, ugly, little *fact*."[34]

AJ's first Diary entry essentially repeats Spencer's relief theory of humor (fermentation, ejaculation, geyser, outlet, relief) when she describes her reason for writing the Diary in the first place (25). By titling herself "that most interesting being" (25), she pokes fun not merely at her own stature or worthiness as a literary subject but at the self-inflation presupposed by the genre itself (recall her "supreme boredom" with Eliot's published journal [41]). She yokes *carcass* to *sins*, mixing the language of the abattoir with the language of religion and piety (25). The forerunner of the secular diary was the spiritual autobiography, which pitted corrupted flesh against the transcendent spirit. Christianity would explain the existence of pain for women in childbirth, and death for all human beings, in the sin of Eve, a woman seeking knowledge. With quite extraordinary compression, AJ offers a reminder that in an attempt to be philosophers, human beings were afflicted with mortal bodies.

Echoing Spencer's physiology, AJ in her Diary secularizes the source of suffering, locating it within the frail human organism and producing a dialogue between her supple mind and her recalcitrant body. As she reflects back on her efforts to study lessons as a child, exercising her intellectual abilities, she describes the revolt of key organs and body parts: "the pit of your stomach, the palms of your hands, the soles of your feet" (150). "Brain" and "head" made the motions of mind excruciating: "The most impossible sensations of upheaval, violent revolt in my head overtook me so that I had to 'abandon' my brain, as it were. So it has always been, anything that sticks of itself is free to do so, but conscious and continuous cerebration is an impossible exercise and from just behind the eyes my head feels like a dense jungle" (149–50). Yet despite this apparent dualism, AJ frequently figures consciousness as itself a material entity: a muscle that may be strained, fatigued, exercised, or overstretched. When something captures her attention, her mind grasps and takes hold—almost literally. Of the man, who may or may not be drunk, hired to pilot her Bath chair, AJ writes, "I wish my mind were not so cramped upon Somers, but his spine does make the most blood-curdling oscillations from the perpendicular" (42). As her impression of British hypocrisy increases—it "leave[s] a dent in the mind"—she consults HJ's opinion, "not wanting," she writes, "my view to become cramped upon conclusions" (88, 87). Though she herself doesn't find Mark Twain's *A Connecticut Yankee in King Arthur's Court* especially funny, she is more derisive of the response of English critics, who stiffen at the American writer's irreverence toward Arthurian legend. She writes, "To let the wit play lightly about what has long been taken with solemnity is a somersault for which the muscles of their minds are not limber eno'" (78). Repeatedly, AJ notes "how fatally the want of humor cripples the mind" (45); conversely, she revels in moments of expansion, no matter how homely: "One's wavering little individuality stands out with a cameo effect and one has the tenderest indulgence for all the abortive little *stretchings out* which crawl in upon the memory" (208).

As with Spencer's relief theory of humor, there is a hydraulics to AJ's enlistment of her "small" life for literary purposes. Like Dickinson's croaking "frog," a humble physical form (a woman, a brain, a "scribbler," as Edel called AJ's notebook) that stretches to contain the vast, the multiple, the immaterial: this is AJ's definition of a joke. Katharine Loring, the untiring manager of her medical care and domestic affairs, is AJ's figure for this. "Notwithstanding the wear and tear of Time and the burden of three invalids upon her soul and body she seems as large a joke as ever, an embodiment of the stretchable, a purely transatlantic and

Figure 2. Photograph of Alice James and Katharine Peabody Loring, c. 1889–90 at Royal Leamington Spa; of Loring's presence in his sister's life, Henry James remarked: "There is about as much possibility of Alice's giving Katharine up as of giving her legs to be sawed off" (quoted in Linda Simon, introduction to *The Diary of Alice James*, 12–13). By permission of the Houghton Library, Harvard University: MS Am 1092.9 (4598).

modern possibility" (56). (HJ echoes his sister's assessment, referring to Loring as "the heroic, the colossal Katharine" [*WHJ*, 264].)

In AJ's household, the joke is often on her—and she records such moments with special relish. A brief entry (dated 12 January 1891) begins as a comment on the busy schedule of her stalwart companion: "Katharine is a most sustaining optimist; she proposed writing for me this morning. I said, 'Why, you won't have time.' 'Oh, yes, I'm not going until twelve, and by that time you are always back again in bed, fainted'" (164). What begins as a statement about her friend's usefulness to AJ's imperious will—Loring is a "sustaining" presence who frequently takes dictation as AJ lies in her bed—twists into a wry observation about AJ's all-too-predictable fainting spells. An unruly body that can be counted on like clockwork, a seeming subordinate clearly in charge, rolled together and expressed with brisk economy: these ingredients migrate into the Diary as a sort of Laurel-and-Hardy act of imperiousness meeting its comeuppance.

Deflating the Superiority Theory of Humor

AJ uses her Diary to depict, and also to pop, her own bubbles of self-satisfaction and (fleeting) feelings of superiority. "How men are fated," she writes, "to prick with their own hand the bubble of their pretensions" (75). In this way she mobilizes the hydraulics of Spencer's relief theory of humor to write against the grain of the diary as a vehicle for the performance of an interior self. Here is an extended entry in which AJ depicts the interior motions of consciousness, her ballooning sense of vanity, followed by her socially chastened egotism. She inaugurates the anecdote by claiming the broad philosophical sweep of her experience: "It's amusing to see how, even on my microscopic field, minute events are perpetually taking place illustrative of the broadest facts of human nature" (48). What follows transpires while AJ is being dressed by Bradfield:

> Yesterday Nurse and I had a good laugh but I must allow that decidedly she "had" me. I was thinking of something that interested me very much and my mind was suddenly flooded by one of those luminous waves that sweep out of consciousness all but the living sense and overpower one with joy in the rich, throbbing, complexity of life, when suddenly I looked up at Nurse, who was dressing me, and saw her primitive, rudimentary expression (so common here) as of no inherited quarrel with her destiny of putting petticoats over my head; the poverty and deadness of it contrasted to the tide of speculation that was coursing thro' my brain made me exclaim, "Oh, Nurse, don't you wish you were inside of me!"—her look of dismay and vehement disclaimer—"Inside of you, Miss, when you have had a sick head-ache for days!"—gave a greater blow to my vanity than that much battered article has ever received. (48)

The lyrical depiction of ethereal consciousness in "this sublime moment" is interrupted first by a reminder that AJ's (undepicted) body is lying prostrate while she is being dressed, and then by her healthy helper's reminder of a recent migraine: "The headache had gone off in the night and I had clean forgotten it" (48). The limpid motions of consciousness are here arrested by the exigencies of the physical body: just as AJ was, as she puts it, "feeling within me the potency of a Bismarck," she was instead rendered "powerless before the immutable law that however great we may seem to our own consciousness . . . my glorious role was to stand for Sick headache to mankind!" (48). AJ's consolation lies precisely in abandoning the puffed ego and instead "to sit by and watch these absurdities"—which, she concludes, "is amusing in its own way" (49). The vignette itself enacts the incongruity and absurdity that it describes, offering the oddly fractured perspective of the self sitting beside itself, laughing. What remains is an ego that, as AJ writes of her dwindling supply of money, demonstrates "the greatest capacity for diminishing itself and yet still existing" (49).

Indeed, AJ not only puts into practice Spencer's hydraulics of humor, she invokes him as a model for first-person writing that effectively manages the problem of egotism. She recounts in full an anecdote from Spencer's *Autobiography* in which the philosopher/psychologist engages in a battle of wits with Huxley, the scientist known as Charles Darwin's bulldog for aggressively making the public case for Darwin's evolutionary theory. "H[erbert] S[pencer] one day in talking to Huxley, said that the only thing to hope for was to make a little mark before one died, to which Huxley—'Oh, no matter about the mark, if one only gives a shove.' At first it makes Huxley seem the bigger animal of the two, which he is no doubt, but surely H[erbert] restores the balance by repeating it to his own harm" (84). Spencer's understatement about his intellectual influence—merely making a "little mark"—is trumped by Huxley's more egotistical and characteristically bellicose assertion about giving a "shove." (This is precisely what the notoriously sarcastic Huxley did when he debated the bishop of Oxford over Darwin's theories, pushing back against a religious worldview in favor of Darwin's scientific account of human origins.) AJ clearly finds the exchange amusing as well as telling: while Huxley's riposte appears to trump Spencer's, Spencer turns out to be the "bigger" by repeating the story in his memoir, at his own expense—by making himself "small." AJ, moreover, adds a layer of wit in her telling, by referring to Huxley—often caricatured as a monkey by religious opponents of Darwin's theories—as the bigger *animal* of the two.

Special notice is given throughout the Diary of people willing to laugh at themselves, with particular delight at those (often piously religious) who don't manage to get the joke. AJ tells of an acquaintance's play on words, and his literal-minded auditor: "Dr. Ogle tells the following—he once told a story in which he said, 'I am in the hands of an unscrupulous Providence.' Some half an hour later, a man came up to him and said, 'A little while ago you said, "I am in the hands of an unscrupulous Providence," you must have meant to say, an inscrutable Providence.' The Doctor must have felt himself *then* in the hands of an inscrutable Providence!" (158). Wordplay requires speed and a mind that can pivot. Dr. Ogle offered a small witticism—a play on the correct term "inscrutable"—only to have an auditor "correct" his mistake after a laughable lag time. AJ then gives the failed jest another spin, jokingly inflating the doctor's dismay at his audience's cloddishness. In the same entry, AJ includes an irreverent comment on the ultimate takedown of a haughty British aristocrat: "The ways of Providence *is* peculiar," she writes: "The substance-full Lady Rosebery dies and a rag-tag like me is left fluttering in the breeze! It must be a strangely muddled moment when it begins to dawn upon the Personage that they are not all there. . . . Imagine having to begin to learn there that you are simply an atom and not in your essence a future Prime-Ministress of the Great Little Kingdom" (158). As she increasingly takes aim at the "big," AJ begins to innovate on Spencer's theory of humor.

Over the course of her Diary, rather than emphasize Spencer's "descending" incongruity—a downward shift of scale in which "consciousness is unawares transferred from great things to small" (400)—AJ experiments with the *ascending* potency that comes with the splitting of the self into both narrator of the Diary and character within it. When she learns of Nurse's tendency to quote her opinions during intellectual disputes with other staff, she records, "Imagine the inflation for my American human accident consciousness in suddenly finding itself a substance apart, a 'Better,' an 'Authority' whose quoted word carries paralysis and finality to the arguments of the Steward's room" (156). The self surprised by itself, momentarily shifting perspective and seeing the world afresh or askew: this describes the beginning of AJ's empowering innovation on Spencer's theory of humor. Relief, for AJ, comes from the embodied awareness of a shared worldview despite being a "substance apart."

Rigidity and the Comic

WJ, in his chapter on habit in *The Principles of Psychology* (1890), notes that human beings tend to fall into routines, creating grooves in the nervous system that take away conscious deliberation and smooth the way for automatic behaviors and attitudes: "*Habit diminishes the conscious attention with which our acts are performed.*"[35] Bergson, in his essay on the comic spirit, argues that humor takes root in that human tendency toward mechanical responses and rigidity. For Bergson, the material body is the culprit, a dumb weight on the more ethereal mind. You have, "on the one hand, the moral personality with its intelligently varied energy, and, on the other, the stupidly monotonous body, perpetually obstructing everything with its machine-like obstinacy" (25). The mind can follow suit, becoming similarly inelastic: "It consists in seeking to mould things on an idea of one's own, instead of moulding one's ideas on things,—in seeing before us what we are thinking of, instead of thinking of what we see" (90).

Joking, by this account, is a practice that aids thinking by unstiffening our theories: precisely the work of philosophical pragmatism, as theorized by WJ: "*Theories thus become instruments, not answers to enigmas, in which we can rest*. . . . Pragmatism unstiffens all our theories, limbers them up and sets each one at work."[36] Humor, like pragmatism, assists observation, by suddenly bringing to awareness the frameworks, ideas, and preconceptions we bring to any encounter with the world around us; joking is empirical at its root, serving as a counteractive to the very situatedness in our own dogged viewpoint that is the ultimate substrate of humor. "This rigidity is the comic," writes Bergson, "and laughter is its corrective" (10). The comic spirit dislodges us from our circumscribed points of view and sends us tumbling down into the mud with creatures clothed in similar flesh and with shared sensibilities. This is what AJ means when she observes, "It's amusing to see how, even upon my microscopic field, minute events are perpetually taking place illustrative of the broadest facts of human nature" (48). The "tiny explosions of humor that we call jokes," Critchley argues, "return us to a common, familiar world of shared practices."[37]

WJ, perhaps preoccupied with his own expanding career and nuclear family, recognized yet misconstrued AJ's power, casting it as *potential* energy and (bizarrely) projecting it into a future when, divested of a body, she is dead. He offers this sentiment as consolation upon hearing of her diagnosis of breast cancer: "When that which is *you* passes out of the body, I am sure that there will be an explosion of liberated force and life till then eclipsed and kept down."[38] AJ lived her adult life in frequent pain, with a rarely flickering awareness of being a body. This has led biographers to argue that she was a professional invalid. Yeazell concurs in almost the same language as WJ, that AJ pursued a "covert career in mortality" (24), and even the insightful Strouse writes that "her miserable health *was* her career" (291). Recent critics have persuasively responded to earlier scholarly judgments and have emphasized AJ's intellectual contributions as the postmortem triumph of a sparkling mind transcending the constrictions of the invalid role.[39]

Empowerment in these accounts entails not just the substitution of Victorian conceptions of invalidism by AJ's heroic self-definition but the displacement of a disabled body by a supple mind. These accounts in fact conform closely to WJ's account that "some infernality in the body *prevents* really existing parts of the mind from coming into their effective rights at all, suppresses them, and blots them out from participation in this world's experiences, although they are *there* all the time."[40] As he concludes in the quotation above, death will mark the mind's liberation from the hampering body. But AJ's potency arises expressly in, through, and because of her body. She riffs on Darwin and Spencer, while anticipating Bergson, when she wonders in her Diary: "It makes one curious to know, if in a generation or so, a Darwinian or Spencerian adaptation may not take place, in the physical woman; their progression is now altogether by jerks, a pulling of the string—how interesting if in time the interrupted current of their speech and motion should [instead] take to itself . . . undulating suppleness and flow" (173). As she follows this speculation with "how wild can be the fancies of the unimaginative female!" (173), AJ seems convinced that for women the encumbrances of sheer femaleness are as unavoidable as men's interruptions of them.

Immanuel Kant saw humor as a way for the purely intellectual to give a form of massage to the body. Our minds, tickled by incongruity, produce a "movement of the viscera," enlisting "the business of life in the body, the affect which moves the viscera and the diaphragm, in a word the feeling of health (which otherwise cannot be felt without such a stimulus), which constitutes the gratification in which one discovers that one can get at the body even through the soul and use the latter as the doctor for the former."[41] This perspective, in which a cognitive appraisal sends the body into healthy gyrations, offers a reverse of aesthetic judgment, in which sensory perception produces an internal experience of harmony. Other philosophers of humor are more attentive to the potentially jolting, even violent aspects of the bodily disruption that extreme incongruity can produce. "Laughter is an explosion expressed with the body," writes Critchley (9); for Bergson, the comic spirit "contracts, expands and shakes our limbs, whilst all other relations leave the body unaffected" (4).

Using humor, AJ insists on the smallness and the anti-aesthetic aspect of her literary output. When WJ suggested that her letters from England merited collection or even publication, her sisterly reply walks a line between delight at the praise and deprecation: "What you say of my letters is quite just, don't fear to be florid or excessive, for like Dr. Holmes I can never have enough, but I must confess to having rolled over in my bed with laughter at the suggestion of the collection of '*documents humains*.' Imagine the millions of the Empire being labeled and pigeon-holed by a creature whose field of vision is densely populated by a landlady, a hosp. nurse and 2 Bath-chairmen [wheelchair pushers], one perpetually drunk! It is too funny!!" (158–59).[42] Critchley has written of comedic sparring, "Humour is an exemplary practice because it is a universal human activity that invites us to become philosophical spectators upon our lives. It is practically enacted theory."[43] AJ first embraces then laughs off WJ's (perhaps patronizing) assessment. She reinscribes his comment as a joke by amplifying it. First, she likens herself to the literary titan Oliver Wendell Holmes—yet winks at Dr. Holmes's famously puffed-up ego and legendary diminutive stature. Second, she figures the worldwide British population as tiny specimens sorted by a "creature" propped up by a wobbly staff of four. There is both a conceptual and a rhetorical aspect to AJ's shift into the terrain of joking: the conceptual disjunction of scale and power is matched rhetorically by the clincher "one perpetually drunk!" WJ's high praise (notable, as he was a vocal and unabashed critic of HJ's late style) is hyperbolically endorsed and then chaffingly dismissed by his bed-ridden sister—whose humorous performance slyly affirms the power in her prose that her brother had discerned in the first place.

Existential Bruises: Alice James's Pain and Peirce's Secondness

For AJ, humor bears witness to the startling fact that thinking and awareness are above all *events* that reverberate both within an individual and among others. When people laugh together, the experience ripples outward, in a way that is connective (cognitively and viscerally) yet harbors an element of detachment, marking a difference from the mirroring associated with empathic responses. At times, AJ as onlooker to her own experience claims superiority over her embedded self undergoing events. In the entry of 18 July 1890, an imagined auditor ("Inconnu," French for *unknown*) is implicitly invited "in" by AJ's confiding narrative voice, with a jesting incongruity about the strength one needs to weather bodily pain: "How well one has to be, to be ill! These confidences reveal to you, dear Inconnu, so much mental debility that I don't want to rehearse herein my physical collapse in detail as well" (129). There is a doubleness here, for despite the self-deprecating scruples, AJ claims the worthiness of recounting her "physical collapse," for "this last prostration was rather excessive and comic in its combination, consisting of one of my usual attacks of rheumatic gout in that dissipated organ known in the family as 'Alice's tum,' in conjunction with an ulcerated tooth, and a very bad crick in my neck" (129). The perfect storm of physical insults, mitigated by a "very small dose of morphia, the first in three years," provided the means for her to sustain her experience and observe it at the same time: to, as she writes, "steady my nerves and *experience* the pain without distraction" (129).

Shari Goldberg has brilliantly described how the existential aspects of pain (in her case, from migraines) resituate the experiencing self: "The symptoms, the pain, are not discrete discomforts that appear and demand treatment. They are ways of experiencing the world that shift one's axis, one's orientation. The symptoms and the pain and the shift may even all be indistinguishable, or identical."[44] This shift in worldview is what AJ leverages the Diary to convey, including the weird expansion that can transpire as the pen records the distress of what Goldberg calls the "bodymind." AJ writes, "There is something very exhilarating in shivering whacks of crude pain which seem to lift you out of the present and its sophistications (great Men unable to have a tooth out without gas!) and ally you to long gone generations rent and torn with tooth-ache such as we can't dream of" (127). The compressed, prostrated body in pain here undergoes an imaginative extension.

Close Distance and Far-Removed Proximity

As Cynthia Davis has eloquently described, AJ experienced persistent pain—something that can be glossed over by readers working with a psychoanalytic framework.[45] F. O. Matthiessen went so far as to write, "Since AJ died just prior to the development of the psychoanalytical techniques which might have been of some use to her, it is not possible to be sure to what extent her ailments were physical and to what extent purely psychic."[46] Given the omnipresence of bodily suffering in the James family (and in the nineteenth century more broadly), it is striking that Davis's is the first account that centers pain and its alleviation to an understanding of the siblings generally and AJ in particular.[47]

The terrible irony, of course, is that a hermeneutic of suspicion produces its own suffering. AJ was precise on this point. She was scathing about the thoughtless comments of "the well": acquaintances who—even while trying to be sympathetic—have "no conception of their cruelty" when querying the not-well:

> A while back I was greatly enjoying a friend from home who went far back and in whose presence the past revived for a bit, when suddenly she removed herself to the planet Mars by asking me whether I was in pain anywhere at that moment. She stood at the foot of the sofa, but she had no gift to divine that pain was as the essence of the Universe to my consciousness and that ghastly fatigue was a palpable substance between us. How could she?—We were emotionally blended, but what common ground had we physically and especially as I had bluffed off all her investigations! (77)

The anecdote is striking for its juxtaposition of spatial proximity ("she stood at the foot of the sofa") and psychological intimacy ("we were emotionally blended") with existential distance ("she removed herself to the planet Mars"). AJ to some extent forgives her visitor's lack of understanding, acknowledging that she herself "had bluffed off all her investigations," presumably by not going into great detail about her discomforts. (That said, AJ was, after all, confined to the sofa during the whole visit, so her friend was not the keenest of therapeutic detectives.)

Contemporary anthropologists have developed a term to describe tight affective relationships present among human beings and our evolutionary kin, primates: *mutuality of being*. Though "grooming and proximity" may be involved, Barbara J. King describes mutuality of being as a particular form of connection: "More than just spending time together, the individuals remain emotionally and cognitively taken up with each other's lives even when they are not together."[48] This sort of relationship is more than a friendship, needn't entail a romantic or marital relationship, and is not limited to kinship groups: it is what comes about when individuals are "co-present in each other."[49] AJ's writings make vivid the mutuality of being that existed between her and Loring and express this deep kinship with her far-flung brother WJ. HJ, a more active presence in her life, surprised his sister by bringing the elder brother to visit after a separation of five years. WJ's presence brings up not just memories of the past but also the *feel* of the family as a sensibility and collective point of view: "What a strange experience it was, to have what had seemed so dead and gone all these years suddenly bloom before one, a flowing oasis in this alien desert, redolent with the exquisite family perfume of the days gone by, made of the allusions, the memories and the point of view in common, so that floating particle sense was lost for an hour or so in the illusion that what is forever shattered had sprung up anew, and existed outside of our memories—where it is forever green!" (51–52). Mutuality of being entails a consanguinity of past experiences that shaped "the point of view in common"; AJ here describes a collective memory that is sensuous as well as perceptual, freshly catalyzed when the three siblings find themselves surprisingly together in AJ's English boardinghouse.

Embodiment, Reflexivity, and Kinship

Far more frequent than moments of nostalgia are jokes and amusing anecdotes that use humor to draw a strong line between intimates and outsiders to AJ's world. When a group of officiates arrives from the American consulate in

Birmingham to oversee the filing of AJ's last will and testament, she becomes overwhelmed with the mix of strangers and members of the household and loses consciousness.[50] What follows—in the Diary entry for 17 February 1890—amounts to Victorian slapstick:

> The most amusing scene followed. I lay in a semi-faint, draped in as many frills as could be found for the occasion, with Nurse at my head with the thickest layer of her anxious-devoted-nurse expression on, as K.[atharine] told me after, when thro' a mist I vaguely saw five black figures file into my little bower, headed by the most extraordinary little man, all gesticulation and grimace, who planted himself at the foot of the bed and stroking my knees began a long harangue to the effect that he and his wife had both "laid upon a bed of sickness" which seemed to constitute uncontrovertible reason for my immediate recovery. (89)

The scenario continues in this vein, with the men coming and going and "becom[ing] tangled in as much resounding red-tape as the creature [the American consul] could reel off for the occasion" (90). The whole scene, AJ writes, was "so curious for me, just like a nightmare effect and I felt as if I were assisting at the reading of my own Will, surrounded by the greedy relatives, as in novels" (89–90). She lampoons an earnest witness to the signing, who took her job so seriously that she refused to look at AJ's face because (as the woman later told Loring) "she felt as if she 'ought to keep her eye fixed upon Miss James's *hand!*'" The witness judged the entire scene "the most picturesque and American!"—a combination that AJ found hilarious: "I think it is the first time," she writes, that descriptors "which are usually supposed to neutralize one another so completely, were ever conjoined" (90).

In this proleptic deathbed scene, AJ calls attention to her body's prostration, creating a scenario in which her physical person is at center stage, even itemizing the group's weird attentiveness to her knees and hands. Her perspective is doubled, creating a structure of reflexivity: on the one hand, she is the body in bed looking up at the leg-stroking executor; while on the other, she is the voice narrating the "amusing scene," looking back over the antics from above ("as in novels"). AJ's first-person perspective is supplemented by Loring, who had passed along *her* view of the pained expression of Bradfield ("Nurse") along with the female witness's silly comments. The Diary thus incorporates others' responses to the anecdote, enacting and encoding experiences "begotten of real life and akin to art," as Bergson puts it (19). The Diary entry ends with

AJ quoting HJ's response to her bravura oxymoron (the welding of *picturesque* and *American*): "You can't say you've done nothing for your Race since you've brought that about in your own person" (90). With obvious satisfaction AJ incorporates Loring's and HJ's amused and amusing additions into her Diary.

AJ's Diary throughout deconstructs the notion of privacy. Much as AJ's close companions bolstered her physically—assisting with mobility, domestic chores, intimate care—so the Diary is textually scaffolded by the contributions of familiar others. In this way, the text becomes a field of (re-)creation, carrying with it the double valence, the cloistered-yet-social aspect of *play*:

> On the one hand, man plays in the real world and knows himself to be playing even as he plays (unlike the schizophrenic, who cannot tell the difference). On the other hand, play is not subordinate to the serious purposes served by all other human activities. Seen from within, the play world is unrelated to anything outside itself. . . . The play world possesses its own internal space and time, which set it off from the real world, but without concealing it. This capacity to exist in two different spheres at once is uniquely human. It enables the player to withdraw temporarily from the real world, and to assert his freedom by recreating it imaginatively, without losing touch with reality.[51]

As with play, there is a meaningful yet permeable boundary between AJ's Diary and her domestic world, and between her clandestine creativity and the accomplishments of her far-flung family. AJ also subverts another of the diary's prime affordances: its immediacy and foreclosure of hindsight.[52] She leverages the diary as a play space for the lively depiction of consciousness as it shuttles forward and backward through time and contends with interruptions and absurdities that compel reflexivity. Thomas Nagel's writing on the absurd is helpful here: "Humans have the special capacity to step back and survey themselves, and the lives to which they are committed, with that detached amazement which comes from watching an ant struggle up a heap of sand. Without developing the illusion that they are able to escape from their highly specific and idiosyncratic position, they can view it *sub specie aeternitatis*—and the view is at once sobering and comical."[53] And while its subject matter taps into quotidian life, AJ's Diary is nonetheless an outward facing document, always positing an interlocutor and indeed an audience and engaging in spirited colloquy about topics from British imperialism to childbirth. Humor becomes an essential mode that makes palpable AJ's experience of a life lived in and through bodily disability, an existence that threatens to mire her in a "mass of subjective sensations" and "emotional borborygmus"—aka gurgling intestines (176). Humor, joking, and laughter, as deployed in the Diary, sets in motion the way that consciousness seeks to navigate a shared world, even as it all-too-frequently runs aground on the stubborn material conditions of the self it only partly pilots.

Bergson illuminates how Jamesian laughter confirms a reverberative conduit among disparate persons: "You would hardly appreciate the comic if you felt yourself isolated from others. Laughter appears to stand in need of an echo. Listen to it carefully: it is not an articulate, clear, well-defined sound; it is something which would fain be prolonged by reverberating from one to another, something beginning with a crash, to continue in successive rumblings, like thunder in a mountain. Still, this reverberation cannot go on for ever. It can travel within as wide a circle as you please: the circle remains, none the less, a closed one" (3). AJ's "going off" at the signing of her will serves as a Bergsonian "crash" even with those (like WJ) who are not present: "However spontaneous it seems, laughter always implies a kind of secret freemasonry, or even complicity, with other laughers, real or imaginary," Bergson writes (3). The diplomatic personage, in AJ's telling, is ironically shrunk to an alien "little man, all gesticulation and grimace" (89), while Loring and HJ reside comfortably in the circle of camaraderie, contributing to and amplifying the humor. Solidarity, straddling the merely bodily or purely psychical, provides an anodyne to absurdity.

Corporeal Contact Zone

In relation to HJ in particular, AJ articulates a form of intimacy that playfully corporealizes their closeness. Rather than seek AJ's verbal account of her well- or ill-being during his frequent visits, her brother "hangs on to whatever organ may be in eruption and gives me calm and solace by assuring me that my nerves are his nerves and my stomach his stomach" (104). Her bodily condition is profoundly acknowledged as an existential fact precisely by not being cast into a narrative: "[Henry] never remotely hinted that he expected me to be well at any given moment, that burden which fond friend and relative so inevitably impose upon the cherished invalid" (104). The attitudes toward another's persistent pain lie along a continuum: the incomprehension of the casual visitor, entailing unbridgeable existential separation between persons; the overheated, "amusing" sentimentality of the distant brother WJ, writing in the dark from across an ocean; and the sympathy and bodily comprehension of the *ami intime*, entailing an unspoken compassion that collapses the separation between persons. These uncompromising options, however, leave little analytical space for expressing or thinking about the experience of pain, discomfort, or suffering in its many forms.

We can see that humor accounts for AJ's particular explosive power as she practices novel forms of embodiment while deploying quotidian literary forms. Instead of drawing on dominant nineteenth-century modes that veil the palpitating, fleshly body along with its pains and frailties—familiar social tropes of delicacy, invalidism, and sentimental suffering—AJ uses humor to startle, wrong-foot, and occasionally inflict gut-punching surprise in the text. She comes by this pugnacious, even pugilistic energy honestly: as the youngest child and only girl in a competitive, fast-talking family that included four older brothers, "a small sister" (as HJ called her in *A Small Boy and Others*) had been from an early age an audience to the jesting of menfolk.[54] During her childhood, a young WJ sent his sister letters that were at once flirtatious and patronizing, addressing her as "You lovely babe," "Charmante Jeune Fille," and "Perfidious child!" (Strouse, 52). James family humor, by all accounts, was a masculine sport: quick, sharp, ironic. HJ recalls that Henry James Sr. could be "comically aggressive" (*Small Boy*, 87). Alice-teasing was a brotherly pastime, with James family acquaintances occasionally following suit. According to HJ, when the "great humorist" William Thackeray visited the United States to give lectures on English humor, he visited the Jameses in Cambridge. Upon meeting AJ, the imposing man "laid his hand on her little flounced person and exclaimed with ludicrous horror, 'Crinoline?—I was suspecting it! So young and so depraved!" (*Small Boy*, 58).[55] AJ was not the only target: Thackeray mocked HJ about his too-tight little boy blazer: "My sense of my jacket became from that hour a heavy one" (*Small Boy*, 87).

Bergson noted that much humor stems from misfitting clothes and appliances—an absent-minded man sitting on the hat he placed on the chair, a large clown riding a tiny bike: "We perceive how easy it is for a garment to become ridiculous. It might almost be said that every fashion is laughable in some respect" (19). The larger point is that the supple, weightless, immortal *soul* finds itself "clothed" by the awkward, clumsy *body*. The human imagination, the dreamy self, identifies with the suppleness: "When we see only gracefulness and suppleness in the living body, it is because we disregard in it the elements of weight, of resistance, and, in a word, of matter; we forget its materiality and think only of its vitality, a vitality which we regard as derived from the very principle of intellectual and moral life" (24). The human tendency to feel ethereal is, however, frequently caught up short by the material world, often in its most humble form—a silly hat, a tight shoe, a sore tooth, an uneven step (or the proverbial banana peel): "Let us suppose, however, that our attention is drawn to this material side of the body. . . . Then the body will become to the soul what, as we have just seen, the garment was to the body itself—inert matter dumped down upon living energy. The impression of the comic will be produced as soon as we have a clear apprehension of this putting the one on the other" (24–25). Bergson is intent in this essay on understanding the nature of humor. He also lays the groundwork for an important ontological insight: how it is that minds can "meet" in a common world, by bumping into sudden shared insights.

In her Diary, AJ revels in logging scenarios that portray the formality and conventionality of British manners colliding with their more practical American counterparts. In an entry composed a few months before she died, AJ describes an Englishwoman she met who "was a refined mortal, and although fifty years of age, embodied still as K.[atharine] said, the Wordsworthian maiden, having that wearying quality which always oozes from attenuated purity" (173). The entry continues, "It seems that on one occasion I told her that Father had hated all forms and ceremonies, which she took to be an intimation that I had been born out of the bonds of holy wedlock. This doubt had devastated her breast for long, until she was driven to ask K. who with one burst of laughter restored me to virtue and the commonplace; but she was not so immoral as to keep the joke to herself, as she told the poor lady she would" (173–74). Here maidenly British virtue suffers a takedown, being endowed instead with a bawdy, bodily texture: purity and doubt might "ooze" or "devastate the breast." (In this way, AJ rhetorically reconfigures the qualities of her cancer as a moral failing—afflicting someone else.) The "forms and ceremonies" that Henry James Sr. disparaged to his children were, for Bergson and AJ, the very ground for humor: "There," Bergson writes, "we have rigidity over again, clashing with the inner suppleness of life" (22). Loring's "one burst of laughter" activates the Bergsonian principle that "the ceremonial side of social life must, therefore, always include a latent comic element, which is only waiting for an opportunity to burst into full view" (22). At this point in her life, AJ had handed the task of physically inscribing the Diary to her friend, who—in a delightful moment of self-referentiality—turns out to be the hero of the anecdote. Loring restores order by first laughing at the lady's mistake and then breaking her white lie not to tell (an "immoral" promise, as perceived by the gossipy AJ). Loring aligns morality and affection by sharing the anecdote with AJ, an action that also supplies the joke's satisfying punchline.

Laughter marks disconnection—here, between a lady's view of AJ as illegitimate offspring and her "commonplace" social legitimacy—but also affirms connection. In Loring's burst no actual information is conveyed; just as in the

Diary entry, nobody's internal consciousness is described. One must imagine the lady's shock at the unflappable Loring's sudden hilarity. What *is* transmitted is the pleasure—first Loring's, and AJ's in quoting her—at the world suddenly appearing rearranged, and the affirmation of *kinship* among the laughers: including the reader, perhaps AJ's projected "Inconnu," who is also in on the joke. The sense of connectedness across bodies is the point. The philosopher Ted Cohen urges that the affirmation of a subjective experience, the sense of something individual and unique being also shared and in that sense *in* the world (and not in an isolated self, mind, or existential being), is a crucial aspect of why we tell jokes: "I think that what you want is to *reach* me and therein to verify that you understand me, at least a little, which is to exhibit that we are, at least a little, alike."[56]

Loring's laughter redounds onto AJ, who experiences an echo of the original burst. Her answering delight, the inscription of the anecdote in the Diary, completes the reverberation, marking the solidarity of two middle-aged women weathering together the vicissitudes of domestic life.[57] AJ delights in their shared sensibility: "A friend said to K. the other day: 'You always look so serious, we can never tell whether you are joking or not, I think there ought always to be a twinkle in the eye'—'Yes,' said K., 'as warning this is a joke'" (166). Relationality, corporeality, reflexivity, and the sudden, quasi-cognitive recognition of change: these are the conditions of possibility for laughter, which begins "with a crash" (according to Bergson, 3) or a "crack" (according to AJ) that, rather than creating trauma, is expanded and diffused as another's fleshy self shudders and shakes in response.

Wisecracking—Literally

In "On Being Ill" (1926), Virginia Woolf puzzles that illness is not among "the prime themes of literature," given that bodily distress is attended by monumental shifts in consciousness.[58] Illness, she writes, often remaps one's orientation to the world, both outwardly—disclosing to its sufferers "undiscovered countries"—and inwardly—revealing "wastes and deserts of the soul" (101). Whereas theorists of illness such as Susan Sontag have centered their inquiries on life-threatening conditions (for example, cancer, tuberculosis, AIDS), Woolf's emphasis is on decidedly quotidian ailments, from headache and flu to a painful, inflamed mouth. At the dentist's office, she writes, "We go down into the pit of death and feel the waters of annihilation close above our heads and wake thinking to find ourselves in the presence of angels and the harpers when we have a tooth out and come to the surface in the dentist's arm-chair and confuse his 'Rinse the mouth—rinse the mouth' with the greeting of the Deity stooping from the floor of Heaven to welcome us" (101). Thus does a rotten tooth, with its punishing ache and (literally) wrenching treatment, offer the occasion for a homeopathic taste of "annihilation" in the form of nitrous oxide. For want of a crown, a self—along with the pain that anchors it to the earth—is momentarily lost.

Woolf's essay throughout hits the minor notes of human experience: "Of all this daily drama of the body there is no record. People write always about the doings of the mind" (101). The essay urges that the quotidian life of the body has largely eluded literary expression (Woolf cites Proust as an exception). From one perspective, Woolf's point is well taken. If great literature is about the human voice at its most lyrical and expressive, the figure of the dental patient with another person's hands in her mouth, gagging and drooling from the tools used to wrench tooth from socket, would appear not just anathema but an actual obstruction to elevated enunciation. If there is one place that seems free of aesthetic or philosophical significance, it is the dentist's office, the province of bile, spit, blood, pus, and pain.[59]

Though Woolf could not have known it, however, the expressive terrain of the dentist's armchair is precisely what AJ maps in her Diary. Composed in the years 1889–1892, the Diary was first published in 1934, eight years after Woolf's essay. In an entry dated 15 September 1890, AJ invokes the precise occasion that Woolf would describe: the uncomfortable, unglamorous experience of tooth extraction.[60] "I had a tooth out the other day," AJ writes, "curious and interesting *like a little lifetime*—first, the long drawn drag, then the twist of the hand and the crack of doom!" (137, emphasis added). In this incongruously playful entry, dentistry becomes a dramatic scenario of existential significance, although the phrase "*little* lifetime," with its scalar qualifier, at the same time quashes the rhetorical grandiosity.

The "plot" of AJ's anecdote picks up where Woolf's leaves off, *after* the anesthetic expectation of "angels and harpers" meets the reality of the postsurgical patient. AJ's extraction ends with a surge of laughter rather than the exaltations of sublimity: "Katharine and Nurse shaking of knee and pale of cheek went on about my 'heroism' whilst I, serenely wadded in that sensational paralysis which attends all the simple, rudimentary sensations and experiences common to man, whether tearing of the flesh or of the affections, laughed and laughed at 'em. As long as one doesn't break in two in the middle, I never have been able to see where the 'heroism' comes in" (137). Whereas Woolf urges the spiritual possibilities inherent in debility and even dentistry, AJ translates (or better, deflates) "the crack of doom!" into an occasion for wisecracking.

One can read this anecdote therapeutically. There is, undoubtedly, a crucial element of relief in the laughter of the patient: though her tooth parting from her jaw "break[s] in two," AJ herself does not; the pain and prostration of a visit to the dentist turns out to be neither horrible nor heroic. The extraction anecdote for AJ, never married and by her accounts a "flaccid virgin" (36), holds up a dark mirror to a more commonly celebrated "tearing of the flesh" for nineteenth-century women, the scene of childbirth. The rewriting of minor dental surgery as comedy serves as corporeal critique: the very notion that everyday bodily fragility or brokenness is in any way noble is made into a joke. AJ here and throughout her Diary refuses the persona of the ethereal invalid, just as she resists the tradition of a woman's diary being a place for affirming a sentimental intimacy with those who share a domestic world. Instead, unnervingly, she "laughed and laughed at 'em."

Whence the laughter of the invalid? For AJ, laughter has its root in shock, in a moment of existential surprise—sometimes delight, sometimes the reverse—at the persistence of self in the face of that which threatens, but fails, to tear it apart. In *The Essence of Laughter* (1855), Charles Baudelaire describes the doubleness of laughter, which is "essentially human" and "essentially contradictory," offering "at one and the same time a sign of infinite greatness and of infinite wretchedness."[61] It is the self somehow enduring a sudden corporeal intimation of its own mortality and yet living to tell the tale. The transformation of such appraisals from pure evanescence to something that is both durable and obliquely sharable requires a certain practice of the self. Baudelaire's sharpest insight captures this notion: "The comic, the power of laughter, is in the laugher, not at all in the object of laughter. It is not the man who falls down who laughs at his own fall, unless he is a philosopher, a man who has acquired, by force of habit, the power of getting outside himself quickly and watching, as a disinterested spectator, the phenomenon of his ego" (148). AJ in her Diary repeatedly presents herself as both the one who falls and the one who laughs at her own fall.[62] Her laughter responds to the resilience that springs from a site of exquisite vulnerability. "Those Grimaces called LAUGHTER," Thomas Hobbes writes in *Leviathan* (1651), are caused by "the apprehension of some deformed thing in another"—including one's prior self.[63] In her Diary AJ frequently refers to herself as "grotesque"—a deformed thing—and surgery further fractures her bodily integrity, yet existentially she endures the extraction not just intact but exultant. In the dentist's chair, she is doubly prostrate as both central character in the sketch and its chronicler, for she wrote (and sometimes dictated) much of her Diary from a horizontal position. To distill this humorous Diary entry to its basic structure: by withstanding dental amputation AJ achieves a form of stand-up, in which her on-site as well as her (imagined future) audiences bear witness to her quotidian triumph while they—and not the patient—twist in discomfort.

Bumping Up Against Hard Facts

Charles Sanders Peirce helps to describe the nature of AJ's translation of bodily impact into a form of philosophical triumph. A close colleague of WJ, Peirce argued that human knowledge fell into three categories. What he calls "Firstness" corresponds roughly to sensory perception; the world arriving for and immersing an individual. "Thirdness" refers to ideas or concepts; the world taken at a distance, cast into the form of human thought and language. To these recognizable psychological categories Peirce added another crucial category, "Secondness," which "is the conception of being relative to, the conception of reaction with, something else."[64]

Secondness provides a framework for thinking about the philosophical significance of AJ's humor. Peirce's middle category beautifully captures a sine qua non of laughter: the intransigence of the world and the people in it as it bumps—often literally—against the human organism: "[There is a category] which the rough and tumble of life renders most familiarly prominent. We are continually *bumping up* against hard fact. We expected one thing, or passively took it for granted, and had the image of it in our minds, but experience forces that idea into the background, and compels us to think quite differently. You get this kind of consciousness in some approach to purity when you *put your shoulder against a door and try to force it open*."[65] Secondness lays bare the fact of human embodiment and thus one's placement within the concrete world of things and persons; it supplies "a sense of externality" (169). This recognition doesn't arrive in the form of a concept but announces itself concussively.

Peirce's "conception of being relative to" thus plants otherness at the center of not just self-consciousness but human experience. Secondness marks the surprise of sudden relation, of an ego encountering something beyond itself, poking even the most abstracted daydreamers or disapproving personages out of their cerebral fantasies and into a richly stocked material environment. Peirce writes, "If, while you are walking in the street reflecting upon how everything is the pure distillate of Reason, a man carrying a heavy pole suddenly *pokes you* in the small of the back, you may think there is something in the Universe that Pure Reason fails to account for."[66] Secondness places relationality and corporeality—both poker and poked—at the core of human experience. (As we shall see, WJ picks up on "the poke" when analyzing children playing with sticks; in HJ's *Daisy Miller*, it takes the form of young men wielding alpenstocks and umbrellas.) Secondness describes a change of perception that is not yet a full-blown idea but that entails resistance (as opposed to habituated accommodation) and therefore agency: a small, durable pushing back against the world. AJ embraces this zone, asserting that "the only thing which survives is the *resistance* we bring to life and not the strain life brings to us" (90). Resistance answers both philosophical idealism and scientific materialism. When Peirce affirms that "shock is a volitional phenomenon" and that "there must be an element of effort in experience" (169), he is establishing the corporeal groundwork for Secondness as crucial for both thinking and transformation: "It is the compulsion, the absolute constraint upon us to think otherwise than we have been thinking that constitutes experience" (170). Laughing together at that which separates us—our distinctive embodiment, our private perceptions—simultaneously figures the dissolution of this separateness.

Peirce's category, while not reducible to cognition, is crucial for human knowledge of the world, lending palpability and salience to subjective feeling and providing salutary correctives to received wisdom and social conventions.

> Besides the lower consciousness of feeling [Firstness] and the higher consciousness of intuition [Thirdness], this direct consciousness of *hitting and of getting hit* enters into all cognition and serves to make it mean something real.[67]

> All experience and all knowledge of that which is, independently of being represented . . . are utterly unintelligible as long as your thoughts are mere dreams. But as soon as you take into account that Secondness that *jabs you* perpetually in the ribs, you become aware of their truth. (130)

Above all, Secondness is the expression of interruption, which in turn opens onto the possibility of transformation. This is not only an ethical or a sociological point but also a philosophical one. Crucially, Secondness extends beyond the realm of disembodied thought: it sutures both individual feeling (Firstness) and general rules and concepts (Thirdness) to lived experience. Peirce affirmed the irreducibly material *jab* that shakes us out of solipsistic dreams and conceptual rigidity. Such jabs are the lingua franca of siblings; they are also the purview of AJ's Diary, which tips sideways the verticality of social norms (well versus ill, men versus women, famous versus "Inconnu") to create a horizontal playing field.[68]

At the core of Peirce's epistemology we find the bare condition for agency and the logical grounds for human knowledge—as well as the conditions of possibility for what Hobbes called the "passion which hath no name," laughter.[69] The insistence on indexicality—the burst, the crack, the poke, the jab, the kick, the hit, the bump, the push—assigns *impact* a key place in Peirce's thought, and also offers a clue about the unexpected humor riddled throughout AJ's Diary. Edel incisively (if rather judgmentally) referred to the "bite" in AJ's prose (18). To cast Edel's observation in less pejorative terms, I would instead call attention to the elements of play: AJ's Diary is social, situated, embodied, spontaneous, and autotelic. Her edgy writing embraces the interruption and redirection manifested by laughter and by Secondness. Like the carom of a billiard ball, the physical contact implied by humor marks an intellectual swerve and allows for fresh, unhabituated insight. Peirce urges that Secondness also establishes the essential, if rudimentary, condition for agency: in being shifted out of alignment or concussed, there is an implied element of destination or of *pushing back* against the doggedness of what one (inevitably, in this shared world) runs up against. Secondness, in this respect, is more akin to physics than psychology and refuses the adhesiveness of empathy or sticky sentimentality.

Humor creates a contact zone that, in bringing about an abrupt shift to the play frame, can bruise as well as educate (or frankly, can educate through bruising). AJ's responses to WJ's sympathy provide a case in point. When in 1886 WJ writes a letter of condolence to his sister—"You poor child!" (*Death and Letters*, 116)—and imagines her "stifling slowly in a quagmire of disgust and pain and impotence," AJ thanks him for his "fraternity and amusingness" but throws his words back at him: "Kath. and I roared over the 'stifling in a quagmire of disgust, pain, and impotence,' for I consider myself one of the most *potent* creations of my time" despite the absence of a "group of Harvard students sitting at my feet drinking in psychic truth" (116–17). The startling reversal, in which AJ meets her brother's earnest sentiment not with mirroring sorrow but with hilarity, implies that the arrow of instruction has been similarly polarized, with AJ usurping the teacher's chair and the Harvard professor suddenly finding himself sitting at her feet.

Laughter: Sounding the Note of the Minor

Riffing on roughhousing, laughter, and instruction, AJ's joking enlists elements operative in the world of the child. In a period marked by the cultural assimilation of evolutionary theory, the minor notes of humor accentuate the centrality of child development and adaptability to theories of consciousness. As nineteenth-century natural scientists observed, human beings have notoriously protracted childhoods, because—unlike for other animals, ranging from turtles to zebras—relatively little is "hardwired" for human infants: knowledge, know-how, and capacities for survival and flourishing are acquired over years of education and experimentation. Children in the process of learning make surprising, often enchanting, mistakes—misprisions that, in their obliquity from adult expertise, point up unstated assumptions underpinning adult logic and knowledge. In one exemplary entry in the Diary, AJ recounts WJ's attempt to educate his son Harry on religious matters: "Some years ago, when Harry was five or thereabouts, Wm. undertook to explain to him the nature of God and hearing that he was everywhere asked whether he was the chair or the table. 'Oh, no, God isn't a thing He is a spirit, He is everywhere about us, He pervades'—'Oh, then he is a skunk!' How could the word 'pervades' suggest anything else to an American child!" (145). The humor of the anecdote arises from unexpected reversals. The religious teachings of WJ go delightfully awry: omnipresence is embodied in furniture, and divinity is equated with the stink of a skunk. AJ registers her delight at little Harry's literalness, and his unwitting deflation of God and, by extension, his father's religious lesson. What would normally be self-evidently "big"—God, a little boy's father, an eldest brother—is rotated by the operation of the joke into something disproportionally little. Conditions that would typically convey insignificance—being uneducated, a small child, a younger sibling, a girl, an invalid—are elevated by the operation of humor to be temporarily and surprisingly superior.

The interaction of bigness and smallness in this joke from AJ's Diary points toward the interaction between mental and bodily experience, and to the structural—and not just thematic—interplay between child and adult in joking. Freud maintained that humor's dependence on sudden reversals (for example, esteemed professor versus ineffective Sunday school teacher) and on a slippage between the incorporeal and the corporeal (for example, a pervasive spiritual presence versus a pervasive odor) point to a "whole number of connections" that affirm "the relation of the comic to the child."[70] Humor involves "an awakening of the infantile"; Freud argues that adult laughter at another's goofiness can be translated into words this way: "'That is how he does it—I do it in another way—he does it as I used to do it as a child'" (225). A mini-recapitulation narrative is frequently bound up in a successful joke.

The glee expressed in AJ's punch line to the anecdote, "How could the word 'pervades' suggest anything else to an American child?" marks an adult freemasonry with WJ; both, as adults, can share a chuckle at little Harry's delightful naïveté. But the punch line also marks AJ's fellow feeling with, and delight at, her nephew's takedown of his father, since both she (little sister) and Harry (little son) have weathered condescending tutelage at the hands of WJ. The joke makes clear that both AJ and Harry, by virtue of the "littleness" that places them lower on the social pecking order, and through a childlike appreciation for literalness, have the capacity to unsettle familiar (and familial) hierarchies. Joking illuminates the status quo and also serves as the means for disrupting it. The joke, as recorded in AJ's Diary, is thus both record and instrument of disruption.

Before they come of age, young people are designated as *minor*: lesser in stature and status, not yet in possession of fully developed social and legal agency. Writing of the United States in the nineteenth century, Karen Sanchez-Eppler has remarked: "The figure of the child demarcates the boundaries of personhood, a limiting case for agency, voice, or enfranchisement," while the diary offers "a model for recognizing value and a capacity for asserting social meaning."[71]

AJ, the youngest and only girl-child in the family, experienced firsthand precarious independence, making her attuned to difficulties of women's existence: especially those who are young, poor, or overworked. In the first year of the Diary she pays attention to the growing family of Charlotte Brooks, a local woman who helps to clean her living quarters. AJ focuses on Becky Brooks in particular, a young girl who experiences both the dependency of childhood and the unrelenting burden of caregiving: "Eliza, who was a permanent appendage of Charlotte's person, whilst she did the house-keeping and errands, has become an excrescence upon the spindly body of white, pinch-faced Becky, aged ten years. Eliza is two and has never walked yet; she must be a bracing burden. Lavinia, who had a good place as slavey somewhere, returned home after the baby's birth for very joy at its advent, sacrificing her place" (41). These entries emphasize the corporeal burden of caregiving, figuring children as almost parasitical: "Nurse met Becky Brooks and her *hangers-on* in front of the Pump Room. She had Eliza, the excrescence, of course, on one arm and was dragging by a red scarf *pinned* round his neck an unfortunate dog with her other hand; four of the others were of course tugging at the scarf so that Becky's slender person often was upholding five others" (33). AJ in her Diary demonstrates familiarity with running a household while also being the recipient of care. Acknowledging her class status and financial independence, AJ nonetheless draws a comparison to "Eliza, the excrescence," describing her own physical being as an "appendage to five cushions and three shawls" (81). She describes her move to England, where HJ was living, in these terms: "I crossed the water and suspended myself like an old woman of the sea round his neck where to all appearances I shall remain for all time" (104). In this way, AJ calls attention to "the minor" not as a stage to pass through (presumably, toward one's *majority*) but as a way of being in the world, a view from the perspective of the dependent, the small of stature, the physically frail. AJ is the first to note that her troubles lie not in grand tragedy but merely in "being ill" and "at home among the anaemic and the fagged" (36).

"Her Expatriation Aided Her"

Characteristically, AJ takes the (diminished) concept of the minor and expands it. The Diary entry about the "appendage" Eliza Brooks is preceded by an entry touching on Ireland's analogous relationship to England. The power of sovereign England, for AJ, depends on false piety and rank hypocrisy, in contrast with the dark irony and rich sense of absurdity that characterizes the subaltern. "The absolute want of humour in the Briton at large," she writes, "is the secret of the Irish question" (30). Indeed, her enthusiasm for Charles Parnell, the Irish minister and primary spokesperson for Home Rule, is a running theme in the Diary. Edel in his "Portrait of Alice James" rightly observes, "Her expatriation aided her"—though he sees her vitriol toward the English as a mere foil "on which to discharge her bitterness" (17). This comment on character misses the twining together of constriction and resistance in potent, self-referential prose. AJ's passion for politics is inextricable from her bodily experience. AJ upbraids WJ and Alice Howe Gibbens James for not commenting on "the elections, showing how different yr insides must be from mine, wh. cramp themselves so convulsively over every little public event here. I seem perfectly grotesque to myself, a wretched, shriveled alien enclosed between four walls . . . an emotional volcano within, with the outward reverberation of a mouse & the physical significance of a chip of lead-pencil" (151). Through identification with the deterritorialized person, AJ affirms that the person without standing—the expat, the colonized, the bedridden—is cursed and blessed with exclusion, forced into linguistic resourcefulness, and able to occupy a decentered position that produces clarity through obliquity.

The most abject location can, when leveraged, become a site of comic power. Sontag, in *Illness as Metaphor*, described the existential experience of sickness through the figure of dual citizenship, hinting that everybody, by virtue of having a mortal body, has access to an alternate territory, what she calls "that other place": "Illness is the night-side of life, a more onerous citizenship. Everyone who is born holds dual citizenship, in the kingdom of the well and in the kingdom of the sick. Although we all prefer to use only the good passport, sooner or later each of us is obliged, at least for a spell, to identify ourselves as citizens of that other place."[72] By charting the view from her own darkly comic "seats of power"—the Bath chair, her chaise longue piled with pillows, the dentist's chair—AJ's Diary announces itself as a site for thinking about what Deleuze and Guattari call a minor literature.[73] They argue that literature written in the minor mode "deterritorializes" language and estranges recognized literary forms, instead giving voice to discordant intensities, "conjunctions, exclamations, adverbs; and *terms that connote pain*" (*Kafka*, 22). AJ conveys the crack of the extracted tooth, the cracking up of the patient, the truncated pronoun, *'em*: in these ways, AJ deterritorializes language by "liberat[ing] a living and expressive material that speaks for itself and has no need of being put into a form" (*Kafka*, 21). The anecdote in the Diary has no preamble; it forwards no plot; it rounds out no character. It neither lyricizes (as with Emily Dickinson) nor naturalizes (as with such writers as Frank Norris) a moment of physical rupture. AJ's surprising hilarity contrasted with others' empathic shock inoculates her own experience from the pitying praise of those who would compress the grinding experience of the chronic invalid with the epithet "brave."

The dental entry offers a striking depiction of the push-me-pull-you rhythm of intimacy: AJ's companions collectively wince at the surgery, marking their empathic attachment to her, while the patient's laughter marks her triumph despite—or rather, through—brokenness. In contrast to this evanescent wholeness, AJ frequently records her sense of herself as partial, an amputated body part or a being composed of disobedient organs. She is a "humiliated appendage" to her "better half Katharine" (151) or (perhaps riffing on hysteria as a wandering womb) she is a disassembled being, having to tow her "stomach and heart back into harbor" (74) after a shock. She persistently falls apart: the internal experience of "violent revolt" during nervous attacks forces her, she writes, "to 'abandon' my brain, as it were" (149). In the dentist's chair, however, AJ's solitary laughter registers the fleeting existential sense of distinct, autonomous selfhood. Contentless and primal, the experience expands beyond the psychological to the ontological, affirming a rarely experienced state of being.

This dislocating shift into existential terrain is abrupt and incongruous, given the nature of the woman's diary as a genre focused on the daily and the domestic. Two brilliant scholars of the Jameses have, in comments that could be read as disparaging, accurately put their critical fingers on the "minorness" of AJ's literary contribution. Edel remarked on the bitterness and the "bite" in AJ's Diary, casting her as a diminished figure whose smallness beside her towering brothers was accompanied by an oversized ego.[74] Ross Posnock, similarly, describes AJ as a foil for her brothers by virtue of her "adamant resistance to the vulnerabilities and relaxations of vagrant curiosity."[75] These observations tend to come from a psychological sense of the hardness, sharpness, self-absorption, and acerbity of the authorial voice.

Like Edel, recent critics have credited the potency of AJ but have been kinder: Haley French, for instance, observes AJ's "frequent assertions ... of the superiority of her perspective on the human condition."[76] Superiority theories of humor, however, depend on a position of well-being that AJ persistently lacks. To be sure, she is a middle-class woman with the finances to keep a small household despite not earning a wage. Any delusion of economic grandeur was thwarted, though, when Aunt Kate died and AJ received a copy of her will: "I see she has deemed it best to single me out from amidst all her heirs by simply leaving me a life-interest in the *objects* wh. she has bequeathed to me.... A life interest in a shawl, with reversion to a *male* heir, is so extraordinary & ludicrous a bequest that I can hardly think it could have been seriously meant" (*Death and Letters*, 175). The bulk of the estate, including property and liquid bank accounts, went elsewhere: her aunt submitted AJ to a familial form of deterritorialization. To WJ, executor of the will and prime beneficiary, AJ emphasizes this double expatriation, stating, "I have absolutely declined to stretch out a skinny arm, 3000 miles, & grasp, with my bird-like claw" (172) the few household items Aunt Kate had (temporarily) bequeathed her. "I am sure you will allow me my little joke, even tho' it be at your expense," AJ writes. "My amusement, let me hasten to add, didn't lessen my *extreme satisfaction* at your good-fortune" (171). AJ launches a scorching riposte that twists the gender politics of WJ being the primary (male) beneficiary—of (among other items) Aunt Kate's *shawl*:

> Your heirs & assigns should give me the shawl, renouncing their rights of reversion in it, & making me its absolute possessor. I may, or I may not, leave it to you in my will, but if I should, ... you must look upon it & accept it with any ravages wh. moth & rust may have brought about. I might make a condition of doing so, that you shd. drape yr. manly

> person in it at my funeral—or, better still, wrap it about you to protect you from the breezes on the wharf when you perform that unaesthetic duty, wh. may some day be yrs., of passing my skin & bones thro' the Custom House. (175)

AJ mockingly adorns her oldest brother in drag, exploiting the potency of self-abasement. She inhabits legal discourse only to torque it, make it grotesque, with the figure of a beshawled WJ overseeing the repatriation of his sister's "carcass" (as she terms it, in her very first Diary entry). "Skin & bones": AJ dreams up what Deleuze would later call the body without organs, crossing the ocean to be officially processed and repatriated by the older brother. No wonder WJ asked HJ, after receiving telegraphed word of their sister's death, if he was sure she was really dead—such was AJ's vitality, she seemed enormous, un-snuff-outable. Such is the affective, linguistic, and corporeal intensity of AJ, who called herself a "Barnum monstrosity" (63) and whose Diary shocked and delighted WJ and HJ. As Deleuze has aptly written, "Even unfolded and laid out flat, the monsters still haunt us."[77] One thinks both of Edel's description of AJ's Diary—written in "scribblers"—and of AJ herself, prostrate and powerful.

Hobbes believed that the distance between an onlooker's ease and well-being and someone else's sudden discomfort triggers the former's relieved delight. "The passion of laughter" is "nothing else but a sudden glory arising from sudden conception of some eminency in ourselves, by comparison with the infirmities of others, or with our own formerly."[78] In the race that constitutes life, Hobbes writes, "to see another fall, [is] disposition to laugh" (60). Similarly, Baudelaire noted that a bystander's mirth can be provoked by another's bodily mishap, giving the example of "a man falling on the ice or on the road"—a now iconic scene of slapstick comedy.[79] AJ's bouts of laughter not only point up her position of abjection but also put the lie to the superiority theory *tout court*. In a letter to a friend, dictated to Loring, AJ says, "I have been trying for the last weeks to be able to write to you, with my own goose-quill, but I have now left such hopes behind: you will, however, be able to hear through the hand of Katharine the quavering chirp of Alice" (*Death and Letters*, 197). Loring's hand, in AJ's riffing, serves as a ludic microphone for the meager sounds of the (birdlike? insect-like?) "dictator." As AJ writes to WJ, when morphine fails to ease pain "cachinnation is the sole resource" (199).

Thinking in terms of a minor literature allows us to acknowledge the strangeness and audacity of AJ's reimagining of the diary as a performative platform—a slightly delirious play space—rather than just a transcription of events.

The dental entry is exemplary. After her laughter, the tooth-extraction vignette simply stops. With no transition, and without even a paragraph break, AJ then launches into a different story, apparently on the thin thematic thread of dentistry. "Harry had a most eccentric accident in Florence," she writes, when he "was seized after dinner with a very severe pain in his throat" that he chalked up to "having had a bad tooth-ache" (137). (Despite the Diary's formal conceit of being tied to the calendar and thus linked to public time, there is no indication of when HJ's "eccentric accident" transpired, or when he told his sister about it.) The entry continues, "The next day he spent with the dentist, and went in the afternoon from the hotel to stay with [his friend] Dr. Baldwin, his throat becoming more and more sore so that he immediately said to the Doctor, 'You must look at my throat'—'Why, you have got something sticking in it and it's green!' He tugged and tugged and brought out a long haricot vert which had wound itself about the root of his tongue, which was already beginning to ulcerate. Think of the dentist, gazing into his mouth all the morning, not having seen a green object" (137). In retelling her brother's story, the Diary repurposes it to serve the theme of tender mouths exposed to (bungling) professional eyes and hands. The anecdote of the legume turns on the absurd ineptitude of the dentist but also calls attention to the incongruity of AJ's witty, eloquent brother painfully tongue-tied by a string bean.

After weaving in HJ's story, the entry concludes with the following one-liner, which leaves behind entirely the Diary's formal claim to report the journal keeper's experience or state of mind: "Emotional expression is infinitely rich and varied of form—the moonlight causes a Yankee butcher to say to his wife—'It's such a beautiful night I can't lie still another minute for I must go out and do some slaughtering'" (137). The cheerful alignment of beauty and butchery, framed by a statement suggesting the sublimity of human sensibilities, abruptly breaks with aesthetic and logical norms of not just diary keeping but narrative. This final joke serves as a gloss on the Diary itself, which contains a minefield of jarring anecdotes that surprise, entice, and deflect, rather than a cumulative record of events and feelings that divulge the recesses of a private psychology. Just as she rejected the "pendulous shape" of George Eliot's journal (41), AJ in her remark on the dullness of the private journal inoculates against this sin with a slightly gross linking of writing and bodily excretion: "If I make this a receptacle for feeble ejaculations over the scenery what a terror it will be" (37).

Sontag's essay calls for a discourse of the body, one that eschews the obfuscations and evasions of metaphor. AJ, writing almost a century earlier, offered just such a literature: through disruption of form, disjunction of logical temporality, and moments of arresting detachment when we most expect sentiment and the fiction of connection. Sinor, building on the work of other critics, has argued that the diary form tends toward parataxis, the piling up of particulars; she argues that this rhythm "is quite literally the grammatical equivalent of tick, tick, tick" (156): a feminine domestic life unfolding in time.[80] AJ's Diary, however, disrupts the quotidian with exclamatory moments of surprise and with the stretching and shrinking of time and space. The "dental entry," taken as a series of comic anecdotes, proceeds through a succession of intense sensations uncertainly aligned with figures of bodies in different states of discomfort, decay, or disassemblage. The potential for pathos or even horror is present (an ulcerated throat, a flayed carcass) but deflected; instead, in each case the potentially volatile affects are dissipated through the effect of humorous dissolve. Each anecdote turns on an incongruity: passivity recast as heroism, dental expertise that is blind, and sublime transport expressed by carving a corpse.

Mouthing Off

The moments are played for humor, somewhat brutally. Bergson maintains that the comic spirit erupts in "the absence of feeling" (2), meaning, primarily, sympathy with its problematic claims of fellow feeling. "To be a sort of stranger *within* his own language," write Deleuze and Guattari (*Kafka*, 26): this is the situation of AJ, who deterritorializes the diary as a genre. In her hands, a feminized, private, subjective form of writing becomes explosive and strangely *public* in its orientation. Loring and Bradfield are frequent audiences: both at different moments actively assist with the creation of the Diary, providing material for anecdotes, conveying gossip and insights, and even helping to inscribe the entries.[81] More radically, dramatically recounted anecdotes implicitly posit an audience through seeking to catalyze a laugh. Of a grand physician, who eight years earlier kept her waiting and shamelessly does so again, AJ writes, "I said to K., . . . 'he will make the same exclamation when he comes into this room.' When hark! The door opens, and a florid gentleman enters, and 'the *late* Sir Andrew' falls upon our ears, followed by the self same burst of hilarity [on his part], rippling down to us, thro' all these years. Imagine the martyrdom of a pun which has become an integral portion of one's organism to be lugged through life like the convict's ball and chain" (226). AJ takes the doctor's joke and weaponizes it, turning his ball-and-chain pun into a pointed riposte. The Diary entry moves forward, like a comedian's routine, by (almost literally) keeping the ball rolling: "They are all terrible, with the globular manner, talking by the hour without *saying* anything, while the longing pallid victim stretches out a sickly tendril, hoping for some excrescence, a human wart, to catch on to, but it vainly slips off the polished surface, as comforting and nourishing as that of a billiard ball" (226). The Diary juxtaposes AJ-the-writer's fierce wordplay with demoralizing moments of obstructed articulateness. Such moments body forth a visceral experience that exists solely on the page. The reader is positioned as the Yankee butcher's wife, startled awake to be the bemused auditor of an absurd panegyric that—like a dream—is defused as well as diffused in the telling, emptied of communicative import.

There is a sonic element to the Diary, fostered by its conversational tone, its frequent invitations to laugh or exclaim, and its extraordinary number of exclamation points and question marks. In many instances AJ uses two or even three exclamation points in a row, as when she quotes a visitor, who had confided in Bradfield about her physical state: "'I was so glad to see Miss James looking better yesterday when I called, there is less going away of her face in weariness and pain!!'—Oh, my eye!!!" (69). Here, three voices combine: the visitor's statement, passed along by Nurse, set on the page by AJ. The conversation is three times removed, a quotation of a quotation within a quotation—we can almost see the three exclamation points as a diacritical index of AJ adding her own voice to that of the other two. Her ejaculation—"Oh, my eye!!!"—torques away from the auditory to a phrase referencing a different sense organ in a moment of sheer concussive expression.

The Diary's physically expressive style, filled (to return to Deleuze and Guattari's terms) with "cries, gasps" and "exclamatory to the highest degree" (*Kafka*, 26), is a key characteristic of a minor literature. AJ cites the paucities of the body as finally a source of expression: "If the aim of life is the accretion of fat, the consumption of food unattended by digestive disorganization, there is no doubt that I am a failure, for as an animal form my insatiable vanity must allow that my existence doesn't justify itself, but every fiber protests against being taken simply as a sick carcass . . . whilst from the whole has flowed perpetually those succulent juices which exude at the slightest pressure from the human comedy" (*Kafka*, 183). As Deleuze and Guattari suggest, it is as if the merely biological functions (for example, eating, digesting, plumping) must be leveraged for the body's true voice, its full expressivity, to make it into language: "The mouth, tongue, and teeth find their primitive territoriality in food" (*Kafka*, 19). AJ affirms the sustaining succulence of humor, writing of one experience that "the whole episode was so shot thro' with the golden thread of Comedy, that we grew fat with laughter" (224). The body parts for communication and collectivity, capable of mobilizing language, can also project the body's state outward through the primal testimony of laughter, wails, sighs, or groans: "In giving themselves over to the articulation of sounds, the mouth, tongue, and teeth deterritorialize. Thus, there is a certain disjunction between eating and speaking, and even more, despite all appearances, between eating and writing. Undoubtedly, one can write while eating more easily than one can speak while eating, but writing goes further in transforming words into things capable of competing with food. Disjunction between content and expression. To speak, and above all to write, is to fast" (*Kafka*, 19–20). The gaping mouth of laughter marks the body's most basic articulateness. AJ, with alliterative determination, writes, "Oh Lord, how thankful I am I didn't take to refined spinsterhood, to be able, if only once in one's life, to call a spade a spade is more productive of labial & mental health & decency than all the prunes & prisms & prudish evasions of a lifetime" (*Death and Letters*, 188). Transpiring across space and inviting echoes, the "labial" exercise of laughter provides a form of relational sustenance in the face of existential paucity. No wonder AJ takes the time to record one of Loring's otherwise random observations: "K. beheld a female child thereof purchasing a ha'porth of ice cream, which being dabbed upon a bit of newspaper she laid on the palm of her hand and transferred with infinite satisfaction to her alimentary canal by means of lingual gymnastics" (190). The sweet-soaked newspaper harkens back to AJ's joke about an edible Paris paper that was easily digested.

The concept of a minor literature helps to explain the oddly jumbled contents of AJ's Diary, which crisscross registers to bring the domestic in disjunctive contact with the political. Within a short entry dated 22 March 1890, she wonders at British widows who remarry quickly, expresses outrage at British politicians' indifference to starving Irish tenant farmers, pokes fun at Otto von Bismarck's colossal egotism, and discusses Christmas trees with Nurse. Domestic relations and current world politics jostle equally for space in the compressed entries (102–4). As Deleuze and Guattari write, "Its cramped space forces each individual intrigue to connect immediately to politics. The individual concern thus becomes all the more necessary, indispensable, magnified, because a whole other story is vibrating within it. In this way, the family triangle connects to other triangles—commercial, economic, bureaucratic, juridical" (*Kafka*, 17). AJ's Diary, with its tales of despotism in Europe and lusty widows whose "moral flesh must be as healthy as that pink substance of which they are physically compact" (102), bodies forth and puts into practice this theory of a minor literature.

AJ takes up a postcolonial stance, as her brothers would note; she writes as an American Irishwoman, speaking sarcastically of the atrocities carried out by high-minded Britons on peasants of all stripes. Of Henry Stanley's ostensible rescue mission in the Congo from 1887 to 1889, a thinly veiled and disastrous bid to establish a British foothold in Africa, AJ is lacerating: "So revolting to all mankind, my dear Briton, is your pervasive 'virtuous' pose of rising superior to the normal man with your 'brotherly love,' [and] 'civilizing processes.' . . . Retribution cometh swiftly! The Emin Pasha Relief Expedition bubble has been pricked. What a stench in the nostrils! What pin-points of *result* from it all save the melting down of 800 Zanzibari porters into 240!" (152). While it was happening, the Stanley expedition was lauded among the British public as a rousing humanitarian triumph. AJ writes as news of massive casualties and disease among the native populations began to appear. She eviscerates the phrases of empire with scare quotes, then follows with her own satirical, sensory expostulations that invoke disgust: a "revolting" superiority, a "pricked" bubble, a "stench in the nostrils," the "melting" of human bodies. A minor literature trades in such intensities: "To make the sequence vibrate, to open the word to unheard-of inner intensities—in short, an asignifying, intensive use of language" (*Kafka*, 22). In the Diary, attention to rot serves as a reminder of debased imperial politics as well as the corporeal substratum of existence.

As portrayed in the Diary, dental anesthesia, idealized propaganda (Stanley's *In Darkest Africa* was a best seller), and the language of sympathy might obscure but could not eradicate the body's fleshy contact with the world. AJ's distaste for hypocrisy and excessive emotion takes on a sticky materiality as she describes charity workers "floundering in a bog of sentimentality" (191). Her withering metaphors at moments turn on herself, often in comparison to Loring's robust competence. The entry for 13 April 1889 reads in its entirety, "K is so excessive in the normal that she seems to me at moments to be barely a rudiment. The Anaemic are so fed by the vanity of emotion and sensation that they become like bloated fungi of the morbid" (193).

Politics and prostration are linked in AJ's visceral responses to news of Irish independence. Her delight at a local election that favored an Irish nationalist politician is manifested as an agonizing bout of physical incapacitation from dyspepsia—causing her to joke that Ireland's emancipation confirms her own vassalage to her stomach. "How strange 'twould be not to be under the dominion of that mighty organ, save digestively," she writes. "No fiat of the fateful three was ever more irresistible than the decrees sent forth by that pivot of my being! Mentally no fate appalls me, but morally no crawling worm was ever so abject as I am before the convolutions of that nest of snakes coiling and uncoiling themselves" (101). In entries that report on affective experience and then reflect on the incongruities—here, surprised delight expressed through physical agony—the Diary models a form of audience-oriented self-appraisal. "Imagine," she instructs, "my 'going-off' on hearing the result of the . . . election!" (101). Such distilled, eruptive moments in the Diary serve as small catapults into the daily life of an invalid, pointing up the uneasy relations between the vulnerable body and the acrobatic operations of consciousness that record the keeping together of body and mind "hanging as it were by a cobweb to Sanity!" (101).

The Drama of Domesticity

AJ pays attention to the slender filaments and minute particles on which life depends. Casting her physical being as "my little rubbish-heap," she refers to her existential precarity during an influenza epidemic of 1890: "An infant bacillus would make one bite of me!" (78).[82] Living in cramped rented quarters (she speaks of "my centimetre of observation" [88]), AJ rhetorically diminishes her body and imagines it housed in a tiny container. An advocate of cremation, she instructs Loring: "Me ashes are to be put in an urn, and sent home" (88). Final dispensation, she cautions, is not to be "as a parlour ornament for William's new house," however; Loring is to transport her cremains to the family plot in Cambridge (88). A benefit of cremation, she reflects, is the desiccation of the body; she won't become seasick when Loring "carrie[s] home the urn in her top berth," since her stomach—"that portion of me, hitherto so susceptible to the dread thing"—would be "reduced to ashes" (89). In sprightly prose she writes, "It seems delightfully clean to elude in this way that early riser, the unpleasant wurrum [worm], and I am greatly in hopes that 'The worms crawled in / And the worms crawled out,' will not be true of my return to dust" (89).

Dust serves as a figure for the reduction of human flesh to its smallest visible form. The delicate dance of being, for AJ in the Diary, becomes the occasion for an internal domestic theatrics, when even asking a servant to do a domestic task—dusting a mantelpiece, for instance—requires a complex internal choreography: "I debated at dawn for a couple of hours or so as to whether I should stir up my palpitating heart and Jumping-Jack of a stomach by remonstrating with Clarkey and request her to transfer the thick layer of 'matter in the wrong place,' which ornaments the mantel-shelf, to some other portion of the cosmos, but my 'amiability' had its way as usual—for what are the woes of dust as compared to an acrobatic stomach!" (73). Agency and action are disassembled; things fall apart; coherence fails. (Dust itself, largely composed of skin cells, hairs, and other bodily detritus, marks the decomposition of the human form in material terms.) The will is cast as a frazzled director marshaling intractable body parts (heart, stomach) to form a resolution (get rid of dust), which in turn would require an outside body to carry out. Broken down into its component parts, the corporate process is stretched out in time, and a decision that would normally take a blink of an eye takes "a couple of hours." Meanwhile, space expands absurdly, as a tiny domestic distance is measured in relation to "the cosmos." With the arc of intention-action-result thus expanded and inflated, the synaptic breakdown becomes explicable. What from the outside would appear as inactivity, merely lying in bed, is narrated as a dramatic colloquy among desire, will, and organs. And the final result, the default decision *not* to tell the servant to dust the mantle, is consolidated into a tidy psychological package: what the patient presents to the world and to herself is labeled "amiability," the character trait of being agreeable, serene, nondemanding. Which is absurd, given the *Sturm und Drang* of the exhausting internal process.[83]

AJ's entry is thus much more than mere reportage on unsuccessful domestic duties. The anecdote shines a spotlight on the drama—at once cognitive and corporeal—of simple decision-making. It reveals the thinness and inaccuracy of the psychological terms by which we seek to understand the actions of other persons. Bergson in *Matter and Memory* (1896) casts consciousness along a continuum: "According to the nature of the play that is being acted, the movements of the players tell us more or less about it: nearly everything, if it is a pantomime, next to nothing, if it is a delicate comedy. Thus our cerebral state [physiological movements] contains more or less of our mental state [consciousness broadly construed] in the measure that we reel off our psychic life into action or wind it up into pure knowledge. . . . [P]sychic life may be lived at different heights, now nearer to action, now further removed from it."[84] Action, whether it be the broad pantomime of dusting or the delicate comedy of reflecting, involves *force* that leverages all available resources of the human organism. Deleuze describes Kafka marshaling his energies in these terms: "He understands his body as the means while in bed to cross thresholds and acts of becoming, each organ 'being under special observation'" (*Kafka*, 30).

Writing provides the stage for distinguishing between reflection and action. For AJ, the morning's "delicate comedy" of bedridden doubt and paralysis translates into a broad "pantomime" of a Diary entry—the humorous tussle with stomach and heart—in the afternoon. She gives the morning's nonevent a plotline based on cost-benefit analysis, in which the "woes of dust" lose out to the more aversive pressure of dyspepsia. The retrospective reframing—that doing nothing stemmed from "amiability"—packs a small feminist punch. It points up the absurdly low stakes of domestic work—to dust or not to dust?—while also sardonically commenting on the turbulent bodily activities hovering in the somatic background of the disembodied feminine performance of imperturbability.[85]

Daniel Kahneman, an economist whose work encompasses cognitive science, points out in *Thinking, Fast and Slow* (2011) that "the mental work that produces impressions, intuitions, and many decisions goes on in silence in our mind."[86] Bodily action is the thinking-made-concrete of what Kahneman calls "the experiencing self," working quickly and intuitively to evaluate situations and accomplish tasks. AJ's recalcitrant body occludes swift, habit-driven solutions to dust (the absent-minded sweep with a cloth, even the verbal request to tidy up). "In such cases," Kahneman writes, "we often find ourselves switching to a slower, more deliberate and effortful form of thinking" (13). AJ in her Diary, recounting the experience, occupies the perspective of the "remembering self" in relation to the "experiencing self," imbuing drama, surprise, conflict, and resolution that transpires at the level of the text. The body, along with the inconsequential objects that help to prop it up in the world, are (she deadpans) essential to "the conduct of life—the angle of one's cushions or the number of one's shawls" (115).

The minorness of domestic travails for AJ serves as a reminder of her dependence—of her own less-than-full majority. Freud describes the complex, less pleasurable laughter that comes from playing the adult with respect to oneself: "We appear to ourselves comic 'as a child' when we meet with a comic disappointment."[87] This describes the second comedic movement of the "dusting" anecdote, in which AJ the narrator—playing the role of adult to her childishly delighted self—comically describes her chagrin at being reminded of her physical ailments. Her expansive consciousness is brought short by her insubordinate body. Alice-as-writer, in her Diary, mocks the triviality of the feelings that seemed so monumental to Alice-as-character: the joke is on AJ, and she knows it.

AJ cut her philosophical teeth in the last three years of her life in her Diary. In her reimagining, the genre represents (to quote Deleuze and Guattari) a "literature of the other, the underprivileged and marginalized" by speaking a "deterritorialized language, appropriate for strange and minor uses."[88] AJ's Diary models narrative comedic calisthenics that are shaped into shareable form. The body is at the center of this humor, visible not just thematically but also through concussive expression. Accordingly, the text dispenses with encrypted subtleties, along the lines sketched by Deleuze and Guattari: "What in great literature goes on down below" the surface text, "here takes place in the full light of day" and "absorbs everyone no less than as a matter of life and death" (17).

The Cosmic Joke: Consciousness and Dissolution

AJ in her Diary was not just documenting an individual pathology. She was establishing herself as a practitioner of high-stakes humor, developing a lived philosophy of human existence unfolding in the face of mortality. For despite her technical mastery of the pace and structure of joking—juxtaposition, irony, timing, wordplay, hyperbole, set-up, and punch line—AJ at middle age was the antithesis of a performer in the usual dramatic sense. In her final decade she largely viewed the world from a horizontal position, from her bed or couch. "Life is simply a huge joke!" she exclaims in one entry (56), expressing delight at the sudden, startling return of Loring to England after spending time in the United States. Itself a startling, incongruous formulation, the exclamation is also uncomfortably ambivalent: does she mean that human existence in general is funny, surprising, disruptive—like a joke? Does she mean that her existence in particular is risible, pathetic, insignificant, worthless—a *mere* joke? Both interjection and outcry, these six words are simultaneously an affirmation of life and a caution about its fragility and absurdity. There is scarcely an entry in *The Diary of Alice James* that does not include a joke; there is scarcely an entry that does not also touch on death.

In this respect, AJ uses the Diary as an experimental space to reflect on her particular condition—her recalcitrant legs, palpitating heart, "jumping-jack of a stomach," agonizing toothache, hair-trigger nerves. Further, she broadcasts the insights that speak to the human condition, wisdom exquisitely available to someone afflicted with recurrent symptoms that leave her prostrate. John Limon has written persuasively about a version of stand-up comedy that has its (ironic, unstable) foundation in abjection: "First, I mean by it [abjection] what everybody means by it: abasement, groveling prostration. Second, I mean by it what Julia Kristeva means: a psychic worrying of those aspects of oneself that one cannot be rid of, that seem, but are not quite, alienable—for example, blood, urine, feces, nails, and the corpse. The 'abject,' in Kristeva's term of art, indicates what cannot be subject or object to you."[89] Limon theorizes this state as both a descriptor of a particular first-person experience and something that is expressed comedically: "What is stood up in stand-up comedy is abjection," he writes. "Stand-up makes vertical (or ventral) what should be horizontal (or dorsal)" (4).

AJ theorizes her own experience in strikingly similar terms. She reflects back on a time she "broke down," groping for ways of describing feeling "abjectly impotent" (149): "As I lay prostrate after the storm with my mind luminous and active and susceptible of the clearest, strongest impressions, I saw so distinctly that it was a fight simply between my body and my will, a battle in which the former was to be triumphant to the end" (149). Here she describes dissociation in which mind looks on as will and body battle it out in a "never-ending fight" (149). The experience she calls falling "into pie" (150) designates the process by which the normally coordinated elements of self—mind, body, will—work at cross purposes. This lack of coordination she traces to "physical weakness, excess of nervous susceptibility," with the result that "the moral power pauses, as it were, for a moment, and refuses to maintain muscular sanity" (149). This is a rare, noncomedic formulation of AJ's physiopsychology, cast in response to WJ's "The Hidden Self" (1890). Notably, she describes how as a girl "the most impossible sensations of upheaval, violent revolt in my head overtook me so that I had to 'abandon' [WJ's term] my brain, as it were" (149). Here is the closest she comes to stating why she turns to humor, and to the affordances of the Diary, as a way to stage her philosophizing. Especially in the latter half of the Diary, the humor frequently works aphoristically to expose the eccentricity of human beings' material, mental, and moral existence.

Threefold Embodiment

Clear that "conscious and continuous cerebration is an impossible exercise" (149), AJ turns to aphorisms to express existential truths. The following pseudo-maxim from the Diary splices together our (narcissistic) desire to see ourselves clearly and the (Gorgon-like) consequences of actually doing so: "What an awful loss it is that we can't see our own follies, they must be so much more exquisite than any one's else, but as vanity is what keeps the world agoing, after one or two convulsive laughs, the game would certainly be up!" (45). Lingering within dark humor is visceral awareness of mortality—something that habituated life suppresses. The anthropologist Helmuth Plessner (born the year that AJ died, 1892) provides an understanding of laughter that helps elucidate AJ's ludic philosophy. Plessner argues that human beings are unique in their threefold experience of embodiment: this involves *being* a body, *having* a body, and *reflecting on* the body.[90]

Plessner, like AJ before him, construes selfhood as irreducibly eccentric, never fully whole or present, though this unstable structure can be obscured in the course of normal life. Laughter manifests a sudden awareness of the clash of these aspects. During periods of health and well-being, these aspects of embodiment rarely conflict. This détente, however, can be disturbed, with one or another aspect of embodiment taking momentary precedent, thereby lighting up the essential instability of the whole structure. For instance, as Elaine Scarry has argued, in moments of excruciating pain one is all too aware of *being* a body, to the exclusion of *having* and *reflecting on* a body; she calls this "world contraction" and describes it thus: "The objects of consciousness from the most expansive to the most intimate, from those that exist in the space at the very limits of vision to those that exist in the space immediately outside the boundaries of the body . . . all in one patient rush are swept through and annihilated. It is in part the horrible momentum of this world contraction that is mirrored in the sudden agonized grimace of a person overcome by great pain or by the recognition of imminent death."[91] Scarry is describing what happens to a person who is being tortured. This horror is of course far removed from the experience of the comic. Yet just as aesthetic experience has a kinship with other moments of transcendence, so humor—which often has a valence of muted violence—has a kinship with physical pain, and with mortality itself.

AJ's Diary is pocked with anecdotes and jokes that, in homeopathic form, force the irreducibility of being a body into the foreground of human experience. Here is a darkly comic anecdote recorded by AJ: "I never can forget this . . . which I read at the age of fifteen. A witness was asked to describe the appearance of the body of a man who was supposed to have been murdered. She said that 'He looked pleasant-like and foaming at the mouth'" (60). The incongruity of the homespun epithet "pleasant-like" being so closely linked to "foaming at the mouth" marks the unbridgeable chasm between social niceties (in which one presents to the world an amiable facial expression and well-regulated figure) and the unpleasant, animal truth of the fluids, tissues, and reflexes that make up our material bodies. What is most striking is that AJ records this bare-boned newspaper item in her Diary *a quarter century* after she read it, suggesting it captured something essential for a girl on the cusp of adulthood.

Embodying the Incongruity Theory of Humor

AJ's self-portrayal in the Diary—an ailing spinster who is also darkly hilarious, a personal Diary that is written for an audience, a trail of jokes tinged with both delight and despair—leverages the Incongruity Theory of humor. In this account, jokes and the laughter they provoke in human beings mark the human recognition of inaptness, inharmoniousness, and inconsistency. "In everything that is to provoke a lively, uproarious laughter," writes Kant, "there must be something nonsensical."[92] In the Diary, the absurdity often lies in wordplay, as when AJ laughingly records a man misstating, "I am in the hands of an unscrupulous Providence" (158). Many of the jokes in AJ's Diary carry something absurd. A case in point is this anecdote, which in fact leads off a trio of jests that she recorded in an 1889 entry: "Just read this, Two Irishmen in Texas came across a snake and one chopped his head off and kept on pounding at the squirming body, whereupon his friend said, 'Why don't you leave off, it's dead.' 'Sure and I know that, but I want to make the crature sinsible of his misfortune'" (59). Teaching a lesson to a snake is silly; pulverizing its body to make it "sinsible of its misfortune" is ludicrous. But tucked inside the joke's absurdity is an anti-Cartesian insistence on the body's awareness.

Laughing at the joke marks the uncomfortable awareness of a darker truth, an even more profound mistake: bodily death trumps consciousness every time, in all species. While it is possible to lose consciousness and live, it is not possible to die and retain consciousness. In a later entry, AJ intensifies the joke, turning it on herself. When her stomach pain becomes unbearable, she calls for HJ, who, she writes, "immure[s] himself, without a murmur, in my squalid indigestions" (135). They consulted a physician and "extracted the consoling answer to 'Can she die?' that 'They sometimes do'" (135). With dark humor AJ writes, "This is most cheering to all parties—the only drawback being that it will probably be in my sleep so that I shall not be one of the audience, dreadful fraud! a creature who has been denied all dramatic episodes might be allowed, I think, to assist at her own extinction" (135).

By joking about sleeping through her demise (what most would call "a good death"), AJ calls attention to the true existential problem: that death eradicates the very consciousness that could bear witness to the event. These jokes affirm that *being* a body is primary, while *reflecting on* the body is secondary—wisdom that is not packaged as a concept but registered corporeally. The pulverized snake and its human concomitant, the chuckling, grimacing human being laughing at the joke, index the body's preeminence—something that, in another turn of the screw, it takes a human frontal lobe to appreciate. Darwin, in *The Expression of the Emotions in Man and Animals* (1872), noted that "the imagination is sometimes said to be tickled by a ludicrous idea; and this so-called tickling of the mind is curiously analogous with that of the body."[93] Tickling, the application of a light touch on sensitive skin to achieve explosions of laughter, notoriously involves intimacy and play with an edge of violence.[94]

These jokes are, in the context of AJ's Diary, preparatory for even more serious incongruities to come. In the entry dated 31 May 1891, AJ writes about being told she has untreatable breast cancer: "To him who waits, all things come! My aspirations may have been eccentric, but I cannot complain now, that they have not been brilliantly fulfilled. Ever since I have been ill, I have longed and longed for some palpable disease, no matter how conventionally dreadful a label it might have" (206). Critics have tended to read this jubilant-sounding entry as an apt psychological response, one that confirms AJ practiced a "career" in death and herself yearned to die.

AJ sought external validation for her firsthand experience of pain. The key term here is "palpable"—able to be touched or felt from the outside (not just available to interior sensation, also known as *interoception*). Having been told that her bodily experiences—"the monstrous mass of subjective sensations"—are hers alone, AJ welcomes the medical acknowledgment of the body's potency: "I was always driven back to stagger alone under the monstrous mass of subjective sensations, which that sympathetic being 'the medical man' had no higher inspiration than to assure me I was personally responsible for, washing his hands of me with a graceful complacency under my very nose. Dr. Torry was the only man who ever treated me like a rational being, who did not assume, because I was victim to many pains, that I was, of necessity, an arrested mental development, too" (206–7). AJ's glee at her cancer diagnosis introduces a new incongruity in this story, for unlike the snake she gets to describe events from her perspective.

The Diary entry is told from the perspective of *being a body* ("an indestructible quantity") rather than *having a body* ("subjective sensations" for which she was "personally responsible"). This new perspective is registered in the following passage, with a funny formulation: the physician is the agent who finally "endows" her with a body, translating subjective pain into a palpable "lump" and then into "a tumour."

> I have been going downhill at a steady trot; so they sent for Sir Andrew Clark four days ago, and the blessed being has endowed me not only with cardiac complications, but says that a lump that I have had in one of my breasts for three months which has given me a great deal of pain, is a tumour, that nothing can be done for me but to alleviate pain, that it is only a question of time, etc. This with a delicate embroidery of

> "the most distressing case of nervous hyperaesthesia" added to a spinal neurosis that has taken me off my legs for seven years; with attacks of rheumatic gout in my stomach for the last twenty, ought to satisfy the most inflated pathologic vanity. It is decidedly indecent to catalogue oneself in this way, but I put it down in a scientific spirit, to show that though I have no productive worth, I have a certain value as an indestructible quantity. (207)

AJ's "indecent . . . catalogue" (she mentions her heart, her breast, her spine, her legs, and her stomach, along with time periods associated with the difficulties she had with each) mimics a reductive "scientific spirit" that counts, itemizes, and quantifies material existence. No longer an inert, *dis*counted "mass of sensation," AJ reflects on the afflicted body she has inhabited and has *been* for her adult life. Whereas doctors vacillate wildly between denying her physical experience and reducing her to it, the Diary entry gives voice to all three aspects of embodiment: being a body, having a body, and reflecting on the body. As she lies on her deathbed AJ writes, "I shall keep the occasion cheerful by contemplating simply the truly human and topsy-turvey aspect of the situation" (222).

Serious Joking About Suicide

AJ's final Diary entries—following her diagnosis of breast cancer—point toward death. The unavoidability of impending dissolution is the cosmic joke that preoccupies AJ, and that is thematized in her recurrent references to suicide. When she reads about a man killing himself in St. Paul's Cathedral, her jokes are scathing. Ventriloquizing the perspective of a sanctimonious bishop, she notes that it was "inexcusably sloppy" of the despondent man to kill himself in the sanctuary—and speculates that the church leaders may (absurdly) "exercise their highly developed muscles of evasion to wash out the stain of blood by an 'Act of Reconciliation'!" (143). Upon hearing that Edmund Gurney (an acquaintance of HJ and WJ) killed himself, she writes: "It's bad that it is so untidy, there is no denying that, for one bespatters one's friends morally as well as physically" (52). Reflecting on her own thoughts of suicide, she writes: "The most comic and apparently the chief argument used against it [suicide], is that because you were born without being consulted, you would be very sinful should you cut short your blissful career! This had been said to me a dozen times, and they never can see how they have turned things topsy-turvy" (52). *This had been said to me a dozen times.* Buried in the joke is an anecdote described by Edel, in which Henry James Sr. many years earlier "gave AJ his fatherly permission to end her life whenever it pleased her, beseeching her only to 'do it in a perfectly gentle way in order not to distress her friends'" (Edel, 7).

Medical anthropologist Jocelyn Chua in her book *In Pursuit of the Good Life* (2014) has retheorized suicide, diverting attention away from the act itself to the range of rhetorical and experiential forms suicide takes: "In clinical and sociological approaches as much as in popular imagining, suicide has been traditionally conceived as a marker of poor social cohesion, the annihilative act of the atomized individual cut loose of the ties that bind to family, community, society, and to life itself. Rather than begin with the premise that suicide is 'antisocial' in the many uses of the term, this book instead recognizes the ways suicide may be generative of social, political, and moral life."[95] Chua's work argues that, "rather than the termination of life alone" (5), suicide "may generate new ways of living and of living with one another" (190) and gets "folded into the everyday" (110). The presence of suicide in stories, jokes, fantasies, and reports, Chua argues, "animates the ways people live (or fail to live) with themselves and others as they labor to remake and presently inhabit that world together" (23). These meditations, on suicide as a continuum of rhetorical and material practices, are useful as a way to approach AJ's complex practice of living in the shadow of disability and ultimately mortality.

The Diary contains AJ's ludic response to her father's injunction on suicide: "I shall proclaim that anyone who spends her life as an appendage to five cushions and three shawls is justified in committing the sloppiest kind of suicide at a moment's notice" (81). Person as appendage, a "subsidiary organ" to the props that support her: Bergson notes, "*We laugh every time a person gives us the impression of being a thing.*"[96] But AJ's joke also marks the prosthetic power of the small—a mere cushion or shawl—and so returns to the Diary's central contrivance: the capacity of the small to usurp the great. Tucked within the quotidian life of AJ is a scalar theory of joking; or more aptly, tucked within the scalar joking of AJ is a theory of life. Here is Bergson:

> Let us suppose, however, that *our attention is drawn to this material side of the body;* that, so far from sharing in the lightness and subtlety of the principle with which it is animated, *the body is no more in our eyes than a heavy and cumbersome vesture, a kind of irksome ballast which holds down to earth a soul eager to rise aloft.* Then the body will become to the soul what, as we have just seen, the garment was to the

> body itself—inert matter dumped down upon living energy. The impression of the comic will be produced as soon as we have a clear apprehension of this putting the one on the other. (24–25, emphasis added)

HJ believed that consciousness could expand and extend after death, beyond the existence of the physical body.[97] WJ wrote about spirit mediumship, and the persistence of personality beyond the grave; upon receiving word of his sister's death, WJ even suggested to his little brother that he double-check to make sure she wasn't performing a "trance-trick[]" (*WHJ*, 265). Contra her brothers, AJ presents an argument for the insistence of the material in human social existence, for the unavoidable and darkly comedic encrustations of the "irksome ballast" that bring to ground a life and in so doing keep us operating at a human scale.

Life-S(e)ized

There is potency in the diastolic and systolic rhythm of expansion and contraction that characterizes humor in AJ's Diary. The soul brought low by the body is matched by the scion of the prodigious James family being "had" by a "little wretch" (Bradfield, who would never trade places [48]) or sustained by a "colossal" spinster (Loring). The disproportion and interruption produce moments of the grand tripping on the small, the general outstripped by the particular, the ideal brought up short by the material: this "descending incongruity" describes the delight one experiences reading the letters of the fraternal Jameses—HJ and WJ—as they fall over themselves (epistolarily speaking) at the sudden appearance in 1894 of copies of AJ's Diary.

After AJ's death, HJ and WJ exchanged letters reflecting on their sister's "little life, shrunken and rounded in retrospect": "Poor little Alice! What a life" (March 1892, *WHJ*, 265). They did not know of the Diary's existence until two years later, when Loring sent them each a printed copy, adding one for Robertson James and keeping one for herself. HJ continues to lament his sister's circumscribed life—AJ, he said, focused her attention on "too small a scrap of what really surrounded her"—but now he frets that the Diary, swollen with his gossipy anecdotes (by his own admission to WJ, he "brought her the world") and circulated by the "prodigious" Loring, is in danger of becoming big (May 1894, *WHJ*, 307). Here is HJ to WJ, writing from the Grand Hotel in Rome, of the "very dreadful-to-me-to-think-of adventures [the Diary] may have": "The printedness-*en-toutes-lettres* of so many names, personalities, hearsay (usually, on Alice's part, through *me!)* about people &c. has . . . ma[de] me intensely nervous & almost sick with terror about possible publicity, possible accidents, reverberations . . . with the fearful American newspaper lying in wait for every whisper, every echo" (May 1894, *WHJ*, 306). AJ's influence is in danger of expanding well beyond the James family.

As if anticipating her postmortem significance, AJ herself repeatedly refers to her physical and existential smallness, each time coining a joke about her disproportionate prodigiousness. "I remind myself all the time of a coral insect," she writes, "building up my various reefs of theory by microscopic additions" (109). The tiny that accommodates the grand presents a self that is at once ludicrous and insistently, unavoidably interesting. AJ's "life"—both Diary and physical existence—presents itself with undeniably feeble exuberance as an embodiment of the stretchable. Wai Chee Dimock has written that "largeness and smallness preoccupy early James," referring of course to HJ and focusing on the monumental impersonality of Rome in the face of one woman's life.[98]

AJ, by contrast, reminds us that even the biggest, oldest cities—and the manners of the human beings that inhabit them—are social accretions. They are forms—like clothing—and therefore susceptible to comedy when brought in touch with the human existence they would contain. When it comes to a world-historical city facing off against the singular ego of a young woman, here is AJ:

> Ellie Emmet, who is staying with her cousins, the Roses, was driving one day with Mrs. Charles; on the carriage turning into Russell Square, Ellie exclaimed, "this is where Amelia lived," when a shiver of the unusual brought from Mrs. Rose, "Why, do you take London in that way?" I am as much amused . . . as you can be by these microscopic observations recorded of this mighty race; they are as grotesque as the following, in which the infinitesimal and the colossal were never more happily contrasted. When I was in Leamington, one of my friends asked Harry if I were not coming soon to London: he said "No." "What a loss to London," was the dislocated rejoinder. (166)

The friend's unwitting verbal comment was funny because disproportionate: it placed AJ (infinitesimal) on the same scale as London (colossal). But by encapsulating HJ's anecdote—at her own expense—into her Diary, AJ formally re-joke-ifies it: the scale of the Life expands to contain that which would render it inconsequential. Indeed, AJ's scalar negotiation echoes Isabel Archer, who similarly scales Rome to fit her life: "[She] made use of her memory of Rome as

Figure 3. In September 1891, a few months after learning she has inoperable breast cancer, Alice James teasingly blames her friend Katharine Peabody Loring for scheduling a formal portrait: "Like a sheep to the shambles, I have been led by K. to the camera!" (*Diary*, 21). By permission of the Houghton Library, Harvard University: MS Am 1092.9 (4598).

she might have done, in a hot crowded room, of a phial of something pungent hidden in her handkerchief."[99]

But lest we overemphasize its expansive power: AJ's Diary is written during what she called her "mortuary moment" (218); accordingly, it is preoccupied with existential annihilation. She actively puts into practice what Nagel has described as living, clear-eyed, in the face of absurdity: "In viewing ourselves from a perspective broader than we can occupy in the flesh, we become spectators of our own lives. We cannot do very much as pure spectators of our own lives, so we continue to lead them, and devote ourselves to what we are able at the same time to view as no more than a curiosity, like the ritual of an alien religion."[100] Practically every page is punctuated with jokes that themselves clatter the cerebral against the corporeal, even her last entry. In it, AJ wryly casts her pumping heart as a feeble, superannuated employee finally ready to retire: no need for suicide, since, she writes, "I feel sure that it can't be possible but what the bewildered little hammer that keeps me going will very shortly see the decency of ending his distracted career" (232).

The ludic disproportion of a small pump plopped inside a cumbersome body, of a little sister born into a family of masterful brothers, of a transplanted Irish American absorbed by parliamentary debates over Home Rule, of a truncated, one-off Diary in a literary history stretching back to the Epic of Gilgamesh: these provide material, anthropological, political, and formal analogs for the smallness of a human life lived in the shadow of disability and death. As Nagel writes, "In continuing to live and work and strive, we take ourselves seriously in action no matter what we say" (724). AJ's audacity is to investigate the face of absurdity and yet to persist with life-affirming action, penning her Diary and appreciating her beloved friend and brothers, right up to the very end.

Coda: *If you tell a joke in a journal, does anybody laugh?*

Itself a joke of sorts, the question riffs on the philosophical riddle about sense perception and the object world: *If a tree falls in a forest and nobody hears, does it make a sound?* Questions of this sort, called koans, fall into a tradition of philosophical reasoning that takes the form of an ongoing, open-ended conversation between teacher and student. In the Buddhist tradition, philosophical insight is understood as a practice that is dialogical (rather than the work of a solitary mind) and that unfolds over time (rather than being a static truth). As Thomas P. Kasulis writes, "The essence of enlightenment came to be identified with the interaction between masters and students. Whatever insight dhyana might bring, its verification was always interpersonal. *In effect, enlightenment came to be understood not so much as an insight, but as a way of acting in the world with other people.*"[101] We can understand joking in AJ's Diary in similar terms.

As caregivers, interlocutors, and frequent butts of her Diary's humor, both Loring and Bradfield had close physical intimacy with AJ. This interweaving takes literal form in AJ's letters and Diary, in which their handwriting appears. In terrible pain, AJ dictated the Diary's last entry to Loring, something AJ notes in the text itself. One must imagine her close companion writing these lines, in which AJ describes being on the verge of asking her for a lethal dose of painkiller: "I am being ground slowly on the grim grindstone of physical pain & on two nights had almost asked for K's lethal dose, but one steps hesitantly along such unaccustomed ways & endures from second to second" (232). Afflicted with "nervous horrors" that "sear the soul," AJ calls attention to Loring using her hand for the hypnotic technique that she learned to help allay AJ's suffering. Yeazell has observed that Loring's "hand, or its fellow, was also engaged to the very end in taking dictation" and committing AJ's words to paper (49): "These last Katharine has completely under the control of her rhythmic hand, so I go no longer in dread. Oh the wonderful moment when I felt myself floated for the first time, into the deep sea of divine cessation, & saw all the dear old mysteries & miracles vanish into vapour! That first experience didn't repeat itself, fortunately, for it might become a seduction" (232). As AJ devotes some of her last breaths to speaking sentences, her friend poignantly lends her body to the task of materializing them. (Strouse reports that Loring, who suffered from poor eyesight, had learned Braille [193]; perhaps this made her especially skilled at the arts of touch.) Writing to an old friend, Loring conveys her perspective: "She is not any better. I do not see why she is not worse, for she seems to me to have been losing strength steadily, for some time. It is her spirit, of course, that keeps her up—she is interested in everything, and immensely interesting & amusing all the time. She really is *very* clever! I have no doubt you knew that before but it constantly impresses me anew."[102] This passage captures succinctly the existential equation of AJ: as the strength of her body diminishes, her spirit swells and "keeps her up."

The phrase, "immensely interesting & amusing," recalls the first entry of the Diary, when AJ reflexively sutures her narrative voice to her physical being by suggesting that "a written monologue by that most interesting being, *myself*, may have its yet to be discovered consolations" (25). Astonishingly, during her years living in England, as she became increasingly less mobile, less comfortable, and less able to manage the simplest tasks of daily living, AJ's literary output also increased, culminating in the Diary that Loring had printed and placed in the hands of WJ and HJ. AJ was not a novelist, nor was she a psychologist. But she was a writer and an observer, and she shared with her brothers a quick wit and an empiricist interest in the vicissitudes of human mental and emotional experience. In her hands, the journal form becomes a laboratory for examining the unfolding comedy of a restless consciousness locked in, even as it was enabled by, an absurd, losing contest with a recalcitrant, pain-ridden human body.

Thematically, the comedic tone of the Diary could appear jarring, appearing in the diary of a woman for whom life would appear to be no laughing matter. This perspective, however, (mis)aligns humor with a state of mind—joy or happiness—that is then given physiological expression. Plessner notes that this understanding is too dualistic, construing the body as "the enveloping layer, indispensable to life and unavoidable for the purpose of expression, of a being which in its true nature knows itself to be emancipated from this envelope" over which it "has command . . . to the limits of sickness and death."[103] Yet the potent physiological responses of laughing (and crying) have no such "symbolic form": "They make their appearance in uncontrolled and unformed eruptions of the body" (31). Laughter, Plessner urges, sounds forth a primal truth. It is not "a form of expression which could be appropriately compared with verbal utterance"; thus a person "breaks—out laughing," with an emphasis on this idea of breakage (31). Laughter marks "an actual break in his [man's] way of existing," a "brokenness" that is finally irrecuperable to individual psychology and instead marks a relationship of the self to its own embodiment and to the world—including the persons in it—who sometimes scaffold, sometimes threaten the self (32).

The comic spirit pervades AJ's gossipy descriptions as well as her descriptions of gossip—especially the dry, sometimes catty vignettes that HJ invariably passed along, about those in their social milieu, during visits with his little sister. It appears in the form of sardonic asides, remembered dialogue, original and quoted jokes, wry observations, cutting derision, and bleak, black humor about illness, suicide, and mortality—that of friends as well as her own. The comic spirit propels AJ's mocking assessment of the rigidity, cruelty, and ordinary abusiveness she sees in English politics, especially regarding the Catholic Church and Parliament's treatment of Ireland's insurgent leaders. It animates AJ's portrayal of what she perceives as her own weak character, her moral failings as a friend and sister, and her unflinching depiction of the humdrum indignities that stem from the material constraints that the world places on fragile human beings. It propels AJ's respect for suffering souls who die by suicide. AJ, who knew well the pain of existence, explicitly made the decision to live by choice, and to write her life up until the day of her death.

Leveraging the Diary's short, consecutive, atomized bursts of text, AJ writes in a way recognizable to the modern reader familiar with the rhythmic jolts of stand-up comedy. Well before comedians like Lenny Bruce and Lily Tomlin took the stage, pragmatist philosophers were theorizing the operations of mind that shift an audience from a zone of familiarity to a place of cognitive and existential dislocation. This experience is what Peirce called "Secondness": a sudden, stunned awareness that marks a shift in thinking and belief that is viscerally felt but not yet conceptualized. Through the medium of the joke, and by posthumously shocking her brothers with her Diary, AJ inhabited the embodied, proto-cognitive realm of Secondness. As Peirce described this virtual space of shifting awareness, "It would be like unexpectedly hearing a great explosion of nitroglycerine before one had recovered oneself and merely had the sense of the breaking off of the quiet. Perhaps it might not be far from what ordinary common sense conceives to take place when one billiard ball caroms on another."[104]

Humor and laughter allow AJ to navigate the peculiar absurdity of being human. As Nagel writes, "I would argue that absurdity is one of the most human things about us: a manifestation of our most advanced and interesting characteristics. Like skepticism in epistemology, it is possible only because we possess a certain kind of insight—the capacity to transcend ourselves in thought" (726–27). As AJ knew well, and her brothers came to perceive through intimacy with their sister, there is a cosmic jest tucked into the cognitive structure of human beings. Adult consciousness, in particular, often comes to feel apart from and superior to the body, only to be brought up short in finding it is part of, and therefore dependent on, the flesh-and-bone, sentient being that it feels it captains.

This chapter has explored how the comic spirit as staged by AJ offers a method for acknowledging and managing human vulnerability—a survival strategy, of sorts. Leveraging the disjunctive relations between mind and body, and between self and other, the Diary's jarring humor and sparring sensibility carry philosophical implications that were not lost on AJ's two older brothers—who also went on to explore, in different genres and with different resonance, how human beings navigate a shifting and uncertain (social) world. WJ pressed these insights into a collaborative, body-based mode of inquiry in his lectures on psychology; HJ expressed the sensory ambiguities of shared vision in his early comic novels and then in his child-centered and ghostly tales. Those aspects of AJ's life that made things difficult—being the little sister in a family that valued the intellectual work of men, being an ambitious woman in a time of limited opportunities, suffering the vicissitudes of a fragile human organism—granted her a lively sense of the limits and yet persistence of human minds at work and at play. To return to WJ's prescient comment, before he knew of AJ's Diary, "I am as sure as I am of anything that her life has been bearing its fruit, fruit not only for her, I mean, but for life at large" (*WHJ*, 257).

The diary is a literary form fitted to the empirical model.[105] It registers an individual consciousness collecting and recording its worldly engagements: "The diary advertises its links with subjectivity by virtue of the prominence it accords the speaking 'I,' to the point where the first person singular pronoun is often so massively self-evident and redundant as to be able to be elided."[106] The journal thus records the elevation of the individual life—its events, things, objects of attention, relations, feelings, actions, thoughts, aspirations, tribulations—to the practices of scrutiny, data-collecting, recording, analysis, and representation associated with modern science.

It is a fitting incongruity to consider that AJ's Diary bears comparison with WJ's *Principles of Psychology* (1890). WJ himself made the links among journal keeping, psychology, and philosophy in a letter to William Dean Howells: "G. Stanley Hall, leader of *American Psychology*, has written that the book [WJ's *Principles of Psychology*] is the most complete piece of self-evisceration since Marie Bashkirtseff's diary. Don't you think that's rather unkind? But in this age of nerves all philosophizing is really something of that sort."[107] Bashkirtseff's translator and editor described the young woman's diary as "a book in the nude" that sprang from "passionate self-absorption and egoism," yet WJ recognized Hall's analogy to his psychology text as both pejorative and apt, insofar as Bashkirtseff's diary also "lay before us 'the very pulse of the machine,' to show us the momentary feelings and uninvited back-stair thoughts passing like a breath across our consciousness."[108] Psychologists in the 1890s similarly placed the subjective experience of the human mind at the epistemological center of philosophical inquiry. When the motions of consciousness become an object of scientific scrutiny, the personal journal becomes minor literature in the Deleuzian sense: a mode for exploring and broadcasting new insights into human experience. Joking also implicates an audience. Thus the dark humor in AJ's Diary provides not just the author but also the reader with an obliquity of vision that tickles us out of our intellectual and social grooves and gives sudden, transient, third-person perspective on ourselves and our individual, first-person grievances and follies.

Approaching the Diary under the aspect of play downplays the invalid narrative and lights up AJ's fierce philosophical project. Huizinga writes, "To dare, to take risks, to bear uncertainty, to endure tension—these are the essence of the play spirit. . . . Here the ideas of contest, struggle, exercise, exertion, endurance and suffering are united" (51). The sociologist Arthur Frank describes how embodiment makes human beings exquisitely aware of their lived exigence: "Contingency is the body's condition of being subject to forces that cannot be controlled."[109] The experience of limitation that comes from pain, disease, and disability, Frank argues, makes vivid "our shared corporeality" (35) as well as human beings' "perpetual vulnerability to interruption" (57). Through high-stakes humor animated by both affection and misery, the little sister enlists the spirit of play to expand the philosophical potency of the journal as a genre and to embrace the ethical challenges posed by a life lived in the shadow of disability and ultimately dissolution.

CHAPTER 2

"In the Same Game"

Consciousness and the Child in William James's Lectures-Turned-Texts

The plays of children are nonsense, but very educative nonsense.
—Ralph Waldo Emerson, "Experience" (1844)

In "Self-Reliance," Ralph Waldo Emerson profiles one of his most enduring figures: the nonchalant boy who is "independent, irresponsible," and "the master of society" by virtue of his disinterest.[1] Emerson—friend to Henry James Sr. and godfather to William James—presents the egoism, curiosity, and freemasonry of boyhood as metaphors for the sovereignty of individual perception. Following in the Romantic tradition of Jean-Jacques Rousseau, William Wordsworth, and William Blake, Emerson offers the child as a lesson in unfettered judgment. Yet if the elder Emerson's self-reliant boy is a detached watcher "looking out from his corner" (261), we can turn to *Edward* Emerson, the essayist's son, for a portrait of youthful exuberance that is active, engaged, and playfully pugilistic. Here is the younger Emerson's portrait of the James family dinner table:

> The adipose and affectionate Wilkie, as his father called him, would say something and be instantly corrected by the little cock-sparrow Bob, the youngest [son], but good-naturedly defend his statement, and then Henry (junior) would emerge from his silence in defense of Wilkie.

> Then Bob would be more impertinently insistent, and Mr. James would advance as Moderator, and William, the eldest, would join in. The voice of the Moderator presently would be drowned by the combatants and he soon came down vigorously *into the arena*, and when in the excited argument the dinner knives might not be absent from eagerly gesticulating hands, dear Mrs. James, more conventional, but bright as well as motherly, would look at me, laughingly reassuring, saying, "Don't be disturbed, Edward; they won't stab each other. This is usual when the boys come home." And the quiet little sister ate her dinner, smiling, close to the combatants.[2] (emphasis added)

Mary James's comment, as quoted by the younger Emerson, offers a crucial gloss on what is transpiring. The James dining room becomes an "arena" for intense, immersive conversational exploits; as "combatants" the diners emulate gestures associated with battle. The mother's laughter and AJ's smile mark a recognition that—to quote Gregory Bateson—"this is play": the menfolk *seem* at odds, but they are not.[3] Their behavior is marked off as nonserious, and yet what transpires is immersive to those involved. Bateson puts it this way: "The playful nip denotes the bite, but does not denote that which would be denoted by the bite" (180). Because mock jousting can in fact sometimes devolve into actual fighting, however, there is an open-ended, unfoldingness to this sort of game—the rules are not static but instead part of what Bateson describes as "an evolving system of interaction" (192).

Johan Huizinga notes that there is dynamic "rhythm and harmony" operative in play that places it in the realm of aesthetics, even as the qualities of play have real-world effects and are explicable in terms of evolutionary theory: "The element of tension in play to which we have just referred plays a particularly important part. Tension means uncertainty and chanciness; a striving to decide the issue and so end it. The player wants something to 'go,' to 'come off'; to 'succeed' by his own exertions. Baby reaching for a toy, pussy patting a bobbin, a little girl playing ball—all want to achieve something difficult, to succeed, to end a tension."[4] The sense of strain calls forth assessment, response, and adaptation, modeling a deeply social interanimation that finds resolution through "success"—a solution, discovery, or otherwise satisfying sense of progress. "Uncertainty and chanciness" describe the conditions of the natural world mapped by Charles Darwin, with the higher organisms displaying, as Elizabeth Grosz has described, "an openness to the unknown, the capacity to withstand the unexpected as well as the predictable."[5] Play drew the attention of Darwin and other nineteenth-century scientists, insofar as it entails accommodation to new situations, assimilation of patterns through repetition, and a precarious relationship to seriousness, which it can always lapse into (think of the happy screams and giggling of tickling devolving into actual terror). The seeming lightness of play can simultaneously manifest an absorbing, full-bodied experience of new understanding.

The potent combination of play, childhood, and increased capacity describe an attitude toward experience that, within the James family, could transpire at any age. Alice James once described her father as "the delicious infant!" emphasizing that Henry James Sr. employed a method of philosophizing and of parenting that allowed an extraordinary amount of freedom among his offspring.[6] The James patriarch, she writes, "couldn't submit even to the thralldom of his own whim" (57), describing a parent who insisted to his family that whoever officiated at his funeral should "say only this, 'here lies a man who has thought all his life, that the ceremonies attending birth, marriage and death were all damned nonsense,' don't let him say a word more" (217). Radical, sometimes naïve questioning of established forms, and a willingness to go lightly into zones traditionally characterized by seriousness were modeled by Henry James Sr., enacted by AJ in her journal, and developed as a style of teaching and investigation by WJ. Many of WJ's colleagues in psychology and philosophy, both his admirers and his critics, commented on his playful and exuberant attitude in and out of the classroom. George Santayana once complained: "James was no draught-horse patiently pulling the scientific barge along a placid academic canal; rather a Red Indian shooting the rapids with spasmodic skill and elemental emotions."[7] WJ himself acknowledged his aversion to normal, routinized (one might say *grown-up*) philosophical modes, characterized by "a sort of champing of jaws, pawing of the ground, and resettling into the same attitude, like a weary horse in a stall with an empty manger."[8]

This chapter takes seriously WJ's playfulness, seeing it not only as a quality of his character but also as a broader disposition toward experience. As such, it serves as both a method and a theory for describing how the human mind works in relation to other people, to ideas, and to the material world. As we shall see, the curiosity, flexibility, anticipation, reaction, relationality, and ludic openness that WJ both describes and enacts are central to the activity of play. If AJ provides a porthole view of the existential drama of embodied human consciousness, WJ opens multiple doors onto the pugilistic intellectual milieu of nineteenth-century science. Different "combatants" in debates over evolutionary theory—often colleagues and friends of WJ—offer accounts of how human beings come to "mind" the world. Indeed, AJ in the *Diary* remarks dryly on her brother's receptiveness to different points of view: "William expressed himself and his environment to perfection when he replied to my question about his house in Chocorua [New Hampshire], 'Oh, it's the most delightful home you ever saw; has 14 different doors all opening outside.' His brain isn't limited to 14, perhaps unfortunately" (67–68). While WJ's watchwords were openness and plasticity, AJ's acerbic humor offers a reminder that many live their lives with a consciousness of closed doors.

In the next section I consider how, intellectually and affectively, WJ's diverse influences allowed him to move with remarkable ease among different fields of study. Trained in both medicine and science (at Lawrence Scientific School), WJ taught at Harvard in multiple disciplines; he served as a lecturer in physiology and anatomy before his appointment as professor of psychology (in 1876) and later philosophy (in 1881). Moreover, in the wake of Darwin's evolutionary theories, the activities, interests, and inclinations associated with childhood and youth were increasingly understood to provide a window into evolutionary processes. As Melvin Konner writes, "It was apparent to Darwin that his own children came into the world with behavioral adaptations that were products of natural selection and phylogenetic legacies, as shown in his infant diary and other writings."[9] Scientists such as Ernst Haeckel saw in the biological development of the child the evolutionary origins of *Homo sapiens*. Haeckel's theory, later named recapitulation theory, is encapsulated in his phrase "ontogeny recapitulates phylogeny."[10] By this Haeckel meant that the infant's growth to adulthood provided a biological analogy for the transmutation of the species, over vast eons, from simple organism to the top of the food chain. Yet, as Konner observes, for a scientist "play is a biological puzzle . . . combining as it does great energy expenditure and risk with apparent pointlessness" (500). In this regard, play offers "a central paradox of evolutionary biology" (500)—one that WJ embraced, to the puzzlement of colleagues like Santayana.

WJ came of age during the period in which Darwin developed and defended his evolutionary theory, though he assimilated these ideas less through classroom instruction than the experience of being thrown directly "into the arena," to quote Edward Emerson. My subsequent section focuses on WJ's relationship with Louis Agassiz, Darwin's primary antagonist in the United States. In 1865, WJ joined the Thayer Expedition, Agassiz's ambitious scientific trek to the Amazon to collect fish species to support his theologically inspired theory on the stability of species. WJ's letters home to his family, as well as his retrospective reflections on the anti-evolutionary theories of his mentor Agassiz, reveal a young man himself trying to adapt to a challenging physical environment while also working to reconcile two different accounts of biological transformation. These twinned struggles offer an in situ instance of WJ immersed in an expedition that is structured in relation to the ground rules set by Agassiz (to prove that species do not evolve over time) while simultaneously changing the rules of engagement. Hector Rodriguez describes this sort of complex experience as a "dance":

> Experience is inseparable from structured action, which is seldom carried out by an isolated ego. In most situations, the player confronts either another player or some impersonal obstacle. There is always a dynamic interplay of move and counter-move. A squash player must wait to see how the ball bounces back from the wall. This 'waiting to see' indicates an essential feature about the activity of playing: that there is always something *other*, and so play is seldom radically subjective. The experience of the player is partly constituted by this moment of otherness. The player must respond to some event, in the context of a structured situation. Playing consists in a trans-individual process of action and reaction, which often takes on a to-and-fro quality reminiscent of dance.[11]

This "dynamic interplay" describes not just the James family dinner table, but also the eldest son's relation to Agassiz; in turn, the idea of a "trans-individual process of action and reaction" proves essential to WJ's later writings on radical empiricism.

I then turn to WJ's early writings on physiological psychology, in which he engages in a partly playful, partly derisive encounter with Herbert Spencer's ideas about mind as correspondence and develops his own theory of neural plasticity. In his two textbooks, *The Principles of Psychology* (1890) and *Psychology: Briefer Course* (1892), we have the first rumblings of WJ's interactive, demonstration-based approach to the study of consciousness, which captivated both students and wider audiences at the turn into the twentieth century. A project that begins as a startlingly intimate-feeling conversation with readers about a Darwin-inflected physiological psychology evolves over WJ's publications into an increasingly play-centered vision of human action and cognition.

Next I examine the textbooks and essay collections that arose out of WJ's mid-career lectures. The classroom serves as a rich environment within which WJ both develops and dramatizes his engaged, dialogical approach to human understanding. The dynamic, inquiring back-and-forth of pedagogical encounters structure the core insights of *The Will to Believe, Talks to Teachers,* and *Pragmatism.* I then consider WJ's late writings and letters, in which he most explicitly articulates the human search for knowledge and meaning as an unfolding practice that emulates the rhythms of open-ended play. WJ gives form to what his friend and colleague Charles Sanders Peirce referred to as "the play of Musement," a multimodal, collaborative, and affection-soaked way of thinking through philosophical questions. In a brief coda I treat the persistence of WJ's pedagogy and presence across the decades.

Throughout, the method of the chapter is to situate WJ in relation to those who influenced him—family, teachers, colleagues—and also to call on some of the thinkers influenced *by* him, such as Huizinga and Bateson, to elaborate how WJ's "larky" style and emphasis on situated, body-based cognitive adaptation in his lectures-turned-textbooks get written forward in full-blown play theory. Put another way, it is revealing to read WJ backward, through these later thinkers, to light up the rudiments of ludic philosophy in a writer who, for reasons discussed below, himself did not develop an explicit theory of play even during the height of the child study movement at the turn of the twentieth century.

Darwin's Children: Experts in Adaptation, Plasticity, and Cognitive Extension

A passage from AJ's *Diary* captures the boyish exuberance of WJ at the age of forty-seven, on the cusp of publishing *The Principles of Psychology* (1890): "He is just like a blob of mercury, you can't put a mental finger on him. H[enry] and I were laughing over him and recalling Father and William's resemblance . . . an entire inability or indifference 'to stick to a thing for the sake of sticking,' as some said of him once" (57). WJ in the fall of 1889 had planned travels in Europe, which he abruptly canceled, instead heading for England in order to see his sister and brother HJ before returning to Massachusetts. AJ records his impetuous, zigzag comings and goings: "The only necessity being to get home, the first letter after his arrival was, of course, full of plans for his return plus wife and infants!" (57). Not just a succinct profile of her dynamic older brother, AJ's nice turn of phrase—"you can't put a mental finger on him"—marks the alignment of the cognitive with the tactile: a signature conception of WJ beginning with his physiological psychology and extending through his radical empiricism.

Childlike Exuberance

Like the proverbial "boys who are sure of a dinner" (261) from Emerson's "Self-Reliance," WJ was swift in his judgments, perceptions, and affections. AJ's entry in her *Diary* aligns her oldest brother's sprint through different cities and nations with the quicksilver quality of his mind, while noting his similarities to their father—who was "an undisciplined, impulsive, and affectionate man," writes Robert Richardson.[12] AJ's comment about the "giddy whirl" (57) of her brother's dash across Europe recalls the peripatetic nature of the James family's three years of Continental travel in the mid-1850s, with the five children pulled along in the wake of their father's stated desire to "educate the babies in strange lingoes" (Richardson, 21). In *A Small Boy and Others* (1913), Henry James captured the vital sense of his older brother as a boy in motion: "I never for all the time of childhood and youth in the least caught up with him or overtook him. He was always round the corner and out of sight. . . . We were never in the same schoolroom, in the same game . . . he was clean out before I had got well in."[13] For his part, after his whirlwind visit in England, WJ wrote of the encounter with his sister: "She was witty and animated and curious about everything, and the tone of invective and sarcasm[,] which I have always read as shrill and forced in her letters, is uttered in the softest and most laughing way in the world, and gives an entirely different impression" (Richardson, 28). WJ recorded this observation about the in-person softness of AJ's humor, of course, before he was aware of the vigorous comedic mode of the *Diary*, which she was keeping at the time of his stopover.

AJ and the whole James family were well aware that WJ's decade-long writing effort was soon to be published. Indeed, the two siblings' projects overlapped: Paul Fisher notes the echoes between WJ's *Principles* and AJ's *Diary*, observing that "for eight or nine years, he [William] had been working, in an obscurity reminiscent of Alice and her journal, on his 'textbook.'"[14] As discussed in Chapter 1, WJ would come to know the consanguinity of the diary and the textbook, when G. Stanley Hall—disparagingly—likened WJ's two-volume text to the recently published diary of the Parisian artist Marie Bashkirtseff.[15] Jacques Barzun, a more recent and more affirming reader, essentially agrees, praising the "succulent detail" of WJ's prose, quoting his reference to the brain as a "blood-soaked sponge" and to the "shimmering of consciousness."[16] A magisterial tome in length and ambition, *The Principles of Psychology* expanded the meaning of what a textbook could be: not a record of settled belief but an active, almost childlike working out of questions in an engaged colloquy with other thinkers.

Ross Posnock notes that there is something less metaphorical, more literal, in the James brothers' engagement with the child. Here is the key passage from Posnock's *The Trial of Curiosity* (1991):

> [Henry] James knocks "at the door of the past" and plunges into the "world of . . . childhood," as his "instant conductors" "seize every object." The seventy-year-old James has recaptured what [Walt] Whitman also recovers: the avidity and insatiable curiosity of a child. . . . James feels not just his own but also William's "small feet plant themselves afresh and artlessly stumble forward again," "our steps" discovering "the wonder of consciousness in everything." . . . [T]o argue that James's opening pages *recover* the mimetic openness of a 'small boy' is imprecise. As the autobiography reveals, James never loses this perspective. Instead it inheres in what he becomes—a "man of imagination at the active pitch."[17]

The dynamic process of writing and reminiscence—the act of philosophizing with the child in mind—represents youthful avidity and at the same time recapitulates it. The capacity for inquisitiveness counts as both epistemology and adaptation: "*Curiosity*," WJ notes in his *Talks to Teachers*, is "a rather poor term by which to designate the *impulse towards better cognition* in its full extent; but you will readily understand what I mean." He continues, "Novelties in the way of sensible objects, especially if their sensational quality is bright, vivid, startling, invariably arrest the attention of the young and hold it until the desire to know more about the object is assuaged. In its higher, more intellectual form, the impulse toward completer knowledge takes the character of scientific or philosophic curiosity. In both its sensational and its intellectual form the instinct is more vivacious during childhood and youth than in after life."[18] For WJ, the child embodies not a mere metaphor but a set of dispositions, postures, and possibilities, while "for most people in middle life, the sort of intellectual effort required of the average schoolboy in mastering his Greek or Latin lesson, his algebra or physics, would be out of the question" (*TT*, 740).

These statements offer a clue to how we might begin to think through the significance of the child for WJ, as both child and thinker are, by his own account, investigators of "new truths" (*TT*, 740). He frequently invokes the research of James Mark Baldwin, a rough contemporary who investigated the child mind and child behaviors under the auspices of evolutionary theory. Baldwin affirmed that children, in their earliest cognitions, were essentially experimenters in vivo: "The child assumes a form of reality as attaching to his perceptions or images, and forthwith proceeds to test the presumption by experimental action. His action brings into play the coefficients of reality which actually attach to the experience, and thus he converts his expectation into fact. He then accepts the thing as having the reality he had before merely assumed."[19] Child's play provides the ground for the creative arts and the sciences; "Invention, using the term most broadly, and imitation, are the two legs, so to call them, on which the human race historically has walked" (*TT*, 742), WJ writes.

Freedom of (and for) Development

Though not himself a specialist in child psychology, WJ saw children as investigators who test urgent-feeling theories in light of experience, a description that precisely aligns with the everyday posture of youth that late nineteenth-century evolutionary psychologists were elaborating. For Baldwin and others, childhood was increasingly conceived as an essential biological period of physical and cognitive immaturity: a risky but immensely fruitful time of dependence, flexibility, learning, and culture acquisition. Baldwin described small children as embedded in a wildly interesting world populated by resonant objects. Fellow human beings, he urged, were the most fascinating but also unpredictable entities in a child's universe, the central "project" that the immature of the species faced: "Persons are very peculiar objects, very interesting, very active, very arbitrary, very portentous of pleasure or pain. If we consider these objects as fully presented, i.e. as in due relationship to one another in space, projected out, and thought of as external, and call such objects again *projects*, then persons at this stage may be called *personal projects*."[20] For Baldwin, children at an early age don't make strong distinctions between things and persons but promiscuously engage in exploration. They are born with intense, autotelic motivation to probe their environment—all the while tending toward a richer sense of understanding, predictability, and mastery. But playful exploration brings immense peril; in a world of hot stoves, steep stairs, and enticing bodies of water, curious babes are in daily danger. This hardwired precarity makes infancy in general and play in particular a puzzle from the standpoint of evolutionary biology.

The riskiness of childhood understood in evolutionary terms is beautifully encapsulated by Theodora Bosanquet, HJ's amanuensis, who in her 1924 biography of the novelist coined the term "children of light" to describe the novelist's sensitive, preternaturally precocious child characters.[21] In her telling, these figures evolved from HJ's vision of the world as a violent place filled with bloodthirsty brutes: "When he walked out of the refuge of his study and into the world and looked around him, he saw a place of torment, where creatures of prey perpetually *thrust their claws* into the quivering flesh of *doomed, defenseless children* of light. . . . He realized how constantly the tenderness of *growing life* is at the mercy of personal tyranny. . . . His novels are a repeated exposure of this wickedness, a reiterated and passionate plea for the *fullest freedom of development*, unimperiled by reckless and *barbarous stupidity*" (57, emphasis added). With its barbarous predators and quivering prey, this passage from *Henry James at Work* invokes ideas from nineteenth-century natural history, a world "red in tooth and claw"—although in Bosanquet's account it is not "Nature" but a highly refined social environment that ruthlessly destroys its tender members.[22] The children of light represent a different set of values, namely, "growing life" and "freedom of development." These terms, rich in literary significance, are familiar to critics attentive to the complex developmental characters central to HJ's psychological realism.[23]

The puzzle of child's play is in fact a central enigma of evolutionary biology. For many in the nineteenth century, the "struggle for existence" described in *On the Origin of Species by Means of Natural Selection* (1859) pointed to a grim naturalistic world where the governing law was competition for mere survival.[24] Darwin himself, however, resisted the "tooth and claw" narrative, affirming: "There is a grandeur in this view of life . . . from so simple a beginning, endless forms most beautiful and most wonderful have been, and are, being evolved" while "the vigorous, the healthy and the happy survive and multiply."[25] At issue, however, is not just how *Homo sapiens* adapted to a particular environment but a prior question: How did human beings become adaptable *tout court*? Modern geology after Agassiz affirmed that sudden, catastrophic climate changes have been the norm rather than the exception over the millennia of human history.[26] While Darwin attended closely to the macro-narrative of evolutionary theory—the achingly slow process of species transformation across deep time—the scientific psychology that emerged in the final decades of the nineteenth century focused on the theory's *micro-narratives*: the ways in which growth and development played out on the more human scale of an individual life.

WJ, writing about the structure of the nervous system in *Psychology: Briefer Course*, offers a crucial insight into the nature of human beings' capacity for transformation. He draws on chemistry and physics to note that while the particles of matter that make up the body cannot change, "a compound mass of matter can change."[27] Therefore, "either outward forces or inward tensions can, from one hour to another, turn that structure into something different from what it was" (*PBC*, 137). WJ, however, includes the following caveat: "That is, they can do so if the body be plastic enough to maintain its integrity, and be not disrupted when its structure yields" (*PBC*, 137). The human nervous system was the "plastic" structure par excellence. Moreover, human beings are endowed with a peculiar capacity: they can take control of how they transform themselves, by harnessing the fact that "[o]rganic matter, especially nervous tissue, seems endowed with a very extraordinary degree of plasticity" (*PBC*, 138). WJ argued that the development of habits can, over time, become a matter of reflex, transferring design from effortful thoughts to attuned muscles and limbs, thus situating knowledge directly into the bodymind as it performs actions: "Which way does my door swing? etc. I cannot *tell* the answer; yet my *hand* never makes a mistake" (*PBC*, 142). WJ, in other words, provides a neural explanation for how human beings learn and change over the course of a lifetime. In addition, he offers an implicit response to the question of how (internal) mental ideas correspond with (external) things in the world. By his account, the world offers-to-hand certain opportunities, that—akin to doorknobs—can be grasped, put to use, and eventually incorporated into gestures, rhythms, and routines that generate new practices and new ideas. This process is recursive and never concluded. As Bergson notes, when the unduly habituated hand *does* make a mistake it is cause for humor: one thinks of Charlie Chaplin's tramp, who in *Modern Times* becomes so used to fastening rivets that he approaches the breast-centered buttons on a woman's jacket with wrenches at the ready. Laughter, stunned outrage, or both—as WJ found in his interactions with AJ—allows for the disruption of habits and learning to take place.

Newly understood as a functional biological period unique to human beings, infancy and youth thus carried an unprecedented evolutionary advantage: the capacity not just to learn but even to transform oneself, other persons, and the world in relation to experience. Stephen Crane encapsulated this adaptive aspect of childhood in his *Whilomville Stories* (1900) when he wrote, "The boy's mind is flexible; he readjusts his position with an ease which is derived from the fact—simply—that he is not yet a man."[28] The child, by this account, is the quintessential evolutionary subject. There are, however, limits. "Hardly ever is a language learned after twenty spoken without a foreign accent," WJ writes; "hardly ever can a youth transferred to the society of his betters unlearn the nasality and other vices of speech bred in him by the associations of his growing years" (*PBC*, 146). These snobbish words index a limit to WJ's own genial open-mindedness, as well; his thinking is shaped by the invidious exclusions of his cultural and historical milieu.

Taken biologically, childhood can be seen as an evolutionary strategy, offering both a temporal period and a method for developing the cultural capacities—language, learning, and ideally love—that allow humankind and human values to flourish in a volatile and changing world. Literarily, childhood and the child mind illuminate (in the words of Alison Gopnik) "the aspects of our nature that allow nurture and culture to take place."[29] This is not to underestimate the foundation for flourishing, that is, sheer survival, which buys time for growth and development. Bound up with and building on survival are five key aptitudes that, for evolutionary psychology, suture human beings biologically to culture: *experimental play*, which provides dispositional knowledge about one's surroundings; *imagination and imitation*, which accommodate the strangeness of what is and project alternative possibilities for the future; *animism*, a capacious theory of other hearts and minds, which attributes sentience, feeling, motivation, and beliefs even to stubbornly dense entities, for example, bigoted adults; *distributed cognition*, which makes use of objects, practices, and other people as harboring information about the world and its denizens; and *narrative wisdom*, which consolidates patterns, consequences, and affective knowledge into memories, tales, histories, and books. More or less present in all human beings, these dispositions are acutely visible as they are tested, put to work, and refined during childhood, the (relatively) protected period of protracted immaturity. Chapter 3 takes up other human-crafted devices that cultivate and exercise the impulse to play (and even to toy), for example, theater, fiction, and cinema.

Twenty-First-Century Perspectives on Evolution and Childhood

WJ's keynote conception of plasticity highlights immaturity as essential to the processes of evolution as they play out in the human species, forging reciprocal links between biological capacities and cultural productions. Bioanthropologists Richard Wrangham (*Freedom Through Fire: How Cooking Made Us Human*) and Dean Falk (*Finding Our Tongues: Mothers, Infants, and the Origins of Language)* take up the traditional measuring stick of the evolutionist—the size of the human brain, in comparison to that of our ape relatives—and place it in the context of evolutionary sociality.[30] To support big brains and bipedalism (with the smaller pelvises necessary for upright mobility), human beings require a protracted infancy for growth and, most important, for learning, that inefficient yet wildly successful way of adapting to a changing world. Setting aside what Stephen Jay Gould has called the "tooth and claw" evolutionary narrative, contemporary accounts of human origins offer a new emphasis: a tale of high-energy, protein-rich food (to nourish the hungry brain); of attentive, long-term care (to sustain the survival of the uniquely immature creation, the human infant); and of communication across generations (to harvest the innovations of lucky or talented individuals). Food, love, and language: these staples of human culture form the new holy trinity of twenty-first-century evolutionary theory.

By the end of the nineteenth century, childhood proved essential to evolutionary theory. Organisms that were "plastic, intelligent, or imitative," in the words of Baldwin, could quickly accommodate to a challenge or mutation by putting it to work in novel ways.[31] Human beings, by this account, could (by virtue of their biology) push back against biological determinism; they possessed the capacity for self-directed change and for the transmission of these changes. This is what Gopnik means when she writes, "Children are the R & D department of the human species" (11). The answer, then, to "How did we become adaptable?" lies, for evolutionary psychology, in the evolved human capacity to "escape from the constraints of evolution" (7). Dependence frees up protected space for play, testing, and transformation. Imagination contributes to and enables adaptation. Flexibility allows for readjustment. "In short," Dewey affirmed in 1922, "among the native activities of the young are some that work towards accommodation, assimilation, reproduction, and others that work toward exploration, discovery and creation."[32] Learning is both backward looking and forward thinking.

Daniel Dennett, in *Consciousness Explained* (1991), offers an evolutionary account of human consciousness that explicitly draws on the work of Baldwin: "The plastic brain is capable of reorganizing itself adaptively. . . . [T]his capability, itself a product of genetic evolution by natural selection, not only gives the organisms who have it an edge over their hard-wired cousins who cannot redesign themselves, but also reflects back on the process of genetic evolution and speeds it up. This is . . . known as the Baldwin Effect."[33] Childhood is our species' way of capitalizing on the plasticity of the brain, making a virtue of the fact that so many human arts are not fixed or stereotyped at birth. Gould points out that, biologically and psychologically speaking, adults resemble children, rather than vice versa: "Among the usual reasons cited for extreme flexibility of human consciousness are the biological neoteny that probably keeps our brain in a labile, juvenile state and the unparalleled potential of the non-somatic culture that our brains have made possible."[34] Just as adult bodies remain close to hairless and strikingly big headed, so adult brains perpetuate (in no doubt imperfect form) the neotenous, juvenile, brain-flexing capacities of the curious child.[35] Despite myriad distinctions in the cultures of childhood across the planet, as a period of contingency and emergence it is perversely universal, insofar as every adult human being on earth has (in one cultural form or another) passed through infancy and survived. "The most ancient parts of truth," WJ asserts in his second Lowell Lecture on pragmatism, "also once were plastic."[36] In a nontrivial way, this assertion is also true of adults. Moreover, the intense emotions of childhood are an essential part of human beings' cognitive structure, agency, and survival.

One of WJ's earliest essays in fact takes up the centrality of feeling for evolutionary theory. He argues vehemently against Thomas Huxley's dualism and materialism—though not his ascription to Darwin's principles. WJ affirmed that, far from epiphenomenal, feeling and consciousness were central to the lived "success" of both the individual and humankind as a species. In 1879, WJ's lecture "Are We Automata?" was published in *Mind,* refuting Huxley's claim that (in WJ's words) "feeling is a mere collateral product of our nervous processes. . . . Inert, uninfluential, it is allowed to remain on board, but not to touch the helm or handle the rigging."[37] WJ is asserting that feelings—appraisals of aversion or affiliation—are essential to consciousness and, contra Huxley, allow an organism to make choices and thus navigate successfully through a risky world. Why else would evolution have selected such costly cargo as the human brain, if not to better pilot the organism?

The nautical metaphor WJ uses describes the *mindful* aspects of human physiology. The ship (meaning, the human organism) is not reducible to its machinery (body) or to its "captain" (the brain or will) but rather distributes control throughout its navigational system, which includes the crew's shared expertise (coordinated sensations and movements) and its essential destination: to complete the journey (survival) while avoiding disaster (death). Interest and attention, which open onto the world of human preferences and relations, are at the core of human consciousness. In some ways, the ship metaphor risks replicating the mechanistic logic of Huxley's locomotive. There is a key difference, however: human beings are capable of setting sail for no specific destination, even at times risking life and limb in the process. Unlike a train on a track, interest and attention may be expressed in bodily movements that are coordinated, motivated yet non-teleological. When we expend energy without a particular goal or outcome in mind, we generally do it "for the sake" of the activity itself, propelled by curiosity. This autotelic energy is most vivid in child's play;

the pleasure is essential to the activity, motivating engagement in the first place, yet (as WJ critiques) this aspect remains inexplicable on Huxley's terms.

Curiosity behavior affords a new way of thinking about those aspects of human experience that look "merely" reflexive. Dewey, building on WJ's anti-mechanistic argument, relates consciousness to a simple childhood gesture: reaching out a hand to touch a lit candle. In "The Reflex Arc Concept in Psychology" (1896), Dewey urges that the child's attentiveness to the flame—her *interest* in it—does not define the candle as an inert thing but actively creates it as a stimulus, something to be engaged. The reaching and the grasping, he argues, are propelled by curiosity and not random mechanics; the child does not "happen" to bump into the flame but *selects it* out of, as WJ calls it, the "blooming, buzzing confusion" of her environment.[38] "The movement is only for the sake of determining the stimulus, of fixing what kind of stimulus it is, of interpreting it," writes Dewey.[39] Only after the fact, described from the outside (and indeed from the perspective of the experienced adult, for whom over time the seeing-reaching-interpreting has solidified into conceptual nuggets and truisms like "candle" and "don't touch"), does the process look like a preprogrammed "series of jerks" (360). As WJ emphasizes, everything turns on that all-important act of attention—perhaps better encapsulated by the more affectively charged term "enticement."

Whereas Huxley saw consciousness as purely private and internal, WJ evolved a way of thinking about mind that extends beyond the brain and even beyond the skin. Andy Clark—influenced by the work of both Dewey and WJ—describes this process as "supersizing the mind": "Fluently using a stick, we feel as if we are touching the world at the end of the stick, not (once we are indeed fluent in our use) as if we are touching the stick with our hand. The stick, it has sometimes been suggested, is in some way incorporated, and the overall effect seems more like bringing a temporary whole new agent-world circuit into being rather than simply exploiting the stick as a helpful prop or tool."[40] This "agent-world circuit" offers a different way of answering an age-old question about consciousness: how things out there in the world "get into" the mind understood as being enclosed in the skull. Karl Groos, in *The Play of Man* (1899), leaps from the walking stick example to the use of a pencil to augment learning: "Carrying a walking-stick is another playful satisfaction in which the hand's sensation of contact has a part, while the lead pencil, small as it is, will sometimes satisfy the demand for 'something in the hand.'"[41] Pencil users succeed in "sharpening their wits by the sensation of contact" (10). Clark's description of an "agent-world circuit" is a modern update on Dewey's conception of how children learn, in a full-bodied, curious encounter with and manipulation of the stuff they find around them.

Body-Based Empiricists at Birth

Clark describes the practice by which very young children come to occupy their bodies "fluently," and gain knowledge of the world through a playful mode known as "body babbling" (35), which involves such actions as "grasping, poking, pulling, sucking, and shoving" (17). Such "babbling" makes evolutionary sense. Because human bodies grow and change and occupy a range of environments, "it is simply good design not to permanently lock in [hardwired] knowledge" but instead "to deploy plastic neural resources" that allow young children and their less agile adult counterparts to become adept at inhabiting different places, tasks, situations, and relationships (269). Human beings in general and children in particular come to know their own capacities—and indeed, to know their own and others' minds—by tuning in to their environments and social situations, testing ways of occupying, transforming, and flourishing in them. Knowledge of the world arrives through the senses: this was the theory and the practice of Henry James Sr. in dragging his family across Europe. He writes about his own childhood in his *Autobiography*: "I lived in every fibre of my body. The dawn always found me on my feet; and I can still vividly recall the divine rapture which filled my blood as I pursued under the magical light of morning the sports of the river, the wood, or the field."[42]

In his *Essays in Experimental Logic* (1916), Dewey theorizes the full-bodied way that children learn as a form of cognitive extension: "Hands and feet, apparatus and appliances of all kinds are as much a part of it [thinking] as changes in the brain. Since these physical operations (including cerebral events) and equipments are a part of thinking, thinking is mental, not because of a peculiar stuff which enters into it or of peculiar non-natural activities which constitute it, but because of what physical acts and appliances do: the distinctive purpose for which they are employed and the distinctive results they accomplish."[43] From this perspective, the active engagement with toys and tools is not external to thinking and knowledge acquisition but constitutive of it. As Clark puts it, "Human minds and bodies are essentially open to episodes of deep and transformative restructuring in which new equipment (both physical and 'mental') can become quite literally incorporated into the thinking and acting systems that we identify as our minds and bodies" (31).

The full-bodied, object-oriented way that children learn would become a touchstone idea for WJ, who writes in *The Principles of Psychology*: "Certainly a child newly born in Boston, who gets a sensation from the candle-flame which lights the bedroom, or from his diaper-pin, does not feel either of these objects to be situated in longitude 71 W. and latitude 42 N. . . . The flame fills its own place, the pain fills its own place; but as yet these places are neither identified with, nor discriminated from, any other places. That comes later. For the places thus first sensibly known are elements of the child's space-world which remain with him all his life" (vol. 1, 681–82). WJ speaks here of an infant's earliest feelings, which offer the material for object relations and eventually abstract thinking in relation to time and space. As a baby continues to interact with his environment, the world coalesces into meaningful people and places. For Baldwin, this capacity to grapple with and to make connections constitutes the rudiments of child's play. Play, for Baldwin, is a high-stakes activity of profound evolutionary significance. An "impulse of extraordinary strength and persistence, and of corresponding utility," play allows for "genuine novelties of adjustment" that in turn contribute to "the actual saving of its life."[44]

Baldwin has been credited with anticipating the field of epigenetics, which investigates how acquired behaviors can be transmitted between generations, but for our purposes Baldwin's signal contributions lie in this key insight: through play children don't merely learn about their milieu, they *learn to learn better*. The autotelic act of playing—engaging in time-consuming, repetitive behaviors with no immediate profit or purpose—is exceedingly "expensive," in evolutionary terms. Over time, however, playing itself leads to a version of "economizing" though the acquisition of language and concepts. Gopnik clarifies this point in *The Philosophical Baby* (2009): "using our heads instead of our hands" conserves energy and time, while also expanding the problem-solving ability exponentially. As a human being grows and matures, the wisdom of experience can be consolidated into human-constructed tools, "short cuts" such as words, concepts, and books. Human beings then continue to play with these new linguistic tools, by thinking about our own thinking, building newer and better tools to think with, and creating spaces and processes that further aid our toolsmaking and thinking-about-thinking. Over time and through practice, this recursive play cultivates competence and eventually something like expertise: as Clark writes, "We tune the way we use these tools by building educational practices to train ourselves to use our best cognitive tools better" (59).

In *The Scientist in the Crib: What Early Learning Tells Us About the Mind* (2000), Gopnik makes explicit the analogy between young children's sensuous empiricism and the work of scientists. Babies are good investigators, engaging in intensive exploratory experiences to achieve a body of knowledge. A question arises, however: how can knowledge of the world continue to emerge past childhood, unless adults manage to approximate the delighted bafflement of the young? Gopnik points to the experience of travel: "An adult in a strange place is like a baby in many ways. There is a great deal of new information available at once. And the traveler is not in a good position to make 'top-down' decisions beforehand about exactly what kinds of information are going to be relevant. Like the baby, the traveler's attention is likely to be caught by external objects and events rather than determined by her own intentions and decisions."[45]

It is with these musings in mind, about what the experience of the child can illuminate about the operations of consciousness and the acquisition of knowledge through somatic encounters, that we turn to two exemplary experiences in the scientific education of WJ. The first experience happened when he was a young medical student who impulsively took a break from his Harvard studies to set sail to Brazil, a voyage that transformed him from a bookish young man into a traveler. The second transpired when he was a professor with his own graduate students, when he made the acquaintance of a young woman—Helen Keller—who impressed him as a sensory explorer who conceptualized the world afresh through the sense of touch. Both encounters involved great mutual affection and helped him to develop his own pedagogical approach—leading one admirer to write in 1911 that WJ was "in short, primarily, though not exclusively, an educational psychologist."[46]

Learning to Doubt (One's Elders): Louis Agassiz and Herbert Spencer

When the American Society of Naturalists met at Harvard in 1896, WJ was invited to present a lecture on Agassiz, the preeminent natural scientist of his day and WJ's former teacher. The gathering of scientists took place in the Museum of Comparative Zoology, known around Cambridge as the Agassiz Museum in honor of its founder. Founded in 1859, the year that Darwin published *On the Origin of Species*, the museum's vast collection of organisms was arranged to affirm Agassiz's vision of how the natural world came into existence.[47]

WJ came of age as older understandings of the human mind were being challenged by the findings of researchers in the experiment-based field of physiological psychology. Scientists turned to the study of children for clues about the species history of *Homo sapiens*; Darwin himself inaugurated the child study movement with the publication of "A Biographical Sketch of an Infant" in the journal *Mind* in 1877.[48] In a time of epistemological rearrangement and rupture, and an intensified interest in science-inflected theories of education, WJ in 1896 was faced with a delicate situation: how is a leading light in these fields to acknowledge the problematic contributions of his early mentors and intellectual influences?

Failed Theorist, Successful Teacher

WJ's lecture honoring Agassiz was a tricky task to pull off graciously. Agassiz, who had died two decades earlier, was known for his stunning capabilities as a zoologist, geologist, and spokesperson for the field of natural history. Yet Agassiz was also a staunch creationist. Beginning in the 1830s, he had devoted his career to establishing the proposition that species were ideal and unchanging, reflecting the mind of God. He actively refuted the key tenets of Darwin's theories: (1) that individual organisms vary one from another, and "the variations are transmitted to his offspring"; (2) that "the agency of natural selection" ensures that organisms best adapted to a specific environment were most likely to survive and reproduce; and (3) "that species are the modified descendants of other species."[49] Survival, Darwin argued, was dependent on how well organisms could cope with environmental pressures. Agassiz instead saw species as ideal forms—he called them "conceptions" in the mind of God—and dismissed the idea that higher forms evolved from lower forms.

For Agassiz, it was design on the part of a supreme deity, not the impersonal engine of natural selection, that was expressed in what he saw as the natural world's unchanging order: "The combination in time and space of all these thoughtful conceptions exhibits not only thought, it shows also premeditation, power, wisdom, greatness, prescience, omniscience, providence. In one word, all these facts in their natural connection proclaim aloud the One God, whom man may know, adore, and love; and Natural History must in good time become the analysis of the thoughts of the Creator of the Universe."[50] A charismatic scientist commanding great social prestige, Agassiz single-handedly helped stall the assimilation of Darwin's theory of evolution in the U.S. context by at least a decade. WJ had had a front-row seat to Agassiz's influence, for he had been part of the naturalist's highly publicized Thayer expedition to Brazil in 1865, which Agassiz had cast (both before and after the trip) as his crowning achievement as a zoologist.

Indeed, debunking Darwin—the idea that species transformed through adaptation, and that there were hereditary links between different species—was Agassiz's impetus for leading the expedition to collect specimens from the Southern Hemisphere. Agassiz wrote at the time, "I am often asked what is my chief aim in this expedition to South America? No doubt in a general way it is to collect materials for future study. But the conviction which draws me irresistibly, is that the combination of animals on this continent, where the faunae are so characteristic and so distinct from all others, will give me the means of showing that the transmutation theory is wholly without foundation in facts."[51] As the tide turned toward Darwin's account of natural history, Agassiz planned a rear-guard action to locate the empirical evidence for his idealist theory among the myriad fish species populating the massive Amazon River and its tributaries. Agassiz sought to refute the "development theory," but he was above all an observer and an empiricist; even then, lecturing aboard the ship taking the team to Brazil, Agassiz emphasized the method:

> If the facts are insufficient on our side [for divine creation], they are absolutely wanting on the other. We cannot certainly consider the development theory proved, because a few naturalists think it plausible: it seems plausible only to the few, and it is demonstrated by none. I bring this subject before you now, not to urge upon you this or that theory, strong as my own convictions are. I wish only to warn you, not against the development theory itself, but against the looseness in the methods of study upon which it is based. Whatever be your ultimate opinions on this subject, let them rest on facts and not on arguments, however plausible. This is not a question to be argued, it is one to be investigated. (43–44)

Demonstration and investigation were Agassiz's core methodological ideals, and the stated goals of the Thayer Expedition (named for the man who was its primary sponsor), which included twenty-three-year-old WJ, newly embarked on medical studies at Harvard and an avid reader of Darwin.

Fast-forwarding thirty years, when in 1896 WJ stepped to the podium to honor Agassiz, his one-time teacher's theory that species were ideal forms existing in the mind of God had been thoroughly refuted—to large extent by the work of the members of the American Society of Naturalists who constituted WJ's primary audience. When he delivered his address, he was far from the uncertain student he was when headed to Brazil. He was cresting the top of his field, approaching in psychology and philosophy the level of prestige of his august professor of natural history. In his address, the former student sidestepped entirely the question of the *content* of Agassiz's ideas and instead called attention to the deceased scientist's lingering epistemological influence. Agassiz, WJ remarked, had a disarming "habit of naming his occupation simply as that of 'teacher,'" a role that became the central theme of WJ's address to the Society.[52]

Agassiz's reach and popularity were extraordinary, extending well beyond the realm of higher education and the international community of natural scientists into the common schools in the United States. As WJ would emphasize, Agassiz's hands-on methods were famous; as Agassiz himself wrote, "In 1847 I gave an address at Newton, Massachusetts, before a Teachers' Institute conducted by Horace Mann. My subject was grasshoppers. I passed around a large jar of these insects, and made every teacher take one and hold it while I was speaking. If any one dropped the insect, I stopped till he picked it up. This was at that time a great innovation, and excited much laughter and derision. There can be no true progress in the teaching of natural science until such methods become general."[53] To know the grasshopper was to come into bodily contact with the jumpy creature, not just to study abstractions expressed in diagrams, models, or statistical charts. William Dean Howells likely had Agassiz in mind when he advocated adopting the perspective of an empiricist (the avatar for literary realism) rather than an idealist in *Criticism and Fiction* (1891): "I see that you are looking at a grasshopper there which you have found in the grass, and I suppose you intend to describe it. Now don't waste your time and sin against culture in that way. I've got a grasshopper here, which has been evolved at considerable pains and expense out of the grasshopper in general; in fact, it's a type. . . . It isn't very much like a real grasshopper, but it's a great deal nicer, and it's served to represent the notion of a grasshopper ever since man emerged from barbarism."[54] Howells's "artificial grasshopper" was a shibboleth for the Romantic tradition in American literature.

WJ centered his remarks not on Agassiz's deeply ingrained idealism but on his devotion to the empirical methods of modern science. While his former professor's theories reinforced traditional religious arguments about divine creation, Agassiz's teaching methods (WJ emphasized) shocked and transformed an institution that had been instrumental in conveying received truths to the next generation and upholding authoritative traditions, that is, public schools:

> Agassiz's influence on methods of teaching in our community was prompt and decisive,—all the more so that it struck people's

> imagination by its very excess. The good old way of committing printed abstractions to memory seems never to have received such a shock as it encountered at his hands. There is probably no public school teacher now in New England who will not tell you how Agassiz used to lock a student up in a room full of turtle shells, or lobster shells, or oyster shells, without a book or word to help him, and not let him out till he had discovered all the truths which the objects contained. Some found the truths after weeks and months of lonely sorrow—, others never found them. Those who found them were already made into naturalists thereby—the failures were blotted from the book of honor and of life. "Go to Nature; take the facts into your own hands; look, and see for yourself!"—these were the maxims which Agassiz preached wherever he went, and their effect on pedagogy was electric.[55]

Agassiz had profound influence on Emerson, and vice versa: the Swiss-born scientist put into practice the wisdom of "The American Scholar," turning from books to the concrete particulars of the natural world.[56] The student's body was the sounding board for the sensory education of eye and hand (and nose: the marine specimens Agassiz had students work with, sometimes for weeks on end, were notoriously smelly). In WJ's remarks, Agassiz the scientist remains a man of faith: he "preached," he was motivated by "devotion," he was a seeker of "truths." Yet the object to which he consecrated himself, in the former student's subtle handling, is the empirical approach itself. In approaching his subject through the lens of method, WJ subtly points up for his audience a great poignancy: Agassiz as a teacher laid the practical groundwork for his students to refute empirically his idealist narrative about the natural world.

The Thayer Expedition to the Amazon, 1865–66

WJ knew whereof he spoke. While attending lectures at the Lawrence Scientific School in Cambridge, he was offered a place in 1865 on Agassiz's expedition to Brazil. He was well prepared for the journey, intellectually; he had read thoroughly *On the Origin of Species*, with its meticulous unraveling of Agassiz's belief in original design: that God created species as eternal and unchanging, and that the material particulars of organisms were flawed and ephemeral representations of divine order. Richardson provides an apt turn of phrase when he writes of WJ's time as a student at the Lawrence Scientific School, "What we

Figure 4. At the age of twenty-three, William James joined the Thayer Expedition to Brazil, led by the charismatic anti-Darwinian scientist Louis Agassiz; WJ weathered smallpox and temporary blindness, concluding, "My forte is not to go on exploring expeditions." By permission of the Houghton Library, Harvard University: MS Am 1092 (1185), 9.

are watching is often the assembly of new playing pieces, the acquisition of new vocabularies, new ways to know, as much as the acquisition of new information" (59). Practically, however, WJ had no experience with the rigors of collecting hundreds of fish and aquatic organisms, or the physical hardships that came with trekking thousands of miles through a South American rainforest by ship, steamer, canoe, and foot. The privations of the trek were a radical departure from WJ's classroom experience to date. WJ, however, put both modes of knowledge acquisition—didactic lectures and immersive fieldwork—to good use.

Agassiz went to the Amazon with a deductive destination already in mind: to accumulate and tag a vast array of creatures—primarily fishes—to support his conception: that the natural world provided a portal to "the free conception of the Almighty intellectually matured in his thought before it was manifested in tangible external forms."[57] WJ went as a student, shaky in his recently chosen medical career and skeptical about Agassiz's passion to refute Darwin's theories as well as about the man's personal grandiosity. Upon first attending a lecture by Agassiz while studying in Cambridge, WJ had written home, "He is evidently a great favorite with his audience and feels so himself"—though he goes on to affirm, "I should like to study under him."[58]

Plunged into close proximity with the great man, in the extraordinary and overwhelming physical environment of the Amazon, WJ was drawn in. He wrote home, "Agassiz is one of the most fascinating men personally that I ever saw. I could listen to him talk by the hour. He is so childlike" (*Letters*, 59). Part way into the trip, however, after a serious bout of sickness, WJ felt alienated: he struggled with the sense that he was a man of intellect rather than action, and anticipated cerebral homesickness, the "pining after books and study" (63). Sick and depressed, he wrote home that he had made a mistake, as he was "now certain that my forte is not to go on exploring expeditions" (58). Yet this same, somewhat despairing letter expressed a realization: that grand and even grandiose ideas must be tested concretely—"on the ground"—to ascertain their validity.[59] He was speaking of an egocentric problem, his own uncertain sense of vocation as a student, but his words also spell out a method for learning through the uncomfortable affect of doubt, and even error: "Here on the ground the romance vanishes and the misgivings float up. I have determined to listen to them this time. I said that my act was an expensive mistake as regards what I anticipated, but I have got this other *edification* from it. It has to be got some time, and perhaps only through some great mistake; for there are some familiar axioms which the individual only seems able to learn the meaning of through his individual experience" (*Letters*, 63). The term "expensive mistake" uses the economic language that permeates the writing of all the Jameses.[60] Yet it also invokes a mode of thinking essential to evolutionary accounts, in which a given feature of an organism—the growth of antlers, say—is presumed to be an "expense" that has some functional "payoff." In this instance, WJ affirms that doubt about one's vocation—which had been merely floated along by "enthusiasm, and the romance of the thing"—prompts worthwhile digressions to ensure that bad ideas are weeded out precisely by living through and feeling the full physical impact of their untenability (63). In a sense, he describes how learning happens sometimes through the inefficient process of *unlearning*. Despite the term "mistake," the realization has positive effects, for it provides WJ with "this other *edification*": not simply that he won't be a field naturalist but that axioms *as such* must at times give way to the test of experience. Such discoveries are indeed expensive, though in this case WJ has the intense, full-body demands of the expedition to thank for weeding out a romantic idea that (he believes) could have sent him in a disastrous direction.

This edification may be scaled up even further. In an important sense, WJ has Agassiz to thank for his discarding an idealist theory about natural history.[61] The younger man's "great mistake" in at least tacitly assenting to Agassiz's theories was short lived and transpired at the beginning of his career. Agassiz's greater mistake was to cement an early belief—as early as the 1830s he developed his idealist theory about species stability—and allow it to persist, despite mounting evidence to the contrary, to the culmination of a long and august career. WJ instead embraces uncertainty, on the new belief that axioms can occlude the truths lived out through on-the-ground experience. He ends up affirming the empirical method that Agassiz could never quite line up with his Romantic, *Naturphilosophie*-inspired conception that species were ideal forms. On an experiential level, the contingencies and challenges of travel to the Amazon, merged with WJ's first-person observation of the expedition leader's obdurate faith in a fixed and increasingly untenable idea, helped to make Agassiz's student a Darwinist.

WJ expresses this shift in a letter to his father just three months later, in which he admits that Agassiz is someone he can learn "on" rather than learn from. WJ had contemplated quitting the trip, but he famously decides to remain once he realizes that Agassiz is a person to learn from experientially rather than dogmatically. WJ mimes his teacher's style while eschewing his ideas: "I see no reason to regret my determination to stay. 'On the contrary,' as Agassiz says, as I begin to use my eyes a little every day, I feel like an entirely new being. Everything revives within and without, and I now feel sure that I shall learn. I have profited a great deal by hearing Agassiz talk, not so much by what he says, for never did a man utter a greater amount of humbug, but by learning the way of feeling of such *a vast practical engine* as he is" (*Letters*, 65, emphasis added). WJ (who suffered temporary blindness during his travels) both experiences and watches his own evolution, such that his experience as a student indexes and embodies some of Darwin's principles about plasticity and transformation. Darwin's ideas about the engine of evolution—heredity, variation, natural selection—explain from a biological standpoint how *populations of organisms* change and adapt. The theory is exterior to the lived experience of individual creatures. To explain how *persons* change and adapt from a psychological standpoint, a different "engine" is called for, one that is "practical" and involves a "way of feeling." Such a theory is at core subjective and personal: in enlisting an individual's attention and interest, it is more a practice than an axiom. And, in a loose analogy to species transformation, what emerges from WJ's encounter with the magnetic environment Agassiz creates is a revolution of perspective that leaves the student feeling like an "entirely new being"—a moving experience lived somatically as well as intellectually.

To return to the professor at the lectern in 1896, half a lifetime removed from his Amazon travels: WJ is now an esteemed philosopher and psychologist looking back on his youthful time aboard ship with Agassiz. From this backward-looking perspective, WJ emphasizes less his mentor's mistaken belief that species are unchanging and instead describes Agassiz's successful practice as a transformer of young men. "While on the Thayer expedition, I remember that I often put questions to him about the facts of our new tropical habitat, but I doubt if he ever answered one of these questions of mine outright. He always said: 'There, you see you have a definite problem; go and look and find the answer for yourself.' His severity in this line was a living rebuke to all abstractionists and would-be biological philosophers."[62] WJ brings the eye of the Darwinian naturalist to bear on Agassiz, explaining that his "view of Nature was saturated with simple religious feeling," a creationist perspective that found "the most sympathetic possible environment" at the theologically oriented community at Harvard of the 1850s (*Memories*, 15). The intellectual and cultural environment, however, has changed: "In the fifty years that have sped since he arrived here our knowledge of Nature has penetrated into joints and recesses which his vision never pierced. The causal elements [the engine] and not the totals are what we are now most passionately concerned to understand" (14). Yet the memory of Agassiz is, WJ concludes, a "breath as of life's morning, that makes the world seem young and fresh once more" (15).

Rejecting Spencer's Correspondence Theory

In his scientific education, WJ was influenced directly by Agassiz, but in his wider reading Herbert Spencer was a potent intellectual source. Before Darwin's theory of evolution, there was Spencer's, first articulated in the British thinker's textbook *The Principles of Psychology* (1854–55). Seeking to understand the operations of consciousness in biological terms, Spencer argued that all organisms change in response to environmental pressures. "Progressive adaptation," he writes, "became increasing adjustment of inner subjective relations to outer objective relations—increasing correspondence between the two."[63] Spencer's correspondence theory, in which an organism's actions are shaped by the environment, accounted for why "the stationary polype [*sic*] with outstretched tentacles, contracts on being touched."[64] The polyp provides Spencer with a model of how human beings grope for an idea: "Whenever a group of inner relations, a cognition, is completely conformed to a group of outer relations, a phenomenon . . . there is what we call an *understanding* of the phenomenon" (375). Mental processes, Spencer argues, are bodily reflexes to bring that which is outside the organism *inside*; as one's perceptions accumulate, he continues, the store of understanding is enlarged. In this way thinking becomes progressively more complex over an individual's lifetime (and over the phylogenic "lifetime" of a species). States of consciousness become compounded over time, attuned to the complexity of the environment.

WJ was first captivated by Spencer's treatment of mental processes in biological terms; as Richardson reports, WJ praised Spencer's "revolutionary insistence that since mind and its environment have evolved together, they must be studied together" (179). A few years after Spencer published his *Psychology*, he expanded his correspondence theory in *First Principles of a New System of Philosophy* (1860), stating that not just living organisms but all systems (natural and human-created) tended inexorably toward greater complexity, on a course toward ultimate perfection: "*Evolution is a change from an indefinite, incoherent homogeneity, to a definite, coherent heterogeneity; through continuous differentiations and integrations.*"[65] For Spencer, these biological truths had ethical implications: "The continuous adjustment of the vital activities to the activities in the environment, must become more accurate and exhaustive" (84), thus pointing toward "that advance in enlightenment which characterizes human perfection" (420).

WJ soon became repulsed by Spencer's passive conception of the mind's mechanical "adjustment" to a static environment. In the younger scholar's first article, published in *Popular Science Monthly* in 1878, he pushed back against the man who compared himself to Aristotle.[66] Spencer's "great task" was to prove "that mind from its lowest to its highest forms is a mere product of the environment."[67] WJ argued instead that mind was dynamic, something between an actor and an action, between noun and verb, which he called a knower. The knower, he wrote, "is not simply a mirror floating with no foot-hold anywhere, and passively reflecting an order that he comes upon and finds merely existing nor was that world itself inert and unchanging."[68]

Stylistically, WJ takes up Spencer's terms and then turns the tables on him. For instance, he emphasizes Spencer's static, quasi-mathematical account of mind by repeated use of the term "formula" to refer to Spencer's "formula of correspondence," emphasizing the way that Spencer abstracts away from particulars to create "an average sense of mankind" and a "statistical" account of intelligence ("Remarks," 896). WJ challenges these ideas by then adopting the concept of the equation and exploding it from the inside. "The knower is an actor, and coefficient of the truth on one side," he writes, and then balances the statement: "whilst on the other [side] he registers the truth which he helps to create" (908). Rhetorically he takes Spencer's equation (that mind and environment correspond or "equal" each other) and "multiplies" both sides of the mind/world equation by a "coefficient" that is, ostensibly, the same: the "knower." Mathematically, such a procedure is unimpeachable. But WJ cannily places the knower on both the subjective side (mind) and the objective side (world), and by doing so contaminates the latter. In this way, with a jesting application of an algebraic principle, he creates a ludic moment of incongruity, pointing up the illogic of Spencer's assumed separation of mind and world.

This early essay serves, in my terms, as a troping device, enacting an argument that proceeds by way of clever turns, wordplay, juxtapositions, and personifications. Throughout the essay, WJ flexes his prose to portray both mind and world as active agents in a dynamic exchange. He likens consciousness to a citizen who is also a player: "There belongs to mind, from its birth upward, a spontaneity, a vote. It is in the game, and not a mere looker-on; and its judgments of the should-be, its ideals, cannot be peeled off from the body of the cogitandum as if they were excrescences, or meant, at most, survival" (908). Mind, he urges, "bring[s] independent interests into the game" and thereby injects "subjective spontaneity" into its relationship with the environment (898). The minds of human beings do not have a "monotonously narrow passion" for survival (898) but have a multitude of interests "that make survival worth securing" (899). Powerful among these are "the social affections" and "all the various forms of play" (899). In articulating his disagreements with Spencer, WJ uses metaphors that have what we might term the flavor of the older man's ideas about evolution: that it involves a "struggle for existence" that results in the "survival of the fittest." Antonello La Vergata has argued that Spencer's writings succeeded in "spoiling and ossifying the richness, variety, and flexibility of Darwin's concept."[69] With youthful effervescence, WJ turns Spencer's concepts this way and that, demonstrating an adaptable, elastic wit. Mustering his arguments against Spencer, WJ engages in verbal sparring and treats scientific debate as a form of sport or contest.

Play, for WJ, provides a category of active experience where Spencer's understanding of the mechanistic imperatives of biological entities founders. WJ's conception of "the game" instead describes experience as a zone where human beings work out nondeterministic rules based on their own values and interests. Surprisingly, he notes, the struggle that is life may, in fact, contradict the brute imperative of survival itself. WJ observes that, in games of honor, the contest may result in the demise of a player and still count as a "win." Society admires a hero, he argues, one who willingly enters a battle "even if headlong courage, pride, and martyr-spirit do ruin the individual" (900). Huizinga affirms this connection between games and war, writing that "ever since words existed for fighting and playing, men have been wont to call war a game."[70] For Huizinga, such high-stakes, adaptive play is soaked with both peril and meaning: "Fighting, as a cultural function, always presupposes limiting rules, and it requires, to a certain extent anyway, the recognition of its play quality" (89). Blood sports, for WJ, encapsulate the ultimate refutation of Spencer's arguments by pointing up the *non*-correspondence of human and biological value. As he puts this insight: "'It is death to you, but fun for us,'"—with the "us" being humankind generally ("Remarks," 900).

The point, WJ suggests, is that there is no universal, determining, dispassionate, disinterested mind in existence to passively "correspond" with a preset environment. He thus figures a relationship between mind and environment that is contingent, uncertain, and unfolding: a field of play that is conditioned by individual interests on the one hand and the salient opportunities afforded by the environment on the other. WJ unsettles Spencer's understanding of mind as a "regulative law of thought" (901). "The umpire," he concludes, "bring[s] a standard of his own upon the scene" (901).

By Latinizing the noun for mind—cogitandum—WJ makes it *sound* physiological, like a region of the brain. Yet he playfully locates consciousness in the body, simultaneously riffing on and disputing the materialist reduction of mind to brain (cerebrum) situated in a snug internal location (cranium). He argues that the processes of the mind are bound up with the body—for example, impulses, emotions, and affections—that in turn cannot be dissected from the world. "The margins of James's copy of [Spencer's] *First Principles* he decorated with such remarks as 'absurd,' 'trebly asinine,' 'curse his metaphysics,' and 'damned scholastic quibble,'" writes Richard Hofstadter.[71] WJ's creative formulations dramatize the precise point he is making: that consciousness is a player in the high-stakes game of knowing, not just accommodating but selecting and assimilating what the field of play presents.

Moreover, WJ affirms, the mind's field of play—the "external" environment—is similarly active, turbulent, selective, and invested. He makes this point in a manner that was, at that time, close to outrageous: by refashioning his classroom as a pugilistic venue for engaging with Spencer's textbook *Principles of Psychology*. Richardson describes how the young professor, in his course "Natural History 2: Physiological Psychology," "allowed himself some fun" (178) as he took apart the esteemed man's arguments and notoriously clunky prose style. Lecturing to his students about his own understanding of mental states, WJ "soon found himself in vehement, almost outraged opposition to Spencer," Richardson writes (178). Exasperated by the closed determinism of Spencer's definition of evolution, and further exasperated by his abstract phraseology, WJ restated Spencer's definition for his students: "Evolution is a change from a no-howish untalkaboutable all-alikeness to a some-howish and in general talkaboutable not-all-alikeness by continuous sticktogetherations and somethingelse-ifications" (Richardson, 179). WJ acts out the way in which an "environment" includes not just natural objects and laws but also ideas and impassioned advocates. Michael P. Lempert quotes an extraordinary letter of June 1878 that WJ sent to his lifelong friend James Jackson Putnam: "Your insolent card of May 13 reaches my eyes (by a strange coincidence) just as I return from the last crowning lecture of the course in wh. poor Spencer has been shaken in my jaws as a mouse is shaken by a tiger (as soon as the latter can conquer his native timidity and once fairly take hold of the mouse). The course (I need not say) closed amid the tumultuous, nay, delirious applause of the students."[72]

Here, the younger and less established thinker plays with the idea that he is a "tiger" to Spencer's "mouse." WJ jokes that he must overcome "his native timidity" before finishing off "poor Spencer" by "shak[ing] him in his jaws." Casting himself as a timid tiger, he tempers (ever so slightly) his grandstanding—though perhaps he is laughing at Spencer's notorious "survival of the fittest" understanding of evolution. He clinches his point, that both "sides" of Spencer's axiom—mind on the one side, environment on the other—are neither disinterested nor disengaged, by telling Putnam, "Would I were part of his [Spencer's] environment! I'd see if his 'intelligence' could establish 'relations' that would 'correspond' to me in any other way than by giving up the ghost before me! He and all his myrmidons, disciples and parasites! Down with the hell-spawn of 'em!" (37–38). Given the extent to which Spencer's theories provided the foundation for social Darwinism, a pernicious set of justifications for grotesque, race-based inequalities, WJ's letter to Putnam can be seen as darkly prescient. As Hofstadter observed, "Spencer's was a system conceived in and dedicated to an age of steel and steam engines, competition, exploitation, and struggle."[73]

Sensory Psychology and Object-Oriented Pedagogy

The year 1879, when WJ's jousting with Spencer was circulating in the scientific community, is often cited as the foundational year for the creation of modern psychology: it is when William Wundt opened the first experimental laboratory devoted to psychological research, in Leipzig, Germany. G. Stanley Hall is credited as opening the second, at Johns Hopkins University, in 1884. (Hall, in fact, was WJ's student, having earned the first Ph.D. in psychology granted by Harvard, in 1878.) Yet it is equally worth noting that, a few years earlier, in 1875, WJ established an experimental psychology *demonstration* lab at Harvard, a hands-on space to supplement a lecture course entitled "The Relations Between Physiology and Psychology." For WJ, new ways of thinking about the human mind and human behavior took on practical, concrete form in and through his teaching, where the science of psychology transpired in relation to students. No mere "sage on the stage," he saw teaching as a space where theory and practice came together in acts of transmission.

WJ's disagreements with first Agassiz and then Spencer began to articulate a set of actions and ideas (he called them "flights" and "perches") associated with the inquisitive student mind in action: habitual acceptance, uncomfortable doubt, curious engagement, skeptical testing, and (one hopes) delighted arrival at a provisional conclusion or perch. This is the sort of experiential, tactile, sensory education that can transpire in a scientific expedition, field of battle, or playing field. It can also unfold in a laboratory or classroom where lively discussion is encouraged. It is quite another thing, however, to translate vital, still developing psychological knowledge into textual form. And when the material is precisely *about* the dynamic ways in which human beings come to "mind" the world, the degree of difficulty is intensified.

Establishing The Principles of Psychology

For WJ, psychology itself was a field under construction, a *science-manqué*. Upon publishing *Psychology: Briefer Course* in 1892, WJ wrote:

> It is indeed strange to hear people talk triumphantly of "the New Psychology," and write "Histories of Psychology," when into the real elements and forces which the word covers not the first glimpse of clear insight exists. A string of raw facts; a little gossip and wrangle

> about opinions; a little classification and generalization on the mere descriptive level; a strong prejudice that we have states of mind, and that our brain conditions them: but not a single law in the sense in which physics shows us laws, not a single proposition from which any consequence can causally be deduced. This is no science, it is only the hope of a science.[74]

As a discipline, the field of psychology was in its infancy. And, like a baby learning to walk, psychology was seeking its bearings, hoping to use ideas drawn from physiology and physics as compass points. What is the relationship between brain states and states of consciousness? Between ideas in the mind and things in the physical environment? WJ in his writing for the classroom sought to instantiate a method for navigating the relationships between mind and brain, on the one hand, and self and world, on the other. In his magisterial *The Principles of Psychology,* the emphasis on discerning the dynamic results of how sensations and perceptions work—how human consciousness helps pilot an embodied self through the world—plays out in terms of tactile encounters. He frequently uses the metaphor of navigation in describing how consciousness works. The metaphor aptly applies to WJ as a thinker: he used others' theories as waypoints as he sought to establish psychology as a provisional body of knowledge. He drew promiscuously on physiology, biology, and philosophy. This new inquiry into the "how" of consciousness became a sort of dead reckoning, a forward-facing mode of inquiry that used previously determined positions (known appropriately as fixed points) to advance. WJ quotes extensively from other thinkers, those with whom he agrees and those his textbook is correcting. These philosophical conversations become a model for the textbook as a colloquy between author and reader, imagined centrally as professor and student.

As a Harvard instructor, WJ jokingly noted that the first class in psychology he attended was his own. So new was psychology as a distinct field of study, he was a professor at the podium rather than a student in the lecture hall. A second irony, less amusing to WJ at the time, was that his promised textbook on the new science took not the (already expansive) two years he had anticipated to complete but rather twelve. He had received the assignment in 1878, and it wasn't until 1890 that the long-awaited *The Principles of Psychology* (*PP*) appeared in print. In the preface, WJ announced: "The treatise which follows has in the main grown up in connection with the author's class-room instruction in Psychology."[75] Disparaging the textbook's startling size—at fourteen hundred pages, "the work has grown to a length which no one can regret more than the writer himself"—he surprises with a statement of the book's premise that is as succinct (and indeed Delphic) as the text is long: "That thoughts and feelings exist and are vehicles of knowledge" (*PP*, vi).

In the opening pages WJ challenges readers' expectations about the textbook to come. "It is mainly a mass of descriptive details" (vii), he writes, sidestepping the role of omniscient authority. Those familiar with Spencer's earlier, identically entitled *Principles of Psychology*, for instance, would be ready for the text's organization to advance the author's theory about the nature of mind. WJ subverts this expectation in a simple sentence: "The reader will in vain seek for any closed system in the book" (*PP*, vii). WJ instead plays the role of a peer, not just the presenter of information but a sort of reader's coach, pointing out potential shortcuts and urging that the book be tailored to individual interests. He advises readers that the more recondite chapters on brain anatomy, or those that use complex schemata to set forth a neurological pathway, could simply be bypassed. "By judiciously skipping according to their several needs," he writes, "I am sure that many sorts of readers, even those who are just beginning the study of the subject, will find my book of use" (v).

Barzun picks up on the novel, "do-it-yourself" pedagogical tone of *Principles*. Of the experience of reading the textbook for the first time Barzun writes, "One looks back on those introductory pages and diagrams with something like the affection one feels for the unfamiliar rules that taught one a new game or the complex instructions for assembling a useful and diverting piece of equipment, except that there the game and the equipment have been ours from birth, and the wonder is that after so long a use we are learning to thread their intricacy for the first time."[76] Barzun captures the delightful conundrum of what it feels like for the mind to become aware of its own operating instructions. The central affects are affection and wonder: the pleasure of encountering the familiar, and the uncanny sense of seeing freshly its extraordinariness. For readers, approaching thoughts and feelings "from the point of view of natural science" is an experience at once estranging—with its "unfamiliar rules" that include looking at two spots on the page cross-eyed in order to see them blur together as one—and strangely intimate, as both the introspective method of inquiry and the entity under scrutiny "have been ours from birth" (*PP*, v). The text offers increasing familiarity with "the equipment" of perception (for example, senses, organs, and mental states) as it rehearses older philosophical understandings of human consciousness. Taken as a whole, Barzun argues, "the *Psychology* gives us along the way a virtual history of the warring conceptions of the mind since Plato" (37).

The textbook also introduced the voice of WJ to an international audience. When *The Principles of Psychology* was published, in 1890, it arrived with fanfare and was generally greeted warmly—not least by his family. As we saw in my Introduction, AJ penned the following in 1891: "One day, talking about some good reviews of William's *Psychology*, which reprobate his mental pirouettes and squirm at his daring to go lightly amide the solemnities, H.[enry] said, 'Yes; they can't understand intellectual larking'—I remember the *Spectator* once describing some of Father's flights from the Commonplace as 'coarse.'"[77] Two years after publishing *The Principles of Psychology* in two magisterial volumes, WJ came out with a compact, classroom-friendly version: *Psychology: Briefer Course* (*PBC*). He wrote to HJ at the time, "My psychology seems to be a great success so-far; and I am quite sure that the 'briefer course' will practically be *the* book used in the colleges."[78] The shorter work addressed this conundrum: How precisely does one convey a "living understanding of the mind" (*PBC*, 4) *to* the active, assimilating minds of students studying psychology and seeking to master a body of knowledge? This particular concern raises questions not just about the contents of the text, nor solely about the most efficacious or lucid mode for the presentation of ideas, but also about method. WJ's stated concern with providing a "living understanding of the human mind" highlights the importance of *how* the material is conveyed. The act of communication—the relationality between minds, the sharing of understanding—is key to the ideas conveyed. In the case of *PBC,* Barzun's metaphor of the textbook as instruction manual for a useful and diverting piece of equipment is apt: with the twist that consciousness is both the device to be understood and the vehicle of understanding.

WJ is explicit in the preface that *pedagogy* is a motivation for publishing the shorter volume: "In preparing the following abridgement of my larger work, the *Principles of Psychology*, my chief aim has been to make it more directly available for class-room use" (*PBC*, 3). By leaving out the more scholarly material from *Psychology* ("polemical and historical matter . . . metaphysical discussions and purely speculative passages . . . book-references . . . [and] all the impertinences"), WJ organized the chapters into "a good pedagogic order" (*PBC*, 3). The classroom was in fact a space of great interest to the physiological psychology that emerged in the second half of the nineteenth century, which focused on the child mind as an object of study. As Sally Shuttleworth observes, "The child is thus to be studied not simply for its own sake but as an entry point for all the emerging historical disciplines of evolutionary biology and psychology, anthropology, and historical philology."[79] The child study movement of Hall and others gathered much of its data about the behavior of children from the reports of teachers based on their classroom interactions. WJ in *PBC* was not interested in the statistical studies of Hall and others; nor was he particularly focused on the subject of children's minds or the nascent field of developmental psychology. Rather, the emphasis on understanding "the faculties needed for steering us in this world of mixed variety and uniformity" (*PBC*, 13), means that pedagogy, for WJ, was folded in as a key aspect of the study of mind—not merely as an after-the-fact vehicle for the dissemination of psychological knowledge. The Greek root of *pedagogy* translates as "I lead the child," and WJ was determined that this text would lead students of psychology *through* what he termed the "zig-zag" process of attaining understanding (Richardson suggests that WJ became "lastingly fond of the term" from his childhood reading of an early form of graphic novel entitled *Voyages en Zigzag*, written by Rodolphe Toepffer, a nineteenth-century Swiss schoolteacher).[80]

It is a tricky business both to convey a baseline set of ideas and principles *and* to activate a student's sensory assimilation of the material. The first chapter of *PBC*, entitled "Introductory," provides a study in WJ's technique for doing precisely that. Using the deductive structure of a Protestant sermon, he initiates the chapter with a quotation from an authoritative text, a definition of psychology from Professor Ladd: "the *description and explanation of states of consciousness*" (*PBC*, 11). WJ rehearses the precepts of physiological psychology, following Spencer in a basic premise of the British thinker's *Principles of Psychology* by adopting an evolutionary perspective, that "since mind and its environment have evolved together, they must be studied together."[81] WJ further establishes that physiology, the study of the functions of the human organism, provides the context for studying "mental science." To study the mind, he affirms, one must take into account the motions of the body: "All mental states . . . are followed by bodily activity of some sort" (*PBC*, 14). In *PBC* he thus adopts the "general point of view" of "'natural science'" (3), shifting the study of the mind from deduction and introspection to the empirical methods of experimental and laboratory science. He points out that, for the new psychology, the conclusion that there exists a "uniform correlation of brain-states with body-states" is "a law of nature" (15). The organizational structure for the introductory chapter, again, is that of a sermon: in a few swift paragraphs he establishes the *text* (definition of psychology), provides *context* and *circumstances* (evolutionary biology, physiology), and establishes *doctrine* (the "law of nature" that mind and body are correlated). New wine decanted into an old bottle.

Yet at the same time WJ is describing these Darwin-inflected "rules of the game" he is also providing the method for challenging them. Regarding the "uniform correlation of brain-states with body-states," he is careful to "quote" this idea rather than simply state or affirm it (15). He matches the authoritative statements with his own voice, which speaks more provisionally, more descriptively of the process by which one might arrive at the "law" that mind states and body states are correlated. Consciousness, he points out, is easily altered by "a blow on the head, by rapid loss of blood, by an epileptic discharge, by a full dose of alcohol, . . . or by a fever" (34–35). "Taking all such facts together," he writes, "the simple and radical conception dawns upon the mind that mental action may be uniformly and absolutely a function of brain-action" (15). WJ here eschews the standard textbook approach to conveying knowledge through the deductive postulation of ideas. Instead of a general law, he substitutes a descriptive narrative by which an idea "dawns" on an inquiring mind. Then, he reinforces the textbook's experimental nature by backing away from the "simple and radical conception" he had himself introduced. He backtracks, translating this "too sweeping a statement" into something more tentative and ad hoc. By the end of the introduction, we no longer have a law; instead, the premise of physiological psychology serves as the "working hypothesis of this book" (15), a "provisional point of view" that will "require several generations of psychologists to test . . . with anything like minuteness" (16).

A Classroom Between Two Covers

From the very beginning of *PBC*, WJ models the method by which the mind encounters, assimilates, questions, and recalibrates in relation to the world of events and ideas. In a method that distinguishes his approach as both daring and amusing, he uses as his "case" the structure and content of the psychological wisdom under discussion. He affirms that "the student will remember that the Sciences constantly have to take these risks [adopting an unproved postulate] by zig-zagging from one absolute formula to another which corrects it by going too far in the other way" (16). As goes psychology as a field, navigating restlessly to and fro, so goes the human mind.

The topic of precisely how to convey knowledge takes especially palpable form in the chapter entitled "The Structure of the Brain," when WJ admits the difficulty of casting the brain's convolutions into words: "A verbal description is absolutely useless," he writes. He supplements the text with his own pen-and-ink drawings of labeled brain regions, but these figures are, he admits, merely schematic and two dimensional. What is needed, instead, is "a good topographical mind" to comprehend the brain's enfolded structures, which are hard enough to understand "even when they are followed with eye and hand" (93). Minds know the world through bodily senses that locate the knower in space. What is needed to learn, it turns out, is precisely the functional harmonizing of psychological and physiological capacities—the coordination of mind and body in the context of an environment. It is this immersive milieu that the text seeks to approximate.

WJ points out that the book's structure moves from more concrete and familiar elements of human mental life—such as the operation of the senses, and the physiological elements of the brain and nervous systems—to those "which we naturally come to know later by way of abstraction" (3). In this regard, the textbook in its organization recapitulates the developmental understanding of the human mind that the content of the text would convey. An infant is familiar with the textures of sensory experience; only "later" do we reflect on mental activities such as reasoning, will, and ethical decisions. The text of *PBC* isn't just based on wisdom gained from experiments; it is itself an experiment, a nascent attempt to capture the mind in action without rendering it in static terms. Professor/writer and students/readers are thus united in a shared endeavor, which may be "stumblingly carried out" (4), as the author admits. Form follows function in WJ's pedagogy; what is conveyed is not inert information but experiences of the mind navigating and seeking to grasp the ways in which the world works.

How exactly does human consciousness work? For WJ, the answer lies in bodily contact with the object world. Chapters on the physical senses—sight, touch, and the like—thus not only inaugurate the study of physiological psychology, they also enlist the students directly in exercising the sense in question. Chapter 3, entitled "Sight," includes a long footnote recommending that students supplement a good textbook on the anatomy of the eye with their own, hands-on dissection of "a bullock's eye, which any butcher will furnish" (35). Both seeing and hearing, WJ argues, are aptly "characterized as organs of anticipatory touch": "The chief function of our eyes and ears is to enable us to prepare ourselves for contact with approaching bodies, or to ward such contact off" (68). Through analogy to technology of visual reproduction WJ explains how human eyes, through the action of muscles and ligaments, are able to focus on objects near and far: "In photographers' cameras the back is made to slide, and can be drawn away from the lens when the object that casts the picture is near, and pushed forwards when it is far" (39). Bodies situated in particular conditions and endowed with consciousness are the means by which we navigate space and thereby come to provisionally understand the world in which we exist.

But to take a step back: how can these ideas be made real to students, sitting in the "camera obscura" (35) model of their own consciousness, reading a textbook? Barzun poses the problem this way: "Think of the eye, too busy to see how it performs its own seeing; all it can ever see of sight is the dissected optic nerve on the laboratory table, the retina, lens, and other parts, no longer seeing."[82] This self-reflexivity and zigzagging between subjective experience and objective detachments is precisely what WJ sets out to achieve. For one thing, he reminds readers of *PBC* of the situatedness of their disembodied-seeming experience—which is, of course, *reading a textbook*. They are using their eyes to study his diagrams of the anatomy of the eye. WJ points out a conundrum: how can our experience feel unified and complete, when key senses—eyes, ears, even nostrils—come in twos? He calls his readers' attention to the strangeness of this normally uninterrogated state of affairs, in which "we hear single with two ears, and smell single with two nostrils, and we also see single with two eyes" (*PBC*, 40).

The reader, temporarily called out of the seemingly effortless process of passing eyes over the page to absorb information, is thus primed for further investigation. With binocular vision, precisely because of the positioning of the organs of sight, there are optical tricks that can produce unexpected experiences of doubleness; these, in turn, bring to awareness the operations that are normally occluded. These moments of estrangement bring "knowledge of" rather than "knowledge about" the phenomenon of sight. In the text WJ offers simple optical illusions, small exercises for students to pause over and try to accomplish. These require active attention and attempts. For instance, one diagrammatic exercise involves two dots of about two millimeters each, positioned on the page with angled lines bisecting them; the text further includes instructions of how to hold the book and look intently at the dots, focusing and adjusting the page distance from the eyes until the two distinct lines fuse into a single image—an X (45). (The technique is similar to one that all kids play with at some point, crossing their eyes and reveling in the distorted world that suddenly appears.)

Readers of the textbook thus spend time on their own embodying the sensory principles under discussion, going through the small exercises offered and then pausing to read and reread the explanation. WJ takes the instruction a step further, however, pointing out that it's odd we don't note such experiences of visual doubling in vivo, as they take place in normal life—such as focusing on a distant spot, which causes objects near to us to appear double. (Holding up a finger near your face, then focusing across the room, reveals this effect.) "The answer to this is that *we have trained ourselves to habits of inattention* in regard to double images" (44). The textbook, with its tiny auto-experiments, jolts the reader's complacency: what seems to be "natural" seeing is actually the result of years of acclimation, making us unsurprised at the apparent "doubling" of a near object and thus unable to "see" it. Use of the stereoscope, which WJ approximates through his simple dot-and-line drawings, calls attention to the habits of attention and interest that dictate how we see the world. Through the intervention of artifice, we are offered an oblique (or zigzag) experience of how we see; not unlike the practice of tacking in sailing, one diverts attention in order to arrive sideways at a destination. As WJ was undoubtedly aware from his early training in studio art, a similar technique is used to teach drawing: turning a picture of a face upside down disrupts habitual vision and can make a copyist draw more to life, with eyes positioned surprisingly at the center of an oval (and less like a habituated, smiley-face conception of what a human countenance looks like). Thus we can "see" how we see by virtue of obliquity, through the successful coordination of hand and eye.

In other chapters, WJ uses different pedagogical techniques to enlist readers in embodied, sensory experience while they learn about the nature of embodied, sensory experience. The chapter on the structure of the brain includes labeled diagrams, for instance, such as a pen-and-ink drawing of the brain visualized from below, where it meets the spinal column. In the schematic diagram, the brain locations that correspond with specific sensory nerves or regions are marked accordingly, for example, "olfactory," "facial," "pneumogastric," "auditory." In a footnote to the chapter's title, "The Structure of the Brain," he notes: "This chapter will be understood as a mere sketch for beginners. Models will be found of assistance" (84), meaning that students must supplement the drawing with three-dimensional models of the brain, cast in plaster. In the footnote WJ goes so far as to recommend where to purchase such models and to warn about the cost. (The best, he opines, can be obtained from a purveyor in Paris, Monsieur Jules Talrich of No. 97 Boulevard St. Germain—well worth the cost of 350 francs [84].)

In a chapter entitled "The Perception of Space," WJ marvels at the adult capacity to have "definite and apparently instantaneous knowledge of the sizes, shapes, and distances of the things amongst which we live and move; and we have moreover a practically definite notion of the whole great infinite continuum of real space in which the world swings and in which all these things are located" (316). The ability to map a physical space or to merely conceive of a three-dimensional object, by holding a conception of it in mind (even before ever having made acquaintance with the particular location or the specific object), is distinct to human consciousness. In an epigraph to "Consciousness as a Problem in the Psychology of Behavior," the psychologist Lev Vygotsky quotes Karl Marx, who affirms, "from the very beginning, the worst architect differs from the best bee in that before building the cell of wax, he already has built it in his head."[83] But how is the human imagination to grasp its seat, the human brain? In lieu of an actual physical space, WJ in *PBC* presents the chapter on the structure of the brain rhetorically as if students were present in a dissection lab, inspecting the organ with hand and eye: "The way really to understand the brain," he asserts, "is to dissect it" (87). The text enlists readers' spatial sense, first going so far as to "place" tools in the readers' hands—a saw, a chisel, a blunt curved instrument—that are intended first to bring the organ into visibility (by allowing for the liberation of the organ from the protective skull); and second, like the walking stick of a blind person, to allow the cautious exploration of the cerebral terrain:

> The first thing is to get off the skull-cap. Make two saw-cuts . . . by actual trial, one will find the best direction for the saw-cuts. It is hard to saw entirely through the skull-bone without in some places also sawing into the brain. Here is where the chisel comes in—one can break by a smart blow on it with the hammer any parts of the skull not quite sawn through. When the skull-cap is ready to come off one will feel it "wobble" . . . The brain in its pia mater should now be carefully "shelled out." Usually it is best to begin at the forward end, turning it up there and gradually working backwards. The *olfactory lobes* are liable to be torn; they must be carefully scooped from the pits in the base of the skull. . . . It is well to have a little blunt curved instrument expressly for this purpose. Next the *optic nerves* tie the brain down, and must be cut through. (88)

Anatomy in the chapter is presented through a series of commands that situate the reader's experience of the brain both spatially and temporally. These directives give shape to a scenario of movement, the handling of an object on a stable surface (presumably a lab table). Commands that imply the coordination of hand and eye introduce a series of linked paragraphs: "Turn next to the ventral surface of the medulla. . . . Now cut through the peduncles of the cerebellum. . . . Now bend up the posterior edge of the hemispheres, exposing the corpora quadrigemina" (92).

Published in 1892, *PBC* represents WJ's thinking at its most physiological; accordingly, the writing is the most expressive of physical movements familiar from choreographed laboratory dissections. I am arguing that this mode of writing can itself be construed as a troping device meant to allow readers—presumably students—to turn text into experience: to "grasp" the material in a sense that is not merely metaphorical. Experience arrives as a compound, WJ asserts, not made up of bits: "'But,' the reader may say, 'is not the taste of lemonade composed of that of lemon *plus* that of sugar?' No! I reply, this taking the combining of objects for that of feelings" (193). The narrative voice is that of Professor throughout, coaxing, commanding, and collaborative. After explaining a quirk of vision, WJ instructs, "To verify this, let the reader stare fixedly before him as if through the paper at infinite distance, with the black spots in Fig. 8 in front of his respective eyes. He will then see the two black spots swim together, as it were, and combine into one" (41). To describe the operation of habit, he calls attention to absurd mistakes: who, he asks, has not "taken his latch-key out on arriving at the door-step of a friend?" (142). By calling readers' attention to their jingling keys and swimming dots, or assuring that "when the skull-cap is ready to come off one will feel it" (88), he is creating instances of the "sensory stimulus" (101) and bodily acts of perception under description.

Ekphrasis is the aesthetic term for translating one art form—a painting, for instance—into another medium—say, a poem. Sensory simulation is the neuropsychological equivalent of ekphrasis: it is the substitution of one sensory experience into another, such as the translation of visual or auditory stimuli into tactile sensation. The Braille system of lettering, which substitutes raised dots for the letters in the alphabet, is an example of sensory substitution—and one that was of interest to WJ. In a letter to Helen Keller, he affirmed that the human sensorium itself was an extraordinary means for engaging "the Great world": "It makes no difference in what shape the content of our verbal material may come. In some it is more optical, in others more acoustical, in others more motor in nature. In you it is motor and tactile, but its functions are the same as ours."[84] Melding the sensory with the intellectual is the aspect of feeling—the delight of discovery, and the hunger to know more. WJ describes the education of Laura Bridgman, who had lost sight and hearing at the age of two (fifty years before Keller). Repeatedly feeling the raised letters her teacher had pasted on the surface of familiar things to name them, Laura suddenly understood: "Accompanied by a radiant flash of intelligence and glow of joy," the blind girl connected touch to sign to thing.[85] "From that moment," WJ writes, "her education went on with extreme rapidity" (939).

Invented in the early nineteenth century, Braille was understood to be a military rather than a prosthetic device; it was used for communicating messages during nighttime battles and was originally called "night writing." Only later did Braille become a means for individuals with impaired vision to read books without the assistance of a sighted individual. Similarly, by mid-century telegraphic technology translated textual information into a series of electrical impulses, dots and dashes, that could be transmitted across vast spaces. The twentieth-century neurologist Paul Bach-y-Rita specialized in technologies to translate topographical information into tactile form to allow blind individuals to navigate the world (to, for instance, become a world-class rock climber). For Bach-y-Rita, *writing itself* "ought to be considered the original precursor [to high-tech inventions], because it enabled the previously auditory experience of the spoken work to be presented visually."[86]

Evolving Consciousness

WJ's commitment to the texture of experience—its singular lived qualities—set him on a lifelong quest to unsettle the clumps into which human beings tend to coagulate things, ideas, and happenings, whether by abstraction, generalization, or universals. For WJ, in the beginning are states of consciousness that are caught up in the sensory and affective nature of "adorable things" and not inert or predigested concepts. "Why," he asks, "from Socrates downwards, philosophers should have vied with each other in scorn of the knowledge of the particular, and in adoration of that of the general, is hard to understand, seeing that the more adorable knowledge ought to be that of the more adorable things, and that the *things* of worth are all concretes and singulars" (*PBC*, 232). He takes the idea of Heraclitus—that we never step into the same river twice—and affirms it at the level of perception. This raises a question: why are we not continuously in a state of surprise at the "novel" appearance of familiar things, such as one's own armchair? Doesn't our recognition of the chair affirm its sameness, or (if we are agnostic about the persistence of objects) the sameness of our perception? WJ answers no, for the very reason that a particular perception of "sameness" is itself an addition to a perception: "Nothing can be conceived as the same without being conceived in a novel state of mind" (232). Seeing a familiar thing is an experience infused with new feelings and associations: "My arm-chair is one of the things of which I have a conception; I knew it yesterday and recognized it when I looked at it. But if I think of it to-day as the same arm-chair which I looked at yesterday, it is obvious that the very conception of it *as* the same is an additional complication to the thought, whose inward constitution must alter in consequence" (232). WJ's idea, that what is apprehended is qualitatively unique, explains his notion that there is never a bright line between a sensation and a perception, which "merge into each other by insensible degrees" (21). He posits that a pure sensation, the very first germ of experience, "*can only be realized in the earliest days of life*" (21).

WJ then backs away even from this claim, however. For even the most rudimentary sensation—"a mere *this*" (23)—"leaves its 'unimaginable touch'" (21) on the newborn's sense organs, what he calls the "dumb awakening of consciousness" (23). From the merest tickle comes a world: the very first sensation that an infant gets *is* for him the outer universe (23). In this regard the child is parent to the adult: "The universe which he comes to know in later life is nothing but an amplification of that first simple germ which, by accretion on the one hand and intussusception on the other, has grown so big and complex and articulate that its first estate is unrememberable" (23). In short, for WJ, sensations are cognitive, placing the infant in relation to the object world, giving rise to what he calls "knowledge of acquaintance" or "sensible knowledge" (22). Over time "sensible knowledge" shades into "knowledge about," the object of which we dub a perception although it is merely a richer, more complex sensation. This increasing complexity marks growth, which can eventually lead to mastery—with the following caveat: "The best taught born-blind pupil . . . yet lacks a knowledge which the least instructed seeing baby has" (22). Learning is built into the structure of sensation.

Yet hot on the heels of WJ's emphasis on the "adorable" particulars ("that no two 'ideas' are ever exactly the same" [157]) is a resistance to the standard empiricist's understanding of complex ideas being composed of simpler ones, like so many bricks spackled together to make a building. His famous conception of the "stream of thought" affirms that ideas—which exist in the world as apparently stable, distinguishable entities—emerge after the fact, separated out from what he calls the "apperceiving mass" (308). Likening consciousness to a bird's motion, which involves both flights and perches, WJ observes that the "resting places"—ideas such as *armchair*—are simply more accessible in human experience. To describe the flights, which he also terms relations, he uses the resonant metaphor I discussed in my Introduction: the attempt to capture "the feeling of relation" is "in fact like seizing a spinning top to catch its motion" (160). A "kaleidoscope revolving" (162) can be stopped to give a stable image, he agrees, but how does one grasp the revolving? Empiricists such as David Hume, he contends, mistakenly "deny the reality of most relations" and instead treat ideas like so many "dominoes in a game," juxtaposed "but really separate" (161).

Children, WJ affirms, are a portal for accessing the flights that make up experience because they have the "congenital impulse" to be interested in "strange things, moving things" (214). Lessons from the schoolroom become an occasion for theorizing the nature of attention. "Sensitiveness to immediately exciting sensorial stimuli characterizes the attention of childhood and youth," WJ writes in *PBC* (214). The coordination between a person and the object world, a process that obtained for adults as well as children, is illuminated by the absorptive tendencies of youth, making "the child seem to belong less to himself than to every object which happens to catch his notice" (214). In a wonderful discussion that condenses the insight of Charles Schultz that adult voices often appear as so much undifferentiated noise to "mind-wandering schoolboys," WJ observes that lapsed attention can be suddenly kindled: "I remember classes in which, instruction being uninteresting, and discipline relaxed, a buzzing murmur was always to be heard, which invariably stopped for as long a time as an anecdote lasted. How could the boys, since they seemed to hear nothing, notice when the anecdote began?" (215). He concludes that, because the prior discussion lacked vital interest, it flowed in and directly out of a pupil's awareness; whereas when "the words awaken[ed] old thoughts" and became suddenly salient, attention was arrested and the student's attention focused (215).

WJ's emphasis on action locates change as the core of mental life. Yet in the context of nineteenth-century science it is not just biological beings with nervous systems that are capable of movement and adjustment. As Elizabeth Grosz has written, for chemists and physicists as well as evolutionary biologists, "matter is imbued with a dynamism or activity," and nature itself is "construed as force, provocation, activity, or incitement" rather than "an inert passivity onto which life, culture, and the human impose themselves."[87] Ice cubes melt, river rocks wear away, apples fall from trees, sunflowers turn their faces toward the sun. In his *Psychology,* WJ at the outset distinguishes two sorts of purposive movement. The first, simpler sort of action he describes is rote and determined, the province of non-sentient entities. He gives the example of iron filings that move toward a magnet. The second sort of action, which is creative and flexible, is the province of beings with consciousness: "If now we pass from such actions as these to those of living things, we notice a striking difference. Romeo wants Juliet as the filings want the magnet; and if no obstacles intervene he moves towards her by as straight a line as they. But Romeo and Juliet, if a wall be built between them, do not remain idiotically pressing their faces against its opposite sides like the magnet and the filings with the card. Romeo soon finds a circuitous way, by scaling the wall or otherwise, of touching Juliet's lips directly" (7).

The romantic metaphor is resonant and telling. Human beings adjust to their environment not only in terms of survival and sustenance but also in relation to their beloved others. Affection names the dynamic state of "being affected" or feeling the impress of the world: to use the formula that WJ set forth, it denotes the relation of the inner accommodating the outer. Emotion literally evokes the movement (-motion) of inner to outer (-e): the impress of the self on the world. The scene that WJ cites includes a statement that encapsulates the poles of *human* (and not electromagnetic) attraction and repulsion: "Love goes toward love, as schoolboys from their books / But love from love, toward school in heavy looks" (act 2, scene 2). Human beings are uniquely ingenious in devising solutions because their capacity for interest and desire motivates their creativity. For WJ, human beings' sensation of touch marks a capacity that (like a kiss) ever so slightly transforms both the kisser and the kissed.

But what do we make of Shakespeare's schoolboys, with their antipathy to school, despite their penchant for meaningful contact with resonant objects? WJ's colleague Dewey addresses this conundrum in his work on education. For Dewey, the relationship between play and pedagogy was structured on a paradox: on the one hand, play was essential to a child's engagement with the world and served as an epistemological activity; on the other, instrumentalizing play (harnessing it for specific teleological ends) eradicated its spirit. Shakespeare's schoolboys, running from their books and reluctantly trudging toward school, serve as a foil for the powerful attractive pull of play that manifests as interest, passion, or love. Play in its richest sense cannot be taught, and Dewey disparaged the tendency of adults to interfere with play or to interpret it in light of adult values and goals. If teachers supply materials, he urged, "the child must make them really his own, and then act upon them as his own, or else he is simply going through certain external motions, into which possibly the adult may read an ideal or a spiritual significance, but which are either sensation or mechanical to the child."[88] In response to those who would characterize play as an activity that is not serious, Dewey—as does Bateson, who follows him—embraces the paradox. Play for Dewey should be understood under the banner of "occupation" in the capacious sense that Adolf Meyer developed the term. "To the child, his play is his activity, his life, his business," Dewey writes. "It is intensely serious. He is absorbed, engrossed in it" (339).

Talking to Teachers and to Students

WJ writes in the idiom of play, and at key moments in the *Psychology* he invokes childhood and youth, especially in the chapters on habit and attention. On the one hand, children are exemplary creatures for understanding the iterative effects of habit. WJ quotes Henry Maudsley, who writes: "Think of the pains necessary to teach a child to stand, of the many efforts which it must make, and of the ease with which it at last stands, unconscious of any effort" (*PP*, 141). On the other hand, children are creatures of novelty: "Sensitiveness to immediately exciting sensorial stimuli characterizes the attention of childhood and youth" (214). This point, however, is quickly followed by its significance for adulthood: distractedness persists for many "to the end of life," and work only "gets done in the interstices of their mind-wandering" (214). Yet notably WJ's *Psychology* does not take on the question of play directly. What is the explanation for this significant omission?

For one thing, play as an autotelic activity falls broadly under the category of aesthetics. In *Principles* he sets forth key topics that the text will not address, despite their interest for the field of psychology. WJ calls attention to his "exclusion of the important subjects of pleasure and pain, and moral and aesthetic feelings and judgements" (v), suggesting that these were omitted to help save space. To some extent, the omission of play points up WJ's emphasis on developing a psychology of the adult, rather than the child, mind.

G. Stanley Hall's Recapitulation Theory of Play

Yet this hardly explains why WJ neglects to investigate an activity that preoccupied scientists and psychologists in the late nineteenth century. There is another explanation, perhaps more salient, that lies with his relationship to his student G. Stanley Hall. Chair of the psychology department at Johns Hopkins University, Hall was best known for his research on adolescence and youth. In this capacity, he set forth one of the more elaborate theories of play—one that was, however, intellectually sloppy and likely to elicit WJ's derision. In theorizing why human beings play, Hall offers the (tautological) answer that youthful creatures play because they are young. "All are young at play and only in play, and the best possible characterization of old age is the absence of the soul and body of play," Hall writes. "Play is always and everywhere the best synonym of youth."[89]

Having thus sidestepped the question of why children play, Hall addressed himself to the question of what play is, and the nature of its particular pleasures. Play, he writes, "is the purest expression of motor heredity" (77), and therein lies its delight: "In play we feel most fully and intensely ancestral joys" (79). To understand what Hall is getting at, one has to grasp his career-long commitment to recapitulation theory—an idea popularized by anti-evolutionary scientists such as Agassiz, and one that Darwin largely repudiated. Some scientists, such as Haeckel, however, were both committed Darwinists and recapitulationists. The theory affirmed that the history of a particular species was a linear unfolding from simple to complex (and thus ideal) form, and that the development of any particular organism in the species from fertilized egg to birth recreated the unfolding of the species (on a vastly collapsed timescale). Haeckel's theory is sometimes called his Biogenetic Law.[90] Agassiz took this idea further, urging that the growth from infant to adult similarly recapitulated the species history. He used this notion to argue that races deemed inferior were simply arrested at a lower stage of development: notoriously, he suggested that an adult of a "less advanced" race was analogous to a youth of a "more advanced" (that is, white) race. This account of play was based in large measure on the theory developed by Groos, who argued that in play people practice for or experiment with serious situations by vicariously reconstructing them.

Despite his general acceptance of Darwin's theory of evolution, Hall continued to embrace recapitulation theory, which was central to his understanding of childhood and adolescence. When young human beings engage in play, such as climbing a tree, building a fort, playing with dolls or even just kicking a stone, they unknowingly mime activities that were once crucial to the survival of the species: "I regard play," Hall writes, "as the motor habits and spirit of the past of the race, persisting in the present, as rudimentary functions sometimes of and always akin to rudimentary organs. The best index and guide to the stated activities of adults in past ages is found in the instinctive, untaught, and non-imitative plays of children which are the most spontaneous and exact expressions of their motor needs" (74). Hall indicates that children erupt into play because wielding a stick (say) mimics the "motor needs" of a rude ancestor. Accordingly, it is a fully determined activity. "The pain of toil died with our forebears," Hall argues; "its vestiges in our play give pure delight" (79). (His statement about the disappearance of back-breaking work from the modern world is absurd on its face.) Further, "primitive men and animals played, and that too has left its traces in us" (79). Hall's account of play merely pushes back the question of motivation to prior generations, for it doesn't explain why primitive man would have engaged in play.

Hall's theory of play is thus backward looking; he sees it as an atavism that offers a window on past adult behaviors rather than an activity with significance in the present. It mimes an ancestor's past discharge of energy for a purpose (say, warding off an attack), this time with no purpose. Groos, commenting on the inadequacies of hereditary accounts, argues that for play to make biological sense it must be forward looking rather than dictated by past species activities. Groos urges that "from the biological standpoint," play can be understood as "pre-exercise" for the serious activities that lie in a child's (and the species') future: "Play is an important agent in supplementing instincts, usually tending to render them more plastic, and thus further the opening of new paths for the development of intelligence."[91] For Groos, an activity defined by its distinction from purpose-driven activity nonetheless is directly instrumental and serves the teleological purpose of survival.

Both Hall and Groos dominated the academic study of child's play, and WJ steered clear of their particular sphere of influence. The recapitulationists framed play in biological and functionalist terms; this exterior view neglects the insider experience, the phenomenology of playing, its meanings and its pleasures. While Groos exhaustively describes types of play and affirms the play function of certain adult tics—he mentions "innumerable toying movements of adults, such as rolling bread crumbs and the like" (10)—he has no strong account for the lifelong persistence of behavior that is "preparatory to the central tasks of life" (361). Presumably, a grown-up would eventually stop "practicing" for life and simply live; here, Groos falls back on the notion that the impulse to play is a hereditary instinct (361).

For WJ, the recourse to mechanical impulse is, in the realm of human experience, a non-explanation. It misunderstands the salient aspects of human life, which is sensory, mindful, and meaningful. In the first chapter of *Principles* he explains the psychological criterion for evaluating human behavior: "The pursuance of future ends and the choice of means of their attainment are thus the mark and criterion of the presence of mentality in a phenomenon. We all use this test to discriminate between an intelligent and a mechanical performance. We impute no mentality to sticks and stones, because they never seem to move for the sake of anything, but always when pushed, and then indifferently and with no sign of choice. So we unhesitatingly call them senseless" (8). For a psychological theory of play, on WJ's terms, one would need to do more than describe it, or to speculate about its function. The important question—why play?—points toward phenomenology: what does play *feel* like, such that we make time and expend energy (often lots of it) on a nonserious activity? And why is play something that, while associated with youth, persists in the form of games, sport, joking, and other behaviors (for example, toying with breadcrumbs) that extend into adulthood? Finally, if play is that which isn't serious, what is the role of play in the serious business of education?

The Spell of the Sensuous Life

After the publication of *Principles*, WJ's reputation as a researcher was secured; moreover, his textbook *PBC* was, as he predicted, adopted in classrooms across the country. Capitalizing on this success, he developed an array of popular lectures that directly treated the subject of education. Richardson writes, "These talks, which he presented over and over to audiences mostly of teachers, were shaking down to a set of seven or eight" (341). Like his godfather Emerson, WJ used the forum of the public talk to hone his thinking before publication, tinkering with the order, wording, and mode of presentation. Paul Stob has calculated that, between the years 1891 and 1898, WJ delivered a version of these lectures eleven times at different venues across the United States, from Berkeley, California, to Buffalo, New York.[92] These live performances led to the publication of the lectures in 1899, tellingly entitled *Talks to Teachers on Psychology, and to Students on Some of Life's Ideals*. The essays sustained an element of colloquy and provisionality even in the crystallized printed form. In his first-person encounters with teachers and students, and in the published text, WJ explicitly applies the conceptions of physiological psychology to the practice of teaching.

Because the collected *Talks to Teachers* would result in a slim volume, WJ added three lectures to the table of contents that were aimed not at teachers but at their pupils. *Talks to Students* consisted of three essays that he had delivered to student audiences: "The Gospel of Relaxation," "On a Certain Blindness in Human Beings," and "What Makes a Life Significant." In his early critique of Spencer, WJ had urged that the British thinker's "formula" for mind as passively reflecting the environment problematically "omitted all sentiments, all aesthetic impulses, all religious emotions and personal affections" ("Remarks," 894). WJ argued that any account of the mind must "bring independent interests into the game" (898) while acknowledging that for a human being, "the interests of his fellow are a part of his environment" (899). In "What Makes a Life Significant" he sets forth his clearest statement on what counts as being "in the game" (908) by distinguishing meaningful play from mere leisure activities. The essay, directed to an audience of students, describes a week he spent at Chautauqua Lake, where he was one of the many philosophers and lecturers invited to speak to the cultured audience—made up largely of schoolteachers—who flocked to upstate New York each summer for expansion of mind and body. Founded in 1878, the Chautauqua Literary and Scientific Circle was first organized as a correspondence course and then expanded its intellectual mission, growing into the adult equivalent of summer camp, with lectures, performances, collective meals, and a range of physical activities.[93] In the essay, WJ calls Chautauqua "a serious and studious picnic on a gigantic scale" and "a middle class paradise": "You have magnificent music—a chorus of seven hundred voices, with possibly the most perfect open-air auditorium in the world. You have every sort of athletic exercise from sailing, rowing, swimming, bicycling, to the ball-field and more artificial doings which the gymnasium affords. You have kindergartens and model secondary schools. . . . You have culture, you have kindness, you have cheapness, you have equality, you have the best fruits of what mankind has fought and bled and striven for under the name of civilization for centuries" (863). Chautauqua was, in many ways, the ultima Thule of progressive education, with a large percentage of the "student population" being teachers seeking to expand their own cultural horizons and to infuse the wisdom gained into their classrooms during the working year.

WJ describes Chautauqua as a "sacred enclosure," calling attention to its special geographical location and also its existence outside or even beyond everyday human experience: "A few summers ago I spent a happy week at the famous Assembly Grounds on the borders of Chautauqua Lake" (862–63). The physical location is matched, in his account, by a sense of the alleviation of the exigencies of everyday living, and in this respect Chautauqua would appear to be an exemplary "magic circle," the term that Huizinga uses to describe the unique physical and spiritual location in which play takes place. Huizinga writes,

> All play moves and has its being within a playground marked off beforehand either materially or ideally, deliberately or as a matter of course. Just as there is no formal difference between play and ritual, so the "consecrated spot" cannot be formally distinguished from the play-ground. The arena, the card-table, the magic circle, the temple, the stage, the screen, the tennis court, the court of justice, etc., are all in form and function play-grounds, i.e. forbidden spots, isolated, hedged round, hallowed, within which special rules obtain. All are temporary worlds within the ordinary world, dedicated to the performance of an act apart.[94]

Huizinga did not imagine the sort of open-ended, conflict-rich encounters that twenty-first-century game theorists would count as games, and that are difficult to distinguish from "the ordinary world." Jan Simons in "Narrative, Games, and Theory" (2007) observes that game playing (especially but not only online computer gaming and modeling) can transpire in "situations [that] are not separate from, but part and parcel of everyday life, and most of these situations have no clearly defined rules, agreed upon outcomes or fixed values attached to them."[95] WJ taps into the contingency, provisionality, and unfoldingness of a new sort of game situation when he critiques the explicitly marked play space(s) of the New York State summer retreat for being too tame, controlled, and non-agonistic: "At Chautauqua there were no racks, even in the place's historical museum; and no sweat, except possibly the gentle moisture on the brow of some lecturer, or on the sides of some player in the ball-field" (865). It is notable here that the amiable gentleman lecturer (himself), moist of brow, serves as the butt for humorous derision; as we shall see, WJ frequently engages in this sort of meta-reflection or self-reflexive joke as he sought to make the public talk a venue for high-stakes play.

For WJ, play is expressed in a practice such as hiking, in which the path is not predetermined and the rules are practically nonexistent (beyond a few basic ones, such as putting one foot in front of the other, and making it back to camp without major injury). Rather, the game of hiking (such as it is) simply unfolds across time and space, usually but not always in relation to other games. In "On a Certain Blindness in Human Beings," WJ quotes at length from a book by W. H. Hudson entitled *Idle Days in Patagonia* (1893); in this extended anecdote, taken at second hand, WJ comes close to articulating a theory of play. "It was my custom," Hudson writes,

> to go out every morning on horseback with my gun, and followed by one dog, to ride away from the valley. . . . At a slow pace, which would have seemed intolerable in other circumstances, I would ride about for hours at a stretch. . . . One day, in these rambles, I discovered a small grove composed of twenty to thirty trees, . . . and after a time I made a point of finding and using it as a resting-place every day at noon. I did not ask myself why I made choice of that one spot, sometimes going miles out of my way to sit there, instead of sitting down under any one of the millions of trees and bushes on any other hillside. (858)

WJ's quoting of Hudson goes on for pages along these lines. Hudson describes how his wanderings began to coalesce around certain stopping points—"it was perhaps a mistake to say that I would sit down and rest, since I was never tired" (859). The experience was one of unfolding meaningfulness, of an intense focus without a particular outcome in mind: "My state was one of *suspense* and *watchfulness*: yet I had no expectation of meeting with an adventure, and felt as free from apprehension as I feel now when sitting in a room in London" (859). Crucially, the feelings associated with this temporary pause from work life were not extraordinary, but they were shot through with positive affect. "The state seemed familiar rather than strange," Hudson writes, "and accompanied by a strong feeling of elation" (859). Huizinga offers the term "dallying" to capture this almost erotic sensibility (33)—the "feeling of tension, joy and the consciousness that it is 'different' from 'ordinary life'" (28). Hiking, riding, or what the British call tramping is social, embodied, situated, spontaneous, and autotelic. For Hudson, the sociality transpired in his dog companion and desire to publish his experience; WJ picks up the ball in his essay, and keeps it rolling.

Again, though he doesn't name the practice, which doesn't look like play in the sense of organized sport or games, WJ celebrates the immersion in seemingly nonpurposive activity that begins by placing oneself in a particular place and adopting an attitude of receptivity that he calls a "kind of magically irresponsible spell" (860). From the external point of view, that of someone seeking to be entertained or amused, the game that Hudson describes is a "mere tale of emptiness, in which nothing happens, nothing is gained, and there is nothing to describe" (859). From the point of view of accomplishment, the hours spent this way "are meaningless and vacant tracts of time" (859). Huizinga describes (and derides) this external attitude as "a collapse of the play spirit, a sobering, a disenchantment" (21). From the inside, however, the hours spent tell a different story: "To him who feels their inner secret, they tingle with an importance that unutterably vouches for itself" (859). WJ has been quoting a man's experience of wandering with his dog and horse, yet he takes from Hudson's description a (non)recipe especially salient for youth. WJ writes, "I am sorry for the boy or girl, or man or woman, who has never been touched by the spell of this mysterious sensorial life, with its irrationality, if so you like to call it, but its vigilance and its supreme felicity" (859–60). This is crucial: when watched by another, play can look silly, absurd, meaningless; the internal experience marks it as aesthetic, shot through with a purposiveness intimately known by the player even as the experience cannot be justified or recuperated by appeal to its purpose.

Johns Hopkins professor Adolf Meyer defined the temporal and rhythmic nature of human experience as *never* senseless or mechanistic. Rather, life equally embraces "the big four—work and play and rest and sleep": "Our body is not merely so many pounds of flesh and bone figuring as a machine, with an abstract mind or soul added to it. It is throughout a live organism pulsating with its rhythm of rest and activity, beating time (as we might say) in ever so many ways, most readily intelligible and in the full bloom of its nature when it feels itself as one of those great self-guiding *energy-transformers* which constitute the real world of living beings."[96] WJ considers Whitman an "energy-transformer" par excellence, though the poet's rambling transpires in the city rather than the woods. He quotes Whitman's letters to capture this daily tempo, with the rhythm of activities echoed in the back-and-forth conversational nature of the epistolary genre. Whitman's key term is *occupation*, in its expansive rather than narrow sense of job or vocation. "Shall I tell you about [my life] just to fill up? I generally spend the forenoon in my room writing, etc., then take a bath fix up and go out about 12 and loafe somewhere or call on someone down town or on business, or perhaps if it is very pleasant and I feel like it ride a trip with some driver friend. . . . (Every day I find I have plenty to do, every hour is occupied with something.) You know it is a never-ending amusement and study and recreation for me to ride a couple of hours of a pleasant afternoon on a Broadway stage in this way. You see everything as you pass, a sort of living, endless panorama" (853). WJ offers a gloss on Whitman's "amusement and study and recreation" that is simultaneously a challenge to his reader: "Truly a futile way of passing the time, some of you may say, and not altogether creditable to a grown-up man. And yet, from the deepest point of view, who knows the more of truth, and who knows the less—Whitman on his omnibus-top, full of the inner joy with which the spectacle inspires him, or you, full of the disdain which the futility of his occupation excites?" (854). The emphasis on the hot, first-person experience of joy-filled activity done for the sheer fun of it distinguishes WJ's understanding from the teleological play theory of Hall and Groos.

WJ's most explicit, child-oriented portrait of open-ended play is once again expressed through the powerful words of another author. In an 1888 letter to HJ, he praises Robert Louis Stevenson for his lucid, lovely prose: "I think his Lantern Bearers one of the most beautiful things ever written" (*WHJ*, 198). The passage from the Scottish author that captured WJ's attention described a game from Stevenson's youth, which consisted of his friends prowling the chilly streets while each boy harbored a lantern underneath his heavy coat. A decade after his letter to his brother, WJ quotes the Stevenson passage at length in "On a Certain Blindness": "'Toward the end of September,' Stevenson writes, 'when school-time was drawing near and the nights were already black, we would begin to sally from our respective villas, each equipped with a tin bull's-eye lantern. . . . We wore them buckled to the waist upon a cricket belt, and over them, such was the rigour of the game, a buttoned top-coat. They smelled noisomely of blistered tin; they never burned aright, though they would always burn our fingers; their use was naught; the pleasure of them merely fanciful; and yet a boy with a bull's-eye under his top-coat asked for nothing more'" (844). Far from an organized sport, the game Stevenson describes took a useful piece of equipment and repurposed it for no-use: "The fishermen used lanterns about their boats, and it was from them, I suppose, that we had got the hint; but theirs were not bull's-eyes, nor did we ever play at being fishermen. The police carried them at their belts, and we had plainly copied them in that; yet we did not pretend to be policemen" (844). The game did not involve role-play, nor did it have a specific origin. It nonetheless evolved a recognizable set of loosely held rules, in which boys would greet each other in the street, sniff out the oily burning smell, then unbutton their coats to allow a glimpse of fire as they crouched and chatted in the nighttime. The game is iterative, keyed to the darkening days of fall in England. The lantern-keepers are boys, but, in his essay, Stevenson analogizes the delight of the hidden lantern with the potency of imagination at any age. "Justice is not done to the versatility and the unplumbed childishness of man's imagination," WJ quotes. "With no more apparatus than an ill-smelling lantern I have evoked him [the enchanter or poet] on the naked links" (845).

Adopting an Attitude: William James's Audience-Oriented Essays

In *The Will to Believe and Other Essays in Popular Philosophy* (1896), WJ collects a series of talks that he gave to student groups over the decade. Equipped with Stevenson's term "apparatus," we can consider WJ's talks as devices for enlisting his audiences in a collaborative activity that has aspects of play. As a professor delivering a lesson, he is faced with the challenge of mediating the nonseriousness of play while employing a decidedly serious genre; in the book version, he also transforms the spoken orations into written chapters. These added twists motivate my use of *troping device*, which calls attention to the varied and intense activity—both intellectual and aesthetic—entailed in these turnings. As with most of WJ's talks-turned-texts, the essays in *The Will to Believe* were very lightly edited and sustain the marks of their oral origin, especially in their explicit orientation toward a youthful audience. He wrote a new preface for the book, with the purpose of giving an ex post facto account of how the chapters fit together. Indeed, the brief preface proves to be important in the evolution of his thought, for in it he uses the phrase "radical empiricism" to establish his method. First, by virtue of being empirical, the method is based on observation and thus potentially corrigible in light of future findings.[97] Second, the method is radical, he explains, to the extent that it affirms "the world is a pluralism" and not a coherent, singular whole: "As we find it [the world] its unity seems to be that of *any collection*; and our higher thinking consists chiefly of an effort to redeem it from that first crude form" (447, emphasis added). The world consists not just of things but also of relations among things, and human beings are immersed in this sensory plurality. Just as the book *The Will to Believe* is a concatenation of particulars subsumed under a unity, so is the world a heterogeneity as it is experienced by human beings. In this way, WJ draws a parallel between *his* process (as a writer who seeks to make a coherent collection of his essays) and that which he seeks to articulate: the manner by which the mental acts of human beings make a coherent collection of the polymorphous sensory data the world offers. At the outset, then, he installs the concept of willful editing, arranging, and synthesizing to be at the core of how we experience the world and move within it.

WJ in the preface further aligns his act of collecting and sense-making with human cognition by explaining the essays are bound together not by an abstract theme but rather by an "attitude," a stance—or, to use a metaphor from sport, a *ready position*. "It has seemed to me," he writes, "that these addresses might now be worthy of collection in a volume, as they shed explanatory light upon each other, and taken together express a tolerably definite philosophical attitude in a very untechnical way" (447). Eschewing terms like "postulate," "axiom," and "first-order reasoning," WJ himself adopts a breezy attitude toward a philosophical topic and toward readers—offering not a serious tome but a conversational text steeped in his playful, unconventional, and audacious attitude. At the outset, he takes on the assumption of earlier scientists and philosophers, that the world is a unity ("the doctrine of monism") and is thus knowable from a singular, external point of view (447). He suggests that he and his readers are engaging in a sort of hunt, building on prior philosophical attempts ("brilliant dashes") that left the sought-after prey ("absolute unity") "undiscovered" (447). Affirming that "the universe is wild—game flavored as a hawk's wing" (448), he recruits readers to join in his "love of sportsmanlike fair play in science" (451) and allow for a certain wildness in method and results. This is not without social risk: "Many of my professionally trained *confrères* will smile at the irrationalism of this view, and the artlessness of my essays in point of technical form. But they should be taken as illustrations of the radically empiricist attitude rather than as argumentations for its validity" (448). Rather than offering a settled philosophical position, "these essays light up with a certain dramatic reality the attitude itself, and make it visible" (449)—while also bringing to awareness "the higher and lower dogmatisms between which in the pages of philosophic history it has generally remained eclipsed from sight" (449). WJ takes belief in a closed system and springs it open, revealing the unfoldingness of truth in the making, even as he enters the philosophical fray.

If philosophy generally trades in established truths claiming universality ("dogmatisms"), WJ with his emphasis on *attitude* stakes out for radical empiricism the affective territory of insouciant youth with its paradoxical combination of skeptical detachment and passionate immersion. (This pose conjures the figure of Whitman: "Do I contradict myself? Very well, I contradict myself. I am large, I contain multitudes.")[98] Amusingly, given WJ's claiming the term "attitude" for the cerebral realm of philosophical inquiry, the word's first two definitions in the *OED* refer to the posture of the body, calling to mind the pose that Whitman strikes in *Leaves of Grass*, with arms akimbo. Biographer Ralph Barton Perry described WJ's own posture and sartorial proclivities in flamboyant terms: "He wore bright neckties. He had a highly developed sense of fun, and was usually himself its principle fomenter. He had days of feeling 'particularly larky,' but some degree of larkiness might be expected at any time."[99] Throughout the essay collection, this youthful exuberance is on full display, both in speaker and in audience, as WJ directs his attention to the "passional tendencies and volitions" (464) of the young "students of philosophy" (466) he addresses "here in this room" (462)—using the collective pronoun as he writes of "*our* willing nature" and that "*we* want to have a truth" (463).

WJ situates his essays within the genre of a scholar speaking to students, but gives it a new spin. He specifies that the traditional, often implicit, rules of philosophical reasoning will be brought into the light and tested by the experimental practice of modern science. Deductive logic will clash with the data from experience. WJ's rhetorical interpellation of a we-who-are-in-the-room consolidates a loosely arranged social body disposed toward engagement: the speaker offers the students agency, however, urging that they choose a side as he situates them within a roughly drawn field of practice in search of "truth." There will be no mere sitting in the stands: different accounts must "live in publicity, vying with each other" in the "liveliest possible state of fermentation" (450). Throughout *The Will to Believe* he argues that *taking a side* in certain hotly "alive" questions—such as the second essay's title, "Is Life Worth Living?"—is essential. Both in the preface and in each essay he is explicit about wishing to conscript his listeners to his side, tempting them with a rhetorical jersey emblazoned with the term "open-minded": "I am . . . so profoundly convinced that my own position is correct, that your invitation has seemed to me a good occasion to make my statements more clear. Perhaps your minds will be more open than those with which I have hitherto had to deal" (457). WJ rouses his readers into a state of readiness, situating them in a not-yet-determined state of inclination.

WJ includes meta-reflection at different stages of *The Will to Believe*, acknowledging that while students may *think* they understand the rules of the lecture genre, what they will experience—and are experiencing—is different. The first essay of the collection, which gives the title to the volume, begins with him riffing on the lecture as a form of pedagogy. He lightheartedly recounts a story about how one of his old teachers abruptly catechized his students in class: "Gurney, what's the difference between justification and sanctification?—Stephen, prove the Omnipotence of God!" (475). This exemplary exchange situates the teacher as the communicator of dogma and the student as the magpie of traditional nuggets—with the humor inhering in the instructor's *apparent* enlistment of the student's mind while actually seeking preordained responses. WJ playfully suggests that, in a Harvard class on religion, method (the didactic lecture) and content (the terms of Puritanism) combine to offer determinism with the merest trappings of human agency. Louis Althusser describes interpellation as a form of cultural conscription into relations of state authority, with the citizen's startled response to the iconic hailing of the police offer—"Hey, you there!"—serving to show the unconscious, unreflective internalization of power.[100] By calling attention to such interpellation, WJ startles the students he addresses (adults and youth alike) into awareness of their student-ness—opening space for a choice and a different relationship to settled philosophical wisdom.

Further, the anecdote serves to place WJ's own lecture/text within a historical and pedagogical context. In the past, he reminds his audience, philosophical lectures were modeled on the sermon, where a "sage on the stage" presented an authoritative text and deductively unfolded the significance for the audience/congregation. In a playful chiasmus, he claims continuity with this genre of address, only to wittily rearrange the words, marking a swerve from the genre of the sermon and its logical mode: "I have brought with me tonight something like a sermon on justification by faith—I mean an essay in justification *of* faith" (457). (One is reminded of Abraham Lincoln's famous takedown of Stephen Douglass, where he calls out Douglass's "specious and fantastic arrangement of words, by which a man can prove a horse-chestnut to be a chestnut horse."[101]) WJ torques the context for his talk from Harvard's (intensely theological) past to its (increasingly secular) present and future. In doing so, he mischievously swaps genres, shifting away from the deductive logic of clerical address to the humanistic mode of the essay. Scott Black's thoughts on the essay genre are helpful here: "Less appropriative than participatory, essays register a practice of digestive, assimilative reading."[102] Black observes that essays are exceptionally elastic, often assimilating "one book in another," making essays "less works than workings out" that in turn invite "turnings and returnings" (6). WJ's troping in this opening anecdote happens in a diversity of registers. He turns from God's agency (justification by faith) to a human being's (justification of faith), from sermon to essay, from oratory to textuality, from his words to others', and ultimately from settled dogma to delightfully paradoxical belief in belief.

These opening gestures in the preface and the eponymous first essay of the collection display a level of wit and intellectual élan that helps the reader to forget the writtenness of the text (again paradoxically, for this happens even as they are reading it) and to experience *The Will to Believe* as something more immediate and lively. This willingness to believe is thus not merely the point of the book but a part of its ingenious mechanism, making it an effective troping device. Moreover, insofar as the preface proves an essential "handle" on the device that is the collection of essays, one can admire WJ's talent for using paratext to enhance, transform, and revivify the meaning of a book—and also note that he accomplishes this feat a decade before HJ embarks on his acclaimed prefaces in the New York Edition (more on these in Chapter 3).

On the one hand, WJ interpellates his audience as part of a group. On the other hand, he calls attention to the human tendency to blandly affiliate, both with each other and with particular ideas that we believe simply as a matter of habit. "As a matter of fact," he writes, "we find ourselves believing, we hardly know how or why": "Here in this room, we all of us believe in molecules and the conservation of energy, in democracy and necessary progress, in Protestant Christianity and the duty of fighting 'for the doctrine of the immortal Monroe,' all for no reasons worthy of the name.... Our reason is quite satisfied, in nine hundred and ninety-nine cases out of every thousand of us, if it can find a few arguments that will do to recite in case our credulity is criticized by someone else" (463). In the beginning sections of "The Will to Believe," WJ uses humor, surprise, and irony to shift the ground under the feet of the audience. In the passage above, he sooths his listeners by naming and affirming beliefs that "we all of us" share. It's an eccentric list to be sure—embracing natural science, religion, and politics—though a fair inference, given the Cambridge context of the lecture. Readers, however, may be more diverse and thus likely to abdicate one or more of the attributed beliefs. Whether lulled into complacency or slightly put on guard by WJ's list, the interpellated "we" is clearly a knowledgeable, even elite group, including the august speaker himself. Yet "we" find ourselves the recipient of an unexpected attack: rather than being praised for our perspicacity, we are censured for the twin sins of gullibility and self-satisfaction. WJ uses incongruity and irony to insert a rhetorical knife between the audience's beliefs and (unworthy) reasons. This rhetorical slice is intended to "get a rise" out of the audience, to create uncertainty, puzzlement, or even annoyance: Is he being serious? Where is he going with this? Do I believe what he said? What are my beliefs?

The Method of Abduction

WJ's irony, witticisms, and other rhetorical turns interrupt the flow of the lecture and the flow of thoughts, creating an ever-so-slight moment of reassessment and readjustment. Another name for this affective space is doubt—a moment that disrupts the unreflective acquiescence to what is going on and literally gives pause. This contentless space of slight uncertainty is what Peirce (to whom the essay collection *The Will to Believe* is dedicated), calls "entertaining the question."[103] It is an almost imperceptible, everyday sort of hesitation, neither the cataclysmic doubt of the suicidal person (a figure whom WJ addresses in the essay "Is Life Worth Living?") nor the procedural, totalizing skepticism of the philosopher. Instead, WJ here instantiates a low-key stutter step of uncertainty on the level of "do I want to bite this?" Peirce, with some humor, describes this slight wavering: "You cannot seriously think that every little chicken that is hatched has to rummage through all possible theories until it lights upon the good idea of picking up something and eating it[?]" (CP, 5.591). Our provisional willingness to do the human equivalent of pecking at a curious seedlike object is what Peirce calls *abduction*.

Another way to put this point: WJ in "The Will to Believe" is intent not just on explaining how a hypothesis is "either *live* or *dead*," depending on its "electric connection" with a person's sensorium, but also on actually coaxing his audience into the very *attitude* of abduction, the act of entertaining an idea (458). A mode of logic first described by Peirce, abduction is helpfully contrasted with the other "grand classes of inference," deduction and induction. Deduction, as we have seen, operates from a rule to particular cases, as with a sermon that works from an established rule (for example, a biblical passage) and then elucidates the rule through discussion of particular facts or instances. Induction works from particular facts to a rule, as with the scientific method, which arrives at provisional but persuasive truth by generalizing from a number of cases. Induction, Peirce urges, condenses a bunch of cases into a rule that we then act on;

when opening a door to a strange room, for instance, we may seamlessly reach for and turn a doorknob. Abduction, Peirce urges, is "bolder and more perilous" than either of the other propositional forms; it arises when we face a curious circumstance that feels unsettled and yet we nonetheless make an "inferential step."[104] This addition of pause, uncertainty, or doubt in the course of everyday life provokes the "first process" of abduction, which again is "entertaining the question" (CP, 6.524). Nathan Houser has noted that Peirce inquired of WJ directly, "What passes in consciousness, especially what emotional and irrational states of feeling, in the course of forming a new belief?"[105]

This core experience, the "starting of a hypothesis and the entertaining of it," includes a small but important "preference" (CP, 6.525), which might be better expressed in the less psychological term "inclination." For any given circumstance that we find puzzling—say, coming face to face with an unfamiliar device attached to a door—there are myriad *possible* things to do: speak to it and request entry, perhaps, or try to insert a credit card. But for old-fashioned human beings, the more likely action (if the device is placed to one side of the door, about a meter off the ground) would be to grasp it with one's hand. The mere grasping (on Peirce's terms) amounts to "entertaining the question" of whether the device is a door handle; manipulating it is equivalent to "testing" the hypothesis. Without this crucial coupling of (1) uncertainty (be it ever so slight) and (2) an ever-so-slight inclination toward a hypothesis (for example, grasping) there would be no abduction. "Hypothesis is a weak kind of argument," Peirce explains, but an argument or position nonetheless (*Writings*, 326). By contrast, the logic of induction collapses a bunch of cases into a rule that we then apply more or less widely: "The belief of a rule is habit" (*Writings*, 337). Abduction for Peirce enlists both agency and action, whereas promiscuous use of induction in everyday life tends more to the mechanistic. When we know exactly what to do, or when a proposition is presented that we find utterly persuasive, we can relegate it to habit: it's "dead," solidified by induction (the logic of science) into an uncontested and internalized rule of conduct. It becomes "objective," by detaching itself from the objects and methods and test cases that helped to coalesce it into being. WJ's effort in "The Will to Believe" is to show how much activity and passion is accreted into the "truths" that we *claim* to hold dispassionately.

For Peirce, then, the insertion of doubt or some momentary instability is the sine qua non of the process in which "a hypothesis" is "entertained interrogatively" (CP, 6.524). Otherwise, we generally go about our days more or less unconsciously, on the strength of induction-laden habits. The psychologist James J. Gibson, building on Peirce's theory of abduction, has described the submerged story of how we flow through our days, thinking not just of the human point of view but also of the "perspective" of the objects, persons, ideas, and devices that are presented to human awareness. Whereas habit makes us treat certain elements of our world as given or inert, Gibson contends that there is an "aliveness" to what we encounter. Gibson's term to designate "what things furnish, for good or ill," is of course *affordance*.[106] Donald Norman elaborates on the theory: "An affordance is a relationship between the properties of an object and the capabilities of the agent that determine just how the object could possibly be used. A chair affords ('is for') support and, therefore, affords sitting. Most chairs can also be carried."[107] Depending on the circumstances, we know which to do, sit or carry: when there is a moving truck out front, we lift the chair; when we are tired, we sit on it. WJ in both the volume *The Will to Believe* and the essay "The Will to Believe" could be said to develop a theory of affordances from the perspective of a human being. He does this by saying that a person's sense of a particular proposition being true is metaphorically like a device that "clicks": "You believe in objective evidence, and I do. Of some things we feel certain: we know and we know that we do know. There is something that gives a click inside of us, a bell that strikes twelve, when the hands of our mental clock have swept the dial and meet over the meridian hour" (466). This state of affairs, of comfortable certitude with respect to "some things," implies a readiness to hand that comes with mastery of certain processes and contexts. A carpenter reaches for the hammer when making a door, knowing the right tool and being deeply comfortable in that knowledge; but may reach for the screwdriver when installing a temporary screen. On such settled occasions our "beliefs"—instantiated by the hammer strike or the turn of the screw—are (as WJ puts it) "not in play" (467). Of such instances of accumulated wisdom (through induction), and the comfortable certainty they afford, WJ writes: "We are all absolutists by instinct" (466). By contrast, when we clumsily use a tool for the first time, the experience is "alive" and uncertain—we may strike our thumb or mangle the project in myriad ways. It is this experience of aliveness that WJ cultivates in the book that he dedicated to Peirce.

In these mid-career essays, WJ offered practical advice to Boston-area educators on developing "the impulses and instincts of childhood."[108] He sought to theorize, represent, and indeed put into practice evolutionary insight about child's play: the countless ways in which children engage with, learn from, and mold the world. The indispensable term was *plasticity*—the survival-based responsiveness of an organism to an environment. WJ, with disarming playfulness, makes the connections between the fundamental principle of natural history under Darwin—adaptability—and (to adult eyes) the almost alien plasticity of young children. He wrote to his wife, Alice Howe Gibbens James, following a junket to Boston's aquarium about his surprised delight at encountering a family of octopi: "The impression which will perhaps outlast everything on this trip, was four cuttle-fish. I wish we had one of them for a child—such flexible intensity of life in a form so inaccessible to our sympathy."[109] Hall and Groos are too dogmatic in their commitment to recapitulation theory; Baldwin is less fanciful in his theorizing about the adaptive potency of youth. These writers and thinkers, however, help to account for WJ's evasion of child study; they also light up the significance of his "childish" (or, seriously playful) way of thinking about and encountering the world. WJ succeeded wildly in interpellating his listeners as not just students but fellow travelers.

Philosophy as Play

In his 1906 Lowell Lectures, WJ equates his method with the outlook and character of insouciant youth. "A radical pragmatist," he writes, "is a happy-go-lucky anarchist sort of creature," whose belief in a "loose universe" affects those with a "rationalist mind" as "'simplified-spelling' might affect an elderly schoolmistress."[110] In the second Lowell Lecture, he notes that fellow pragmatist F. C. S. Schiller had, "in influential quarters," been "treated like an impudent schoolboy who deserves a spanking" (516). Figures of children, and of a childlike resistance to "old-fogyism" (WJ's term), are peppered throughout.

So What Is Pragmatism?

Perhaps WJ's most play-centric talks, the Lowell series were delivered twice over the course of three months in 1906–7. The lectures were published a few months later, collected into book form as *Pragmatism: A New Name for Some Old Ways of Thinking* (1907) and advertised as "Popular Lectures on Philosophy." The playfulness is signaled in the title. Rather than invoking formal philosophical categories such as epistemology or theory of knowledge, or established psychological terms such as consciousness or cognition, he starts with a Greek-rooted word (pragmatism) that originally meant "pedantry," only to follow up with a plain-spoken translation in the subtitle. The phrasing invokes novelty ("A New Name") yet follows it up with an incongruity, stating with folksy phrasing that "Old Ways of Thinking" will be the topic at hand. Rather than the proverbial new wine in old bottles, the title purports to serve up old stuff with a new label. Downplaying the claims for the lectures as well as his own authority, WJ continues to innovate on the lecture as a genre, enlisting his audience in a set of incongruities and surprises that engage them in the process of puzzling from the start. In this way he creates a level playing field for what is to come: the active enlistment of his audience's ideas about how thinking itself is a dynamic activity that plays out in the world of things, events, persons, and ideas.

Critics have noted the idiosyncratic and distinctive voice that WJ brings to his writing. Barzun puts his finger on a quality of his prose style: "The effect is of a high-powered conversation in which we hear, agreeably, a voice."[111] Stob explores the strong effect of orality in WJ's lecture-based texts, tracing it back to Greek philosophers.[112] Indeed, the preface to the print edition of *Pragmatism* establishes the book's oral roots in the very first sentence, noting also the iterative element, that the talks had been delivered to different audiences at different locations: "The lectures that follow were delivered at the Lowell Institute in Boston in November and December, 1906, and in January, 1907, at Columbia University, in New York" (481). Yet the concept of orality alone downplays two crucial elements of WJ's lecture practice. First is the element of back-and-forth, of adjustment and recalibration, that is essential to conversation. Second is the aspect of sensory presence, of an embodied person engaged with (and engaging the senses of) the audience. With respect to the dialogical, the preface to *Pragmatism* picks up the title's juxtaposition of high-mindedness and plain-spokenness and translates it into a charmingly doubled narrative voice, one that is in ongoing conversation with itself, calling attention to the process of adjustment, restatement, and clarification. Dashes are plentiful in *Pragmatism*: "The pragmatic movement, so-called—I do not like the name, but apparently it is too late to change it—seems to have rather suddenly precipitated itself out of the air" (481). WJ interrupts his own train of thought to voice an opinion.

This double-voicing prepares the reader for an ongoing colloquy between the forms of philosophical tradition and the activity inherent in WJ's pragmatist approach to truth. He situates his own lectures as part of an ongoing conversation, joking that his "enterprise is a bold one," since "the founder of pragmatism himself [Peirce] recently gave a course of lectures at the Lowell Institute with that very word in its title,—flashes of brilliant light relieved against Cimmerian darkness!" (488). In Greek mythology, the Cimmerians lived in misty darkness near the entrance to Hades (today, WJ might joke about Buffy the Vampire Slayer, set atop a Hellmouth). Riffing on Peirce's opaque style yet also deprecating his own, WJ announces he's willing to "risk" using the same title because "none of us, I fancy, understood *all* that he said—yet here I stand, making a very similar venture" (488). He doesn't actually name "the founder of pragmatism," leaving the audience to whisper among themselves about whom he's talking. Philosophical convention calls for a discussion and definition of key terms, not least the title. Yet prior even to (not) naming the "founder of pragmatism," WJ in the book's preface swerves into a parenthetical statement that critiques rather than defines the key term. At the moment one expects a voice of authority, another voice pipes up offering an expression of taste ("I do not like the name"). To accompany this element of double-voicing is the idea that pragmatism itself is not unified: it's a "set of tendencies" rather than a stable object of inquiry. Tellingly, rather than a settled school of thought, WJ's preferred phrase "the pragmatic movement" invokes motion and change, and he personifies the directional word "tendencies": "A number of tendencies that have always existed in philosophy have all at once become conscious of themselves collectively, and of their combined mission; and this has occurred in so many countries, and from so many different points of view, that much unconcerted statement has resulted. I have sought to unify the picture as it presents itself to my own eyes, dealing in broad strokes, and avoiding minute controversy" (481). WJ unsettles the very idea of a "single" movement by disaggregating pragmatism into "so many different points of view" (481) that share an inchoate awareness of "their" forward-oriented "combined mission," with no sense of foundational principles or axioms (481). He appends to the short preface a reading list of a dozen articles. Similar to his task in *The Will to Believe*, WJ suggests that his task here is to assimilate these points of view and thus "unify the picture as it presents itself to my own eyes" (481).

The book/lecture series is a polyglot assemblage, replacing the opacity of Peirce with clarity, translating the idiom of philosophy into the vernacular, and including the voices of German, French, English, and American thinkers. Scott Black's description of the essay—itself a translation of the French *essai*, or attempt—is once again apt: *Pragmatism* explicitly assimilates (more than) "one book in another."[113] WJ aligns the project of *Pragmatism* with the operation of perception itself, in which the stimulation of multiple senses kindles an awareness that coalesces into an understanding (a "picture" before one's eyes). The new ways of thinking about thinking are subjective, but they are also collaborative and iterative.

In this way, WJ sidles into a key claim: how does one adjudicate the potentially limitless different points of view? In the second lecture, he invokes a camping experience he had with a group of friends "engaged in a ferocious metaphysical dispute" (505). He gives the now-famous example of a spectator trying to see a squirrel clinging to the other side of a tree. In a zoological version of the spinning top, the squirrel shifts position around the tree at an identical pace to the watcher, so that "never a glimpse of him is caught" (505). The group, who could easily be Chautauquans with their "unlimited leisure," argue in circles over the spiraling of man and squirrel: *Does the man go round the squirrel or not?* WJ answers that it depends on what is meant by "going round," a matter of words. But really, he goes on to indicate that it is a problem of framing, of providing context. If the frame is defined by geographical coordinates, the answer is yes; if the frame is defined by the point of view of the circling mammals, the answer is no. From this story emerges an understanding of pragmatism as a practice, a "method of settling metaphysical disputes" (506).

WJ urges that metaphysics, in breaking free from all context, is a form of "unlawful magic" because of its dependence on non-communal "magic *words*" (509). Without a terrestrial foothold, philosophical questions and terms present an "enigma, of which the key must be sought in the shape of some illuminating or power-bringing word or name" (509). Get the right term and "you can rest": "you are at the end of your metaphysical quest" (509). Pragmatism, on the other hand, "performs a concrete function" (519) and actively creates a magic circle within which (1) things can happen, (2) the happenings can matter in particular ways, and (3) those involved can have equal stake in the happenings. To draw on WJ's terms, pragmatism is a "mud philosophy" (527) that "widens the field" (522) and establishes what "conduct" (529) is called for. It may look like "a doctrine of caprice" (599), but that implies dispassion, an "above the fray" (or "in the stands") stance. Instead, pragmatism (personified by WJ as a *she*—perhaps reminiscent of Mary James at the dinner table?) creates the possibility for passionate individual energies—like the ardent campers watching a squirrel—to be put into a common idiom and made meaningful. As WJ writes, "The aim of a football-team is not merely to get the ball to a certain goal (if that were so, they would simply get up on some dark night and place it there), but to get it there by a fixed *machinery of conditions*—the game's rules, and the opposing players" (535). Along similar lines, pragmatism serves as a sort of agnostic umpire, one who comes upon potential players in need of a game (for example, a field of contest with rules and boundaries) and helps to supply one.

The Child as Pragmatist

If pragmatism could be viewed as a sort of an umpire, the pragmatist—on the ground, battling it out—may have more in common with the figure of the player. Both set ideas in play, in concrete and experimental terms. They take up live questions and put to the test what "practical difference[s]" emerge from holding different beliefs, positions, and conceptions. We can, moreover, begin to historicize the connection between the pragmatist and the child, further moving the association from the realm of metaphor—as in Amanda Anderson's suggestion that pragmatists are like annoying teenagers, with an "inappropriately" "casual attitude" and lack of "a certain gravitas"—into the zone of practice.[114] The pragmatist adopts an "empiricist attitude" (508) and "faces forward to the future" (585). As Baldwin affirmed, childhood was increasingly conceived as a crucial biological period of physical and cognitive immaturity and therefore flexibility. "*Curiosity*," WJ notes, is "a rather poor term by which to designate the *impulse towards better cognition*" (740).

The pragmatist—though metaphorical kin to Emerson's "boys who are sure of a dinner"—begins to emerge as actively pugnacious, not just an idealized figure for an unsullied vision or independence of mind. Unlike the uncorrupted youthful detachment that Emerson celebrates, it is the child's embeddedness in a world of persons and things that draws WJ's interest. He cites the pioneering physicist James Clerk-Maxwell, who as "a child . . . had a mania for having everything explained to him, and . . . when people put him off with vague verbal accounts of any phenomenon he would interrupt them impatiently by saying, 'Yes; but I want you to tell me the *particular go* of it!'" (572). WJ knew that the image of the pragmatist "cling[ing] to facts and concreteness" and "observ[ing] truth at its work in particular cases" (516) seemed infantile: "What a childishly external view!" he wrote (with some exuberance)—the search for truth cast as "a sort of rough and tumble fight between two hostile temperaments!" (501).

Age-old philosophical debates about knowledge and reality, in WJ's hands, are pointless when detached from the everyday lives of human beings. Without peril or prize, discussions of truth with nothing at stake are akin to "a general informing his soldiers that it is better to keep out of battle forever than to risk a single wound" (*WB*, 469–70). There is, by contrast, a "depth and wildness" (561) to those pressing questions that are incontrovertibly alive, that engage a person's "willingness to act" (524). (One is again reminded of Dewey's child reaching for the candle, and his proto-theory of affordances—in the beginning was immersive curiosity that motives the seeing-reaching-burning-withdrawing coordination.) The risk-taking child philosophizes in the wild, scaffolding her attempts with useful things, persons, and ideas; adults need to be reminded. "The Will to Believe" concludes with the author adopting the part of a general rallying his pragmatist troops, urging good cheer in the face of daunting epistemological conditions and an uncertain path forward: "We stand on a mountain pass in the midst of whirling snow and blinding mist, through which we get glimpses now and then of paths which may be deceptive. If we stand still, we shall be frozen to death. If we take the wrong road, we shall be dashed to pieces. We don't certainly know whether there is any right one. What must we do? 'Be strong and of good courage.' Act for the best, hope for the best, and take what comes. . . . If death ends all, we cannot meet death better" (*WB*, 479). Juxtaposed with his feminized personification of pragmatism—"her manners are as various and flexible, her resources as rich and endless, and her conclusions as friendly as mother nature" (*Pragmatism*, 522)—WJ's portrayal of the pragmatist is martial, even pugnacious: "I find myself willing to take the universe to be really dangerous and adventurous, without therefore backing out and crying 'no play.' . . . I am willing that there should be real losses and real losers, and no total preservation of all that is" (617). Life understood from the pragmatic posture, he writes, is immersive: "I, therefore, for one, cannot see my way to accepting the agnostic rules for truth-seeking, or willfully agree to keep my willing nature out of the game" (*WB*, 477). HJ picks up the agonistic (not agnostic) figure in his unfinished biography, entitled *The Middle Years*, when he writes that "youth is an army, the whole battalion of our faculties and freshnesses, our passions and our illusions, on a considerably reluctant march into the enemy's country."[115] In turn, WJ in *Pragmatism* echoes HJ (and Bosanquet) in acknowledging life's "bewilderments": "I ask you in all seriousness to look abroad on this colossal universe of concrete facts, on their awful bewilderments, their surprises and cruelties, on the wilderness which they show" (496).

WJ musters the links between play and battle when confronting "the lonely depths" (*WB*, 480) and the "suicidal mood" (499) where one encounters "the base notes of life" (480). In "Is Life Worth Living?" he observes that the neutral stance associated with agnosticism and scientific skepticism can foment a "mistrust of life" (501)—a refusal to enter the field of play in the largest sense. "For my own part, I do not know what the sweat and blood and tragedy of this life mean, if they mean anything short of this. If this life be not a real fight, in which something is eternally gained for the universe by success, it is not better than a game of private theatricals from which one may withdraw at will. But it *feels* like a real fight" (502). Mary Reilly captures the pragmatist spirit and links it to play: "What man needs and demands from life," she writes, ". . . is not wealth, comfort, or esteem, but games worth playing. Critical to being alive is the presence of the challenge, the quest. When man cannot find a game worth playing, he falls prey to acedia."[116]

Acedia—the lack of any care or concern—is akin to *anhedonia*, a term WJ uses in *Varieties of Religious Experience* (1902) to describe "pathological depression," the incapacity to feel pleasure and affection.[117] Its opposite is not merely pleasure or hedonism but rather the stimulation of interest leading to practice and to mastery, what we would now call "flow."[118] Here WJ mentions a colleague's book *The Psychology of Religion* (by E. D. Starbuck), which offers an athletic analogue for the experience—at once cognitive and affective—of a life shot through with meaningfulness: "An athlete . . . sometimes awakens suddenly to an understanding of the fine points of the game and to a real enjoyment of it, just as the convert awakens to an appreciation of religion. If he keeps on engaging in the sport, there may come a day when all at once the game plays itself through him—when he loses himself in some great contest."[119] The idea of the "game play[ing] through him" describes a somatic attunement with the environment that tips toward the full assimilation of the game's constraints by the player—so much so, that he can innovate fluidly and with less effort. Creative agency expressed through action performed in relation to both physical constraints (for example, gravity) and human rules (for example, use a racquet, keep the ball inside the lines): this is the interactive, volitional nature of play, which for WJ emerges as an ideal form of human vitality and expression.

The pragmatist, by this account, is plunged in the midst of experience-with-constraints, a state most vivid during youth. Accordingly, the child in WJ emerges as an indigenous, curiosity-driven and object-oriented philosopher, what we might call (following the brilliant cognitive anthropologist Edwin Hutchins) a "pragmatiser in the wild."[120] Children, evolutionary psychologists observed, were smaller versions of "men of science preferring to turn their backs on metaphysics as on something altogether cloistered and spectral, and practical men shaking philosophy's dust off their feet and following the call of the wild" (*Pragmatism*, 496). For children, urgent questions are explicitly, indeed *corporeally*, alive or dead: as WJ puts it, "Living things, then, moving things, or things that savor of danger or of blood, that have a dramatic quality—these are the objects natively interesting to childhood, to the exclusion of almost everything else" (*Talks to Teachers*, 767). Philosophy, for WJ, all too often allowed its practitioners to "jump about over life instead of wading through"; the latter, he urged, should involve "putting off our proud maturity of mind and becoming again as foolish little children in the eyes of reason."[121]

Contemporary responses to WJ's pragmatism emphasized its instrumentality and critiqued what some saw as its crude voluntarism.[122] Richardson writes that "many philosophers seem to have felt WJ was saying a person could believe, and call true, anything he or she found convenient."[123] Yet we have seen, by tracing figures of play in WJ's texts-turned-lectures, that understanding and belief emerge as active, embodied, situated, and social processes. Moreover, there is a crucial autotelic aspect to WJ's approach: the precursor to arriving at provisional truth (or as WJ would put it, believing our beliefs) is to care, to engage, to enter an arena in the first place. This feature of being "in the game" is the sine qua non of his thinking, writing, and teaching, connecting his pragmatic method to his radical empiricism through an ontology of human experience predicated on the raw capacity for interest. "'We have to take a leap in the dark'" (*WB*, 478), he affirms, though his genial and insouciant style obscures the existential difficulty of what he describes.

Peirce, in Richardson's account, had his own "elegant answer" to misguided critics: "For people who say that pragmatism means believing anything one pleases. If one could believe what one pleased that would be true. But the fact is one cannot" (494). A logician more than a psychologist, Peirce leaves it at that. WJ points to the prior question, not of confidence in a particular truth, but of believing as such. He writes of Tolstoy in a period of catastrophic melancholy, who lost all belief and with it the very ground of reality: "These questions 'Why?' 'Wherefore?' 'What for?' found no response" (*Varieties*, 143). Teleological accounts of pragmatism—succinctly captured in WJ's aphoristic "By their fruits ye shall know them, not by their roots" (26)—misunderstand the full phenomenological fruits of philosophizing with the child in mind. Lurking within WJ's energizing words is a real concern with "psychical neuralgia" (138), an "abode of shadows" (137) that offers human beings an abyssal sense of living in a world without foundations.

Peirce, in his concept of musement, describes a practice that is a philosophical form of meditation. This explicitly autotelic experience points up a paradox within pragmatism and offers a kind of remedy to the sick-souled impasse that WJ seeks to avert. As Elizabeth F. Cooke affirms, on the topic of Peirce on play, "free play of mind contains absolutely no purpose, yet undergirds all purposeful advancement in the community of inquiry, since musement supplies inquiry with its novel insights. So the pragmatist theory of inquiry, defined primarily by its teleological end, appears to be grounded in a most unteleological thought process."[124] Turning to Peirce, in fact, provides a way to further elucidate the paradoxically not-fruitful fruits of philosophical inquiry I have been suggesting hide in plain sight in the play of WJ's writings.

The Play of Musement

The idea of contest, central to WJ's pragmatism, is a key aspect of play. Huizinga traces the etymological links between play and struggle: "Who can deny that in all these concepts—challenge, danger, contest, etc.—we are very close to the play-sphere? Play and danger, risk, chance, feat—it is all a single field of action where something is at stake (40). Huizinga extends the analogy to urge that there is a "sportive character of philosophy" (153), where "the argument goes back and forth like a shuttle and, in its flyings, epistemology takes on the appearance of a noble game" (149). WJ uses the language of rhythm and contest when he describes the "practical consequences" that arise from "true ideas"—meaning, ideas that have successfully emerged from an inward, sensory, yet umpire-like process of "veri*fication*" (making true): "The connexions and transitions come to us from point to point as being progressive, harmonious, satisfactory. This function of agreeable leading is what we mean by an idea's verification" (*Pragmatism*, 574). In this regard, the language of play doesn't only provide a set of well-worn metaphors for WJ the pragmatist. It is both source and model for adult ways of interacting with the world, of weathering strangeness, testing beliefs, seeking "'satisfaction'" (589), investigating other minds, learning through experience, and making meaning.

WJ attributed the term "pragmatism" to Peirce, though the latter favored "pragmaticism."[125] Indeed, collaboratively teasing out a philosophical problem was for Peirce a method that fell under the auspices of play. WJ admired Peirce's quirkiness as a philosopher, and also appreciated his puzzling, ludic style of conversing. Joseph Brent describes how WJ referred to his friend as "that strange and unruly being" (16), a character trait that the precocious Peirce himself claimed (at the age of fifteen!) as essential to his philosophizing: "If I should turn old fogy or obedient lad my life would in troth and indeed be a failure. For on not doing it is my whole theory built."[126] WJ picked up on this image, likely from conversations with Peirce, lamenting what he called "old-fogyism" in philosophy. For both men, this term figured a form of rationalism, of low-stakes, armchair musing on questions of knowing and being, with a dogged commitment to being right trumping the active, involved question of moving forward and plowing new ground.

Peirce, much later looking back on his life and assessing himself as a philosopher, was emphatic that his prime contribution derived from his youthful inquiries, "that happy accident that I early hit upon a METHOD of thinking, which any intelligent person could master" (323). This sense of his method as easily practiced is itself a sort of joke, since Peirce was known for his abstruse writings. He himself roots his talent for high-wire feats of inscrutable logic to a character trait: "Add to the elements of whatever success I have had that I have [been] always unceasingly exercising my power of *learning new tricks*—to keep myself in possession of the childish *trait* as long as possible. This is an immense thing" (323).

Philosophizing and friendship, for Peirce, were intertwined. Brent writes of Peirce's early camaraderie with Horatio Paine ("the dearest friend of Peirce's young manhood") as they delved together into Schiller's *Aesthetic Letters*: "The intimacy between Peirce and Paine involved much more than giving in to the temptation to do mischief. It was a romance of searching minds inspired by Schiller's idea of *Spieltrieb*, what Peirce later called 'the play of Musement'" (53). When entering the "play of Musement," Peirce writes, one begins with awareness that gives way to colloquy: "Impression soon passes into attentive observation, observation into musing, musing into a lively give and take of communion between self and self."[127] It is a matter of "open conversation," though not "a conversation in words alone, but is illustrated, like a lecture, with diagrams and with experiments" (CP, 6.460–61). Brent explains that "in this play, the Muser does not create by the force of imaginative power but, instead, experiences an aspect of reality represented in a sign and guesses at its meaning by means of the instinct of hypothesis" (330).

For Peirce, in the play of musement all aspects of human sensate experience are put to use, not just reason and logical analysis. (Brent uses the phrase "instinct of hypothesis" advisedly, to refer to modes of knowing that include, but are not limited to, the exercise of reason.) Peirce is explicit about this: "There is no kind of reasoning that I should wish to discourage in Musement; and I should lament to find anybody confining it to a method of such moderate fertility as logical analysis. Only, the Player should bear in mind that the higher weapons in the arsenal of thought are not playthings but edge-tools. In any mere Play they can be used by way of exercise alone; while logical analysis can be put to its full efficiency in Musement" (CP, 6.461). Peirce elaborates on the paradoxical combination of philosophy as a form of serious play by invoking, like WJ, the metaphor of navigation—albeit a mode of sailing that is open, wayward: a fully absorbing endeavor where the destination cannot be known in advance.

One needs, he suggests, to truly be "at sea"—to not be fully aware of either the rules of play or the goal, both of which instead unfold in the process. He phrases this idea explicitly as a form of colloquy: "So, continuing the counsels that had been asked of me, I should say, 'Enter your skiff of Musement, push off into the lake of thought, and leave the breath of heaven to swell your sail. With your eyes open, awake to what is about or within you, and open conversation with yourself; for such is all meditation.'" (CP, 6.461). The genre that best captures the activity that Peirce describes is the lecture—more various in its appeal to the material urgencies of the world than just talk. By equating meditation and conversation, and likening this method of inquiry to a multimodal lecture, what at first could sound like solitary musing becomes engaged with the world beyond itself. Musement is thus absorbing, urgent with worldly consequences. For the "lake of thought" to be an arena for play it must allow for consequences: for Peirce, it must be possible (within the practice of philosophy) that the skiff could founder, lose its way, or even sink.

Peirce's association of navigation and the genre of the lecture affords a conception of philosophical inquiry that is social, pleasurable, and based in practice. As one former student wrote of Peirce, "He had the pedagogic gift to an unusual degree": "The terms of equality upon which he met us were not in the way of flattery, for they were too spontaneous and sincere. We were members of his 'scientific' fraternity; greetings were brief, and we proceeded to the business that brought us together, in which he and we found more pleasure than in anything else."[128] For Peirce, the play of philosophy—"a certain agreeable occupation of mind"—made such colloquies a form of kinship, a "fraternity" practiced under the sign of fun, "in which he and we found more pleasure than in anything else." Peirce himself later wrote fondly about his friendship with Paine, when they spent "every afternoon long months upon it, picking the matter to pieces" (53). Peirce's tendency to turn every conversation into the play of musement startled HJ, when Peirce called on him during a trip to England. Peirce wrote to WJ, "I see your brother very frequently. He is a splendid fellow. I admire him greatly and have only discovered two faults in him. One is that his digestion isn't quite that of an ostrich & the other is that he isn't as fond of turning over questions as I am but likes to settle them and have done with them. A manly trait too, but not a philosophic one."[129] In an ever-shifting environment, people are in constant need for new truths as tools for thinking. In this regard, philosophical questions are almost always in play, and musement is an ongoing activity.

As we heard earlier, in *Pragmatism,* WJ wrote that Schiller had been "treated like an impudent schoolboy who deserves a spanking" (516). Schiller, like Peirce, actively took up the question of play, arguing for its centrality as a core instinct in human life. In his *Letters on the Aesthetic Education of Man* (1794), Schiller addresses his reader as "you," indicating that what he wishes is a colloquy on philosophical matters; most intently he wishes to explain his divergence from Kantian aesthetics in elevating play over the beautiful. "But what is meant by a mere play," Schiller queries, "when we know that in all conditions of humanity that very thing is play, and only that is play which makes man complete and develops simultaneously his twofold nature? What you style limitation, according to your representation of the matter, according to my views, which I have justified by proofs, I name enlargement."[130] In Schiller's exposition, the senses respond to immediate stimulus, while reason shapes the world into knowable wholes. As he puts it, "The sensuous impulsion requires that there should be change, that time should have contents; the formal impulsion requires that time should be suppressed, that there should be no change" (74). These powers play out in relation to the world of objects: "The sensuous instinct wishes to be determined, it wishes to receive an object; the formal instinct wishes to determine itself, it wishes to produce an object" (74). The sensuous instinct operates like Spencer's mind: it accommodates itself to the environment. The formal instinct, by contrast, assimilates the material of the world to its own design. Far from being an activity of a certain developmental phase, play for Schiller offers the essence of what it means to be human: "Man only plays," he affirms, "when in the full meaning of the word he is a man, and he is only completely a man when he plays" (79).

Schiller's writing on play profoundly influenced Huizinga, who emphasized the experience of play as irreducible and autotelic—an end in itself. Play is fun; that is why we do it. Following Darwin, scientific explanations for ludic behavior centered on the idea that play is rehearsal; as with the wrestling of wolf cubs, it is understood to serve the biological need for survival or the social need for cohesion. Known as extrinsic theories of play, these functionalist accounts are teleological and imply that other activities could serve just as well. Huizinga emphasized that physiology and psychology fell short of explaining "what actually is the *fun* of playing? . . . The intensity of, and absorption in, play finds no explanation in biological analysis" (2). Fun, he argues, is "an absolutely primary category of life" that "cannot be reduced to any other mental category" (3).

For Peirce, musement is a way of attending without having a goal; its findings—that which it lights up—are neither right nor wrong. Cooke writes that "the kind of evaluative claims that the individual makes in musement, especially at this noticing stage, are not truth claims, but claims regarding what is interesting, puzzling, and worth thinking about some more."[131] Musement is thus in partnership with abduction, which, Peirce writes, "makes its start from the facts, without, at the outset, having any particular theory in view, though it is motived by the feeling that a theory is needed to explain the surprising facts" (CP, 2.106). To have a feeling of puzzlement, one must have some beliefs about the world: musement thus points inward, bringing to awareness one's own values and expectations, even as it points outward, animating a desire for a fresh understanding. Musing, by this account, makes us interesting to ourselves, mediating lively curiosity that is not simply "put to use" in philosophy, science, and aesthetics, but that supplies the precondition for these pursuits in the first place.

Coda: "I Read Him for Work and for Play"

WJ didn't succeed in helping Peirce land a permanent job, but the two sustained an almost lifelong friendship, having met as young men at Lawrence Scientific School in 1861. Nathan Houser describes how, "late in 1910, after James's death, Juliette Peirce wrote to Alice [Howe Gibbens] James that her husband 'has not been the same since the loss of his earliest and best friend' and asked if she would please send Charles a copy of James's *Talks to Teachers*, which he had never read but now wanted to."[132] Seeking consolation for her aging and bereaved husband, Juliette asked for the work where WJ most explicitly turned his attention to the passion and plasticity of youth. Both men were talented and eccentric educators, and exactly who was student and who was teacher changed in topsy-turvy fashion over the decades they knew each other.

WJ shifted among callings (artist, physician, scientist, philosopher, psychologist) to emerge from youthful uncertainty about his career to beloved Harvard professor. His intellectual legacy is equally heterogeneous, as scholars working in philosophy, neuroscience, and literary studies claim him as a key forebear. Almost a century after his death, an admiring introduction to a volume on WJ's contribution to educational psychology offers striking evidence of the warmth and affection he continues to elicit. Entitled "William James: Our Father Who Begat Us," the essay explains,

> This is a volume about one hundred years of contributions to educational psychology, and so I have quite reasonably been instructed to outline and evaluate the legacy left by James to present-day education and educational psychology.... Before I begin, however, let me put

> my bias clearly on the table. I can claim no sense of objectivity about this man or about his work. For over 30 years, I have been smitten with William James. I read him for work and for play. I read him for guidance. I read him for inspiration. I read him when my spirits are low. I read him to discover what I really think. I read him to learn. I am never disappointed.[133]

Within this commentary we can hear something unusual in an academic article, an undertone of warmth that exceeds the conventional, cool affect of mere admiration.

WJ's body of work, in this account, is not just useful but also inspiring, stimulating, pleasurable, reassuring. It offers what D. W. Winnicott—a key figure in the next chapter—called a "holding environment," the subjective experience of emotional cohesiveness, allowing the feeling of safety that affords risky exploration. The passage above adumbrates a zone of experience that will prove important for thinking about the literary creations of HJ. Though it isn't registered in any standard taxonomy of the passions, this lively affective texture is more interactive than amusement, more action based than pleasure, and more terrestrial than joy. It is a peculiar zone of inquisitive enjoyment, which at its simplest is mere *fun*, though in its unfoldingness—and in its profoundly ambivalent nature—I am calling *toying*.

CHAPTER 3

Play Is the Thing

Toying with Vision in Henry James's Pedagogical Works

> We find certain things about seeing puzzling, because we do not find the whole business of seeing puzzling enough.
>
> —Ludwig Wittgenstein, *Philosophical Investigations* (1953)

When Henry James's play *The American* opened in London on 3 January 1891, Alice James (who was with HJ in London) and William James (who was home in the United States) held their breaths in anticipation. Aided by the transatlantic telegraph, word of the first performance's modest success circulated swiftly among the siblings, prompting this delighted reply from Cambridge, Massachusetts: "A telegram from Alice this A.M. announces 'unqualified triumph—great future author—ovation.' I am almost as glad as you are, and hope that it is only the beginning of a sort of Sardou or Dumas career. It will of course inspire you with the 9 or 90 other plays which you have in mind."[1] *The American* was adapted from HJ's novel of the same name, as was his play *Daisy Miller*, which never made it into production. It is poignant to read WJ's ebullient missive, speculating about the "9 or 90" plays HJ had "in mind," in light of what came to pass four years later, in 1895: the disastrous opening night of *Guy Domville*, HJ's first (and last) original play staged before a London audience.

By 1890, HJ was eager to experiment with the theater, confiding his hopes to AJ and conveying his delight that *The American* had "worked its calculated spell upon you."[2] Leon Edel uses the same terms of enchantment for the novelist's lifelong affection for the theater: "Henry was taken to the theatre at an early age, and thereafter, for sixty years, he was a consistent (and consistently critical) playgoer. He was a stage-struck boy, a stage-enamored young student, a serious-minded drama critic, and in middle life an anxious playwright. The theater never lost its fairy-tale spell for him."[3] For Walter Benjamin, the ritual of artistic presentation—the physical presence of spectators for a performance or showing—is what creates the spell or "aura" that constitutes the special, vivified nature of art. Dramatic performance, for Benjamin, manifests more explicitly what is true in other instances (for example, viewing a painting, or reading a novel) because it bodies forth the person-to-person rapport between performers and viewers in the seats. "The artistic performance of a stage actor is definitely presented to the public by the actor in person," Benjamin writes, thus cultivating a reciprocity that allows "the stage actor to adjust to the audience during his performance" in a shared time and space.[4] In the case of drama, the writer's vision cast into dialogue and stage directions is embodied by players and put into action.

Yet, at the premier of *Guy Domville* on 6 January 1895, Benjamin's model art form presented an aesthetic problem that became a personal horror story. Critics and biographers have observed that HJ, whose late works spoke to an elite group of dedicated readers, did not have an easy time managing the in-person demands of a theater populated by a diverse audience of vocal strangers. His loyal sister had died in the interim between *The American*'s modest success and *Guy Domville*'s proscenium premiere: "Without Alice to encourage him and comfort him—without Alice fretting for a telegram from him, even—Harry premiered his second play" only to find himself "booed off the stage" during the curtain call.[5]

Literary scholars have noted that the mid-1890s were a turning point for HJ, marking a period when his fiction eschewed the encounter with physical places and persons—the densely detailed realm of literary realism—for the "bodiless" realm of the modern novel of interiority. Virginia Woolf is among these observers. Commenting on HJ's "The Friends of Friends" (1896), in which a character who has died to serves as the story's focalizing consciousness, Woolf writes, "And yet—does it make very much difference? Henry James has only to take the smallest of steps and he is over the border. His characters with their extreme fineness of perception are already half-way out of the body. There is nothing violent in their release. They seem rather to have achieved at last what they have long been attempting—communication without obstacle."[6] For many critics, the relationship between corporeality and consciousness in HJ's fiction is one of inverse proportionality over the years of his career, with the pervasive, free-floating consciousness that forms the narrative point of view of his late work *The American Scene* (1907) effectively eclipsing bodily presence.[7] From this perspective, dead persons offer a case in point: stretching from Woolf through Martha Banta to the collection *Henry James and the Supernatural* (2011), ghosts in HJ's fiction have been understood to be figures for the operations of consciousness, frequently that of the author himself, unencumbered by the physical body.[8] Kristin Boudreau, for instance, writes, "If the beings that appear to him [HJ] are not always the ghosts of dead persons—in some cases we might call them the ghosts of past experiences—they nonetheless assume the identity of disembodied consciousness."[9] Whether projections, memories, or figures for repressed desires, ghosts in HJ are understood centrally as specters of disembodiment.

And indeed, the matter of bodies is put on display with HJ's foray into the London theater scene. It is worth noting that the production of *Guy Domville* foundered not only on the dramatic flaws of the script but also on the actors' corporeal performance. Edel describes how the players on opening night, sensing the increasing impatience and restlessness of the audience, struggled on. Encumbered by their costumes and mannered lines, they produced awkward humor and broadcast unscripted embarrassment. The actress portraying Mrs. Domville, Marie Saker, became "unnerved" with what the young theater critic George Bernard Shaw called her "Falstaffian make-up" and conveyed to the audience her mounting "discomfort" with her costume, "a voluminous skirt of black satin over a pannier crinoline of huge dimensions" and "an enormous hat" (*GD*, 93). The face of the lead actor, a man known for his striking good looks, twisted into a crooked smile that "displayed his nervousness."[10] According to Shaw, a light-hearted scene involving two characters trying separately to get the other one drunk projected instead "the sobriety of desperation" (*GD*, 95). The audience jeered at the actors' discomposure, deepening it.

There were, Edel notes, essentially two audiences in the house that night: one comprised of HJ's friends, fans, and members of London's cultured classes; the other composed of the less decorous public who knew little to nothing about the author. The first audience honored the convention of realist theater, that there was a "fourth wall" that allowed them to spy on—without being a part of—events transpiring on stage. The second did not, and instead actively responded during the performance: not just with murmurs and restlessness but with inappropriate laughter, derisive sounds, and even vocal interjections. A moment meant to be poignant—the lead crying out, "I am the *last*, my lord, of the Domvilles!"—generated a quip from the audience that triggered an explosion of laughter: "It's a bloody good thing y'are" (*GD*, 96). *Guy Domville*'s dispiriting opening night provided a case study in Henri Bergson's theory of humor: that a body acting mechanically kindles the comic spirit. (WJ's consoling letter to his brother—that HF's failed play will "be regarded as a larky kind of thing, and a joke, to have tried your hand and failed at that sort of job" (*Letters*, 316)—must have touched a tender spot.)

Scholars of HJ have aligned his backing away from the theater with a modernist creation myth. Citing 1895 as a pivot point, Henry Popkin states: "Henry James wrote for two theatres: for the commercial stage and for the [idealized] theatre of the mind."[11] David Kurnick writes that, by leaving behind the sweaty publicity of the London stage with its intractable audiences, HJ succeeded "in the creation of the novel of interiority," a literary form that faces away from collective experience and takes refuge in the incorporeality and individuality of novelistic consciousness.[12] Theater studies has challenged one implication of this formulation, that disembodiment and interiority are necessary conditions for literary merit. Sharon Marcus writes, "The belief that drama is only aesthetically worthy if it approximates literature, and can become literary only by leaving theater's corporeality, popularity, and ephemerality behind, has few explicit adherents today."[13]

This chapter challenges the other implication regarding art and (dis)embodiment, to argue that HJ's attempt to make it big in theater provides an analytical lens for illuminating three important things about his later work. First, HJ's experience with dramatic arts helps explain a key shift in his career: namely, his interest in narrative fiction featuring children. After 1895 HJ largely turns away from the theater as a place to stage plays and turns to narrative fiction as a place to stage play.[14] Children—appearing in novels, short fiction, and autobiographical writings—serve as exemplary figures for thinking about the relational and embodied nature of consciousness.[15] Second, HJ's move away from theater highlights his interest in new media that appeal to a wider, collective audience as he experiments with the psychophysiology of seeing. The emergence of cinema, or the "photoplay," coincides with this final period of HJ's career, with the first public "cinematograph" showings taking place in 1896. His interest in technologies of vision centers on fascinating, proto-cinematic devices that, following Benjamin, we might call early implements of "mechanical reproduction": the stereoscope and the thaumatrope, known collectively as philosophical toys.[16] Third, HJ's turn to these new technologies of vision offers a way to rethink, on the one hand, the ambiguous, apparently disembodied nature of apparitions; and, on the other hand, the durable materiality of images and their tangible effects on those who encounter them. These tales call attention to the affects, palpitations, and impacts of human corporeality: uncanniness and horror, to be sure, but also surprise, pleasure, and sheer vitality. HJ the playwright's encounter with the theater and early cinema of London's West End, and HJ the novelist's engagement with the embodied mind's theater of play, I argue, are two sides of the same coin.[17]

Twining together the playwright and the spinner of tales shines light on the technological and experimental nature of later works. The next section sets the stage by examining *Daisy Miller: A Study* (1878) as an early exploration of *toying*, the creative use of tools to explore and thereby come to understand the possibilities offered in enticing new scenarios. This early work, which HJ adapted for the theater, demonstrates the limits of melodrama (and the limits also of *boys*) for affording flexible, object-oriented mind play. HJ's excited missives conveying the thrill and danger of "going public" with his play *The American* provides the occasion for enlisting D. W. Winnicott's account of child's play. Winnicott's conception of the transitional object offers a lens for seeing the *Guy Domville* experience as not just *a* failed play but as *failed play*.

I then focus on experiments with focalization in *What Maisie Knew* (1897) and the fine line between thauma (wonder) and trauma (wounding). Ranging among his child-centered works, I examine HJ's interest in pedagogical relationships in light of Victorian toys: beguiling, sometimes creepy objects that, when affordant, dramatize the emergence and co-creation of meaningful perceptions through imaginative play. As I go on to explain, *The Turn of the Screw* leverages a form of cognitive playfulness—modeled by the children, and structured into the tale—that balances things that delight and things that distress. This discussion lights up the way that HJ designed *The Turn of the Screw* to function, in the hands of readers, as a troping device analogous to a philosophical toy. I describe the story as a hands-on quasi-classroom that depicts and enlists a push-me-pull-you experiment in training perception. I then turn to "The Jolly Corner," arguing that this late story updates HJ's earlier experiments in embodied vision by recruiting techniques and tropes from early cinema. A brief conclusion reflects on what AJ called the "first-timeness" of certain resonant experiences and concludes with a succinct definition of Jamesian play: "pleasure under difficulties!"

Playing with Reality: Inflexible Props and Transitional Objects

It might be going too far to blame the demise of *Guy Domville* on the actress Mrs. Sacker's voluminous hat—but it played its part. In the philosophy of humor, the hat makes a frequent appearance; in particular, the sort of hat that has evolved so far beyond the zone of use and practicality as to actually impede its original purpose. Herbert Spencer inaugurates *The Physiology of Laughter* (1860) with the query "Why do we smile when a child puts on a man's hat?"[18] Answer: an unexpected contrast of ideas that produce tension, and then a gush of relief when we realize the triviality of the contrast. Bergson urges that clothes in general and hats in particular materialize social forms that constrain a person's movement. The comic emerges from "some rigidity or other applied to the mobility of life, in an awkward attempt to follow its lines and counterfeit its suppleness."[19] All clothing carries the possibility of the comic: "It might almost be said that every fashion is laughable in some respect. Only, when we are dealing with the fashion of the day, we are so accustomed to it that the garment seems, in our mind, to form one with the individual wearing it. We do not separate them in imagination."[20]

But if something makes us aware of the discrepancy between the body and the appurtenances that mime its shape, all bets are off. A comedy of manners set in a different period—for example, *Guy Domville*—presents a peculiar peril: "Suppose, however, some eccentric individual dresses himself in the fashion of former times: our attention is immediately drawn to the clothes themselves, we absolutely distinguish them from the individual, we say that the latter IS DISGUISING HIMSELF,—as though every article of clothing were not a disguise!—and the laughable aspect of fashion comes out of the shadow into the light."[21] We could say with Bergson that laughter with respect to clothes arises from a particular sort of failed mimesis. What is laid bare is *not* the body: a person whose clothes are torn from his body is an object of pity, not of humor. What is funny about outdated fashion is the laying bare of the masquerade, of the artifice and routinization of everyday life. As Bergson writes, "Already, the stiff and starched formality of any ceremonial suggests to us an image of this kind. For, as soon as we forget the serious object of a solemnity or a ceremony, those

Figure 5. In the studio of Mathew Brady, a young Henry James poses for a daguerreotype with his father, Henry James Sr.; when William Makepeace Thackeray mocked his outfit, HJ recalls, "My sense of my jacket became from that hour a heavy one." By permission of the Houghton Library, Harvard University: MS Am 1092.9 (4597.6).

taking part in it give us the impression of puppets in motion" (22). As we saw with Alice James, stiffness and starchiness are challenged by a burst of laughter; further, they are capable of being ironed into suppleness by the activity of play.

Daisy Among the Boys

Stiffness, the quality of being resistant to change, is the inverse of plasticity. Rigidity can be useful, however, if one wishes to probe at a comfortable distance—or to harm. The uses and abuses of stiffness are precisely what is at issue in *Daisy*

Miller: A Study.[22] The novella's introductory scene amusingly compares two ways of navigating an environment through an interaction between two young American males. Winterbourne, the focalizer of the story, is a worldly feeling young man of leisure whose occupation in Geneva—"studying"—is ironically introduced with scare quotes (*Tales*, 4). Randolph, his erstwhile sparring partner, is Daisy Miller's comical little brother, who is indifferent to the educational aspects of the Grand Tour he is on with his mother and sister. Winterbourne has been sipping coffee in the garden of a Swiss hotel; seeing the boy's pretty sister, the young man pumps the boy for information, seeking an introduction. Randolph, impishly wielding a stick, engages in his own preferred mode of introduction and exploration: "He poked his alpenstock, lance-fashion, into Winterbourne's bench and tried to crack the lump of sugar with his teeth" (*Tales*, 5). With a sugar bowl at hand, Winterbourne engages in a light colloquy, all the while supplying the boy with lumps. There is an undertone of violence in the scene, as stick pokes and sugar cracks: "He carried in his hand a long alpenstock, the sharp point of which he thrust into everything that he approached—the flowerbeds, the garden benches, the trains of the ladies' dresses." Winterbourne's digs are conversational: "'If you eat three lumps of sugar, your mother will certainly slap you,' he said." Playacting the adult, Winterbourne is a naughty supplier of sweets: "'Take care you don't hurt your teeth,' he said, paternally," as he doles out sugar. The scene offers amusing, mutually satisfying parallel play: "The child, who had now got astride of his alpenstock, stood looking about him. . . . The little boy had now converted his alpenstock into a vaulting pole, by the aid of which he was springing about in the gravel and kicking it up not a little" (*Tales*, 5).

Randolph's play probes boundaries, setting the scene for Winterbourne's own verbal (and social) boundary-crossings with respect to Daisy. The scene's humor lies in the *apparent* incongruity of rough-housing boy and decorous gentleman, who nonetheless are amusingly congruent in their quests: by scene's end, both become acquainted with the "sweet thing" that they are after, sugar for the boy, Daisy for the young man. Even the most urbane of men once were boisterous lads, the scene lightly suggests: "Winterbourne wondered if he himself had been like this in his infancy, for he had been brought to Europe at about this age" (*Tales*, 5). By placing Randolph and Winterbourne on a continuum, the story aligns their different epistemological tools, the probing stick and the only slightly more subtle probing questions. In both, mixed in with curiosity, fun, and the pleasure of new relations is the serious potential for harm.

In his *Talks to Teachers on Psychology* (1899), WJ explains how children's propensity to handle (and indeed to mouth) objects announces the action-oriented alliance of bodies, minds, and the physical world: "Up to the eighth or ninth year of childhood one may say that the child does hardly anything else than handle objects, explore things with his hands, doing and undoing, setting up and knocking down, putting together and pulling apart . . . that acquaintance with the properties of material things, which is really the foundation of human consciousness."[23] Knowledge of the world emerges in relation to concrete, physical properties; ideas themselves can be understood in light of their invitation to be grasped and handled: "To the very last, in most of us, the conceptions of objects and their properties are limited to the notion of what we can *do with them*." WJ concludes, "A 'stick' means something we can lean upon or strike with" (*TT*, 747). Not merely a phallic symbol, a stick embodies a set of concrete affordances, from toy to prop to weapon. What one can do with a stick is explicitly in play in *Daisy Miller*.

The novella creates a comedic play frame in which fiddling with sticks and toying with young ladies form two slightly divergent points on a male developmental timeline. A week before Winterbourne and Daisy face off in the Colosseum at the story's climax, the "pretty American flirt" astutely likens Winterbourne to a grown-up equivalent of Randolph's alpenstock: "I noticed you were as stiff as an umbrella the first time I saw you" (*Tales*, 44). Having pushed and prodded and teased the young man in Switzerland and then Italy, Daisy's remarks become more pointed. Yet the metaphor of the umbrella—a prop that, like a cane, is often played for humor—keeps her banter light.

HJ, however, takes *Daisy Miller* the novella in a different direction, scaling the metaphors away from play toward violence. The climactic scene transpires in the Colosseum, a site of blood sports; and Daisy's response to Winterbourne turning his back on her invokes fencing's *touché*: "'He cuts me!'" (*Tales*, 46). Winterbourne, for his part, acts and thinks as though he is in a melodrama: first, expressing dismay at "a delicate young girl lounging away the evening in this nest of malaria"; then letting rip an aggrieved insult, "What a clever little reprobate she was, and how smartly she played at injured innocence!" Winterbourne, vacillating between a damsel/strumpet dichotomy, can flex his stiff imagination only so far in understanding the play of flirtation, exploration, and affection that Daisy initiates. In this early work by HJ, the tutelage of Winterbourne is secured—if it is—in the crudest of terms, by the death of the object of his admiration.

HJ, in killing off Daisy at story's end, translates a light comedy of manners into moralizing melodrama. In so doing, he illuminates the potentially brutal consequences of refusing to see flirting as play, as a give-and-take between equals with the telos of fun (rather than prurient knowledge or moral judgment, both encapsulated in Winterbourne's boring, irrelevant question, *Is she innocent?*). Published in 1878, *Daisy Miller* is an early—might one say boyish—attempt on the author's part, for just as Winterbourne weaponizes the proprieties, HJ leverages the limited affordances of melodrama as a blunt instrument for making a point about the dangers of inflexible thought and action. In so doing he replicates something of the violence inherent in rule-bound Victorian gender roles—which the story ostensibly holds up for ridicule. A few years after publishing what would be his most popular work, HJ changed the ending of *Daisy Miller*, as well as its subtitle, to revise it into a play. In *Daisy Miller: A Comedy*, Daisy and Winterbourne marry. The play did not make it into production, but HJ did publish the new version as a story in the *Atlantic* in 1883.

Staging The American

It wasn't until 1890 that the novelist turned his full attention toward becoming a successful writer of plays. As James Wood has written in the *Atlantic*, "The story of Henry James's fruitless flirtation with the theater has been so often told that it has become folkloric, invoked and repeated by generations of marveling Jamesians."[24] Perhaps it's going too far to point out the proleptic analogy between HJ's "fruitless flirtation" and that of his lively, lovely character Daisy—though David Lodge in *Author, Author!* (2004) did fictionalize and play for humor HJ's own colossal misadventure with boisterous theatergoers.[25] Edel's sympathetic portrayal of *Guy Domville*'s opening night instead emphasizes the playwright's surprise and horror: "The novelist, having heard the applause [from his sympathizers in the audience], came forward shyly, hesitantly; and at that moment the gallery exploded. Jeers, hisses, catcalls were followed by great waves of applause from that part of the audience which esteemed James and had recognized the better qualities of the play. The two audiences had declared war. The intellectual and artistic elite answered the howls of derision; the howls grew strong in defiance. . . . James faced this pandemonium; his dark beard accentuated the pallor of his face and his high bald dome."[26] HJ is here described as vulnerably embodied, sweating and horrorstruck in the glaring incandescent stage lights. For all his social prowess among American expatriots and London cultural elites, he was exceedingly shy and anxious when it came to encounters with a wider public. Edel argues persuasively that this face-to-face encounter was traumatic for the diffident writer, who left the stage (as one of the actors later described it) "green with dismay" (*GD*, 99). The call for "author, author!" had sounded as if the audience wished to pay homage to the genius of the playwright, but instead it became an occasion for the theatergoers to noisily render their communal verdicts.

In light of this experience, one can see how the separation of author and reader (via novels), and of actor and audience (via cinema), might offer blessed antidotes to the unruliness of live drama. So, we can understand that what Benjamin (citing Pirandello), rebukes as a defining structure of alienated aesthetics might be welcomed by HJ as an authorial refuge: "The film actor . . . feels as if in exile—exiled not only from the stage but also from himself. With a vague sense of discomfort he feels inexplicable emptiness: his body loses its corporeality, it evaporates, it is deprived of reality, life, voice, and the noises caused by his moving about, in order to be changed into a mute image, flickering an instant on the screen, then vanishing into silence. . . . The projector will play with his shadow before the public, and he himself must be content to play before the camera."[27] The technology of projection offers the "shadow" of action that has happened in the past. As we know, HJ's notorious curtain call was not his debut as a playwright; it is shadowed by the author's prior, much more agreeable, experience with the theater.

Almost exactly four years earlier, on 3 January 1891, HJ had made his mildly successful foray into the theater with the adaptation of his novel *The American* for the London stage. In a letter he wrote a few hours before the play opened, he told WJ of his and AJ's shared palpitations about the impending event: "We are resting and quaking today," HJ writes, though he admits that "the omens and auspices are good—the theatre is bad but big & every seat in it has been taken for a week. The principal London critic, Wm. Archer, of the weekly *World* (I will send you his pronouncement,) is coming down & can scarcely get one" (*Letters*, 250). The production itself, HJ admits, was far from lavish; with some trepidation he notes that the play was now out of his hands and in the hands of the actors and audiences, though he wistfully hopes that its "intrinsic vitality"—what Benjamin would call its aura—will persist: "The play will owe nothing whatever to brilliancy of interpretation, & the mounting is of the meagrest—it will all, if the thing isn't damned, be a success of *intrinsic vitality*. . . . [W]e had yesterday a supreme, complete, exhaustive rehearsal, during which I sat in the stalls watching & listening as to the work of another: the result of which (I boldly say it—on the untried eve,) was a kind of mystic confidence in the *ultimate life* of the piece—. . . I think it has a *strong life*" (*Letters*, 250, emphasis added). In this moment of anticipation, HJ sits in the audience and watches actors embodying the characters he had developed in his novel *The American*. Sitting in the empty, darkened theater, his feeling of authorship recedes as he adopts the perspective of an audience member, "watching & listening as to the work of another."

The language HJ uses to describe the play is identical to what James Mark Baldwin uses to describe (child's) play and (adult) aesthetic objects. In *Thought and Things* (1906), Baldwin writes: "The construction bears the face value of what it is: a limited and struggling life. It seems reasonable —after we find it so, at any rate—to expect that an imitation of the real, thus produced and so used, will not be merely a dry, hard context representing an objective order; but that it will have, in its very release from the dead and inanimate, a certain rebound, vitally-semblant and more-inclusive richness of meaning."[28] Applying Baldwin's formulation to *The American,* HJ bears witness to his "construction" being "release[d] from the dead and inanimate" and taking "vitally-semblant" form on the stage, as a sort of externalized, phantasmagorical presence.

In his earlier novel *The Tragic Muse* (1890), HJ theorized the spectator's role in theatrical productions. The novel's focalizing character Hyacinth Robinson expresses how a riveted audience member vivifies inert stage properties by acts of imagination kindled by intensified stage lighting and newly darkened auditoriums: "His imagination projected itself lovingly across the footlights, gilded and colored the shabby canvas and battered accessories, losing itself so effectively in the Active world that the end of the piece, however long or however short, brought with it something of the alarm of a stoppage of his personal life. It was impossible to be more friendly to the dramatic illusion" (*GD*, 41). Cognitive theorists contend that a successful stage play overrides an individual's awareness of everyday narratives, allowing her to bracket contradictory information: "When spectators 'live in the blend' of a performance, . . . they temporarily put aside their knowledge that the actors have other lives outside of their immediate role-playing and that the characters began initially as words on a page, for instance."[29] While bracketing alternative narratives, viewers nonetheless draw on their own affective experiences in vivifying the actions on the stage—the "conceptual blending" described by Bruce McConachie, and elsewhere by Mark Turner.[30]

Baldwin roots this capacity for appreciation in the emergence of play in young children: "The player as much as says to himself, *this is real, or would be, but for the fact that I know that it is not*."[31] This practice is "semblance," and the fully exposed doubleness is crucial: "Not only is the child using his imagination, but he is also aware that the construction is imaginative" (*Thought*, 112). Baldwin uses a theater metaphor to describe the twinned seeing and seeing *into*:

"Consciousness, even while busy with the play objects, casts sly glances behind the scenes, making sure that its firm footing of reality is not entirely lost. There is a sort of oscillation between the real and the semblant object" (112). Of course, thoroughly naïve spectators might find themselves utterly immersed in the conceptual blend and unable to "oscillate," cognitively speaking. Mark Twain memorably cast Huckleberry Finn as just such an audience member anxiously viewing a seemingly dangerous circus act.[32] Baldwin explicitly connects what otherwise looks like mere punning: between play as an imaginative practice associated with children, and play in the sense of dramatic performance keyed toward adults.

The Substance of Illusion

Baldwin, along with WJ, influenced the English pediatrician D. W. Winnicott, who affirmed the centrality of object relations in children's psychological development.[33] Winnicott in *Playing and Reality* (1971) provides language to capture HJ's oddly doubled experience of watching his play from the stalls.[34] "Of every individual who has reached to the stage of being a unit with a limiting membrane and an outside and an inside," Winnicott writes, "it can be said that there is an inner reality to that individual" (2). Psychology as a discipline concerns itself with the nature of that "inner world," which "can be rich or poor and can be at peace or in a state of war" (2). Winnicott goes further, however, to posit a third zone of being, what he calls "an intermediate area of experiencing, to which inner reality and external life both contribute" (2). The co-constitution of inner and outer, he argues, provides the emergent self not only with a healthy sense of resilience but with an even prior need, a sense of reality. This "intermediate state" Winnicott describes can be supported by an infant's "transitional object," a material entity that the child endows with significance. A transitional object helps an infant to do two things: first, to recognize her (inner) power to assimilate and to shape experience—often expressed by the child damaging, ingesting, or defacing the object; and second, to confirm the object's independent (outer) power—manifested through the persistence of core qualities such as texture, smell, warmth, and feel. This second element secures a child's sense of the solidity of the world beyond the self, revealing that a beloved thing "has vitality or reality of its own" (5). The transitional object offers important mediation for a child, allowing for a healthy and secure psychology grounded in a sophisticated ontology.

To return to HJ's thrilled response to seeing *The American* on stage: witnessing his novel bodied forth by players in a theater carries the potency of a transitional object. The production transpires in the world, suffused in texture, scents, colors, movement, aurality, warmth. Rightly combined, even "the meagrest" properties can express the "intrinsic vitality" that the playwright seeks, from the glow of the lights to the gestures of the actors to the rustlings of the audience (*Letters*, 250). And indeed, there is overlap, for Winnicott, between the animism of a child's relationship to transitional objects and the affecting qualities of powerfully wrought creative productions. For Winnicott, the child, the artist, and the religious mystic each possess a capacity for creating a magic circle: for arranging and providing the conditions for stolid materials to be animated. Winnicott coins the term "substance of illusion"—only an apparent oxymoron—for this process: "I am therefore studying the substance of illusion, that which is allowed to the infant, and which in adult life is inherent in art and religion. . . . We can share a respect for illusory experience, and if we wish, we may collect together and form a group on the basis of the similarity of our illusory experiences. This is a natural root of grouping among human beings" (3). The products of the imagination, when vitally rendered and affectingly staged (whether a published novel, painting in a gallery, or theatrical production), take substantial form and become sites of collective experience. In the theater, actors, script and physical properties operate in unison under direction to draw an audience in. When writing about drama, HJ often invoked mechanical metaphors to describe this compound, collective instance of creating. He described, for instance, his ideas for a "pretty three-act comedy" as the "machinery" of the plot, with a character's secret providing "one of the big wheels of the action."[35] (HJ, echoing an idea from WJ's tops metaphor, muses over the construction of the story as if he were engaged in carpentry: "I've wanted a hinge for that, a pivot and a platform. . . . I must hammer at it—that is turn it round a bit.")[36] In his letters about *The American*, HJ records his delight at the play's material manifestation. His was the glee of the child who, having set a toy in motion, experiences both proprietary pride and the wonderment that the thing runs on its own.

And indeed, Winnicott notes a danger in creative acts—one that will become pertinent in the later discussion of *The Turn of the Screw*. The impulse toward collective sharing of an illusory experience, characteristic of the child's playing with a transitional object as well as the artist's creating an aesthetic experience, "becomes the hallmark of madness when an adult puts too powerful a claim on the credulity of others, forcing them to acknowledge a sharing of illusion that is not their own" (3). Johan Huizinga writes that any element of force undercuts a central aspect of the experience: "First and foremost [. . .] all play is a voluntary activity. Play to order is no longer play: it could at best be but a forcible imitation of it. By this quality of freedom alone, play marks itself off from the course of the natural process."[37] Although he doesn't name the process as play, Paul Armstrong has eloquently argued that HJ's most ambiguous stories enlist "an endlessly extending exchange of views"—a rhythm of reciprocation that resembles the back-and-forth collaboration of play.[38]

Play, for HJ, is a name for manifesting imagination in and through the obduracy of the material world. Terry Castle, in her article on eighteenth-century phantasmagoria productions, historicizes the modern conception of consciousness as essentially inward: "From an initial connection with something external and public (an artificially produced 'spectral' illusion), the word ['phantasmagorical'] has now come to refer to something wholly internal or subjective: the phantasmic imagery of the mind."[39] Castle continues: "But in another highly paradoxical sense, ghosts now seemed more real than ever before—in that they now occupied (indeed preoccupied) the intimate space of the mind itself. The paradox was exactly like that achieved at the real phantasmagoria: ghosts did not exist, but one saw them anyway. *Indeed, one could hardly escape them, for they were one's own thoughts bizarrely externalized*" (58, emphasis added). Castle is referring to a strange feature that accompanied the creation of new technologies of projection, in particular the magic lantern: they provided a model of consciousness in which a dark box (that is, the mind) could be filled with images that had no material manifestation (that is, ghosts). By some accounts, the novel works precisely in this way, dropping fictional images into readers' minds.

By virtue of translating his popular novel *The American* into a play, HJ explicitly sought to reverse the phantasmagorical model of both consciousness and aesthetic production. He sought to materialize his "ghosts"—via actors, stage properties, lighting, and so on—and thus to enjoy, and to capitalize upon, the experience of having his creation dramatized and his "thoughts bizarrely externalized." While a thrilling prospect, one that could net him both critical acclaim and financial reward, HJ worried about the translation of words on the page to embodiment on the stage. He concludes his preperformance message to WJ by asking for his brother to pray for him: "God grant that tonight—between 8 & 11 (spend *you* the terrible hours in fasting, silence & supplication!) I don't get the lie in my teeth. Still I *am*, at present, in a state of abject, lovely fear . . . I am *too* nervous to write more" (*Letters*, 250). As Stephen Nachmanovitch notes, "Artists, as they play, are simultaneously bidding for approval and sometimes begging for survival."[40] (Indeed, HJ admittedly had monetary aspirations; one letter to AJ reads like a balance sheet as he tallies potential theatrical earnings.)[41]

Following the debacle of *Guy Domville*'s opening night, HJ offered a post-mortem on his career as a playwright and a dig at Oscar Wilde's newest dramatic success, which had opened the same night in 1895: "There is nothing, fortunately, so dead as a dead play—unless it be sometimes a living one [that is, Wilde's]" (*LHJ*, 160). Edel has set the tone for much writing about the *Guy Domville* debacle, arguing that the dramatic arts were ultimately too coarse, too corporeal, for HJ: "Women," Edel writes, "were ethereal creatures to put into fiction; but in the stage wings they were flesh and blood, with greasepaint covering the flesh, and beads of sweat on top of the paint" (*LHJ*, 106). Further, argues Edel, the imperatives of directors and producers encroached on HJ's solitary mastery. Kurnick describes the critical consensus on HJ's theatrical failure, that it gave birth to the modern novel's insistent interiority, over and against the collectivity, corporeality, and publicity of the stage: "In [HJ's] scenic method theater is remade as metaphor. James's theatrical debacle has become one of the better-known critical allegories for the birth of the modern novel . . . confirm[ing] our sense that the privileged subject of modern literature is the psychic interior."[42] Instead, we might consider that his foray into the theater opened HJ to proto-cinematic modes of representation, which made different claims on the human sensorium. His theatrical travails left him with a similar conceptualization yet the exact opposite value judgment to that which Benjamin would later affirm in "The Work of Art in the Age of Mechanical Reproduction." HJ's experience with *Guy Domville* pointed up the problem of material properties that remained doggedly intransigent—for neither the rowdy nor the decorous audience did *Guy Domville* succeed in casting a spell.

In recoiling from the theater, HJ didn't eschew the corporeality of aesthetic experience or consciousness, nor did he abandon the ideal of collective experience. His pleasure watching in a dark theater anticipates the experience of an audience member in a cinema. It is worth noting that, as WJ's Harvard colleague Hugo Münsterberg writes in the first psychological study of what he terms the "photoplay," "the decisive step was taken when pictures of the Edison type were for the first time thrown on a screen and thus made visible to a large audience. That step was taken 1895 in London. The moving picture theater certainly began in England."[43] Not surprisingly, HJ's first major publication after *Guy Domville* was *What Maisie Knew*, a novel that embraces the proto-cinematic nature of consciousness even as it emphasizes the sensory, outward-focused aspects of learning to feel one's way through a world of tangled relations. In it, HJ reminds us that, in the 1890s, consciousness figured in terms of a magic lantern was neither passive, nor solitary, nor disembodied—though it did require a steep learning curve and present a new set of cognitive conventions to master.

Maisie, Morgan, Miles, and Flora: Flipping the Educational Script

Midway through *What Maisie Knew*, one of Maisie's former governesses, now her stepmother, promises that the young girl's formal education is about to begin:

> "You shall have such lessons as you've never had in all your life. You shall go to courses."
> "Courses?" Maisie had never heard of such things.
> "At institutions—on subjects."
> Maisie continued to stare. "Subjects?"[44]

The conversation continues in this vein, as Maisie puzzles about the building blocks of a conventional education. The humor lies in the child's innocent incrimination of her governess-turned-stepmother, through a set of questions that reveals that the former Miss Overmore hasn't managed to fulfill the rudiments of her post, whether that be instructor or parent. Incongruously, rather than the adult quizzing the student, it is Maisie who catechizes her elder. With most topics of education "put off from week to week" and many "that they never got to at all," Maisie's education transpires largely outside the schoolroom *(Maisie*, 51). The narrator reports that the child "saw more and more; she saw too much" (43), a clause that may sound quantitative—suggesting she was an overfilled receptacle—but that carries a moralizing message. The child is privy to what HJ calls "ugly facts": the parents' distaste for monogamy as well as their mutual desire to foist caregiving responsibilities on the other (23). *What Maisie Knew* nonetheless turns out to be a novel of education for both the central character and the author, who are not so much enlightened as themselves sources of enlightenment, in a sense that is almost literal.

A Novel Projecting Device

In *Maisie* HJ tests a new technology of narrative projection by narrowing the focalizing consciousness to a single figure, a small girl who from birth is audience to the adult machinations and romantic partner changes happening around and indeed through her. Maisie is the novel's number one spectator and also a catalyst to the action—her physical presence "in the thick of the fight" is essential to her dawning consciousness and to HJ's narrative scheme: "Only a drummer-boy in a ballad or a story could have been so in the thick of the fight. She was taken into the confidence of passions on which she fixed just the stare she might have had for images bounding across the wall in the slide of a magic-lantern. Her little world was phantasmagoric—strange shadows dancing on a sheet" (*Maisie*, 39). With parents fighting for her custody, Maisie is not shielded from their skirmishes. In this respect she occupies an extraordinary, embedded position: present for their battles, she is akin to a war correspondent, except that she lacks a clear sense of what is transpiring around her. Her "small expanding consciousness" registers what goes on, and while it's clear to the reader that adults are carrying on child-free encounters "off-stage," only what Maisie was present for is directly narrated (24). HJ emphasizes the symmetrical, recursive structure of the to-and-fro plot, as Maisie is "entertained in rotation" by her parents, "rebounding from racquet to racquet like a tennis-ball or a shuttlecock" (23). An object of sport for the parents, Maisie functions as the narrative's ambulatory projection device. Unlike an inert object, Maisie learns, loves, and grows. Her "active, contributing, close-circling wonder . . . provides vitality and variety" as she strives to enlarge the circle of care around her (31). She is in this regard a transformer: she cleanses events of the adults' base motives even as she fine-tunes her understanding.

In describing Maisie's vision, HJ references the magic lantern. This early cinematic device used an internal light source (the lantern), translucent slides, and a concave mirror to project figures on a flat surface: the "images bounding across the wall," from the quoted passage. Along with the mirror and the lamp, magic lanterns were equipped with wheels. Though the slides were themselves static, the images produced could be set in motion by human manipulation. The Royal Polytechnic Institution in London, for instance, had four huge lanterns that allowed for the projection of short narratives: by shifting from one lantern to another, rolling the lanterns forward and backward, and modulating the light source, operators could create a "dissolving view" that simulated motion and transformation. The Polytechnic promoted magic lantern shows as an entertaining form of education; they took place in the institution's "Temple of Science" with the motto "Science for All," so that audiences might view various new technologies or attend a lecture on chemistry as well as view a magic lantern show.[45] The narrative's reference to Maisie's world as phantasmagoric invokes a particular variety of magic lantern show, which true to its Greek root projected phantasms—ghosts, goblins, vivified skeletons, and other apparitions—in a place of congregation (*agora*). In these shows, death itself was cleansed of its morbidity to become fodder for amusement. As Castle has ably demonstrated, the term "phantasmagoric" has in modern usage become a metaphor for strange, dreamlike, and generally hallucinatory subjective experiences.[46] *What Maisie Knew* returns the metaphor to its technological roots by conjuring the older meaning of a proto-cinematic public performance: "It was as if the whole performance had been given for her—a mite of a half-scared infant in a great dim theatre. She was in short introduced to life with a liberality in which the selfishness of others found its account and there was nothing to avert the sacrifice but the modesty of her youth" (*Maisie*, 39). Maisie, as with infants more generally, experienced herself at the center of a "blooming, buzzing confusion" (to quote WJ), experiencing what goes on around her as a show put on for her benefit. The narrative slyly suggests that, as with an actual phantasmagoria, the gruesome machinations transpire with tawdry publicity, as adults who should be caregivers use the child as an unwitting go-between for their infidelities. Maisie at this early moment in the novel is transfixed by the drama she sees, just as she would be at a magic lantern or nickelodeon production in a "dim theatre": the play of light and shadow, and the darkened space, are crucial elements of both childhood perception and early cinema.

HJ explicitly aligns his own compositional process with the child focalizer's perceptions, using terms resonant of early cinema.[47] HJ describes the process of looking back on the novel from his editorial position as "the old problems and dimnesses—the old solutions and little findings of light" (*GD*, 117). The light that figures the successful work of imagination is not aligned with the intensity of sunlight (or the passive glow of moonlight, as Nathaniel Hawthorne once described it, in the preface to *The Scarlet Letter*). Rather, the light must be kindled and controlled: "I was in presence of the red dramatic spark that glowed at the core of my vision and that, as I gently blew upon it, burned higher and clearer" (*Maisie*, 24). One of the earliest publications describing the magic lantern and other optical devices was entitled *The Great Art of Light and Shadow*, written by a German Jesuit priest in the seventeenth century.[48] HJ uses the language of optics when describing the novel, referring to Maisie as a lens in his Notebook, "a dim, crooked little reflector" (162).

This mirroring isn't static; the vision transforms as it rolls out in time. The narrative consists of "a series of moments" that serially reveal each "stage" of Maisie's dawning awareness.[49] The language of drama—including HJ's own stated "scenic method" and commitment to the "*march of an action*"—shades into that of early cinema. Entertainment featuring early projection devices enthralled audiences with familiar, repetitive movement such as soldiers marching, children on a seesaw, or windmills turning. As Nancy Bentley has described in *Frantic Panoramas,* the practice of unspooling images to achieve seamless motion became increasingly common in the 1890s.[50] "Magic lanternists, artists, and craftsmen . . . created more complex slides to simulate movement. And they developed a variety of ways to use images to tell stories and create dramatic effects. Audiences, in turn, became used to the lanternist's tricks, and the terror originally inspired by the phantasmagoria was gradually replaced by a more modest thrill and an excited curiosity about how the visual effects—ancestors of today's special effects—were done."[51] Creating early cinematic productions with magic lanterns involved the operator handling multiple devices to create a series of unfolding moments, while in turn audiences became as interested in the production's effects as the narrative itself.

The involvement of operators' bodies in the process of creating new visual experiences is a crucial aspect of the new technologies. Critics' emphasis on reflection and vision in the work of HJ has tended to emphasize disembodiment, overlooking another metaphorical register that is strikingly apparent both in *What Maisie Knew* and in the preface to it, which calls attention to the kinesthetic agency of the artist. As HJ and his readers were aware, early instruments of projection (magic lanterns and panoramas, as well as smaller devices such as kaleidoscopes and zoetropes) involved wheels that depended on human beings turning them to elicit the effect of motion.

Indeed, after emphasizing the "pictorial glow" of his initial conception, HJ's preface shifts to more tactile metaphors. He acknowledges that while a divorce plot with a child at its center could be a study in misery, if the "facts" of the couples' (un)couplings are properly *turned*—both by the artist and the child character—other possibilities may emerge: "The light of an imagination *touched by them* [facts] couldn't help therefore projecting a further ray, thanks to which it became rather quaintly clear that, not less than the chance of misery and of a degraded state, the chance of happiness and of an improved state might be here involved for the child, *round about whom* the complexity of life would thus *turn to fineness*, to richness—and indeed would have *but so to turn* for the small creature to be steeped in security and ease" (*Maisie*, 24). This passage draws on two different meanings of the verb "to turn." Attending to the structure of his narrative creation, HJ figures the child character as a (passive) pivot and also an (active) transformer: the plot *turns* around her, and in turn she *turns* ugliness into fineness. The difficulty lies in balancing the plot's tawdriness with the child's fineness of imagination.

Turning refers to something that is actively created; one might use a felicitous turn of phrase, or turn a piece of wood on a lathe. The object created, whether a table leg or a top, is symmetrical about a central axis. Similarly, one can position a torch or lantern to create a pool of light, a circle of visual salience. HJ in the passage describes the tentative gropings of a creative consciousness assembling its materials and hoping that the experience would lead not to shock or to a mere unfocused "muddle" but rather to "fineness" and even "happiness." Light must be mastered, analyzed, and controlled. "Sketchily clustered even, these elements gave out that vague pictorial glow which forms the first appeal of a living 'subject' to the painter's consciousness; but the glimmer became intense as I proceeded to a further analysis. The further analysis is for that matter almost always the torch of rapture and victory, as the artist's firm hand grasps and plays it" (*Maisie*, 24). What was merely a "glimmer," available to the visual sense, transforms into something more intense, more richly vivid, when "the artist's firm hand grasps and plays it."

I am emphasizing here how the glow of imagination is paired with the effortful, manual activity of *making*, a persistent theme across HJ's prefaces. Critics have linked the cinematic in *Maisie* to the rise of consumer culture built on illusion. Christina Britzolakis makes this point about Maisie, that "her 'sharpened sense of spectator-ship' is an effect of powerlessness and exclusion rather than of aesthetic choice; she suffers 'the doom of a peculiar passivity' (101), immersed in a game whose rules she does not understand, and to which she remains ultimately peripheral."[52]

But Maisie, crucially, is not merely a device (though her parents may treat her as such). She learns; she engages; she plays with what materials she has. What was once a "buzzing confusion" becomes more explicable, and she becomes adept at reading the adults' once-baffling actions and manipulating them into relations of care. Learning to "read" proto-cinematic entertainments for nineteenth-century audiences was not dissimilar; historians of film describe how spectators quite quickly assimilated magic lantern conventions, delighting in the ghosts that appeared and rarely jumping out of their seats when a train seemed to come straight at them. Knitting together a "series of moments" is something that happens at the level both of the artist/operator and of the spectator; making and viewing early cinematic productions involved assemblage, an embodied, enraptured stance that also left room for (as HJ puts it) "analysis" (*Maisie*, 24).

Establishing Rules of the Game

As a young child, Maisie is a repository of impressions that lack a sense of significance. As time passes, however, she gleans practical knowledge from the intriguing adults around her. Later, she thinks back over earlier interactions to which she bore witness: "She found in her mind a collection of images and echoes to which meanings were attachable—images and echoes kept for her in the childish dusk, the dim closet, the high drawers, like games she wasn't yet big enough to play" (*Maisie*, 41). HJ uses the "as if" configuration that Baldwin indicates is an essential formula for play. The narrative itself is being doubly playful here, first, by likening Maisie's storage of ideas to things stacked in a closet and, second, by figuring the objects as games and books, vehicles for imaginative play. These items, tagged to different ages, mark her maturation. The same is true for words and ideas: Moddle the nurse "put away" Maisie's parroted phrases (presumably, hushed the child), but they remain in her memory: "The great strain meanwhile was that of carrying by the right end the things her father said about her mother—things mostly indeed that Moddle, on a glimpse of them, as if they had been complicated toys or difficult books, took out of her hands and put away in the closet. A wonderful assortment of objects of this kind she was to discover there later, all tumbled up too with the things, shuffled into the same receptacle, that her mother had said about her father" (41). Maisie's adaptive process here—of seeing, selecting among, and reinterpreting things over time—mimes HJ's editorial process in the prefaces, as he looks back over, rearranges, and reinterprets his early works.

Maisie's father manifests a negative kind of flexibility that is thematized in the novel as permissiveness. Beale persistently offers statements and experiences that, in their ambiguity, are ironically affordant. Maisie's cognitive capacity for second-level awareness—to feel, and to know she feels—arises early and explicitly in a scene involving her father. Regarding her parents' divorce, the nurse Moddle had repeated to the child, "'You will feel the strain—that's where it is; and you'll feel it still worse, you know'" (40). Maisie is thus on the lookout for this phrase—"the strain"—and registers when her father uses it in her presence. Maisie takes the moment as a shared one, a point of connection because of "her father's telling her he felt it [the strain] too" (40). Amusingly (and horrifyingly), her father in this instance is telling his daughter that *she* is a strain: he is drawing an equivalence between her burden (being tossed between two parents) and his burden (having to look after her). The dark humor in the scene, for the reader, comes from the clash of two different psychological modes: Maisie's love and empathy, on the one hand; and on the other, her father's unapologetic narcissism. Maisie attributes empathy to her father (he feels her strain) and, reciprocating, feels sorry for his suffering. Beale, on the other hand, cares only about his own woes and carelessly tells the child she is its source. Yet the outcome of even bad parenting here is Maisie's intensified compassion and her feeling of increased competence about sharing a sentiment with her father.

If the process stopped here Maisie would remain a kindhearted, if not particularly intelligent, character. But the very next sentence enfolds the future, in which Maisie comes to reread the encounter and understand the nature of her father's sorrow: "It was only after some time" had passed that Maisie could look back and "attach to the picture of her father's sufferings . . . the meaning for which these things had waited" (*Maisie*, 41). The meaning, presumably, is that her father, unwilling to be burdened by her care, was foisting his daughter off on his ex-wife. Maisie, as kids do, eventually sees her parents' flaws (Beale's being perhaps more pronounced than most). Yet the more interesting point is twofold: first, even despicable adults can provide object lessons for a child to "learn on"; and, second, that an earlier understanding can be supplemented by a later one—just as HJ as editor can have a richer experience of the novel he wrote looking back on it a decade later. Indeed, HJ is explicit that stepping back from immersion and rereading experience transforms the agony of mere existence into something that resembles play: "[This] sharpened sense of spectatorship was the child's main support, the long habit, from the first, of seeing herself in discussion and finding in the fury of it—she had had a glimpse of the game of football—a sort of compensation for the doom of a peculiar passivity" (*Maisie*, 101). Omri Moses puts his finger on the way that characters in James's late fiction navigate their social arrangements to arrive at—rather than manifesting already established—interests. Like Maisie, "They show a capacity to experiment, revealing to us the malleability and unpredictability of their possible interests."[53] *What Maisie Knew* calls attention to the myriad affordances even a toxic environment yields to a questing consciousness. The self-same experience or statement as "the strain" can sustain different understandings—for example, Maisie's generous one as well as her father's selfish one—without one being more apposite than the other. Thinking in terms of affordances allows us to see the child exerting a form of imaginative agency: rather than merely accommodating herself to the adults, she seeks to assimilate them to her needs and to her way of feeling. Mrs. Wix, for instance, may deplore the plunging necklines preferred by Maisie's mother, with the understanding that Ida Farange is sexually promiscuous. Maisie, by contrast, interprets the clothing as a telltale for predicting her mother's movements: "She was always in a fearful hurry, and the lower the bosom was cut the more it was to be gathered she was wanted somewhere else" (*Maisie*, 88). Maisie in this way turns her mother's risqué outfit into a device with which to mark time and organize her world.

Ida, despite her expressive décolletage, is the less affordant of the parents: she may be promiscuous, but she is not permissive. She bristles with sharp objects: "The next moment she [Maisie] was on her mother's breast, where, amid a wilderness of trinkets, she felt as if she had suddenly been thrust, with a smash of glass, into a jeweler's shop-front, but only to be as suddenly ejected with a push and the brisk injunction" (*Maisie*, 126). Appropriately, Ida excels at billiards, a game of precision and concussive smacks; unlike Beale, she makes no jokes and eschews irony. Unmaternal, Ida is nonetheless the rare adult who gives Maisie helpful advice about playing games: "'You had better indeed for the future, miss, learn to keep your thoughts to yourself'" (45). Ida puts into words "exactly what Maisie had already learned": to adopt the proverbial poker face.[54]

Maisie's experiential learning, humorously, is akin to Dewey's promotion of "sense-training and object lessons and laboratory exercises."[55] The "scientific experimental method" placed the child at the center of a new epistemological framework in which, Dewey urged, "knowledge is a mode of participation" (210). Of course, not everyone was thrilled with the laboratory model of a student-centered classroom. In an article entitled "Mental Conservation of the Child," a professor of education bemoaned the lack of a coherent curriculum. Dewey's ideas, he writes, have "landed even the theorists, to say nothing of the administrators and teachers, in a jolly, topsy-turvey land. It would be difficult and discouraging to say clearly where the children were being landed."[56] The question of "landing" is apropos for Maisie, whose parents toss her back and forth, sometimes playing keep-away, other times hot potato, regarding custody of the child: "The day was at hand, and she [Ida] saw it, when she should feel more delight in hurling Maisie at him [Beale] than in snatching her away" (*Maisie*, 46). Ida is clever, and she is aware of and frustrated by the clash of her rules with those of Victorian mores: "the real end of all their tugging would be that each parent would try to make the little girl a burden to the other—a sort of game in which a fond mother clearly wouldn't show to advantage" and "begot in Ida Farange an ill humour of which several persons felt the effect" (46).

Meanwhile the adult "spectators" of the couple's machinations take pleasure in being privy to the perverse rules of Ida's and Beale's games. Brad Evans extends this prurient delight to the reader: "One of the great delights of *Maisie* comes from the troubling mismatch between what she knows and what we know."[57] These shadowy adult figures, however, remain largely unaware that Maisie is in fact toying with them: "Nothing was so easy to her as to send the ladies who gathered there [at Beale's] off into shrieks, and she might have practiced upon them largely if she had been of a more calculating turn" (*Maisie*, 54).

Maisie learns to withhold, sharpening her acuity by acting out imaginative exchanges with her doll Lisette: "In the presence of it [the doll] she often imitated the shrieking ladies. . . . She could only pass on her lessons and study to produce on Lisette the impression of having mysteries in her life" (55). Maisie learns how to play on the adults around her, all the while demonstrating more advanced ethics than her grown-up counterparts by confining her experiments to a doll rather than other characters.[58]

Toying with Teachers

The 1890s are distinguished for being the decade of HJ's most memorable child characters: Maisie, of course, but also Morgan ("The Pupil"), Miles and Flora (*The Turn of the Screw*), and Nanda (*The Awkward Age*).[59] Since each fictional child is equipped with an instructor, these works could be termed HJ's pedagogical tales; even Guy Domville, the protagonist of the eponymous stage play, was a live-in tutor, though his little ward "Geordie" has no lines and apparently the character wasn't cast. Yet these works turn the tables on the student-teacher relationship: not just with respect to who is learning from whom but also on what counts as education in the first place.

In *The Turn of the Screw* the governess's description of her pupils in action in the schoolroom blurs the line between instruction and amusement: "They performed the dizziest feats of arithmetic, soaring quite out of MY feeble range, and perpetrated, in higher spirits than ever, geographical and historical jokes."[60] The children exhibit great fluency and ingenuity as they repurpose the dry materials of education for the purposes of pleasure (one feels the contrast with the grim lessons of Charles Dickens's Gradgrind). Miles and Flora treat facts as flexible tools that in turn dazzle and inspire their governess, herself a young woman with an education but with few prospects who was pressed into service at an early age. *The Turn of the Screw* is designed such that the governess embraces both the perspective of the adult (as narrator of the story) and that of an untested young woman of roughly Winterbourne's age (from *Daisy Miller*). The narrator reflects back on her novitiate as an instructor, when she entered "service for the first time in the schoolroom" (*Screw*, 4). Her sense of her task is Deweyan: she was to "watch, teach, 'form' little Flora" (8)—a string of verbs that suggest she understood her occupation to include observation and instruction at the behest of the more creative act of "formation." Dewey is explicit about the aesthetics of teaching as cultivation rather than indoctrination:

"Where anything is growing, one *former* is worth a thousand re-formers" (emphasis added).[61] Indeed, the governess admits that, from her very first, somewhat breathless day on the job, she and her pupil Flora avoided the schoolroom: "Lessons, in this agitation, certainly suffered some delay. . . . I spent the day with her out-of-doors; I arranged with her, to her great satisfaction, that is should be she, she only, who might show me the place" (*Screw*, 9).

The governess's guide to her new position is her diminutive charge, who orients her to the household at Bly. While doing so, the pupil takes in knowledge not *from* her teacher but *about* her: "I reflected," writes the governess, "that my first duty was, by the gentlest arts I could contrive, to win the child into the sense of knowing me" (*Screw*, 9). Flora's situation echoes that of Maisie. Though "Maisie knew everything . . . that could be known" about Mrs. Wix's sad life, there "were many [subjects] put off from week to week"—presumably, history and Latin and geography—"that they never got to at all" (*Maisie*, 51). Miss Overmore is no better. She identifies with her pupil, saying they are both "good quiet little girls" (*Maisie,* 53). Indeed, in the absence of instruction from Miss Overmore, "There was also the solution of a second governess, a young person to come in by the day and really do the work" (*Maisie*, 56).

Instead of teaching, these educator-characters take up their role explicitly as a test or experiment in their own circumscribed, ambiguous existences. In "The Pupil," Morgan's tutor, Pemberton, is "modest . . . even timid; and the chance that his small scholar might prove cleverer than himself had quite figured, to his anxiety, among the dangers of an untried experiment" (*Tales*, 189). In each pedagogical tale, the instructors express doubt about their ultimate control over both their charges and the educational "environment," which are households—or, in the case of "The Pupil," a series of transient spaces—not of their possession. (*The Awkward Age*, by contrast, has a "female adolescent" making her way in society and "far removed from . . . the nursery and the schoolroom.")[62] A contemporary commentator describes the vexed role of the governess, who shoulders responsibility without authority: "She must live daily amidst the trials of a home without its blessings; she must bear on her heart the sins she witnesses and responsibilities that crush her . . . she must be ever on her guard; let her relax her self-restraint for one moment, and who shall say what mischief and misery might ensue to all from one heedless expression of hers."[63] Readers quickly become aware that the ersatz adults are neither the prime educators nor—to pick up the stories' language of experimentation—the principal investigators. Rather, Mrs. Wix, Pemberton, and the unnamed governess in *The Turn of the Screw* are the object of the children's tutelage and experimentation.

As mediators of knowledge, the pupils help to facilitate their instructors' entry into their new, complicated, even baffling domestic milieus.

In addition to being keen watchers, children in HJ's fiction turn out to be expert in imaginative entertainment, whether playing with an instrument, games, or make-believe. Maisie, a more talented musician and artist, "could play more pieces [on the piano] than Mrs. Wix, who was moreover visibly ashamed of her houses and trees and could only, with the help of a smutty forefinger, of doubtful legitimacy in the field of art, do the smoke coming out of the chimneys" (*Maisie*, 50). Morgan's tutor (with telling ambiguity about who is "he" and who is "him," who is teaching and who is learning) "wondered if he should be able to teach him to play, though his mother had said it would never do and that this was why school was impossible" (*Tales*, 189). The governess of Flora and Miles, in retrospect, notes not just the flipping of the teacher/student role in her relationship with the children but also the substitution of amusement for schoolwork: "Lessons with me, indeed, that charming summer, we all had a theory that he was to have; but I now feel that, for weeks, the lessons must have been rather my own. I learned something—at first, certainly—that had not been one of the teachings of my small, smothered life; learned to be amused, and even amusing, and not to think for the morrow" (*Screw*, 14).

Troping Devices and the Potential for Trauma

HJ in the preface to the *New York Edition* looks back on *What Maisie Knew* and "The Pupil" with the pride and technical know-how of a master craftsman, inviting readers to admire "my design; which design [became] more and more attractive as I turned it over" (*Maisie*, 26). There is an invitation here, to consider the work of HJ's pen (or, more accurately, typewriter) as itself a device, one with complex machinery that affords further play for the reader. In taking up the text, the reader accepts the invitation to "grasp and play with it," a phrase that captures the dual sense of both words, which refer equally to manual and cognitive attempts at understanding and (through iteration) expertise. Just as Maisie the "little wonder-working agent would create, without design, quite fresh elements of this order," so the reader is encouraged to emulate "the play of the child's" imagination in engaging with HJ's child-centric tales (*Maisie*, 25).

Jean Piaget argued that human beings interacting with the things and persons in their world seek to balance *accommodation*—one's bodily and cognitive conformity to the world as it is found—with *assimilation*, the creative rearrangement of the environment to suit one's self-directed needs and desires.[64] When both elements of the adaptive balance are equal, homeostasis (to use biological terms) and contentment (to use psychological ones) are the result. In a coercive environment, accommodation takes the day; for play to happen, assimilation—the imprint of the self on the world—dominates the equation. HJ is explicit that, for Maisie, the exquisite balance tips in the right way, toward assimilation; he thus for most of the novel gives precedence to the cleansing power of Maisie's consciousness over the bullying coercion and instrumentalism of the adults. The emphasis on play in the preface directs the reader: rather than offering a tragedy or morality tale, HJ's works featuring children are suffused with "a broad and rich comicality" (*Maisie*, 30)—or as he puts it in the preface to *The Awkward Age*, "jocosity" (7).

The metaphorical alignment of playing and reading is not far-fetched. But: in what sense is a tale a toy, something that has "moving parts" that one can explore and activate through manipulation? We can begin to think through this question by considering the nature of toys in the nineteenth century. Maria Edgeworth, in her 1798 treatise on children's education, writes suggestively about the toy store of the future. Such a shop would, she imagines, offer material supplies that children would use to construct things, with these acts of creation as an essential part of playing: "A rational toy-shop should be provided with all manner of carpenter's tools, with wood properly prepared for the young workman, with screws, nails, glue, and emery paper, and a variety of articles which it would be tedious to enumerate; but of which, if parents could readily meet with a convenient assemblage, they would willingly purchase for their children."[65] Edgeworth distinguished between the "Good Toy" and the "Bad Toy," with the former characterized by its link to cognitive expansion. She approved, too, of toys that were also tools, promoting coordination and gamesmanship: "Tops, kits, hoops, balls, battledores and shuttlecocks, ninepins, and cup and ball, are excellent," she opined. Bad toys were mimetic, expensive, fragile, and above all inert, frustrating the desire for movement and happenings of all sorts (Edgeworth likened Bad Toys to bad servants). These playthings not only promoted unseemly commercial desires in children for gilded replicas of adult life, such as "the finest, frail coach-and-six," they didn't "go." Such a carriage, she urges, a child can only "drag . . . cautiously along the carpet of the drawing-room, watching the wheels, which will not turn."[66] Such toys forced accommodation to their features and resisted assimilation to the child's purposes.

Clearly, HJ did not think of his stories as carriages or dolls. Rather, he spoke in terms of structure, design, devices, and experimentation. *In the Cage*, for instance, is an "experimentally-figured situation" (akin to a twenty-first-century story told all in tweets) that "puts into play" the once familiar figure of the telegraph operator who taps others' messages into a machine.[67] HJ writes that the conception of a typist serving as a medium for romantic exchange of messages between a lady and a gentleman "kindled" his artistic imagination: "This wonderment, once the spark was kindled, became an amusement, or an obsession, like another" (154). The apposition of *amusement* and *obsession* places the affective tenor in the spiral of play, while the interest in the relationship between person and device enlists the concept of toy: "an object, especially a gadget or machine, regarded as providing amusement for an adult."[68]

At the turn of the twentieth century, as Henry Ford's workers were assembling high-priced toys for adults, a cartoonist was turning out ludic devices that embodied—and made fun of—American appetites for machinic amusement. Rube Goldberg, born in 1883 and trained as an engineer, published his first cartoon of what would come to be known as a "Rube Goldberg machine" in 1914. By 1931, the Merriam-Webster dictionary had a new entry in his name: "A Rube Goldberg machine is a contraption, invention, device or apparatus that is deliberately over-engineered or overdone to perform a very simple task in a very complicated fashion." Goldberg in his drawings made creative use of the six basic types of machines: the level, wheel and axle, pulley, screw, wedge, and inclined plane. His ludic creations obeyed the basic rules and units of engineering: a dropping ball, for instance, never went up. His machines strayed from the values of engineering by virtue of their gratuitous difficulties (dozens of moving parts), incongruous elements (a cat's tail pulling a string, or a feather tickling a foot), and frivolous results (a self-operating napkin, an automatic balloon popper). Goldberg's cartoons conveyed "the valuable lesson in how comedy ensues when one combines the deadly serious and the ridiculous."[69]

Rube Goldberg machines serve as troping devices, tweaking conventional operating instructions and loosening the determinisms of everyday life. A student in Dewey's Lab School who "plays his games and makes his simple and more complex machines" is likewise turning out what Lev Vygotsky calls "tools of thinking."[70] For a child, such a troping device could be any object (including a person) that can be used as a "pivot" to "detach meaning from an object, or a word from an object" (98–99). The action that sets an object and its meaning at odds, that loosens the connection, Vygotsky calls *play*: "In play thought is separated from objects and action arises from ideas rather than from things: a piece of wood begins to be a doll and a stick becomes a horse. Action according to rules begins to be determined by ideas and not by objects themselves" (97). It is "in play," Vygotsky urges, that "things lose their determining force" (96) and instead can be assimilated to other purposes—purely for the fun of it.

Adam Phillips writes that ideas themselves–like things—can be in play, noting that some "facts" are affordant, while others are excessively rigid and dogmatic:

> We are continually being told the facts of life . . . and yet only some of the facts seem at all nourishing; we can copy them—remember them and reproduce them—but we can't make anything sufficiently our own with them. They are, in other words, minor traumas; not subject to inner transformation. It is the antitransformational objects that are the most dispiriting. Those objects we have no interest in transforming—and so are of no interest—or those objects that demand that we do not transform them but merely abide by them. Absolute obedience is a fear of interest. A trauma, one could say, is a set of bewildering, unconscious instructions.[71]

For a material analogue, one might point to a straitjacket, which for horror ranks among the worst of antitransformational objects; it forces obedience by trapping the wearer's arms into a parody of an embrace, unable to do harm but equally unable to grasp the simplest object.

What have Rube Goldberg machines, psychoanalytical theory, and entrapment have to do with reading fiction? The terms that accrue around "antitransformational object"—trap, trauma, rigidity, obedience—are central to Shoshana Felman's analysis of HJ's *The Turn of the Screw*. At the beginning of her essay "Turning the Screw of Interpretation," Felman asks the question "What does the act of turning a screw have to do with literature?"[72] The famed answer to her question takes no fewer than 113 pages in *Yale French Studies* to deliver. Felman's argument, notably, shifts attention away from the agency of the reader to the coerciveness of the story: "Whichever way he [the reader] turns, he can but be turned by the text, he can but perform it by repeating it" (101). Felman urges that HJ's story is a trap, forcing the reader into an analytical position that repeats the crushing analytical "operation" of the *governess*, which Felman describes as the "suffocating gesture of a tightly closed embrace" (163). Readers by this account are stuck inside the machine of the text that "screws" them: "The manipulator of the screw, who believes himself to be in control of its successive turns, in control of an enterprise of fixity and closure, discovers that, in reality, he himself is nothing but a screw, a cog in the wheel of a machine that runs by itself" (178). As Felman describes it, *The Turn of the Screw* is an exemplary nontransformational object, forcing acquiescence.

What is startling about Felman's influential essay is that *performatively* the essay demonstrates how extraordinarily affordant the story is, while *thematically* it affirms the coerciveness of the story. In a way, Felman treats the story like a child who wishes to engage and to play, while she—the serious adult—goes to Rube Goldberg–level creative lengths to construct an awe-inspiring device (that is, her extraordinary essay) that, with razzle-dazzle lights and sensational effects, sends the equivocal, amusingly self-undermining message "No."[73] This critical performance is clearly fun for Felman, and has elicited applause from a literary-critical audience that admires its moves, but leaves the reader in a bit of a pickle: either literal-minded and duped, or suspicious-minded and caught. Neither is a fun position to be in—which begs the question of why *Screw* for more than a century has been one of Henry James's most consistently read, analyzed, and adapted (for film and television) literary works. (*The Haunting of Bly Manor*, a streaming drama series created by Mike Flanagan, is the most recent adapation, having been released in October 2020.)

We can discern a different way to handle *The Turn of the Screw*, if we approach it under the aspect of play. Vygotsky urges that the key to child's play is collaboration, with the adult following the children's prompts and accommodating herself to what is transpiring. Spontaneity is essential; coerced or rote activity lies outside the realm of play. Moreover, because it is underdetermined, play gives pleasure through iteration: rather than diminishing pleasure, a second or third or tenth go-round can be as delightful or desirable—if not more so—than the first. In fact, most of us engage in some form lifelong play: think of tennis, poker, crosswords, Tetris, or just bantering conversation. This speaks to a unique feature of HJ's story, to which readers (and teachers) tend to return again and again. Play is situated, carrying with it a sense of rules, boundaries, or what Robin Bernstein calls a "script."[74] (Echoing Phillips, I prefer the term "operating instructions," as often these stipulations are nonverbal.) Successful play often has a tempo—both a pace and a rhythm—that, to invoke the fairy tale of Goldilocks and the three bears, is neither too fast nor too slow but somehow just right. There is no ultimate scale for tempo: it is judged affectively by those involved. Too slow tends toward boredom; too fast, toward alarm.

With respect to Miles and Flora in *The Turn of the Screw*, the governess becomes uncomfortably aware that she, as the teacher, *is* the toy (or what I am calling the troping device), as when she writes, "They pulled with an art of their own the strings of my invention and my memory" (49). In terms of the flipping of roles, however, one hears the *governess's* experience tipping away from humor into horror, as the children's fancies come more quickly, the music becomes less controlled, the performances too rapid. In the course of a few sentences the tone shifts from enchantment to misgiving: "We lived in a cloud of music and love and success and private theatricals. The musical sense in each of the children was of the quickest, but the elder in especial had a marvelous knack of catching and repeating. The schoolroom piano broke into all gruesome fancies; and when that failed there were confabulations in corners, with a sequel of one of them going out in the highest spirits in order to 'come in' as something new" (38). From the first line of her narrative, the governess calls attention to the tempo she experienced at Bly: "I remember the whole beginning as a succession of flights and drops, a little see-saw of the right throbs and the wrong" (6). As the story intensifies, the governess emphasizes the suddenness and bizarreness of the children's shifts: "He [Miles] played on a minute before answering . . . breaking moreover into a happy laugh which immediately after, as if it were a vocal accompaniment, he prolonged into incoherent extravagant song" (64).

Whereas the adults in Maisie's world operate by the rules of their tawdry game, the governess in *The Turn of the Screw* is affordant to the point of concern: she offers no daily routine, no educational structure, and no ground rules (or even rules about walking the grounds).The children come and go; perambulations occur; child-initiated play transpires. "I happened to spend [time] in the grounds with the younger of my pupils," the governess recalls; "I walked in a world of their invention—they had no occasion whatever to draw upon mine; so that my time was taken only with being, for them, some remarkable person or thing that the game of the moment required and that was merely, thanks to my superior, my exalted stamp, a happy and highly distinguished sinecure" (28). A sinecure is an easy job, where work can come to be more like leisure, or like play. Ellis Hanson emphasizes that, in *The Turn of the Screw*, "who is the child and who is the adult" is up for grabs.[75] When the governess isn't playing along, she serves (almost like a younger sibling) as audience to Miles's and Flora's amusement: "My attention to them all really went to seeing them amuse themselves immensely without me: this was a spectacle they seemed actively to prepare and that engaged me as an active admirer" (28). The children, perhaps baffled by the governess's endless susceptibility to their shaping, seek to coax her into an active adult role—as Flora did, by the lake at Bly. The narrator writes, "I forget what I was on the present occasion; "I only remember that I was something very important and very quiet and that Flora was playing very hard" (28). The governess's role, which she seems to forget, is of course to be *a caregiver watching a child playing*—all of which is transpiring *next to a body of water* and thus requiring extra diligence, also known as work, on the part of the responsible adult.

Vygotsky affirms that the relationship between the child and adult with respect to toys is crucial, because at first imagination is acted out collaboratively ("externally," as Vygotsky puts it), and only later does the child learn to play symbolically (an "internal" activity). There are thus "two planes" involved: "Every function in the cultural development of the child *appears on the stage twice*, in two planes, first, the social, then the psychological, first between people as an 'inter' mental category, then within the child as 'intra' mental category" (emphasis added).[76] Flora's playing by the lake appears to occupy both planes: physically manipulating two bits of wood to create a toy boat, and (like Maisie) manipulating her caregiver to do her "very important" job and *take care*. Vygotsky writes, "Play provides a transitional stage in this direction whenever an object (for example, a stick) becomes a pivot for severing the meaning of horse from a real horse. . . . [O]ne of the basic psychological structures determining the child's relationship to reality is radically altered" (97). Vygotsky observes that symbolic play involves a doubling that entails "going above," acting more like an adult: "In play a child is always above his average age, above his daily behavior; in play it is as though he were a head taller than himself. As in the focus of a magnifying glass, play contains all developmental tendencies in a condensed form and is itself a major source of development" (102). Playing by the water, Flora is asking that her governess also "play up." Earlier, the governess had observed of herself, "I could succeed where many another *girl* might have failed" (27, emphasis added), underscoring that, not unlike the child she watches, the young governess exists on a cusp. Within the story, the governess flickers between girl and woman; a flicker effect that is mimed by the story's form, which fuses the governess-narrator's backward glance with the governess-character's anxious peering into the future.

The narrative of *The Turn of the Screw*, I am arguing, offers a form of play that (to quote Vygotsky) contains the development of the governess "in a condensed form" through the device of retrospection. Both the governess and Flora are "playing up"—moving from more mechanical to more creative and symbolic play—and doing so under the watchful eye of an older person: "under direct personal notice" (29). The governess watches Flora; but who observes the governess-by-the-lake? Textually speaking, her audience is herself, the narrating governess: "I rather applaud myself as I look back!" (27). In a funny moment (both funny ha ha, and funny peculiar) the governess-by-the-lake who is *living forward* becomes aware of a shadowy spectator who is . . . a governess. The text's flicker effect suggests that the more experienced, more watchful, and frankly sadder caregiver whom the-governess-by-the-lake perceives could be one of two, or both: Miss Jessel or the narrating governess herself. Indeed, the name "Miss Jessel" does not appear in the chapter that ends by the lake. A short interval later in plot time, a couple of pages in text time, the governess spectator (note the double entendre!) by the lake is named by the governess—"Miss Jessel"—who then exclaims, "Oh for the effect and the feeling she might have been as close as you!" (30). The "you" of this affordant statement is her partner in dialogue, Mrs. Grose—but also the reader.

The scene, which transpires across the gap between one chapter and another, switches between at least two temporal planes and two narrative levels (one diegetic, the other extradiegetic): "as the two sides of a coin," to use the phrasing HJ employs in the preface to *The Golden Bowl*.[77] The moment, existing in the plot and also in a readerly space, is uncanny, to be sure, but also fascinating, complex, and ingenious: as Walter Benn Michaels has noted, *The Turn of the Screw* turns on "the emphatic suspension of the ordinary rules" of story operation.[78] The story, as generations of readers are aware, plays with us—and reciprocally, invites us to play with it.

The Turn of the Screw and the Philosophical Toy

The discussion of the scene by the lake to this point has emphasized formal elements. We can also make sense of *The Turn of the Screw* in terms of optics as well as play—two zones of experience that are twined together in the figure of the philosophical toy. This sort of device ranged from the familiar kaleidoscope and stereoscope to the less well known kaleidophone (which made sound waves visible via a vibrating wand) and chronoscope (essentially a stopwatch).[79] In 1827 the inventor Charles Wheatstone praised philosophical toys in these terms: "The application of the principles of science to ornamental and amusing purposes contributes, in a greater degree, to render them extensively popular; for the exhibition of striking experiments induces the observer to investigate their causes with additional interest, and enables him more permanently to remember their effects."[80] Nicholas Wade has described the widespread popularity of these simple devices that instruct and entice: "Philosophical instruments and toys not only advanced visual science, but also engaged a wider public in the phenomena that were displayed, and influenced the ways in which artists represented space and time."[81]

The Retinal Afterimage

The twining together of philosophy and amusement, and of science and art, is made manifest in John Ayrton Paris's *Philosophy in Sport Made Science in Earnest! Being an Attempt to Illustrate the First Principles of Natural Philosophy* (1827). Each chapter treats a selection of devices, which include compasses, magnets, looking glasses, rockets, magic lanterns, fireworks, swings, pinwheels, tops, kites, hoops, shuttlecocks, arrows, ear trumpets, and more. Cast as a novel, the narrative of *Philosophy in Sport* has striking similarities to *The Turn of the Screw*. A schoolboy named Tom arrives home to his family's English estate for summer recess. Having received high marks from his master, Tom claims the prize his father promised: a summer of scientific play on the grounds of Overton Lodge. Like Bly, the estate includes an English great house, a sloping lawn, and meandering paths; these are dotted with busts of philosophers and poets. Tom's quirky father turns his son's "mid-summer holidays" into an exploration of scientific and optical principles through "the philosophy of toys."[82] Tom's little sister, Louisa, joins in for the play-centered tutorials.

A half century before Dewey, the paternal character Mr. Seymour describes the educational adventure he and the children will embark on at Overton: "I have long thought that all the first principles of natural philosophy might be easily taught, and beautifully illustrated, by the common toys which have been invented for the amusement of youth" (13). Seymour deconstructs the play/schoolwork dichotomy, stating that children put more effort, discipline, and thought "in carrying into effect their holiday schemes" (19). He jokes that his approach will repurpose the traditional tools used for schoolroom discipline: "Imagine not, however, that I shall recommend the dismissal of the cane, or the whip . . . but the method of applying them will be changed; with the one I shall construct the bow of the kite, with the other I shall spin the top" (vii). As Daniel Brown writes, "All the adult characters [in *Philosophy in Sport*] provide commentaries on the experiments and children's play, which they draw principally from classical sources, but also canonical British literature and history."[83]

Paris, the author of *Philosophy in Sport*, had another claim to fame: he also invented the thaumatrope in 1824 and published the book partly as a way to publicize the new optical toy (Brown, 33). As Mr. Seymour explains to his children, the thaumatrope—or *wonder-turner*—consists of a "a pasteboard circle" to which "two strings were fastened in its axis, by which the card could easily be made to revolve, by means of the thumb and finger" (340). The toy comes with operating instructions and an explanation, which the character Mr. Seymour reads aloud:

"This philosophical toy is founded upon the well-known optical principle, that an impression, made on the retina of the eye, lasts for a short interval, after the object which produced it has been withdrawn. During the rapid whirling of the card, the figures on each of its sides are presented with such quick transition, that they both appear at the same instant, and thus occasion a very striking and magical effect" (340). Exploiting persistence of vision, in which a *positive afterimage* of an object lingers briefly, the two sides of the rapidly spinning cards fuse in the operator's visual field. If there is the drawing of a cage on one side and of a bird on the other, a third image of bird-in-cage appears when the card is spun quickly at just the right distance from the operator's eyes.[84]

Paris's book was updated and republished by Robert Routledge in 1877. The chapter on the thaumatrope appears early in Routledge's narrative (rather than toward the end, in Paris's edition) and the later edition includes a new philosophical toy, the zoetrope. This device sits on a table and, when spun quickly, creates the effect of figures jumping or dancing. Whereas the thaumatrope creates a fused image for a single user, the zooetrope's moving images are visible to multiple viewers. After showing these toys to Tom and Louisa, Mr. Seymour explains the *negative* afterimage: "There is another very remarkable class of optical sensations which may persist for several minutes after the exciting objects are withdrawn" (63). The key is fixity of gaze: "If we direct our gaze for about thirty or forty seconds towards some brightly-coloured object, keeping the eyes steadily fixed upon one point, so that the images of the object remain during that period of time depicted upon the same parts of the retinae, we may, after the removal of the object, continue to see its shape with perfect distinctness for a longer or shorter interval" (63). With a negative afterimage, the object appears to change color and size, often looming ominously when a watcher shifts her gaze. Louisa exclaims, "That would be very much like seeing a ghost!" but observes, "I do not remember that anything of the kind you mention ever appeared to me" (63). The father says that while such "spectral forms" may appear spontaneously, they can also be *made* to show up "by a simple effort of will": "Keep your gaze riveted on a single point [and] you can at any time summon up these phantasmal forms" (64). The children proceed with the demonstration. They fix their gazes on "gilt ornaments" for a period of seconds then shift their eyes to the ceiling, where each sees the image reappear—"only they now appeared of a bluish color, and much darker than the ground" (64). *Retinal fatigue*, the father explains to the wondering children, causes the images to be magnified and appear in a complementary color, with gold and blue being transposed.[85] (A pathological version of the negative afterimage, in which small objects appear large or vice versa, is known today as "the Alice in Wonderland Disease," named by a neurologist named John Todd in 1955.)[86]

It's fun to consider *The Turn of the Screw* with these optical effects in mind. (This takes the light-spirited lead of HJ in the preface, who emphasizes that the story's "small strength" is that it's "least apt to be baited by *earnest* criticism" [emphasis added]).[87] Early on, the governess describes Flora with "her hair of gold and her frock of blue" (9), and in the scene by the lake, the governess recalls the "great and pleasant shade . . . suffused with the brightness of the hot, still hour" (28). In what sounds like the negative afterimage demonstration from *Philosophy in Sport*, the governess stares intently at Flora ("I held my breath while I waited") and then looks away, at the expanse of water. "After some seconds," she relates, . . . I again shifted my eyes—I faced what I had to face" (29) and (she reports later) saw a "woman in black . . . on the other side of the lake" (30). Later, in a separate encounter in the children's schoolroom, the governess describes the reverse process, how the image of the strange woman fades: "She was all before me; but even as I fixed and, for memory, secured it, the awful image passed away" (57). Ghost, or afterimage? These moments play with color and emphasize the evanescence of the image, with memory—like text—offering a way to "fix" the image.

This shift, from the register of vision to the register of text, is crucial. In the governess's phrasing, the first meaning of *fixed* is *sees*. As the sentence unwinds—"even as I fixed and, for memory, secured it"—we as readers may realize that "fixed" in the governess's statement might also mean *preserved* (not unlike the fixing bath in photographic development). But upon further reflection: "fixed" also means *corrects, edits,* or *touches up*. These two meanings—preserving and changing—are diametrically opposed. With irony and some humor, the word "fixed" is a miniature troping device, serving as a pivot for meanings that spiral off. Don Anderson points in this direction when he writes of HJ's "sober playfulness" in *The Ambassadors*, citing a moment where, by virtue of wordplay on *too* and *two*, "author and reader share a joke that is concealed—by the typography, as it were—from the characters."[88] In sum, the sentence about the governess fixing the image is highly affordant and delightfully *unfixed*. Readers who discern this enter a magic circle and share a playful moment of discovery with the witty and skilled author. The smile of the reader serves as a sort of secret handshake—though the circle of play is open to anyone sensible of (and not worried about) the divergent meanings.

Indeed, the repeated use of *fix* and *pupil* in *The Turn of the Screw* calls attention to the act of seeing *and* to the reflexive act of seeing oneself see—precisely the kind of introspection that was generating studies in psychology labs at the turn of the nineteenth century. This is the "spinning top" conundrum that WJ raised in *The Principles of Psychology*: "The attempt at introspective analysis in these cases is in fact like seizing a spinning top to catch its motion, or trying to turn up the gas quickly enough to see how the darkness looks."[89] Like jokes in the hands of AJ, puns for HJ produce a semiotic flicker effect, creating a sort of third image, that *almost* lets us grasp the top's motion or see the darkness. The terms *fixed* and *fix* appear nineteen times in *The Turn of the Screw*, and *pupils* appears twenty times (by contrast, the singular *pupil* appears just twice). Pupils can refer to students, or to the centers of the eye where the optic nerve connects to the cornea. These two statements by the governess—that the she passed her days "in constant sight of my pupils" (36) and that "I kept my pupils in sight" (43)—are on the one hand unambiguous: she and her students stay close together. These phrasings, however, create an absurd pun, if we take "pupil" optically, to mean the dark center of the iris. How can one see *through* one's eyes and also see oneself seeing? A mirror—or another person's face (as when Mrs. Grose's face gives the governess a "slow reflexion" of her own visage)—shows only the outside, not the introspective experience of seeing (30).

Like a child's riddle, *pupil* harbors its own answer. Anatomically, every human eye has a blind spot in the visual field, called the optic disk, where the optic nerve connects: "The blind spot can be difficult to detect subjectively because of the ability of the brain to 'fill in' or ignore the missing portion of the image."[90] The pun on *pupils* marks textually both the concept of seeing and the concept of the blind spot; the trope is brought to the surface, is made thematic, when the governess wonders if "my pupils practised upon me" (38) and when she refers to "the secret of my pupils" (50). She explicitly wonders whether her eyes are playing tricks on her. Reading childishly for puns, one can discern that the governess's use of *pupils*, like the text's variants on *fixing*, slyly point to the concept of blind spot: that which can't be seen directly.

To become aware of our blind spot, we need a device or technique. These can be quite humble; for instance, as many children learn, if you close one eye and pass a finger across your field of vision, part of it appears, for a split second, to disappear. This weird, momentary erasure is the manifestation of the blind spot. But there are even more ingenious (and fun) ways to see how we see. As Mr. Seymour makes clear to his students, philosophical toys are devices that exploit the anatomy of vision in human beings—binocularity, persistence of vision, apertures for optic nerves, and retinal fatigue—to make us obliquely aware of our embodied seeing selves. *The Turn of the Screw* does the same.

Creepy Christmas Playthings

HJ in the preface recalls that *The Turn of the Screw* was a holiday commission: "I was asked for something seasonable by the promoters of a periodical dealing in the time-honoured Christmas-tide toy."[91] This explanation aligns with the frame narrative: a holiday gathering in which acquaintances, presumably brought together for a week-long house party, gathered around a fire for entertainment. (In fact, the novella appeared serially in *Collier's Weekly after* the holiday season, from January through April 1898.) Upon its publication, Henry describes the story as one of his "small inventions."[92]

For Victorians, the night before Christmas was the heart of the more secular, convivial part of the holiday, involving gifts, parlor games, and skits. More pious duties, such as attendance at church or the giving of alms to the poor and less fortunate, were by contrast largely reserved for Christmas Day. At holiday time each year, the Royal Polytechnic theater featured magic lantern shows "based on traditional stories such as *Robinson Crusoe*, Bluebeard, *Alice in Wonderland*, and, especially at Christmastime, the stories of Charles Dickens."[93] This list overlaps with HJ's "familiars" in the preface, "*Cinderella* and *Blue-Beard* and *Hop o' my Thumb* and *Little Red Riding Hood*."[94] Indeed, Victorians originated the association of the December holiday with entertainment, consumerism, and shopping. By the 1890s, periodicals of all stripes geared up to describe and advertise Christmas gifts for children.

HJ, in the preface to volume 12 of the New York Edition, teasingly emphasizes the link between story and plaything by calling it an "*amusette*."[95] Most critics seem to think this French term refers to a trifle, but the term has an alternate, opposing meaning that hides in plain sight: an amusette is a gun mounted on a swivel.[96] The twining together of amusement and violence captures a key aspect of play—and of *The Screw*. A delightful surprise can shade into shock; the giggles of a friendly tickle may tip into cries of dismay; or the pleasure of repetition may deflate into indifference. Play theorist Scott Eberle seeks to capture this dynamic, using the figure of a spiral to portray six core affects that characterize play, along with the aversive feelings that arise when amusement intensifies beyond the pleasurable: "Imagine play as a spinning galaxy or a pyrotechnic pinwheel spiraling head-on in your direction. The elements—anticipation, surprise, pleasure, understanding, strength, and poise—hug the center of rotation closely. But also picture an imaginary line swirling from each of the elements as a scale that slides into its opposite."[97] Eberle provides a chart (Figure 6)

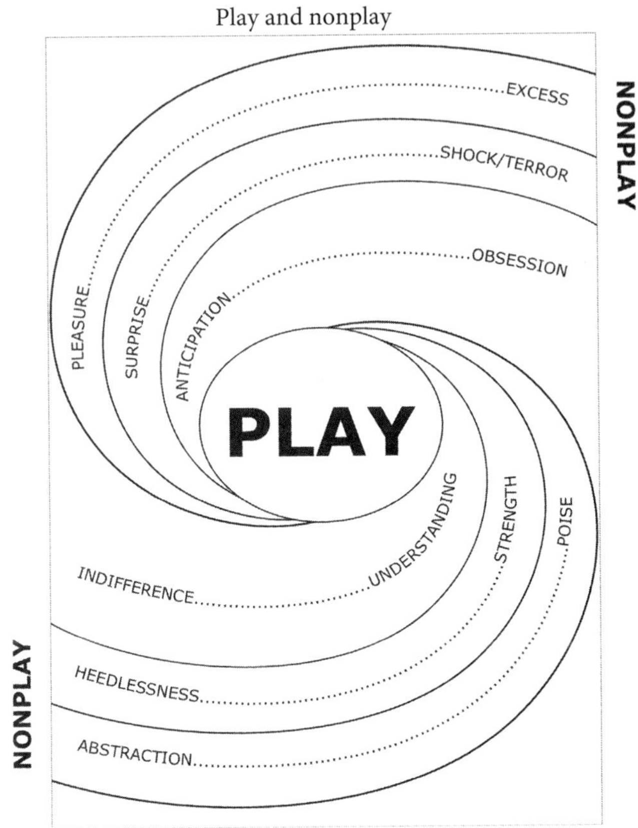

Figure 6. The delightful, life-affirming elements of play may—if the experience becomes too extreme—spiral into aversive, sometimes excruciating forms, as when *surprise* intensifies into shock/terror. Reprinted with permission of The Strong®.

that designates the aversive experience as "nonplay," showing how strength (for instance) can give way to heedlessness.

The chart is suggestive for thinking about the "gun" that is hidden in the French term "amusette." Amusement for HJ by no means forestalls qualities more serious, even foreboding: as he notes, the fluidity of creative play—he calls it "improvisation" in the preface—mobilizes exceedingly strong forces: "Then the waters [of invention] may spread indeed, gathering houses and herds and crops and cities into their arms and wrenching off, for our amusement, the whole face of the land" (172). The odd personification of flood waters as something with dangerous "arms" resonates with the figure of Ida Farange, the fierce game player who is also Maisie's mother: "The sole flaw in Ida's beauty was a length and reach of arm conducive perhaps to her having so often beaten her ex-husband at billiards, a game in which she showed a superiority largely accountable, as she maintained, for the resentment finding expression in his physical violence" (*Maisie*, 37–38). The sentence's alignment of Ida beating her ex in a game and his physically beating her to (in a sense) *even the score* is unsettling in its incongruous escalation: the equation that is not equal emphasizes that the world of play is always embedded in real social relations and inequities. "Play is 'tense,'" Huizinga affirms, pointing up "the deep-seated affinity between playing and battle."[98] In the context of a custody battle, HJ was aware of the exquisite balancing act necessary to keep the character Maisie—and thus the novel—in the realm of the delightful rather than the despicable.

Yet the precarity of positive affects shading into negative ones is part of the pleasure of play, as WJ observed in his critique of the anemic sports at Chautauqua (see Chapter 2). Victorian toy makers were similarly aware. Toys in the 1890s were often infernal little gadgets equipped with the capacity to cross over into a darker zone. The "creeping baby doll" patented in 1871 placed a realistic papier-mâché head on a metal torso equipped with sprockets and screws to monstrous effect; a doll-sized butcher shop came equipped with tiny carcasses hanging from miniature meat hooks; and bird-driven automata encased living birds inside to power the toys' movements.[99] There is a potent analogy to be made between HJ's pedagogical tales and the new-fangled toys that were entering the Victorian market in the 1890s: both were calibrated for amusement but, if tightly enough wound, were capable of entering the nonplay territory characterized by terror.

Examining the Parts of the Device

If *The Turn of the Screw* is akin to a philosophical toy, it is worth taking a moment to itemize the different parts that compose the device. First, there is the frame narrative: this is what begins on Christmas Eve and ends on or about New Year's Eve, and is set in an old house in an unspecified but presumably English location. Second, there is the governess's narrative, which forms the bulk of the story. The conceit is that this narrative is orally delivered, over a series of nights, by a man at the holiday gathering named Douglas. We learn from the unnamed narrator of the frame narrative that after hearing the governess's narrative read aloud, he later copied it down, word for word. Third, there is the preface, published in 1908, a decade after *The Turn of the Screw* first appeared.

On its face, the diegetic chronology of the story is surprisingly simple: beginning on Christmas Eve and concluding a few days later, Douglas first promises to read a story and then does so.[100] But when all the narrative parts are put in motion by the action of the reader—the frame, the governess's story, the preface—the mechanism of *The Turn of the Screw* proves to be artful and ambivalent, "now more complex," just like the mechanical toys of the 1890s. With respect to the frame narrative: at the outset of *The Turn of the Screw*, the holiday gathering consists of adults only (perhaps any children have gone to bed?), though the topic at hand is children: "The story had held us, round the fire, sufficiently breathless, but except the obvious remark that it was gruesome, as on Christmas Eve in an old house a strange tale should essentially be, I remember no comment uttered till somebody happened to note it as the only case he had met in which such a visitation had fallen on a child" (1). In lieu of actual children, attention turns to children as the object of nefarious nighttime visitors. The evening proceeds in this way, priming at once the holiday audience and HJ's readers, as different storytellers take turns spinning yarns by the fireside. The subject of children is set aside, however, and the narrator notes that "some one else told a story not particularly effective" (1).

With the introduction of this judgment—*not effective*—the gauntlet is thrown down. As others offer their stories, the character named Douglas, one of the audience, seems restless, capturing the attention of the unnamed narrator. Douglas, presumably, has a story that *is* "effective," and indeed the tale that he reads to the group a few nights later is the core text of *The Turn of the Screw*. The framing narrative thus has the effect of setting the stage: insofar as the tale Douglas presented to the diegetic audience—those sitting before the fire—is effective, so too will the self-same tale presented to the extra-diegetic audience, that is, readers of HJ's story.

The story is the same, but is the experience? The members of both audiences, those inside the story (characters) and those outside the story (readers) literally receive the same narrative. Felman emphasizes the "blurring of the very difference between inside and outside."[101] The occasion is clearly different, however: the inside or diegetic audience *hears* the story rather than reading it on a page. The inside audience, one imagines, has a shared sensory experience: by a fire on Christmas Eve (replete with smells, sounds, sights, warmth), with a group of companions (murmuring, rustling, reacting), listening to oral delivery (inflected by tone of voice, pacing, delivery, gesture). The difference in audience experience could be likened to the difference between being at a theater for a production and reading the script at home alone in an armchair.

There is another key difference in the experience of what I (following Felman and others) am calling the "inside" and the "outside" audience of the governess's story. The inside audience gets the story in pieces over a few days' time; the outside audience can read it in a single sitting. But, once again, there are rough analogies. In *The Turn of the Screw* the interested yet frustrated members of the diegetic audience must exercise patience, insofar as they are forced to wait a few days for the leather album containing the story written in the governess's hand to arrive. Similarly, historical readers of the *Collier's* serialization of the story had to wait for installments. Even once *The Turn of the Screw* is published in full (in *The Two Magics*, in the fall of 1898), the interested but frustrated extra-diegetic audience must also exercise patience to make sense of the temporal delays written into the conveying of the story: the nested set of time periods and removes, as well as a byzantine twisting of recollections and transcriptions. So the two audiences are neither completely dissociated nor identical in their positions vis-à-vis receiving the story. The fictional and actual audiences, in short, have experiences that are similar but slightly discrepant.

The story's frame thus produces what Felman calls a "cleft" (123), or what I am calling a set of discrepancies, each of which indexes a significant temporal lag. There are more discrepancies that also have a material analogue. Though presumably identical, there are two paper copies of the governess's narrative: the one possessed by Douglas (the red album "written . . . in old faded ink and in the most beautiful hand" [*Screw*, 2]) and the one that the unnamed narrator later transcribes. There are two media for the exact same tale, the (visual) written text and the (auditory) oral one. There are two figures in the frame presenting the story, Douglas and the unnamed narrator. The frame's cleaving between talk and text, and between two speakers, is captured in the odd ekphrastic comment that forms the last sentence of the frame narrative: "Douglas, without heeding me, had begun to read with a fine clearness that was *like a rendering to the ear of the beauty of his author's hand*" (6, emphasis added).[102] The twinned discrepancies in the frame, moreover, prepare the reader to note that the first-person governess's telling is similarly cleft: the older woman narrates the story (backward), and the younger woman lives it forward. Subtle reminders of this cleft are tucked into the governess's telling at various moments. Early on, for instance, the governess directs attention to two distinct moments of seeing: "I have not seen Bly since the day I left it, and I daresay that to my older and more informed eyes it would not appear sufficiently contracted" (9). Toward the narrative's end she confesses that original blurriness may be supplanted by retrospective clarity: "I suppose I now read into our situation a clearness it couldn't have had at the time" (81).

By winding in spans of time, instances of transcription, and multiple tellers, the frame provides operating instructions for how to engage the "device" that is the text. The term "device" is not an arbitrary trope but is offered by HJ when he writes that the tale "is a piece of ingenuity pure and simple, of cold artistic calculation" (172). The frame offers a sort of handle: in my terms, it "turns" the story, winds it up (as it were) for the reader to set it in motion. (The preface stresses that such movements are precisely the point: the story is "an anecdote amplified and highly emphasised and returning upon itself," while "the artistic value of such an experiment be measured by the intellectual echoes it may again, long after, set in motion.")[103] The "inside" audience is explicitly instructed about the engineering principles that structure the mechanism, through a catechism between Douglas and the group that emulates in ludic form classroom instruction:

> "If the child gives the effect another turn of the screw, what do you say to *two* children—?"
>
> "We say, of course," somebody exclaimed, "that they give two turns! Also that we want to hear about them." (1)

Felman argues that the metaphor here is "not mathematizable," and that "Douglas's question is a rhetorical one—an affirmation which in truth does not ask nor call for an answer" (183n.). But this overly sedulous reading misses the point. Crossing conceptual registers, Douglas's query doubles as a joke, with the audience supplying the punch line. For a reader to join the "we"—"we want to hear about them"—affirms *gameness.* It's more like a call-and-response before a match ("Who's going to win?"; "*We're* going to win!!"). J. L. Austin, in *How to Do Things with Words*, gives "I do" (in a wedding vow) as a model performative statement.[104] HJ in *The Turn of the Screw* invites readers to join the game voluntarily, to give consent with enthusiasm (and, contra Austin, without enlisting the authority of the state): to affirm, in essence, "It's my turn!" The governess's later exclamation in the text that "'it's a game'" (47) doubles down on the "diction and tricks" of the frame narrative (see my Introduction in this book). The frame playfully establishes that nothing is singular, not least seeing: vision itself, we are reminded, entails a turning spiral of visual perception and cognition that is situated (like all of human existence) in time.

Reading with the Thaumatrope in Mind

By crossing our eyes, we can make a single object—our coffee mug, say—appear double. HJ in the preface plays with the idea of double vision as a temporal process: seeing now, seeing then. He meditates on the experience of reading back over the stories in volume 12 of the New York Edition. As with his other prefaces, this one begins with the subjective feelings—the "pang of exile" and "nostalgic twinge"—that attend the author's reacquaintance with works that are now "at a distance."[105] As Graham Good has written, HJ's prefaces (and his essays more generally) are as much acts of reminiscence as they are works of criticism: "Previous readings, and their accompanying feelings, are inscribed in the work, so that to re-read is to re-experience an earlier self."[106] HJ acknowledges that, as an author, his "backward vision" entails a discrepancy, between two time periods (the past and the present) and between two points of view that similarly fail to correspond (that of the younger HJ—the writer—and that of the older HJ—the critic).[107]

The Optics of Seeing Double (Without Blurred Vision)

For HJ, editing is a recursive process of seeing (and feeling) his way back into the original composition. In this way, the collected stories offer a portal for a mode of perception that he aptly, oxymoronically, calls a "present revisiting."[108] AJ describes an old desk filled with letters from her deceased parents as provoking just such a revisiting (see Chapter 1). HJ marks the distance between past (which can feel too far away) and present (which can feel too near): "We are divided of course between liking to feel the past strange and liking to feel it familiar, the difficulty is, for intensity, to catch it at the moment when the scales of the balance hang with the right evenness."[109] This balance is partly a matter of proximity, of focusing on something neither too near nor too far away. "I delight," he writes, "in a palpable imaginable *visitable* past—in the nearer distances and the clearer mysteries, the marks and signs of a world we may reach over to as by making a long arm we grasp an object at the other end of our own table" (*Aspern*, x). But the figure of the balance scale, like that of the object at a middle distance, suggests also the visual equipoise necessary for clarity of binocular sight. Without some calibration, HJ's experiments in "backward vision" are askew and "almost reduce at first to a mere blurred, sad, scarcely consolable vision this present revisiting, re-appropriating impulse" (vi).

The issue of blurring with respect to vision is crucial to the parting of ways between physiology (the mechanics of seeing) and psychology (the mental acts that accompany sight). Wittgenstein addresses the question of how human beings bring two diverse images into clarity and depth. Binocular sight involves a complex calibration that includes particular acts of consciousness. It's not as if one could take the image that appears to the right eye and the image that appears to the left eye and overlay them to achieve visual clarity: "It is anything but a matter of course that we see 'three-dimensionally' with two eyes. If the two visual images were fused, one might expect a blurred image as a result."[110] Human vision crucially enlists particular aspects of the mind, not just the cornea and the optic nerve.

At the turn of the twentieth century, cinema provided the occasion for new understandings of human perception. Münsterberg, in his book *The Film: A Psychological Study* (also known as *The Photoplay*), writes that mental acts—"the processes of perception, attention, interest, memory, imagination, suggestion, and emotion" (58)—are essential to our capacity to see. Münsterberg's book is the first thorough exploration of the aesthetics of early film in light of psychological research. In it, the psychologist invokes the earlier experiments by Étienne Jules Marey. In a nonviolent version of an amusette (a swiveling gun), Marey used a photographic gun with a revolving, photosensitive cylinder to shoot twelve images per second in wheel form; when developed, the circularly arranged images could be placed in a device (Marey used a zoetrope) and spun. When positioned at the proper distance from the viewer's eye and turned at the proper speed, the images gave the effect of movement: a pole vaulter arcing through the air, a pigeon taking flight, a dancer twirling. The key for this optical effect, to prevent the blurring together of images, was to present each image in a frame as a brief flash followed by darkness: "The time of the exposure through the opening in the revolving shutter had to be extremely short in order to give distinct pictures. The slightest lengthening would make the movement of the film itself visible and produce a blurring effect. This time was sufficient for the seeing of the picture.... Hence it became essential to transform the continuous movement of the film into an intermittent one" (7). Münsterberg notes that including interruptions, rather than posing a problem for perceiving dynamic motion, was the great innovation that made possible cinematic seeing. The special sort of artificial seeing that allowed human beings to perceive motion—to experience change directly—depended on serial images strung together with enabling gaps.

We can hear in HJ's winces and pangs, and in his desire to grasp an object as with his hand, a sense of the corporeal components of "backward vision."

What HJ describes as his authorial problem of revision Jonathan Crary attributes to a nineteenth-century transformation in the nature of seeing as such, which, he argues, is increasingly concerned with "physiological status of the observer and of vision."[111] Here is Crary: "As observation is increasingly tied to the body in the early nineteenth century, temporality and vision become inseparable. The shifting processes of one's own subjectivity experienced in time became synonymous with the act of seeing, dissolving the Cartesian ideal of an observer completely focused on an object" (98). In Crary's account, "perception and cognition" are "essentially temporal processes dependent upon a dynamic amalgamation of past and present" (98). Vision in this account is not analogous to a photograph, which captures a single moment in time. Seeing for Crary has an element of the duplicate and the duplicitous: for what is the single position from which one could possibly obtain an objective view? "A dynamic amalgamation of past and present" describes what would, in a Cartesian world, appear to be impossible, for how is one to occupy two different time periods in a single moment? For Crary, a particular media technology offers an (ominous) solution: the stereograph, in which two similarly but slightly discrepant images are put into a viewing device that a viewer can look into. The two images activate human binocular vision, giving the passive viewer the *appearance* of depth but without the reality. Stereographic depth is a trick of the eye, and there is no "there" there (to invoke Gertrude Stein's famous phrase).

For Crary, this capacity to "overcome" spatial discrepancy through technological trickery applies equally to temporal discrepancy: because of the mediations of memory, we always see the past darkly, through the scrim of the present. He argues that this dislocation of vision from its objects heralds the modern reign of the psychological and the subjective, in which the past lingers on in consciousness.

Vision itself, for Crary, becomes a form of hallucination, "a vision that did not represent or refer to objects in the world" (141). In the stereoscope, in particular, Crary sees the early workings of a world dominated by images owned and organized by corporate media giants that use human beings as their tools.

The Stereoscope Versus the Wonder-Turner

Recall that we were discussing *The Turn of the Screw* and HJ's act of "backward vision" in the preface, as he sought to align his viewpoint in the present with his perspective in the past. Tom Gunning describes a similar dilemma but offers a solution very different from Crary's: *how could one see both sides of a single coin at the same time?*[112] This playful conundrum had its roots in a jovial if high-powered dinner table conversation involving Charles Babbage (a mathematician credited with developing an early version of a computer) and John Herschel (an astronomer who also experimented with photography). Herschel posed the question about the coin, which Babbage promptly solved: "I took out of my pocket a shilling, and holding it up before the looking-glass, pointed out *my* method."[113] This solution, Herschel said, was too cheap: akin to holding a stereoscope slide (not in the device) and seeing the two pictures side by side. Herschel replied, "'That won't do'; then spinning my shilling upon the table, he pointed out *his* method of seeing both sides at once" (189). Babbage tells a friend, who, he relates, "brought me a beautiful illustration of the principle. It consisted of a round disc or card suspended between the two pieces of sewing-silk. These threads being held between the finger and thumb of each hand, were then made to turn quickly, when the disc of card, of course, revolved also. Upon one side of this disc of card was painted a bird; upon the other side, an empty bird-cage. On turning the thread rapidly, the bird appeared to have got inside the cage" (189). Babbage of course is describing Paris's thaumatrope, or wonder-turner. The person manipulating the strings to spin the disc had the experience of seeing both sides at once. Gunning notes, "Rapidly successive images seem to fuse in time" (499), for an effect he calls *flicker-fusion*.

For Gunning, the thaumatrope as a device is crucially different from the stereoscope. The stereoscope, which fixes the viewer's gaze with a masklike apparatus, renders the viewer passive as it gives the uncanny impression of depth to a two-dimensional image. The wonder-turner, in contrast, enlists core elements of play, by virtue of being situated, embodied, spontaneous, and fun. It is also instructive. "The lessons offered by the thaumatrope," Gunning explains, "depended on the manipulator not only being in control of the device, but also being able to examine its elements both in motion and stillness. Anyone could see that each side of the disk presented only one element of the composite image produced by spinning. Thus, in contrast to the traditional magic trick, whose illusion remains mysterious because the secret is kept close by the prestidigitator, the philosophical toy is a tool of demonstration and demystification. The illusion could be both produced and deconstructed by the child who operated the device, once instructed by a knowledgeable adult" (503). The thaumatrope puts the pleasure and the instruction in the player's hands. Spinning a thaumatrope is social, too, inviting cross-generational play.

In the preface to *The Turn of the Screw* HJ employs the language of the thaumatrope. He describes an idea that "flickers," offering "bare facts of intimation" that the author must "turn"—that is, both shape (in the sense of create) and set in motion (that is, spin). His conception "flickered so for a moment and then, as a light, to my great relief, quite went out. It had flickered indeed but at the best—yet had flickered enough to give me my 'facts,' bare facts of intimation; which, scant handful though they were, were more distinct and more numerous than I mostly *like* facts: like them, that is, as we say of an etcher's progressive subject, in an early 'state.' Nine tenths of the artist's interest in them is that of what he shall add to them and *how he shall turn them*" (*Aspern*, ix, emphasis added). HJ, emphasizing *turning*, innovates on the art of "spinning a tale." While the centrality of the eye places emphasis on visual perception (the impingement of light from without), the involvement of *hands* (in the turning) figure agency and artistic control.

HJ lodges the imaginative source for the story in the object world, precisely at child level. The idea for *The Turn of the Screw* is a "germ"—and since it is "gleaming" in the dust, one might imagine this germ to be a *coin*, à la Babbage and Herschel. It is explicitly a thing that must be handled:

> Such was the private source of *The Turn of the Screw*; and I wondered, I confess, why so fine a germ, gleaming there in the wayside dust of life, had never been deftly picked up. The thing had for me the immense merit of allowing the imagination absolute freedom of hand, of inviting it to act on a perfectly clear field. . . . I find here a perfect example of an exercise of the imagination unassisted, unassociated—playing the game, making the score, in the phrase of our sporting day, off its own bat. To what degree the game was worth playing I needn't attempt to say: the exercise I have noted strikes me now, I confess, as the interesting thing, the imaginative faculty acting with the whole of the case on its hands. (*Screw*, 124)

As HJ describes it, the point is to get the game going; it is an "exercise": meaning a sport, educational activity, or test. The playing field is clear: "the imaginative faculty" is possessed by the author, and also by other players—that is, readers.

A fair question is this: how does reading with philosophical toys in mind pertain to central questions about *The Turn of the Screw*? Critics often note that there are two sorts of readers of *The Turn of the Screw*: those who read it as a ghost story—about a woman who sees apparitions—and those who read it as a psychological thriller—about a woman who *thinks* she sees apparitions.[114] Following the critic Edmund Wilson's diagnosis (in an essay first published during the Freud-influenced 1930s) of the narrating governess as hysterical and most likely sexually repressed, the "ghost story readers" have been referred to as naïve, literal-minded, or *unsuspicious*; whereas the "psychological thriller readers" have been described as skeptical, metaphorically minded, or *suspicious*.[115] One object of analysis, two ways of looking at it, with readers sifting into distinct camps. To see one way is to have the other way unavailable—not unlike trying to see both sides of a coin, at once.

With the thaumatrope in mind, we are in a better position to see how HJ distinguishes between the different sorts of readers. Those who are "unsuspicious" read the frame not as operating instructions but as a précis: they know in advance that they are reading a tale of ghosts appearing to two children. It's as if they perceive a thaumatropic image (bird-in-cage) without awareness of their part in making the two images fuse into one. I call this reading *monoscopically*. A monoscopic reading of *Screw* as a ghost story is neither right nor wrong; rather, it is akin to listening to music in mono rather than stereo, a decidedly less rich experience. The text, however, urges the full thaumatropic experience: having the pleasure of the strange though recognizable image hovering mid-air, *and* the delight of slowing it down, speeding it up, and even stopping the motion altogether to discuss puzzling it through.

The governess herself models both sorts of seeing. Her first sighting of a man in a tower is monoscopic, even static: "The gold was still in the sky, the clearness in the air, and the man who looked at me over the battlements was as definite as a picture in a frame" (16). But this "definite" image is preceded by a different kind of image, an explicitly internal imagination on the part of the governess of a "handsome face" seeing and approving of her. Moreover, the "definite" image is then followed by a series of discrepant images as the governess does a quick "differential diagnosis" of who she is looking at: "I thought, with extraordinary quickness, of each person he might have been and that he wasn't" (16). The narrating governess, looking back on her naïve youthful experience, slows down and even stops the thaumatrope. She presents what she sees and deconstructs the act of seeing. She doesn't adjudicate between them or "fuse" them: she presents both seeings, and in her so doing the cursory reader may stick with the first "definite" two-dimensional (painting in frame) image, while the attentive reader takes into account the whole complex, iterative, differential act of seeing. The discrepancy is experienced affectively, as ambiguity, uncertainty, doubt: a tickling of the mind and a rumbling of the uncanny.

The Method of Demonstration

This first crucial instance of seeing a ghost in *The Turn of the Screw* offers a demonstration of the complexity of quick acts of recognition. Daniel Kahneman, in *Thinking, Fast and Slow* (2011), writes that such acts don't arise in a vacuum but are usually warranted responses to a situation that has "provided a cue."[116] Such "cues" prime those familiar with them, establishing a playing field on which the mind can operate. Kahneman describes how such cues work: "We are not surprised when a two-year-old looks at a dog and says 'doggie!' because we are used to the miracle of children learning to recognize and name things. [. . .] The miracles of expert intuition have the same character. Valid intuitions develop when experts have learned to recognize familiar elements in a new situation and act in a manner that is appropriate to it. Good intuitive judgments come to mind with the same immediacy as 'doggie!'" (11–12). In the context of literary study, genre serves as a cue, alerting readers to exercise their intuition in particular ways. Kahneman states that demonstrations are particularly powerful when studying human affects and intuitions. While skeptics could always discount the findings of experiments by questioning the judgments of the persons involved (both experimental subjects and researchers), "the use of demonstrations provided scholars from diverse disciplines—notably philosophers and economists—an unusual opportunity to observe possible flaws in their own thinking. Having seen themselves fail, they became more likely to question the dogmatic assumption, prevalent at the time, that the human mind is rational and logical. The choice of method was crucial" (9). Kahneman gives this further rationale for working in vivo with demonstration rather than in vitro with experimentation: "We preferred demonstrations because they were more fun" (9). Amusement, he goes on to argue, is not epiphenomenal to the experience of intuition, but—insofar as perceptions of pleasure and pain play such a role in human belief and cognition—an essential part of it.

Spinning a thaumatrope models a form of demonstration. The spinning card invites, exploits, and makes visible the interaction of mind-body-world. To use Donna Haraway's term, the device cultivates "fingery eyes."[117] *The Turn of the Screw* thematically and formally emulates a toy, by delighting and also by lighting up materially how it works. When the governess shares her vision with

Mrs. Grose, she describes the older woman handling the information: Mrs. Grose "visibly turned things over" (48) as she considered the "deep design" (47) the governess presented. The governess, in turn, acknowledges Mrs. Grose's cognitive efforts, when she refers to "the fine machinery I had set in motion" (48). (Here again is HJ, winking at the reader who can see that the governess has also set in motion the "machinery" of the story's plot, of which he is the designer.)

Even as she desperately tries to get Mrs. Grose to see her point of view, the governess does the exact opposite with the children for much of the tale: she tries to *avoid* having them see, thereby short-circuiting the highly educational process of demonstration. When anything interesting or important comes up, the governess diverts and deflects: "We were perpetually coming into sight of subjects before which we must stop short, turning suddenly out of alleys that we perceived to be blind" (49). (Recall Maisie's bemusement when Miss Overmore promises to introduce her to "subjects.") Keeping the children "lost in their fairytale" (46) and offering herself as a "screen" (a two-dimensional surface), the governess tries to enforce monoscopic seeing on the part of the children. Meanwhile her own role develops into that of a principal investigator; using the language of experiment, she takes her pupils as her object of study. "I began to watch them in a stifled suspense, a disguised tension" (27), she affirms, seeking "proofs" (27), awaiting "evidence" (34), evaluating "specimens" (36). She believes her study to be *blind*, a process in research in which the research design is actively concealed from key participants. The governess persists in (the fruitless endeavor of) keeping the children unaware, offering other topics and indeed herself as amusements: "There were things enough, taking one with another, to chatter about, if one went very fast and knew by instinct when to go round" (49). The trio's days go round and round, "almost automatically through the very same movements" (52). Not surprisingly, the children are aware of this truncated, monoscopic education; Miles is explicit in stating, "[I know] not half I want to!" and "I want to see more life" (54).

The story demonstrates, moreover, that the children have a design of their own. The endless frivolity and enforced tranquillity provoke the children to disrupt the cycle of bland amusement, to turn the tables and put the governess "to the test" (26). *Philosophy in Sport* is instructive here, with Mr. Seymour explaining that "play and work, amusement and instruction, toys and tasks, are commonly . . . employed as terms of contrast and opposition—the prevalent notion being that all instruction must necessarily be attended with a painful sense of mental effort, while amusement is characterized by the absence of intellectual exertion. But it may be noticed that a child is sometimes miserable in a room full of playthings, and will often *break his toys*, not from a love of mischief, but for the pleasure he finds in acquiring a knowledge of their internal mechanism."[118] Miles and Flora break the routine at Bly, most dramatically by playing at running away. Running away, of course, is a beloved activity of young children, who may plan doing so for hours but who usually just take a few steps away from the house, sometimes merely hiding inside. Miles and Flora are no exceptions: Miles heads for the front lawn at night, and Flora (more dangerously) lights out for the lake. These small absences can be seen as toyings: to use Mr. Seymour's words, they are "breaks" (or breakouts) that manifest an interest in the governess's "internal mechanism," which she has been at pains to conceal. Each disappearance provokes in the governess what she herself calls an "outbreak," whether a flurry of conversation with Mrs. Grose ("my first outbreak," 33) or a moment of unchecked emotion with the children ("the little outbreaks of my sharper passion," 37). Her outbreaks, in turn, come under the evaluating gaze of both characters and readers. (Indeed, in the frame narrative both Douglas and the unnamed narrator use the term "outbreak" to characterize the story as a whole.) Running away is thus not just mischievous; it is a form of demonstration: a classic child's method of getting a rise out of a caregiver.

What I am calling the children's "demonstrations," while familiar, have complex effects when woven into HJ's narrative. They reveal, exercise, and also help to catalyze a complex theory of mind. Theory of mind is the capacity to anticipate the actions or beliefs of another person; as Alison Gopnik has pointed out, theory of mind involves seeing double: having a hypothesis about another's perceptions or beliefs depends on "children's ability to keep track of their own first-person phenomenology."[119] So while the governess thinks the children are oblivious, we as readers know that they know their own minds precisely because they are adept at knowing the governess's. When the governess asks Miles why he and Flora conspired on a midnight outing he states simply, "In order that you should do this"—that is, "think me . . . *bad*" (45). As Michael Bérubé writes, "We try to read each other by look, posture, expression, gesture. And, to make things more complicated (and/or fun), we know this about each other, so we also try deliberately to produce certain readings in others by feigning certain looks, postures, expressions and gestures."[120] Such (apparent) departures from everyday life is in fact an ingenious method: for grasping motivations and understanding how things work in a baffling, complex, and affordant world.

Indeed, the governess herself tries out the children's strategy of demonstration, absenting herself from church without notice. She, however, is startled by how mildly the children respond when she turns up, as she "had so perfectly expected the return of the others to be marked by a demonstration" (57). The governess's attempt at generating an outbreak fails, revealing that—unlike the children—she has little insight into their minds. The demonstration in fact boomerangs: it further reveals how adept the children are at reading her (they asked Mrs. Grose to say nothing of the governess's absence) *and* shows how it's beyond the governess's capacity to attribute theory of mind to the children. The children's studied actions offer a "sudden revelation of a consciousness and a plan" (56), which the governess can only attribute to an exterior, malevolent agency. When she exclaims that "there are depths, depths!" (30), her statement is perfectly off the mark, insofar as the demonstration makes the unseen—the children's robust theory of mind—visible. Like a clever pun or riddle, the demonstration succeeds in "practically proving" (25) the young governess's incapacity to play along.

What to Do with the Screw

If we play with the device and attend to the dynamic interplay of the two time periods—the governess's two experiences—we experience the oscillations affectively as ambiguity, vertinginous happenings that refuse to resolve. Reading thaumatropically, in contrast, we spin together the two visions to create our own private theater, engaging in the low-stakes tension of how the apparitions appear to us. The experience of oscillation, of flipping between understandings, of (temporary) resting places, of instances of the uncanny: this is the nature of the play, as HJ's ingeniously affordant narrative device enlists our perceptions and interpretations. As with any toy, we can stop the spinning and arrest the play of ambiguity—this happens when we embark on a singular reading or interpretation. (Felman's article is so powerful because it's a multimodal, recursive interpretation that comes very close to miming the play of the tale itself.) Stopping the motion isn't a misuse of the story; just as it isn't a misuse of the thaumatrope to inspect both sides, independently, to understand how it works.

But, when the device isn't spinning, we can't see both stories at once: unless (to extend the thaumatropic dynamic) we hold the device in front of a mirror, in which case we look at "our" side, at the "other" side, and at ourselves looking. (Recall the philosophical discussion between Babbage and Herschel.) This last option, of looking at ourselves looking, is what, finally, I have been doing with HJ's story—allowing it to spin, then stopping the motion to inspect the two sides. It is the rare reader, today, who can occupy the position of reading

The Turn of the Screw as a full-on ghost story—in my experience, these tend to be younger readers. Professional readers (that is, literary scholars and English majors) are at this point true adults, less interested in playing with the story than stopping the play altogether and substituting a "shortcut" interpretation. Another approach is to take the device apart and admire its ingenuity—and go back to playing with it—so as to allow it to demonstrate our own arts of mind as we participate in the spinning of stories. My point is that looking at just one side or the other of a thaumatrope when it isn't spinning "stills" the experience.

The fun of the story, of course, is that it presents like a trick figure: a duck-rabbit or a Rubin's Vase Ambiguous Figure (invented by the Dutch psychologist Edgar John Rubin in 1915).[121] Rubin's experiments in perceptual psychology addressed how we see figure and ground, and the way that certain drawings could surprisingly (and delightfully) shift in a viewer's perception: from two faces in profile, nose-to-nose, to a sculptured vase. Rubin's experiments found that seeing a figure (as opposed to ground) was significantly more memorable to viewers; that the figure seemed closer than the ground (suggesting depth); and that viewers could be primed to see one or the other. Conflicting instructions, Rubin found, led to more variety with respect to *which* figure was seen by test subjects. Most important, viewers rarely get stuck seeing just one way: though it may take coaxing from someone who has "mastered" seeing both the vase and the faces, with time and effort one can succeed in seeing both.

HJ's story in essence takes the static ambiguous figure (vase/faces) and narrativizes it: prompting readers to move beyond the discrepant and therefore *opposite* interpretive options (ghost story OR psychological thriller) and instead to spin them together. The combination, taken thematically, affords a delightful possibility: that private apparitions (hallucinations) can exist in the public world (ghosts). (WJ in similar fashion suggested in *Varieties of Religious Experience* that perhaps a feature of "hysterics" is their capacity to see the "unseen"—acknowledging that "these clinical records sound like fairy-tales.")[122] Pericles Lewis calls such intermediate entities "shared fictions."[123] Simply put, we can both *have an experience* and *share that which occasioned it*, which results in a third thing hovering somehow between: a very real fictive thread of connection. Clever devices beg to be passed along so that others can enjoy the visions it conjures. *The Turn of the Screw* in this way works as a philosophical toy, an autotelic demonstration of the quirks and capacities of the dynamic, context- and time-bound human bodymind complex. Huizinga argues that this sort of play is "far from being merely imitative"; it is *methectic* rather than mimetic, a matter of the audience "helping out" with the creation.[124] "Whether sorcerer or sorcerized,"

Huizinga writes, "one is always knower and dupe at once"—with the crucial addendum: "But one chooses to be the dupe" (23).

My discussion of *The Turn of the Screw* would not be complete without acknowledging that, over the past century, literary critics have largely proved incapable of reading it "thaumatropically"—for the wonder of its turnings. Instead, they have by and large read the tale stereoscopically. The stereoscope has two crucial differences from the wonder-turner, however. First, rather than oscillating two images to achieve flicker-fusion, the stereoscope is static: the device produces a single image of uncanny depth and apparent three-dimensionality. Second, while the thaumatrope calls on a user's skill (to spin the card, at the right speed, at the right distance from the eyes) and thereby demystifies its operation, the stereoscope is used passively and mystifies its mechanism. (It's notable that this wildly popular device is not included in Routledge's edition of *Philosophy in Sport.*)

As we have heard, the stereoscope, for Crary, indexes the conscription of human vision itself to a new regime of power: "It is no coincidence that the stereoscope became increasingly synonymous with erotic and pornographic imagery . . . the very effects of tangibility that Wheatstone had sought from the beginning were quickly turned into a mass form of ocular possession . . . in part responsible for its social demise as a mode of visual consumption . . . it became linked with 'indecent' subject matter."[125] It's worth noting that the modern critical debate over *The Turn of the Screw* turns precisely on the question of erotics and depth psychology, starting with Wilson's analysis of the governess's displaced sexual interest in the children.

As Sharon Marcus and Stephen Best have pointed out, with the rise of Freudian and Marxist methods of interpretation, our reading practices have cast critics as detectives who root out hidden meanings.[126] A "hermeneutics of suspicion," in Paul Ricoeur's phrase, attributes an odd three-dimensionality to a literary work: the idea that there is a "surface" story implies that there is a volume to be plumbed, "depths" of some sort that exist behind, below, or beyond what is depicted. This practice has not just created an intriguing sense of textual "space," it also links textual interpretation with the idea of making depths visible: as Marcus and Best write, "For example, a queer symptomatic reading might interpret the closet, or ghosts, as surface signs of the deep truth of a homosexuality that cannot be overtly depicted" (3). A thaumatropic reading, by contrast, can be thought of as a surface reading that spins—but one that is hard to retrieve given the overwhelming critical accounts that cue us for stereoscopic depth.

While it has been hard for modern critics to credit the playfulness of *The Turn of the Screw*, "The Jolly Corner," written a decade later, is another story. In it, HJ makes a calculated attempt at giving his readers a delightful experience that both "works" and allows us to appreciate the precision of its immaculate design. Which, ultimately, holds a mirror up to (or better, *turns* on) the incredible design of our own embodied selves. The 1908 story draws out the kind of imaginative play that human beings alone are able to condense into resonant expressive objects—what I have been calling *devices*—and to share with fellow players, who in turn can take pleasure participating as vivid life unspools before our eyes.

From Youth to Adulthood in "The Jolly Corner"

The adults in *What Maisie Knew* are expert in the arts of calculation, where their own interests are in play; indeed, it is with an eye to Maisie's income, bequeathed to her by an aunt, that the adults maintain their clutch on her. Ida Farange, especially, "bristled so with calculation" (*Maisie*, 88). Spencer Brydon at the outset of "The Jolly Corner" (1908) experiences his return to the United States from overseas after thirty-three years away as a problem of calculation. Everyone wants to hear how he "reckon[s]" the changes, and he is ready, he says, to "'make answer as I can,'" but he is finding it infernally difficult to tally his thoughts and give such an accounting.[127] "'Everyone asks me what I 'think' of everything'" (*Tales*, 313), Brydon grouses to Alice Staverton in the first line of the story. He has for "a couple of months availed himself of every possible occasion to talk" to her, but he is apparently no closer to closing out his account.

Brydon had, in his young adulthood, sailed for Europe from New York City, the home of his "overschooled boyhood" and "chilled adolescence" (314); one can equate him with Winterbourne from *Daisy Miller*, now late middle aged and returned to the United States. Brydon arrives on the scene an older gentleman, someone who feels he's "lived longer than is often allotted to man" (313). This lengthy absence—practically a lifetime—means that upon his return to New York City, "everything was somehow a surprise" (313). The word "everything" is capacious, referring to the cityscape Brydon finds himself in, to his thoughts and feelings, and perhaps to his own changed perspective, looking at New York through the eyes of a man no longer in his youth. How, the story inquires through the central consciousness, is one to calculate surprise?

Accounting for Change

Surprise—a key affect, as we have seen, for Eberle's spiral of play—registers change, which poses a problem in "The Jolly Corner" because "the great fact all the while" is "the incalculability . . . of change" (313). Brydon faces a twofold difficulty in rendering an account. The first is the problem of proliferation: the moment one gets hold of even a single surprise, a tiny instance of change, myriad others transpire. (Brydon is clearly behind the eight ball here, since he's already two months into his New York residency; his doomed game of "catch up" recalls Tristram Shandy trying to tell his life story from birth, only to find his account receding further into the past as he lives his life forward into the future.) The second problem in trying to account for all the surprise is the problem of belatedness, for change has a short—an impossibly, incalculably short—shelf life. This isn't just an empirical issue of measurement but a philosophical problem: the moment surprise registers in consciousness, its movement is arrested and it's no longer a change. "Like a bird's life, it seems to be an alternation of flights and perchings," as WJ suggests of the fleeting quality of consciousness.[128] A surprise fully accounted for lacks the vital quality that made it a surprise in the first place.

Brydon's middle-aged attempt at accounting for his life manifests the temporal nature of what Bergson in *An Introduction to Metaphysics* (1903) calls duration. We live life in a "succession of states" that refuse quantitative summing up, because life unfolding involves a qualitative flow, "a continuous flux."[129] While we are immersed in living (for example, like Brydon while he was in Europe) we experience "a succession of states, each of which announces that which follows and contains that which precedes it" (11). Only in looking backward can we pluck particular moments of experience out of an integrated whole: "They can, properly speaking, only be said to form multiple states when I have already passed them and *turn back to observe their track*" (11, emphasis added). Bergson uses the figure of two spools of ribbon to express how we experience time: "This inner life may be compared to the unrolling of a coil, for there is no living being who does not feel himself gradually to the end of his roll; and to live is to grow old. But it may just as well be compared to a continual rolling up, like that of a thread on a ball, for our past follows us, it swells incessantly with the present that it picks up on its way; and consciousness means memory" (11–12). At birth, one spool is empty and the other full; toward the end of our lives, the one spool is now almost full, the other almost empty. The latter is Brydon's situation.

Like a bookkeeper building in a margin for error, or an engineer accounting for wobble, Brydon cleverly tries to square surprise with calculation through the concept of allowance. By "allowing, and in the most liberal and intelligent manner, for brilliancy of change," he takes "pains to give surprises so much margin for play" (*Tales*, 313). Margins, in accounting, can be mathematically calculated in terms of differentials, and Brydon puts his mind to the task: "He had given them more than thirty years—thirty-three, to be exact; and they now seemed to him to have organized their performance quite on the scale of that license. He had been twenty-three on leaving New York—he was fifty-six to-day" (313). Brydon affirms that the quantity of surprises was "quite on the scale" he would have predicted, given the length of his absence and his own passage from youth to age. After thus accounting for the surprises, Brydon extends his calculations further, seeking to itemize his "'thoughts'" (the scare quotes are his) about "everything." Yet in this endeavor he notes a problem: "It would have taken a longer absence"—perhaps "it would have taken a century"—to "pile up the differences, the newnesses, the queernesses, above all the bignesses, for the better or the worse, that at present assaulted his vision wherever he looked" (313). At the age of fifty-six, he doesn't have the time to accomplish such a task. Moreover, to accomplish these calculations it would take a "more averted mind"—that is, a mind turned away from the dynamic present and focused only on cataloguing or "piling" up his thoughts. This is what he means when he tells Alice Staverton, "'For, even were it possible . . . my 'thoughts' would still be almost altogether about *something* that concerns only myself'" (313, emphasis added). Brydon recognizes that in accomplishing such a "reckon[ing]"—in accounting simply for "something"—he would have overlooked all that didn't concern only himself. He would have missed pretty much "everything" else—and it is precisely "everything" that he (or any good accountant) seeks to reckon.

In keeping the point of view tightly focused with Brydon, "The Jolly Corner" thus begins with a strange but at least a describable conceit: a character attempting to catch hold of his thoughts about "surprises attending his so strangely belated return to America" (313). But before the first paragraph concludes, it is clear that Brydon's particular concern actually speaks to a larger, indeed a philosophical problem. How could one capture *any* surprise, *any* thought—"anything," in short—without arresting its movement and thus turning the experience of transition into its very opposite, stasis? And if "everything was such a surprise," the inability to calculate a single tiny surprise is equivalent to the inability to reckon "everything"—which is to say, the inability to reckon *anything*. As AJ puts this conundrum: "Truly nothing is to be expected but the unexpected!" (*Diary*, 198).

Seizing a Spinning Top to Catch Its Motion

With Brydon trying to capture surprise on the wing, we have now come full circle, to a key image from the introduction to *Philosophical Siblings*: the game of tops. WJ in his discussion of the stream of thought addresses the very problem that Brydon faces. In *Psychology: Briefer Course*, WJ urges that "consciousness is in constant change" and that this element of undifferentiated flow is its essential quality.[130] To put this point in Brydon's terms, consciousness is not composed of things that could be piled—noun substantives—and could in theory be counted. WJ notes that an older way of thinking about consciousness conceived of ideas as being built up from sensations and perceptions, "as houses are built by the agglutination of bricks" (*PBC*, 152). But (to follow the metaphor) the sturdiness of the house thus built renders invisible that which spackles it together, the relations among the "bricks." In actuality, "the terms related [are] almost naught," WJ writes, while "the feelings of relation are *everything*" (*PBC*, 168, emphasis added). The attempt to give one's *thoughts* about everything (as Brydon does) is to skip over the feelings of relation: "The attempt at introspective analysis in these cases," WJ affirms, "is in fact like seizing a spinning top to catch its motion, or trying to turn up the gas quickly enough to see how the darkness looks" (*PBC*, 160). AJ articulates the conundrum of capturing change with mordant, self-referential wit: "The difficulty about all this dying," she writes, "is that you can't tell a fellow anything about it, so where does the fun come in?" (*Diary*, 223). WJ's analogy for the attempt to grasp feelings of relation—aka "everything"—suggests that rather than stopping the motion one needs instead to find a way of playing along, of joining in the game.

Bergson also invokes child's play to think about catching consciousness in motion. In *Creative Evolution* (1907), Bergson describes the bootless attempt to "catch" change (here figured as smoke): "Before the intervening movement you will always experience the disappointment of the child who tries by clapping his hands together to crush the smoke. The movement slips through the interval, because every attempt to reconstitute change out of states implies the absurd proposition, that movement is made of immobilities."[131] In "The Jolly Corner," while the aging Brydon attends to the changes he perceives, he is perforce turned to the past, while the present continues to unfold—behind his back, as it were. Brydon's assimilating perception is engaged in a lagging, losing effort to create a pile—a stable, visualizable whole—out of moving parts. The language of his thoughts registers Brydon's attempt to create the conditions for "crush[ing] the smoke," translating vague, relative qualities (different, new, queer, big) into sturdier substantives (differences, newnesses, queernesses, bignesses), as if hoping that nouns would be more susceptible to "piling" and thus containment and calculation.

Yet, having established the impossibility of Brydon's endeavor—to "grasp" the irrecuperable interruption of thirty-three years—the story translates the problem of the gap into the solution. Whereas WJ's greatest contribution to psychology lies in his theorizing of flight, relations, and the stream of thinking, AJ was the mistress of the interruption. Her abrupt jokes interrupted—and thereby offered a homeopathic response to—the absurdities of embodied human existence. Not until the very end of her life, however, did she discover the "golden solution of the complex riddle" of ever-alert consciousness, which lay in the brief suspension or time-gap offered by hypnosis (223). And it turns out that herein lies the answer to the puzzle of the "The Jolly Corner": to mind the gap.

Affectively, Brydon upon his return home from overseas experiences the dislocating effects of his deterritorialization. Normally, consciousness is tied inextricably to one's first-person point of view. As WJ wrote, "Within each personal consciousness, thought is sensibly continuous" (*PBC*, 157). There is an exception, however: "The only breaches that can well be conceived to occur within the limits of a single mind would either be *interruptions, time-gaps* during which the consciousness went out; or they would be breaks in the content of the thought, so abrupt that what followed had no connection whatever with what went before" (*PBC*, 158). Lived forward, the changes that moved Brydon from youth to old age would be slow and imperceptible; the same is true for modernizing New York. Because the story begins with interruption—a sudden arrival, after a thirty-three-year gap—the visible difference in both cityscape and Brydon testifies to transition. The rest of the story can attend to the problem of the interval, which can indeed be expressed, albeit mathematically. Calculus (also known as "the calculus of infinitesimals") measures differentials: it is the study of the rates at which quantities change.[132] (More on rates shortly.)

How is one to attend to transition in the unspooling of time and life—and not just to the terminal points of an (uncertain) beginning and an (ever-receding) end? AJ in her Diary made the attempt to capture the process after her diagnosis with breast cancer: "This long slow dying is no doubt instructive, it is disappointingly free from excitements: 'naturalness' being carried to its supreme expression. One sloughs off the activities one by one, and never knows that they're gone, until one suddenly finds that the months have slipped away and the sofa will never more be laid upon, the morning paper read, or the loss of the new book regretted; *one revolves with equal content within the narrowing circle until the vanishing point is reached, I suppose*" (230, emphasis added). But AJ also interrupts her philosophizing with light mocking in the very next paragraph: "Vanity, however, maintains its undisputed sway, and I take satisfaction in feeling as much myself as ever, perhaps simply a more concentrated essence in this curtailment." Strikingly, whereas many think of time in linear terms, AJ's phrasing—"one revolves with equal content within the narrowing circle"—is echoed by Bergson's conception of time unspooling. What AJ calls the "supreme expression" of "'naturalness,'" Bergson terms *vital evolution*—which is not just psychological but an ontological concern, for all matter is in a state of becoming and only appears substantive, stationary, and completed. Nowhere is this more true than with human beings: "That the child can become a youth, ripen to maturity and decline to old age, we understand when we consider that vital evolution is here the reality itself. Infancy, adolescence, maturity, old age, are mere views of the mind, *possible stops* imagined by us, from without, along the continuity of a progress" (312). HJ in "The Jolly Corner," picking up threads from both of his siblings, uses the returned Brydon to toy with our conceptions of aging as a developmental process that passes through preset stages.

What AJ calls "the narrowing circle" toward "the vanishing point," Bergson (and WJ) explain using Zeno's paradox to show that it makes no sense to think of consciousness—or of a person aging—as a set of divisible static units or clearly delineated stages. It is impossible to point to the exact moment of transition from one state (for example, infancy) to another (maturity)—something that the philosopher Zeno in one of his famous paradoxes exploited, by dividing the flight of an arrow into static instants and then concluding that the arrow in flight doesn't move. *If one focuses on states, movement becomes impossible to see.* Here is Bergson's way of getting at this idea (again, echoing AJ's term "slipped"): "The reality, which is the *transition* from childhood to manhood, has slipped between our fingers. We have only the imaginary stops 'child' and man, and we are very near to saying that one of these stops is the other, just as the arrow of Zeno is, according to that philosopher, at all the points of the course" (313). Bergson notes that language, with its emphasis on noun substantives, is ill equipped to represent motion. "The Truth is that if language here were molded on reality, we should not say 'the child becomes the man,' but 'There is becoming from the child to the man.' In the first proposition, 'becomes' is a verb of indeterminate meaning, intended to mask the absurdity into which we fall when we attribute the state 'man' to the subject 'child'" (313). Bergson and WJ thus agree that we can't get from stages to motion; Bergson and AJ agree that our conceptions of stages of life ("man" and "child," but also "woman" and "invalid") "mask the absurdity into which we fall." The key is to begin with motion: what the young philosopher Bergson optimistically phrases as "there is becoming" and what AJ (writing at middle age, afflicted with cancer) calls "this long slow dying."

Kaleidoscope and Cinematograph

Read in light of these ideas, "The Jolly Corner" becomes a device that makes thinkable and visualizable what isn't available to the "naked eye." The story presents irrefutable testimony that, to use Bergson's phrase, "there is becoming": first, we have the character Brydon, who was young but is now old; and, second, we have New York City, which was once a nineteenth-century city and is now a twentieth-century metropolis. Thus we can say that the story weaves together two transformations that transpired at the same time: the aging individual and the changing cityscape (with its attendant altered culture and values). The story thus establishes the foundation for a third question, one that artificially—as a thought experiment—brings together the two transformations: what would Brydon have become had he stayed in New York? "The Jolly Corner" sets up the occasion for trying to think the two changes simultaneously.

To calculate anything, one needs to calibrate the units. Let us designate Brydon, our first-person consciousness, as "our body." Let us present everything that is not Brydon—including people, places, things—as "other bodies." (This should make sense in a moment.) With our units thus designated, we can use Bergson to illuminate what HJ is up to in the story: "There is, between our body and other bodies, an arrangement like that of the pieces of glass that compose a kaleidoscopic picture. Our activity goes from an arrangement to a rearrangement, each time no doubt giving the kaleidoscope a *new shake*, but not interesting itself in the shake, and seeing only the new picture" (306, emphasis added). Brydon, moving to New York, gives his life/kaleidoscope "a new shake." HJ arranged "The Jolly Corner" as a play frame for both seeking the new arrangement and becoming aware of the "shake."

Bergson offers a warning, however: beware the fake shake. He points out a sticky problem, an illusion that he associates with the apparatus of "the cinematograph," what we would now call the cinema, or moving pictures. Rather than experience transformation (what Bergson calls "becoming") from the inside, human beings unassisted tend to grasp at it from the outside: "We take snapshots, as it were, of the passing reality, and, as these are characteristic of the reality, we have only *to string them along* to feel as if we have captured the motion of our thoughts and of the world" (306, emphasis added). This "stringing together" takes shape as any "stage of life" stories. For example, with a bildungsroman we tell about change and about development. Brydon talks about his family property (the jolly corner) in precisely this way, as the site of a sequence of happenings: "the one in which he had first seen the light, in which various members of his family had lived and had died, in which the holidays of his overschooled boyhood had been passed and the few social flowers of his chilled adolescence gathered" (*Tales*, 314). This mini-autobiography offers what we could call *ordinary knowledge* about Brydon by marking out stages that are easily imagined as a series of family photos: Brydon's ancestors, Brydon as a baby, Brydon as a boy, Brydon as an adolescent.

For Bergson, the mechanism of the new visual technology of moving pictures (cinema or photoplay) is infernally good—better than novels—at seeming like *ordinary knowledge* and providing an *illusory* sense of becoming: "Whether we would think becoming, or express it, or even perceive it, we hardly do anything else than set going a kind of cinematograph inside us. We may therefore sum up what we have been saying in the conclusion that the *mechanism of our ordinary knowledge is of a cinematographical kind*" (306). The motion picture, by reeling before viewers' eyes a series of static images, gives the illusion of change but does not capture the experience of becoming. Cinema provides a model for everyday human consciousness, where we essentially take a series of snapshots and then retrospectively string them together as if in an inevitable, cause-and-effect narrative.

Bergson disparaged moving pictures for providing (he believed) a false sense of becoming, a nonvital simulacrum of the lived flow that he called duration. But: however brilliant Bergson might have been about his philosophy of how time and consciousness unfold, he was not exceptionally perspicacious about the technology of film. As Gregory Flaxman has argued, Bergson had a limited understanding of the affordances of film. He was unaware of the potential for moving the camera through space, taking a variety of shots with different angles and depths, and editing the film for juxtapositions and other effects. Flaxman writes, "The cinematographic image that Bergson had witnessed, Deleuze explains, was the product of technology still struggling to unleash its potential."[133] As we shall see, Münsterberg, writing just a few years after Bergson, explored the much more complex relationship between moving pictures, the human sensorium, and lives live in time.

Spencer Brydon: Developer or Designer?

Delightfully, what Bergson couldn't quite see his way to, HJ accomplishes most cleverly in "The Jolly Corner." He leverages the perceptual and philosophical possibilities of early film to create an imaginative scenario that emulates the *motions of becoming*—that which, as I have been arguing throughout this book, is exemplified in the growth of a child and is thematized through iterative experiences of practice, playing, and learning. "The Jolly Corner," as with AJ's Diary, takes the perspective of someone far from the bloom of youth. In his final years, HJ sets aside the exemplary "learner" (the not-yet-adult) and instead looks to the figure of a late-middle-aged man paired with a woman of similar age. Brydon, in trying to reconcile his current state with his younger self, kindles an appreciative awareness of the ever-present, poignant motion of becoming itself—as seen from a position closer to the end of life than the beginning.

In "The Jolly Corner," the concept of the interval—a gap between youth and age, or simply *then* and *now*—is formalized in architectural terms as the difference between the two buildings that Brydon owns. He has possessed, since his original departure, two fairly similar old properties: one situated on a corner, the other a mid-block structure that he is renovating to fit the new fashion. The "jolly corner" he leaves in its current condition—which means, as it was thirty-three years prior. The other house "two bristling blocks westward" is "already in course of reconstruction as a tall mass of flats" (*Tales*, 314). This architectural chopping up and reassemblage into separate units transpires at the edge of the story; Brydon's friend Alice Staverton (along with the reader) visits the modernizing property just once, surveying it while it is under (re)construction.

While the "lesser" property is being subdivided, Brydon discovers that he has a proverbial "mind for business." Supervising the renovation, he is surprised at the arrival "in a *compartment of his mind* never yet penetrated, of a capacity for business and a sense for construction" (314–15, emphasis added). Brydon's mind here *resembles* a building of many rooms or "compartment[s]," while the talent that he discovers inside this structure is, aptly enough, a knack for reassembling homes into apartments.

Or at least, Brydon has a knack for *imagining* the renovated configuration—leaving the work of carpentry to manual laborers. Architecture involves both design and creation, with the gerund "building" embracing both the verbal form of making and the noun form of end product. Brydon's talent involves seeing the present entity as a pivot point between past and future. Staverton suggests to him that, had he stayed in New York rather than move to

Europe, Brydon might have "anticipated the inventor of the skyscraper" (316). (A nice ambiguity, suggesting that Brydon might himself have invented the skyscraper—or been a savvy venture capitalist and backed the actual inventor.) Rather than being a man of leisure, Brydon might have been a man with an occupation. Moreover, he could have been an architect of the present moment in which he finds himself—that slice of time and space (now, New York City) which had so baffled his capacity for description after a hiatus of three decades. Rather than an old fogy (to use one of WJ's terms for the opposite of youthful freshness), Brydon—in Staverton's vision—could have been someone who had helped to bring into being the densely populated and fast-paced city that he now visits as a relative stranger. In contemporary parlance, Brydon could have been a developer, one who remakes a cityscape and becomes rich while doing so. (The term "developer," we can note, resonates with Herbert Spencer's version of evolutionary psychology, with its emphasis on growth as linear progress.)

The concreteness of construction, in the context of the New York real estate market, fuels financial speculation. This strange harnessing of two different conceptions of *construction*, one material (building) and the other abstract (imagining), is registered formally in the text of "The Jolly Corner" through unstable metaphorization. The figures of speech in the story tend to materialize, as is the case when Brydon cogitates on the matter of risk. With the lesser property he is undertaking a substantial renovation, which puts him in peril of either making too much money (which is ethically compromising) or losing too much money (which is financially embarrassing). This situation causes him internal consternation, but it does not stymie his forward momentum: "He loafed about his 'work' undeterred, secretly agitated; not in the least 'minding' that the whole proposition, as they said, was vulgar and sordid, and ready to climb ladders, to walk the plank, to handle materials and look wise about them, to ask questions, in fine, and challenge explanations and really 'go into' figures" (315). Others hammer and construct; he fronts the money. The developer meets the riskiness of his venture with outward aplomb, manifested as a readiness "to walk the plank," a metaphor that signifies meeting one's probable doom with courage. The possibility of financial (and thereby social) gain is rendered with a cliché, as a readiness "to climb ladders." But: as surveyor of the construction site, Brydon is *in fact* called upon to walk across planks and to scale ladders. Insofar as his particular form of work is fronting the money and helping design the apartments, it is "merely" speculative, involving no physical activity, and accordingly takes scare quotes in the text: "his 'work.'" Such speculative activity is linked with loafing—just as HJ "gaped" while WJ acted and AJ lay in bed.

But of course real estate and other financial speculation (the province of those who "'go into' figures") transpires at a level of abstraction that renders capitalists extreme wealth that they leverage to build new and bigger buildings. Real estate as a discursive field provides "The Jolly Corner" not just with a tension between artistic and materialistic value but also with metaphors that oscillate between the figurative and the literal. This oscillation is explicitly, if understatedly, played for humor—and is appropriately registered through the amused gaze of a woman named Alice.

Staverton's notion, that had Brydon taken up real estate three decades earlier he'd be a powerful shaper of the city and extremely wealthy, similarly oscillates between a speculation (something that occupies the province of the mind and has no cash value) and a materialization (something that occupies the province outside the mind and does have cash value). The oscillation happens at the level of the text, with the terms "image" and "figure" as crucial pivot points, denoting both something in the mind *and* a material entity. Here is where the question of whether the jolly corner is haunted becomes salient. The idea of Brydon's possible, alternate self occupying his old home's corridors becomes something he *sees* as an "image" that catalyzes emotion, leaving him just as "thrilled and flushed" as "he might have been [had he been] met by some strange figure, some unexpected occupant, at a turn of one of the dim passages of an empty house" (316). What starts as a metaphor to explain the feeling—he was as excited *as if* he'd run into a stranger in a dark hallway—becomes a sort of internal ghost, a set of feelings that stays with him "quite hauntingly" (316).

In a further materialization, Brydon believes that he might in fact encounter his alter ego (the man who stayed in New York and became a rich developer) should he be able to enter the compartment of his mind where that figure lies, hazily imagined and unrealized. Brydon's thoughts about a potential internal encounter take shape as if outside himself and are presented in the text as a matter of doors. The single image of Brydon's alternate self, the image that left him "thrilled and flushed," becomes a tiny scene, "that of his opening a door behind which he would have made sure of finding nothing, a door into a room shuttered and void" where "in the dusk" he perceives a "quite erect confronting presence" facing him (316).

The *idea* of finding an alternate self behind a door precedes materialization in the story's plot: the actual encounter with a doorknob and then a figure behind it. The mental image takes shape much as the book of a play precedes production or an architectural blueprint precedes construction. The remaining plot of "The Jolly Corner" traces Brydon's efforts to stage a confrontation with his alternate self, the developer-financier-venture-capitalist Brydon-who-might-have-been.

But while the renovation of the first building provides the occasion for an aging man to become the developer he never was, the story's setting shifts to the other property—the jolly corner—and his search for the figure behind the door. Whereas the first building is piled with construction materials and bustles with workmen, the house on the corner lacks furnishings and people (with the one exception of a house cleaner, who only visits in the daytime). No chairs or armoires or mirrors or books occupy the empty rooms of the second dwelling, the one in which Brydon had lived before his departure for Europe.

A Childhood Home Without Properties

Why the need to create this particular form of domestic vacuum, stripped of furnishings? The year before "The Jolly Corner" was published, HJ in *The American Scene* (1907) had described precisely the circumstance in which an American absent from the United States for many years could be beguiled by domestic objects, and in "which, at the turn of staircases and from the walls of communicating rooms, portraits and relics and records . . . laid traps, of a pliantly primitive order, for memory, for sentiment, for relenting irony."[134] Such "traps" were, he had observed, "gross little devices, on the part of the circumscribed past" that prompted shallow feelings of nostalgia (*Scene*, 4). In *The American Scene*, the narrator finds that "the restored absentee" must "brace himself" for newer, open-plan interior spaces, in which the "diffused vagueness of separation between apartments, between hall and room, between one room and another, between the one you are in and the one you are not in, between place of passage and place of privacy, is a provocation to despair" (66).

Contrasted with the perceptual noise of *The American Scene*, the house in "The Jolly Corner" offers a property with few properties. It is old-fashioned, with public space on the first floor and private rooms above. Stripped of furnishings, it presents a "great gaunt shell" (*Tales*, 317)—a phrase reminiscent of *acoustical shell*, a hard structure used in a theater to heighten an audience's sensory experience. The jolly corner, through subtraction, becomes something like a pure form, a series of boxes (rooms, corridors, stairwells) stacked and aligned. The stripping down is registered textually by the term "mere." Staverton serves as the audience sharing in Brydon's impressions of his old home in its stately emptiness: "He spoke [to her] of the value of all he read into it, into the *mere* sight of the walls, *mere* shapes of the rooms, *mere* sound of the floors, *mere* feel, in his hand, of the old silver-plated knobs of the several mahogany doors" (318, emphasis added). The *OED* gives the Latin meanings of the term as "pure," "sheer," "undiluted." In the jolly corner, the moving parts are simple devices: the doors are equipped with hinges and knobs for opening; windows in their sashes could be raised or lowered.

Brydon experiences sensory reciprocity in the stripped-down space. He connects with the past through contact: he grasps a knob "which suggested the pressure of the palms of the dead; the seventy years of the past in fine that these things represented, the annals of nearly three generations, counting his grandfather's" (318). This hands-on, tactile encounter is contrasted with mediated contact: the probing of space with a stick. When Brydon (in an echo of Winterbourne's detachment) taps "the steel point of his stick on the old marble of the hall pavement," his mind diverts into the overstuffed, muddled private realm of image and association (324). Stick in hand, he loses touch. He realizes that he must seek out "big game" without mediating tools, so afterward when he entered the corner property "he did ever the same thing; he put his stick noiselessly away in the corner" (324). With an absence of props, he enters the structural landscape of the building itself and comes into sensory contact with childhood: "the impalpable ashes of his long-extinct youth, afloat in the very air like microscopic motes" (318).

Like Brydon's repeated revisiting of the property, the movement of "The Jolly Corner" is iterative. The story begins at a precise moment of conversation between Brydon and Staverton, and jumps backward to when the two—a few days prior—had visited Brydon's two houses. After this retrospective scene, the narrative then fast-forwards to the present moment, this time locating the two within Staverton's apartment. Her uninterrupted life and his interrupted one are embodied in the attitudes of stasis and movement they respectively adopt: "She was seated by her fire, and before her, on his feet and restless, he turned to and fro between this intensity of his idea and a fitful and unseeing inspection, through his single eye-glass, of the dear little old objects on her chimney-piece" (320). He speculates that the path he chose *not* to take would have "produced some different effect for my life and for my 'form'"—suggesting of course that the shape of his life (its form) would have been different had he stayed put in New York, but also that his physical body (his form) would have been sculpted differently by altered conditions. Brydon's thoughts about the man he didn't become are metaphorized as a flower: somewhere deep inside him, he muses, there exists the bud of an "*alter ego*" (321). He drops the floral metaphor, however, and offers another, that of a medal or disk, which has one side stamped with his actual life, the other with what his life would have been had he stayed in New York. (I will call his alter ego *Brydon Prime* for clarity.). The two-sided medal, each with its own face, is like a coin, with a different figure on either side. Brydon says to Staverton, "'I know at least what I am' . . . ; 'the other side of the medal's clear enough'" (321).[135] But he is curious to view *both* sides, what he is and what he would have been. The question is, how to view both sides together? What technology of vision to employ?

Critic Mark Schiebe, observing that Brydon has a monocle while Brydon Prime wears spectacles, has argued for the stereoscopic motif in "The Jolly Corner": "Henry James' tale may be read as a reimagining of the doppelgänger motif and the related optical trope of 'double vision.'"[136] Yet, as we have seen with *The Turn of the Screw,* the stereoscopic experience is static and artificial, offering the illusion of depth and solidity. Rather, in "The Jolly Corner" HJ pulls off the thaumatropic action that he attempted in *The Turn of the Screw*. Recall that the thaumatrope produces a dynamic image, calling on the agency of the operator to effect the interplay of surfaces *and* to demystify the means by which hand and eye collaborate in creating a composite image. That said, Schiebe is right to note the stereoscopic element in the following conversation when Staverton tells Brydon that she has seen his double, Brydon Prime, prompting Brydon's half-stated query and her reply:

> "You—?"
> "I've seen him in a dream." (322)

Brydon is disappointed, and replies: "'Oh a "dream"—!' It let him down." Here Brydon marks the difference between seeing a figure in one's mind's eye—as in a dream—and seeing a figure in the world. Seeing in a dream is illusory, purely subjective, involuntary, and above all not creditable: stereoscopic. Staverton, however, offers an enigmatic explanation that "spins" her first comment:

> "But twice over," she continued. "I saw him as I see you now."
> "You've dreamed the same dream—?"
> "Twice over," she repeated. "The very same." (322)

Staverton's affirmation that she saw Brydon Prime twice is meant to be convincing, like repeating an experiment and getting the same result twice. The phrase itself—"twice over"—appears twice, adding insistence (with the "over" adding a thaumatropic twist to the simpler term, "twice"). The syntactical spinning continues. Staverton's additional phrase, "the very same," itself has an alternate meaning, a spin-off. On the one hand it affirms that she dreamed the same dream twice, thus she saw Brydon Prime, identically, two times. On the other hand, the phrase could mean that she saw Brydon Prime *just as she is now seeing Brydon*. Fusing these two stipulations brings together thaumatropic possibility: that she is now seeing Brydon twice over.

The Psychology of Cinema

But in what sense does Staverton see Brydon "twice over," or double? Münsterberg in his writings reminds us that, with our two eyes, we see *everything* twice, as it were: "Whenever in practical life we see an object, a vase on our table, as a solid body, we get the impression of its plastic character *first of all by seeing it with our two eyes from two different points of view*" (emphasis added).[137] Münsterberg makes this point about the doubleness of human vision for a particular purpose: to affirm that the phenomenology of the photoplay—its flow, its depth—is not artificial but *precisely the same as everyday sight for human beings*. Staverton saw Brydon Prime twice at different moments—just as she sees Brydon twice at the same moment.

Mind the Gap

In "The Jolly Corner," HJ explicitly invokes the dimensional condition of *time*, which is the essential element in the perception of movement. Münsterberg notes that the human capacity to translate a stream of images into movement—that is, cinematic seeing—involves not just passive optical reception but, crucially, coalescing acts of mind that bridge the gaps between filmic frames. The way a person experiences motion becomes vivid when we compare the screen and the stage, writes Münsterberg: "What is then the difference between seeing motion in the photoplay and seeing it on the real stage? There on the stage where the actors move the eye really receives a continuous series. Each position goes over into the next without any interruption. The spectator receives everything from without and the whole movement which he sees is actually going on in the world of space without and accordingly in his eye. But if he faces the film world, *the motion which he sees appears to be a true motion, and yet is created by his own mind*" (30, emphasis in original). Film, which depends on interruption (the gap between still images), activates the viewer's suturing mental acts. In this respect, watching a film is like reading a book, and both are bodymind experiences: "If we are fully absorbed in our book, we do not hear at all what is said around us and we do not see the room; we forget everything. . . . [O]ur bodily personality works toward the fullest possible impression" (36).

In the visual and dramatic arts, Münsterberg writes, perception is naturally drawn toward the human frame, especially faces and hands. This sort of immersion is difficult if not impossible in a stage play, because of the significant spatial gap between the actors on the stage and the audience in the theater. In an auditorium or acoustic shell, myriad elements vie for attention: "On the stage this [close focused attention] is impossible; there nothing can really fade away. That dramatic hand must remain, after all, only the ten thousandth part of the space of the whole stage; it must remain a little detail. The whole body of the hero and the other men and the whole room and every indifferent chair and table in it must go on obtruding themselves on our senses" (37). It is here that Münsterberg draws out the most significant power of the moving picture, which lies in editing techniques, especially the close-up and parallel action. Focusing the camera in, say, on a close-up of the hand of an actor holding a revolver makes this element of the performance loom large. Rather than artificial, this cinematic feature *mimes human perception*. Like film, "the act of attention which goes on in our mind," Münsterberg writes, "has remodeled the surrounding itself" (37). Note the key term, "remodeled": remodeling is what Brydon carries on materially in the lesser property, in which he stages a transformation into flats. Acts of attention, Münsterberg affirms, are miniature remodelings in which the perceiver shapes the world into distinct objects and into foreground and background, bestowing shape, size, and depth along with meaning and salience.

Moving Pictures

WJ emphasized how difficult it is to "catch real fact in the making, and directly perceive how events happen" (*Varieties,* 449). He sees "the world of generalizable objects" as inert and static, explaining "as in stereoscopic or kinetoscopic pictures seen outside the instrument, the third dimension, the movement, the vital element, are not there" (*Varieties,* 449). To apply these terms to HJ: he configures the "The Jolly Corner" to include "the third dimension, the movement" by recalibrating how time functions in the story. In *The Turn of the Screw*, the temporal distinction between the-governess-as-character living her life forward while at Bly and the governess-as-narrator looking back on her life from a point in the future created a cleft that psychoanalytical readings stepped in to suture. The action of "The Jolly Corner," by contrast, transpires *now*—in a brief slice of the present. It is as if Brydon *is* the older governess, trying to grasp a hold of his virtual (younger, other) self, to see if the experience of looking back and of living forward can be aligned in an unfolding present.

The older technologies of stereoscope and shadow play, in "The Jolly Corner," are associated with Brydon's trivial daytime occupations. Brydon spends his days going through the motions of social life in a distracted manner, with conversation and responses that verge on the automatic: "his gestures of response were the extravagant shadows, emphatic in proportion as they meant little, of some game of *ombres chinoises*" (*Tales*, 323). As the story unfolds, it is Brydon's nighttime wanderings in his old property that take shape as the most acutely interesting. While his body went through the motions of social intercourse, his attention was trained elsewhere: "He projected himself all day, in thought, straight over the bristling line of hard unconscious heads and into the other, the real, the waiting life; the life that, as soon as he had heard behind him the click of his great house-door, began for him, on the jolly corner, as beguilingly as the slow opening bars of some rich music follows the tap of the conductor's wand" (323–24). It is not just that Brydon is absentminded or daydreaming. The syntax here suggests that he becomes a figure for cinema, for a narrative projected over an audience's heads, behind a "great house-door," "on the jolly corner," accompanied by "some rich music."[138]

In a playful nod to his child-centric writings, HJ mixes resonant metaphors of gaming and toying into the text. Brydon's nighttime wanderings become a game, once again not unlike Robert Louis Stevenson's description of boys carrying lanterns under their heavy coats (from chapter 2). Brydon is "playing at hide-and-seek" (326); he muses that "people enough, first and last, had been in terror of apparitions, but who had ever before so turned the tables and become himself, in himself, in the apparitional world, an incalculable terror?" (325). But suddenly the roles flip: "'I've hunted him til he's 'turned,'" Brydon thinks to himself (327). The pursuer is now the pursued. This prompts in Brydon new tactics, in which he spins around, randomly and suddenly, to catch himself being watched. To his dismay, however, the figure he seeks seems equally rapid and elusive: "These manoeuvres recalled to him Pantaloon, at the Christmas farce, buffeted and tricked from behind by ubiquitous Harlequin" (327).

Importantly, Brydon's household rambles involve as much stillness as motion; as many breathless silences as living gestures. To use WJ's terms, his movements have both "flights and perches." Brydon's perambulations echo the movements of the thoughts in his mind: "The house, withal, seemed immense, the scale of space again inordinate; the open rooms, to no one of which his eyes deflected, gloomed in their shuttered state like mouths of caverns; only the high skylight that formed the crown of the deep well created for him a medium in which he could advance" (333). With a hole for light at the top, the "deep well" acts as a camera obscura. Better known as a box-sized device, the camera obscura in its original form was a room. Moreover, the wording in the passage above creates an ever-so-slight kinship with the human cranium ("mouths," "eyes"/"skylight," "deep well"). These "boxes"—both house and mind—offer the "medium" for Brydon Prime to appear. They contrast with the flat, two-dimensional closed door on the top story that had provided Brydon with a screen.

The upstairs floor plan, with its telescoping doors along corridors, is the space of trickery and trompe l'oeil. HJ calls on other aesthetic forms to note their inadequacy to the full apprehension of what has become a moving target. The alter ego makes his appearance downstairs, and the indistinct figure is first compared to a sculpture ("some image erect in a niche," 334) and to a painting ("No portrait by a great modern master could have presented him with more intensity," 334). But these analogies are discarded, and the figure instead takes shape in the black-and-white tiled foyer, where an open door allows sight while the closed front door prevents passage. In what amounts to an architectural box, Brydon first sees the figure he has been seeking "quite as one of those expanding fantastic images projected by the magic lantern of childhood" (334–35). "The vestibule" that "gaped wide" provides a "virtual screen" for a form that materializes and also moves.

Suturing the World of Sight and the World of Touch

HJ in "The Jolly Corner" plants clues that the new technology of the motion picture is a model for enabling his own narrative manifestation of motion, akin to a amoving picture. There is, however, the issue of interruption. As Münsterberg explained, a reel of film spun in front of a viewer would be an unintelligible blur were it not for the flicker effect of darkness interposed between images: "Isolated pictures presented to the eye in rapid succession but separated by interruptions are perceived not as single impressions of different positions, but as continuous movement" (4). This perception of motion is called a "stroboscopic effect" (4), and it is this that HJ emulates in the story.

Brydon's ability to view his alter ego is dependent on "blackouts" or interruptions that are literary analogues to the visual medium. The constant nightly visits to the house brought him no closer to visualizing who he would have been, had he been in continuous residence in New York. Part way through the story, Brydon changes his tactics and absents himself from his nightly perambulations. He does this three times, thus introducing gaps (or *reprieves*) so that he could conduct a differential comparison. The narrator mentions these interruptions twice: "He had made, as I have said, to create on the premises the baseless sense of a reprieve, his three absences; and the result of the third was to confirm the after-effect of the second" (327). These disruptions to the routine provide the essential conditions for the viewing that happens.

Brydon's final reckoning with his alter ego transpires after the second time he's created a "calculated absence" or a gap in his routine. During this time of interruption he begins to perceive that he is being followed as he wanders the four stories. The psychology of film, as Münsterberg writes, has made clear that the sensation of movement is not *merely* the effect of an optical afterimage but also involves a complex assemblage of feeling and association—a "mental mechanism" that can be set in motion by the merest external stimulus: "It is only a suggestion of movement, and the idea of motion is to a high degree the product of our own reaction. *Depth and movement alike come to us in the moving picture world, not as hard facts but as a mixture of fact and symbol. They are present and yet they are not in the things. We invest the impressions with them*. . . . We create the depth and the continuity through our mental mechanism" (30). The crucial element in film is thus the human psychological capacity to blend the flickering image with our first-person bodily sensations. WJ, writing about Bishop Berkeley's theory of vision, states that "the tangible 'feel' of a thing, and the 'look' of it to the eye, have absolutely *no point in common*" (*PBC*, 326, emphasis added). This lack of a "point in common" between one's sensation about a thing and the thing itself captures perfectly Brydon's experience at his very first glimpse of his alter ego's face: "He had been 'sold,' he inwardly moaned, stalking such game as this: the presence before him was a presence, the horror within him a horror, but the waste of his nights had been only grotesque and the success of his adventure an irony. Such an identity fitted his at *no* point" (*Tales*, 335). Brydon falters; his vision is powerless to forge the link or to calibrate the distance between himself and Brydon Prime: "He felt the whole vision turn to darkness and his very feet give way. His head went round; he was going; he had gone" (336).

In this collapse of consciousness, however, the pronouns serve as pivot points that allow Brydon and his double to meet. They are joined in the phrase "the whole vision" that "turn[ed] to darkness," for this *vision* encompasses both Brydon's own viewpoint *and* that which he is looking at, the alter ego. The head that "went round" signifies both his own turning away and that of his mirroring double. Finally, "he was going; he had gone" refers to the departure of his own consciousness and that which his consciousness embraced, the vision of his double. In other words, the final sentences of the long middle section of "The Jolly Corner" provide the "point in common" where Brydon and his double "meet"—though the meeting transpires in darkness. The camera obscura has served its purpose, offering the vision (as it were) upside down, to the single "eye" that pressed itself to the aperture. The vision is private, solitary, unconscious; it recalls AJ's invocation of the "vanishing point" (230).

Hand, Eye, Heart

The question then is, can the meeting of the two be shared? This is the entire subject of the short final section of the story, which narrates Brydon's "rich return of consciousness" (336). Brydon (not unlike an infant) first hears a voice, and then a face comes into view "while he l[ies] looking up at her." His proprioceptive sense is engaged, and he becomes "conscious, yes, of tenderness of support and, more particularly, of a head pillowed in extraordinary softness and faintly refreshing fragrance" (336). It is his own head, and he realizes "that Alice Staverton had made her lap an ample and perfect cushion to him": "Slowly but surely his consciousness grew, his vision of his state thus completing itself: he had been miraculously *carried* back—lifted and carefully borne as from where he had been picked up, the uttermost end of an interminable grey passage" (336, emphasis added). What is striking here is the triple meaning that the sentence achieves, helped along by the emphasized term "carried" and the concluding phrase, "grey passage." First, the sentence means that Brydon has been *carried* along a *grey passage* or corridor. Second, he is *carried* back to consciousness, through a *grey passage* of dawning awareness. Third—playfully—the text has *carried* the character back into the plot, with the long dense paragraph of prose being a *grey passage* (visually on the page). "You brought me literally to life," Brydon tells Staverton, with the statement applying equally well to the author of the story and the reader's act of mind (337).

WJ noted that human beings experience the world not only through vision but also through contact and the sorts of calibration that are possible when the full bodymind is enlisted: "Touch-space is one world; sight-space is another world. The two worlds have no essential or intrinsic congruence, and only through the 'association of ideas' do we know what a seen object signifies in terms of touch" (*PBC*, 328). Crucially, human relations of love and fondness help to suture the world of sight to the world of touch, though of course this takes the effort of connection and calibration: "All such confusions very quickly disappear with practice, and the novel optical sensations translate themselves into the familiar language of touch" (328). Pillowed in Staverton's lap, Brydon "felt her hold him close" and "her eyes were in his eyes" as he states, "'I was to have known myself'" (*Tales*, 338). His tentative gropings toward self-knowledge are here cast into the awkward, forward-and-back verb tense ("was to have known") that oscillates between future and past. Staverton closes the circle: "'You came to yourself'" (339).

The question remains: did Alice's and Spencer's visions of Brydon Prime intersect? The final dialogue transpires as the sun streams onto the physically proximate couple, as they busily work to establish a shared understanding. The fast-paced play of pronouns (him, you, me) offers a literary equivalent to the swiftly moving images of film, creating a continuity (but not an identity) of experience: for of course Staverton's *you* is Brydon's *me*. The slightly differentiated echoes produce a negotiation between what the two see and feel:

> [Staverton:] "Well, in the cold dim dawn of this morning I too saw you."
>
> [Brydon:] "Saw *me*?"
>
> "Saw *him*," said Alice Staverton. "It must have been at the same moment."
>
> He lay an instant taking it in—as if he wished to be quite reasonable.
>
> "At the same moment?" (338–39)

In comparison to similar colloquies in HJ's late fiction there is an added element of physical touch: "At this Brydon raised himself; he had to see her better. She helped him when she understood his movement, and he sat up, steadying himself beside her there on the window-bench with his right hand grasping her left" (339).[139] Not only the dance of dialogue but also movement and gesture become essential pantomime in the passageway of the jolly corner, as the two sit face to face, hands clasped, spinning a shared story.

In the final passages of "The Jolly Corner" we have the return of the hand-and-eye motif from HJ's invocation of the thaumatrope, but this time transpiring in three-dimensional space. The key differences between Brydon and the visualization of the alter ego are twofold: their hands (Brydon Prime's right hand is missing two fingers) and their eyewear (Brydon Prime sports a pince-nez with two lenses, whereas Brydon prefers a monocle). These two items are telling and offer an important contrast: for a stereoscope to create the illusion of depth, one needs two lenses; whereas for a human being to see in three dimensions, a single eye suffices. WJ states, "A being reduced to a single eyeball would perceive the same tri-dimensional world that we do, if he had our intellectual powers" (*PBC*, 327). Brydon Prime, the shadowy image of a bespectacled man who Brydon might have been (a heartless developer), is subsumed to the monocled man holding Staverton's hand.

Coda: Listening to Alice

A person is not a mechanical device; nor, for that matter, is fiction a "trap," to invoke HJ's teasing statement from the preface to *The Turn of the Screw.* "The Jolly Corner" affirms that the fullness of memory, cognition, affection, and sensation supplement the mechanics of vision. We can recall that before Staverton, another Alice gave voice, with humor, to the bodymind complex and its enravelment with beloved others when she wrote of HJ, "He hangs on to whatever organ may be in eruption and gives me calm and solace by assuring me that my nerves are his nerves and my stomach his stomach" (*Diary*, 103). (HJ returns the compliment, writing to WJ that "her style, her power to write—are indeed to me a delight" [*Letters*, 307].) The potency of cinema—and its pertinence for HJ's pedagogical works—rests with the furnishings of the human mind. Though "we see everything with our right or our left eye from different points of view," Münsterberg writes, "even with one eye closed, we see the world around us in three dimensions" (21). And, as "The Jolly Corner" affirms, the capacities that help us to navigate our lives are delightfully activated (and put on display) in resonant works of literature.

While HJ brought a cinematic sensibility to "The Jolly Corner," he never set aside the aspiration to write a successful stage play. In both endeavors, he sought to kindle collective seeing in multiple dimensions, and to make the act of seeing itself an object of awareness. "With habit and repetition," HJ suggests, one might "gain[] to an extraordinary degree the power to penetrate the dusk of distances and the darkness of corners, to resolve back into their innocence the treacheries of uncertain light, the evil-looking forms taken in the gloom by mere shadows, by accidents of the air, by shifting effects of perspective" (*Tales*, 325). Brydon (like HJ) is a lantern-bearer in a reverse phantasmagoria; his nighttime rambles to discover his alter ego are pure play, in that they are situated, embodied, spontaneous, and autotelic. They are also serious-minded and social, involving coordination and care. Sitting together, Staverton and Brydon reveal that they viewed Brydon Prime "at the same moment"—and while Spencer thinks the alter ego is awful, Alice offers a different perspective, asking, "'[Why] shouldn't I like him?'" for kindling their clear-eyed, late-in-life affection. In remarkable fashion, "The Jolly Corner" lives up to its name, with *corner* designating the form of three-dimensionality and *jolly* naming the affect of good cheer—while its verb form "jollying" denotes an encouraging nudge. It is certainly the rare work by HJ that ends with a hug.

Conclusion

"Pleasure Under Difficulties"

This exploration of Alice, William, and Henry James's literary productions has approached their work critically and also under the aspect of play. To quote Johan Huizinga, who has set a keynote for this book, "Our point of departure must be the conception of an almost childlike play-sense expressing itself in various play-forms, some serious, some playful."[1] Over the course of their contrasting careers, each of the siblings—remarkably—kept alive this childlike play-sense; indeed, some of the most affecting scenes of their childhood experiences come in the final months of their lives.[2]

AJ notes the peculiar power of certain memories, puzzling about "what determines the *selection* of memory, why does one childish experience or impression stand out so luminous and solid against the, for the most part, vague and misty background?"[3] She recalls an afternoon from the "summer of '56," which involved a dreary drive with the whole family, "save Wm.," when they went to visit the home of "Mlle. Marie Boningue our governess" (128):

> We were turned into the garden to play, a sandy or rather dusty expanse with nothing in it, as I remember, but two or three scrubby apple-trees, from one of which hung a swing. As time went on Wilky and Bob disappeared, not to my grief, and the Boningues. Harry was sitting in the swing and I came up and stood near by as the sun began to slant over the desolate expanse, as the dready h[ou]rs, with that endlessness which they have for infancy, passed, when Harry suddenly exclaimed: "This might certainly be called pleasure under difficulties!" The stir of my whole being in response to the substance and exquisite, *original*

> form of this remark almost makes my heart beat now with the sisterly pride which was then awakened and it came to me in a flash, the higher nature of this appeal to the mind, as compared to the rudimentary solicitations which usually produced my childish explosions of laughter; and I can also feel distinctly the sense of self-satisfaction in that I could not only perceive, but appreciate this subtlety, as if I had acquired a new sense, a sense whereby to measure intellectual things, wit as distinguished from giggling, for example. (*Diary*, 128–29)

I quote this passage at length because it captures so vividly the back-and-forth rhythm of play. AJ's mind traverses the distance between the present and the past, oscillating like the forlorn swing until her pulse quickens, beating a tempo of "sisterly pride." HJ's quip, a pocket performance for an audience of one, puts a frame around an endless and boring afternoon, creating from inauspicious materials a spark of liberatory energy. Huizinga notes that for the Greeks play included the ideas of "contest, struggle, exercise, exertion, endurance and suffering" (51), which small HJ condenses into "pleasure under difficulties": perhaps the most felicitous (and certainly the most condensed!) definition of play we have yet encountered. In on the joke, AJ feels transported out of the realm of childish things, into the magic circle of shared amusement and recollection. The experience is not just imaginative but also sensory: the adult AJ scents a waft of what she calls "the exquisite *family* perfume of the days gone by, made up of the allusions, the memories and the point of view in common" (51).

Sent outside with the injunction "to play," the siblings express philosophy-worthy wisdom on the absurdity of their situation, their simultaneous thralldom to and exclusion from the drudgery of adult society. Like a memory of sex or death, the moment is suffused with a significance that would be retrievable decades into the future. AJ, writing at middle age, observes that "the things we remember have a *first-timeness* about them which suggests that that may be the reason of their survival. I must ask Wm. some day if there is any theory on the subject, or better whether 'tis worth a theory" (128). WJ, for his part, would observe in *The Varieties of Religious Experience* (1902) that a

> sense of deeper significance is not confined to rational propositions. Single words, and conjunctions of words, effects of light on land and sea, odors and musical sounds, all bring it when the mind is tuned aright. Most of us can remember the strangely moving power of passages in certain poems read when we were young, irrational doorways

> as they were through which the mystery of fact, the wildness and the pang of life, stole into our hearts and thrilled them. The words have now perhaps become mere polished surfaces for us; but lyric poetry and music are alive and significant only in proportion as they fetch these vague vistas of a life continuous with our own, beckoning and inviting, yet ever eluding our pursuit. We are alive or dead to the eternal inner message of the arts according as we have kept or lost this mystical susceptibility.[4]

Aptly, WJ here declines to offer a theory (though he keeps the door open to one); instead, this professor of philosophy and psychology offers a passage that itself reads as a poem.

The present book, both in theme and in method, has been affirming that we can indeed discern a sort of indigenous theory within the siblings' writings, about the existential importance of humor, play, and philosophical toys for human survival and flourishing. "It all comes back to that," HJ writes in the preface to *The Golden Bowl*, "to my and your 'fun'—if we but allow the term its full extension."[5] Play enlists not just the mind but also (as AJ puts it) a "stir of my whole being" (128). To invoke HJ's formulation about Maisie—who knew, and knew that she knew—the three siblings lived, and were astonishingly aware that they did. This wisdom was hard-earned. AJ rivals both brothers in eloquence when, in her final days, she writes, "It is the most supremely interesting moment in life, the only one in fact when living seems life, and I count in the greatest good fortune to have these few months so full of interest and instruction in the knowledge of my approaching death. It is as simple in one's own person as any fact of nature, the fall of a leaf or the blooming of a rose, and I have a delicious consciousness, ever present, of wide spaces close at hand, and whisperings of release in the air" (217). What AJ calls "delicious consciousness," the play theorist Brian Sutton-Smith less poetically calls "a general feeling of viability"—an essential resilience that can be understood on evolutionary terms even if not subsumed within them:

> Sex, like play, may be pleasurable for its own sake, but it nevertheless serves an evolutionary purpose through childbirth. Play is also a pleasure for its own sake, but its genetic gift is perhaps the sense that life, temporarily at least, is worth living. Play we might conceptualize as what I came to call a viability variable, one supplied as a genetically based technique that allows us to triumph over regular, ordinary

> distresses and disasters or, more simply, to feel good about life in general. Perhaps as birth is the evolutionary salute to sex, a general feeling of viability is the evolutionary salute to play. Just as sex, though fun, can also create birth, so, too, can play, which is also fun, create a lively viability. Thus do both fulfill their evolutionary tasks.[6]

The potency of play for the James siblings lies in its utterly grounded power to offer homeopathic doses of (an admittedly oxymoronic) corporeal transcendence. Rather than the awe of the sublime or the loveliness of the beautiful, play engenders a homelier set of affects, which transpire in relation to game compatriots and affirm the "lively viability" of the human endeavor writ small.

NOTES

INTRODUCTION

Epigraph: Frank Sewall, *The Angel of the State: Or, the Kindergarten in the Education of the Citizen: A Study of Pestalozzi, Froebel, and Swedenborg* (Boston: E. A. Whiston, 1896), 106.

1. A note on names: with multiple Jameses in play in this book, identifying the different siblings poses a problem. Using full names each time is cumbersome, while using first names feels too informal. I have followed the lead of F. O. Matthiessen, whose magisterial *The James Family* is still the most comprehensive treatment of the siblings, and use initials for my central figures: Alice James is AJ; William James is WJ; and Henry James is HJ. In quotations, citations, headings, and first appearances in a chapter, the full name is used.

2. Letter from William James to Alice James, 1889, quoted in F. O. Matthiessen, *The James Family: A Group Biography* (New York: Vintage Books, 1980), 303.

3. Alice James, *The Diary of Alice James*, ed. Leon Edel and Linda Simon (Boston: Northeastern University Press, 1999), 51.

4. The first two phrases can be found in an 1891 entry from AJ's *Diary* (217); the last is from a letter WJ wrote to HJ in 1888, quoted in *William and Henry James Selected Letters*, ed. Ignas K. Skrupskelis and Elizabeth M. Berkeley (Charlottesville: University of Virginia Press, 1997), 198; hereafter referred to as *WHJ*.

5. Ross Posnock, *The Trial of Curiosity: Henry James, William James, and the Challenge of Modernity* (New York: Oxford University Press, 1991), 36. Posnock's brilliant and generative study reflects the influence of the Frankfurt School in making the case for HJ as a cultural philosopher. My own book, while deeply indebted to Posnock's work, expands the analytical frame to include a serious consideration of AJ. This broader consideration in turn affords the key insight that "low theory"—a body of thought that includes cognitive science, play theory, and object-oriented philosophy—situates these thinkers as it were "butt-end-foremost," a term WJ used to describe the "humanist position" in *Pragmatism* (1907); in *Writings: 1902–1910*, ed. Bruce Kuklick (New York: Library of America, 1987), 593. I invoke WJ's irreverent phrase to capture the idea of an on-the-ground set of philosophical practices that considers not just the products of the mind but also the situatedness of the physical body.

6. Henry James, *The Ambassadors* (New York: W. W. Norton, 1964), 196. In its intransitive verb form, *toddling* (according to the *Oxford English Dictionary Online*) may refer to a child learning to walk, to a person engaging in a leisurely stroll, or (rarely) to the act of toying or playing with (Oxford University Press, June 2020), https://www-oed-com.libproxy.lib.unc.edu/view/Entry/202820?rskey=a02Ler&result=1&isAdvanced=false.

7. *Merriam-Webster.com Dictionary*, s.v. "ludic," accessed June 2, 2019, https://www.merriam-webster.com/dictionary/ludic.

8. Johan Huizinga, *Homo Ludens: A Study of the Play-Element in Culture* (Kettering, Ohio: Angelico Press, 2016), 19.

9. For a superb, multifaceted discussion of the literary appropriation of scientific experiment in the nineteenth century, see Randall Knoper's introduction to *Literary Neurophysiology: Race, Sex, and Representation in U.S. Writing, 1860–1911* (New York: Oxford University Press, forthcoming 2022).

10. In foregrounding fun, *Philosophical Siblings* offers an alternative to three current approaches to the study of literature: the instrumental cognitivism of a critic like Lisa Zunshine; the universalizing, species-level claims of literary Darwinism (for example, Brian Boyd); and the moral philosophy criticism practiced by Amanda Anderson. For Zunshine, "fiction engages, teases, and pushes to its tentative limits our mind-reading capacity," thus serving a prosocial purpose (*Why We Read Fiction: Theory of Mind and the Novel* [Columbus: Ohio State University Press, 2006], 4). For Anderson, literature and debates within literary criticism constitute reason-based practices for discovering what values we hold, and for exerting, demonstrating, and refining our capacity for judgment and discernment; see *Psyche and Ethos: Moral Life After Psychology* (New York: Oxford University Press, 2018). By contrast, the ludic pragmatism of the Jameses emphasizes that literature offers a play space that first and foremost entices participation. From this initiating act, many "outcomes" are possible—better social skills, more sex appeal, clarification of values—including their exact opposites and (perhaps most radically) nothing in particular.

11. See Nancy Easterlin, *A Biocultural Approach to Literary Theory and Interpretation* (Baltimore: Johns Hopkins University Press, 2012), esp. 24–33.

12. Brian Boyd, *On the Origin of Stories: Evolution, Cognition, and Fiction* (Cambridge, Mass.: Harvard University Press, 2007), 1.

13. WJ wrote eloquently, and from personal experience, about "the morbid mind": when this state of being arises, "all natural goods perish. Riches take wings; fame is a breath; love is a cheat; youth and health and pleasure vanish. . . . Back of everything is the great spectre of universal death, the all-encompassing blackness"; *The Varieties of Religious Experience* (Cambridge, Mass.: Harvard University Press, 1985), 116. With perhaps the exception of HJ, each of the James siblings suffered the chill of what WJ called "the sick soul"; for a biographical account, see Martin Halliwell, "Morbid and Positive Thinking: William James, Psychology, and Illness," in *William James and the Transatlantic Conversation: Pragmatism, Pluralism, and Philosophy of Religion*, ed. Martin Halliwell and Joel D. S. Rasmussen (New York: Oxford University Press, 2015); in *Oxford Scholarship Online*, DOI:10.1093/acprof:oso/9780199687510.003.0006.

14. William James, "What Makes a Life Significant," in *Writings: 1878–1899*, ed. Gerald E. Myers (New York: Library of America, 1992), 862.

15. Brian Sutton-Smith, "Play Theory: A Personal Journal and New Thoughts," *American Journal of Play* 1, no. 1 (Summer 2008): 82–128, 97.

16. The two younger brothers, Garth Wilkerson (Wilky) James and Robertson (Bob) James, served in the Civil War in the storied 54th and 55th Massachusetts Infantry Regiments that enlisted Black soldiers. Both later embarked on nonliterary careers. Wilky James died young, in 1883; Bob James tried careers in the railroad and in farming, finally settling in Concord, Massachusetts, with his wealthy wife and raising a family of four children. HJ described Bob's animated conversation as "'charged with natural life, perception, humor and color . . . the equivalent, for fine animation, of William's epistolary prowess'"; quoted in Jean Maher, *Biography of Broken*

Fortunes: Wilky and Bob, Brothers of William, Henry, and Alice James (New York: Archon Books, 1968), 138.

17. Unsigned two-part review of *The Principles of Psychology* in *Nation* 53 (2 July 1891), 15; (9 July 1891), 32–33. To my mind, WJ in the letter to HJ half lets on his suspicion about the reviewer when he writes, "The second installment was utterly unintelligible. . . . I did n't care a single straw for the matter one way or the other, not even enough to find out who wrote it." Attribution of review to Charles Sanders Peirce in *WHJ*, 258–59.

18. Matthiessen, *The James Family*, 14.

19. Henri Bergson, *Laughter: An Essay on the Meaning of the Comic* (Mineola, N.Y.: Dover, 2005), 3.

20. William James, *Pragmatism: A New Name for Some Old Ways of Thinking* [1907], in *Writings: 1902–1910*, 574.

21. Louis Menand, *The Metaphysical Club: A Story of Ideas in America* (New York: Farrar, Straus and Giroux, 1981), 151.

22. Mary Reilly, *Play as Exploratory Learning: Studies of Curiosity Behavior* (Beverly Hills, Calif.: Sage, 1974), 16.

23. See Leon Edel, *The Life of Henry James*, vol. 5 *The Master: 1901–1916* (New York: Lippincott, 1972); and Colm Toíbín, *The Master: A Novel* (New York: Scribner, 2005).

24. Play—like emotion or humor—is surprisingly difficult to define. Nineteenth-century theories emphasize the physiological and functional aspects of play; that it dissipates surplus energy, that it relaxes and refreshes, or (according to G. Stanley Hall), that it recapitulates primitive behaviors of the human species. Twentieth-century theories focus on the social, cultural, and/or cognitive aspects of play; these thinkers include Johan Huizinga, Jean Piaget, Lev Vygotsky, and Gregory Bateson (among many others). This book affirms that there is a loose affiliation—a *family resemblance*—among the different forms of play. I take my cue from WJ, in his work *The Varieties of Religious Experience* (1902). Rather than seeking "any single principle or essence," he understood his object of study to be "a collective name," and posited that the best way to approach the diversity of cases was to "enjoy[] an intimate acquaintance with all their particularities in turn" (in *Writings: 1902–1910*, 32).

The concept of *family resemblance*, theorized by Ludwig Wittgenstein, is especially apt for the present book given his primary example, *game*: "We are inclined to think that there must be something common to all games, say, and that this common property is the justification for applying the general term 'game' to the various games; whereas the games form a *family* the members of which have family likenesses" (in *The Blue and Brown Books*, quoted in Nicholas Griffin, "Wittgenstein, Universals and Family Resemblances," *Canadian Journal of Philosophy* 3, no. 4 [June 1974]: 635–51, 635.) In fact, George Pitcher has argued that the source text for Wittgenstein's concept of family resemblance may have been WJ's *Varieties of Religious Experience*; see Pitcher, *The Philosophy of Wittgenstein* (New York: Prentice-Hall, 1964), 218.

25. John Dewey, *Experience and Education* (New York: Simon and Schuster, 1938), 32.

26. Bill Brown, *The Material Unconscious: American Amusement, Stephen Crane, and the Economics of Play* (Cambridge, Mass.: Harvard University Press, 1996), 49.

27. I count myself, and some of my earlier work, among these critics; see, for instance, my contribution to *The American Child: A Cultural Studies Reader* entitled "Traumatic Realism and the Wounded Child" (ed. Caroline F. Levander and Carol S. Singley [New Brunswick, N.J.: Rutgers University Press, 2003]: 128–48).

28. Charles Sanders Peirce, *The Essential Peirce*, vol. 2, ed. the Peirce Edition Project (Bloomington: Indiana University Press, 1998), 436.

29. For Reilly, Freud is the ultimate spoilsport: "While the Freudian theory performed a powerful service in decoding unconscious motivation, play comes off badly under the rigid constructs of the theory. The nature of play as a discrete behavior serving adaptive and necessary functions becomes chewed up in the psychoanalytical process" (*Play as Exploratory Learning*, 71).

30. Rita Felski, *The Limits of Critique* (Chicago: University of Chicago Press, 2015), 152.

31. Indeed, the Jameses' texts themselves also invite spinoffs: witness the plethora of filmic adaptations of HJ's works (especially cinematic variations on *The Turn of the Screw*); the surge of references to WJ in contemporary scholarship, ranging from literary studies and philosophy to education and neuroscience; and the (fewer, but no less potent) creative adaptations of AJ's *Diary*, especially Susan Sontag's *Alice in Bed: A Play* (New York: Farrar, Straus and Giroux, 1994). Judith Hooper wrote a novel by the same name, *Alice in Bed: A Novel* (Berkeley, Calif.: Counterpoint, 2015).

32. "Interpretation becomes a coproduction between actors that brings new things to light rather than an endless rumination of a text's hidden meanings or representational failures," Felski writes emphatically, in *The Limits of Critique*, 174. I agree with Felski in this and in her affirmation that non-suspicious readings need not exclude culture, history, and ideology—the "whole envelope of circumstances," as HJ's Madame Merle (from *The Portrait of a Lady*) puts it. Context ("the envelope," or "macrolevel") may set ground rules, but there's room for improvisation, which is what I take Felski to mean when she states the following: "This macrolevel holds the cards, calls the tune, and specifies the rules of the game; the individual work, as a microunit encased within a larger whole, can only react or respond to these preestablished conditions" (156).

33. Paul Armstrong, "Henry James and Neuroscience: Cognitive Universals and Cultural Differences," *Henry James Review* 39, no. 2 (Spring 2018): 133–51, 133. I admire Armstrong's emphasis on the phenomenology of cognition in HJ's works. Armstrong picks up on HJ's language of "flickering," too, though he doesn't trace this idiom to the early technologies of film: "Maurice Merleau-Ponty observes that 'our reflections take place in the temporal flow that they are attempting to capture' (*Phenomenology* lxxviii), and so, when we begin to reflect, we always find a reservoir of unreflected experience already there whose flickering, obscure immediacy we can never fully elucidate" (133).

34. Reading under the aspect of play affords novelty and surprise, something that historicist or cognitivist approaches, taken separately, sometimes close down. In his excellent article "Reading Minds in the Nineteenth Century," Paul Gilmore observes that "many of the readings produced by cognitive literary studies seem, as with other reductionist materialisms such as vulgar Marxism, simply to tell the same story over and over" (331); in *The Oxford Handbook of Nineteenth-Century American Literature*, ed. Russ Castronovo (November 2012): 327–42, DOI: 10.1093/oxfordhb/9780199730438.013.0019.

35. Paul Fisher, *House of Wits: An Intimate Portrait of the James Family* (New York: Henry Holt, 2008), 3. In his review of *House of Wits*, Charles McGrath (like Matthiessen) picks up on the idea of performance, observing that Fisher's book "keeps all the balls juggling." McGrath's largely unfavorable review was entitled "James Clan: A Family with a Load of Baggage," *New York Times* (30 July 2008), https://www.nytimes.com/2008/07/30/books/30book.html.

36. See Jean Strouse, *Alice James: A Biography* (Cambridge, Mass.: Harvard University Press, 1999); Leon Edel, *Henry James: A Life* (New York: Harper Collins, 1987); and Robert Richardson, *William James: In the Maelstrom of American Modernism* (New York: Houghton Mifflin Harcourt, 2006). The philosopher Ralph Barton Perry's masterful *The Thought and Character of William James* (1935), which won the Pulitzer Prize in 1936, clearly set the bar high for future

biographers; Edel also won a Pulitzer Prize and a National Book Award for his work on HJ, while Strouse's and Richardson's biographies both won the Bancroft Prize (among others).

37. Posnock, *The Trial of Curiosity*. For the influence of WJ's pragmatism on HJ, see Richard Hocks, *Henry James and Pragmatistic Thought: A Study in the Relationship Between the Philosophy of William James and the Literary Art of Henry James* (Chapel Hill: University of North Carolina Press, 1974). Hannah Wells reverses the trajectory of influence, asking instead "what Henry gave to William" (35). Her answer is that HJ in his experimental late stories exposes the material conditions—and racial exclusions—on which a modern "pragmatism model of subjectivity" is constructed; "What Henry Gave to William," *Henry James Review* 35, no. 1 (Winter 2014): 34–47, 45. To the best of my knowledge there are no book-length studies of the Jameses that center on AJ. However, important articles and chapters that prioritize AJ's work include Alice Golomb Hoffman's "Writing Siblings: Alice James and Her Brothers," *Psychoanalytic Review* 102, no. 1 (February 2015): 1–32, which argues for "sickness as a source of creativity" (2); Cynthia J. Davis's marvelous chapter, "'No Pain and No Consciousness': The James Siblings on Anesthesia and Suffering," in which pain for AJ and HJ "served to tether the imagination to the material world and infuse its products with the requisite 'air of reality'" (this chapter is part of Davis's study of U.S. literary realism, forthcoming from Oxford University Press); and Elizabeth Duquette's insightful "'A New Claim for the Family Renown': Alice James and the Picturesque," *English Literary History* 72, no. 3 (Fall 2005): 717–45.

38. Joan Richardson, *A Natural History of Pragmatism: The Fact of Feeling from Jonathan Edwards to Gertrude Stein* (Cambridge: Cambridge University Press, 2007); Steven Meyer, *Irresistible Dictation: Gertrude Stein and the Correlations of Writing and Science* (Palo Alto, Calif.: Stanford University Press, 2002). Richardson calls attention to the natural historical roots of both WJ's and HJ's interest in "thinking about thinking and language" (x), with HJ offering in his novels and autobiographies the "linguistic analogue of being lost amidst signs" (xi). Meyer emphasizes the influence of WJ on Gertrude Stein (WJ's student), who attempts to capture in her writing a "sense of immediacy" (8) as well as "the decisive role of processes and procedures, of conjunctive as well as disjunctive relations, in the composition of experience" (13).

39. Paul Grimstad, *Experience and Experimental Writing: Literary Pragmatism from Emerson to the Jameses* (New York: Oxford University Press, 2013); Kate Stanley, *Practices of Surprise in American Literature After Emerson* (Cambridge: Cambridge University Press, 2018). These terrific studies attend to literary works as a "a source of experience" (Grimstad, 12), with Grimstad emphasizing how HJ's late fiction twines together "experience and composition . . . to form a continuity" (93) and Stanley arguing for the textual transmission of a radically empirical capacity for "conductive spontaneity" that "propels the undulating movements of the mind" without seeking to arrest them prematurely into meaning and concepts (45). Jonathan Levin perspicaciously links WJ and HJ through their emphasis on "transitional dynamics of consciousness, language, and action" and the "displace[ment of] stable or coherent identities and meanings" (Durham: Duke University Press, 1999), xii. Gregory Phipps takes a slightly different approach in *Henry James and the Philosophy of Literary Pragmatism* (London: Palgrave Macmillan, 2016), treating WJ as one among other theorists of pragmatism and tracing how HJ's novels reflect or embody the different conceptions. In *Pragmatic Modernism*, Lisi Schoenbach distinguishes WJ and HJ by virtue of their belief in institutions; Schoenbach's study helpfully situates WJ (and Dewey) in terms of "a post-Darwinian conception of the dialectic of habit, in which continuity and adaptation to the environment are continually balanced with positive actions and constantly changing reactions" ([New York: Oxford University Press, 2012], 24).

40. Upon hearing of AJ's breast cancer, WJ advised his sister that her death would liberate her potent spirit from the "infernality" of the body. Her mock-effusive epistolary reply: "I will venture upon the impertinence of congratulating you upon arrived 'at nearly fifty' at the point at which I started at fifteen!" She concludes: "'Twas always thus of old, but in time, you usually, as now, caught up"; quoted in *The Death and Letters of Alice James*, ed. Ruth Bernard Yeazell (Boston: Exact Change, 1997), 194–95.

41. Elaine Scarry, *The Body in Pain: The Making and Unmaking of the World* (New York: Oxford University Press, 1987). Scarry argues that pain reduces the self to inarticulate, isolate, unacknowledged flesh: "Pain comes unsharably into our midst as at once that which cannot be denied and that which cannot be confirmed. [paragraph break] Whatever pain achieves, it achieves in part through its unsharability, and it ensures this unsharability through its resistance to language" (4). My Chapter 1 examines how AJ affirms the expressive shareability of experience that runs counter to Scarry's account of epistemological doubt and linguistic shutdown.

42. Davis, "No Pain and No Consciousness."

43. Bergson, *Laughter*, 1.

44. Henry James, *A Small Boy and Others* [1913], in *Henry James: Autobiographies* (New York: Library of America Press, 2016), 5, 6.

45. In *The Varieties of Religious Experience*, WJ mentions "persons whose existence is little more than a series of zig-zags, as now one tendency and now another gets the upper hand" (157). Biographer Richardson picked up and popularized WJ's term by titling a chapter "Growing up Zig-Zag." For an interesting parsing of "the notion of zig-zag" in WJ's work, see Jeremy Carrette, "Growing Up Zig-Zag: Reassessing the Transatlantic Legacy of William James," in *William James and the Translatlantic Conversation: Pluralism, Pragmatism, and Philosophy of Religion,* ed. Martin Halliwell and Joel D. S. Rasmussen (New York: Oxford University Press, 2014), 199–202 passim.

46. For a terrific account of the centrality of the body to WJ's understanding of experience, see Richard Shusterman, "William James, Somatic Introspection, and Care of the Self," *The Philosophical Forum* 36, no. 4 (Winter 2005): 419–440.

47. Alva Noë, *Out of Our Heads: Why You Are Not Your Brain, and Other Lessons from the Biology of Consciousness* (New York: Hill and Wang, 2010), 32.

48. Sharon Cameron, *Thinking in Henry James* (Chicago: University of Chicago Press, 1991).

49. Paul Armstrong has further expanded the study of consciousness in HJ as both social and ontologically extensive. For HJ, he argues, art offers a field of experience that can produce community and not merely enhance a "private aesthetic realm" (99). Armstrong taps into the language of play when he observes, "Fluid relations can make possible a playful reciprocity based on mutual recognition and engagement, or they can become a field of contest between opponents who would structure them for their own purposes" ("Art and the Construction of Community in 'The Death of the Lion,'" *Henry James Review* 17, no. 2 [Spring 1996]: 99–106, 100).

50. William James, *Psychology: Briefer Course* [1892], in *Writings: 1878–1899*, 138.

51. Karen Sanchez-Eppler, *Dependent States: The Child's Part in Nineteenth-Century American Culture* (Chicago: University of Chicago Press, 2005), xxv, xxvii.

52. Strouse, *Alice James*, 51.

53. Anthony Chemero, "An Outline of a Theory of Affordances," *Ecological Psychology* 15, no. 2 (2003): 181–95, 191.

54. James J. Gibson, *The Ecological Approach to Visual Perception* (Boston: Houghton Mifflin, 1979), 129; quoted in Chemero, "An Outline," 182.

55. Caroline Levine, *Forms: Whole, Rhythm, Hierarchy, Network* (Princeton: Princeton University Press, 2015), 7; see also Terence Cave, *Thinking with Literature: Towards a Cognitive Criticism* (Oxford: Oxford University Press, 2016).

56. Scarry gets at this core of vitality when she writes that even "ordinary and routine artifacts" (she gives the example of a chair) are so "extravagantly excessive in their referential powers that the calculus of projection and reciprocation will seem almost funny"; "the total act of creating," she concludes, "contains an inherent movement toward self-amplifying generosity" (*The Body in Pain*, 318). For a truly wonderful reading of HJ and WJ in relation to the object- and milieu-oriented vitalism of Henri Bergson, see Omri Moses, *Out of Character: Vitalism, Modernism, and Psychic Life* (Chapel Hill: University of North Carolina Press, 2014), esp. the discussion of "relational being," 80–84.

57. William James, "What Is an Emotion?" [1884] in *Collected Essays and Reviews* (London: Longmans, Green, 1920), 257.

58. Writing in 2000, Todd Jackson in his article "Questioning Interdisciplinarity" noted that while "literary study has often welcomed other disciplinary approaches and concepts, this welcome, except in a few cases, has not extended to cognitive science and evolutionary psychology" (*Poetics Today* 21, no. 2 [Summer 2000]: 319–47, 323).

59. These scenes are taken, respectively, from AJ in her *Diary*, WJ in *Principles of Psychology*, and HJ in *The Ambassadors*, describing the character of Lambert Strether wandering the streets of Paris with fresh eyes.

60. Jonathan Kramnick, *Paper Minds: Literature and the Ecology of Consciousness* (Chicago: University of Chicago Press, 2018), 6; also, see Jane F. Thrailkill, "Ian McEwan's Neurological Novel," *Poetics Today* 32, no. 1 (2011): 171–201. Surprisingly, Kramnick doesn't mention the Jameses (or Dewey), forebears of today's cognitive neuroscience in which "the emphasis on motion, skill, and environment broadens the discussion from the ostensibly unchanging nature of the brain to the historically variable conditions of circumstance" (6).

61. Anthony Chemero, *Radical Embodied Cognitive Science* (Cambridge, Mass.: MIT Press, 2009), 183.

62. Huizinga, *Homo Ludens*, 14.

63. Alison Gopnik, *The Philosophical Baby: What Children's Minds Tell Us About Truth, Love, and the Meaning of Life* (New York: Picador, 2010), 7–8.

CHAPTER 1

Epigraph: Henri Bergson, *Laughter: An Essay on the Meaning of the Comic* [1900] (Mineola: Dover Publications, 2005), 19. Subsequent references to this work appear in parentheses in the text.

1. Alice James, *The Diary of Alice James*, ed. Leon Edel (Boston: Northeastern University Press, 1999), 232. Subsequent references to this work appear in parentheses in the text. Katharine Loring had four copies printed: one for herself and one each for WJ, HJ, and Bob (Robertson) James.

2. See Mikhail Bakhtin, "Discourse in the Novel" in *The Dialogic Imagination: Four Essays by M. M. Bakhtin*, ed. Michael Holquist, trans. Caryl Emerson and Michael Holquist (Austin: University of Texas Press, 1981). Bakhtin uses the term "heteroglossia" to signify the myriad registers of discourse and voice within a language, a text, or a genre (the novel in particular): "In the makeup of almost every utterance spoken by a social person—from a brief response in a casual dialogue to major verbal ideological works (literary, scholarly and others)—a significant number

of words can be identified that are implicitly or explicitly admitted as someone else's, and that are transmitted by a variety of different means" (354). For example, AJ frequently lapses into the argot of a servant or a native Englishwoman; conversely, she frequently derides the obfuscations of church or parliamentary officials in moments that are "parodic, and aimed sharply and polemically against the official languages of its given time" (273).

3. Leon Edel, "Preface to the 1964 Edition," *The Diary of Alice James*, xxix.

4. See, for instance, Kristin Boudreau's argument that AJ used her invalidism as a way to critique conventional ideas about sympathy ("'A Barnum Monstrosity': Alice James and the Spectacle of Sympathy," *American Literature* 65, no. 1 [March 1993]: 53–67); Elizabeth Duquette's reading of AJ's skillful use of the picturesque to establish herself as an intellectual within the storied family ("'A New Claim for the Family Renown': Alice James and the Picturesque," *English Literary History* 72, no. 3 [Fall 2005]: 717–45); Natalie Dykstra's discussion of her use of "the sickroom as a means to establish a measure of personal value and freedom with her work of being ill" ("'Trying to Idle': Work and Disability in *The Diary of Alice James*," in *New Disability History: American Perspectives*, ed. Paul K. Longmore and Lauri Umansky [New York: New York University Press, 2001]: 107–30, 109); and Ruth Bernard Yeazell's analysis of AJ's life and writings as forming a "covert career in mortality" (21) in her introduction to *The Death and Letters of Alice James: Selected Correspondence*, ed. Yeazell (Berkeley: University of California Press, 1981), 21. Subsequent references to this work appear in parentheses in the text.

5. Davis argues that, for HJ and AJ, "physical suffering as either an experience or a theme could also in their view impose constraints that served to tether the imagination to the material world and infuse its products with the requisite 'air of reality'" (*The Ache of the Actual: Pain and the Aesthetic of U.S. Literary Realism,* forthcoming from Oxford University Press; internal quotation from AJ's Diary, 173.) In her experiences with doctors, however, AJ found that the lack of organic explanation for her symptoms made her susceptible to their skepticism and did *not* serve as a sort of "earnest money" of the real. Davis situates pain as a rhetorical technique or a literary strategy; her project is "to recover and examine representations of physical suffering that depict it as valuably enabling a refined sensibility and interiority portrayed as distinguishing the most discerning from the more insensible, pain-averse members of the upper classes."

6. *William and Henry James Selected Letters*, ed. Ignas K. Skrupskelis and Elizabeth Berkeley (Charlottesville: University Press of Virginia, 1997), 307.

7. Yeazell, *Death and Letters*, 187, emphasis added.

8. William James, "On a Certain Blindness in Human Beings" (1899) from a series of three *Talks to Students* in *William James, Writings 1878–1899*, ed. Gerald E. Myers (New York: Library of America, 1992), 841–60, 848, 860.

9. Norman Malcolm, *Ludwig Wittgenstein: A Memoir* (New York: Oxford University Press, 2001), 29.

10. Jean Strouse, *Alice James: A Biography* (Boston: Houghton Mifflin, 1980), 276.

11. Yeazell, noting that the Diary was written in different hands, writes that "to subject one's private journal to all this stenographic activity testifies, at the very least, to a certain ambivalence about its privacy" (6).

12. Linda Anderson, in 1996, edited a collection of AJ's letters that almost doubles the number of Yeazell's volume, though it still only includes about two-thirds of the available correspondence. See *Alice James: Her Life in Letters* (New York: Thoemmes Press, 1996).

13. Strouse notes that WJ "referred constantly to her physical attributes"; she gives the following example of a letter he wrote from Paris to his parents, referring to twelve-year-old Alice: "Thousand thanks to the cherry lipped apricot nosed double chinned little Bal for her strongly

dashed off letter, which inflamed the hearts of her lonely brothers with an intense longing to kiss and slap her celestial cheeks" (52–53).

14. Quoted in F. O. Matthiessen, *The James Family: A Group Biography* (New York: Vintage Books, 1980), 209.

15. George Prochnik, *Putnam Camp: Sigmund Freud, James Jackson Putnam, and the Purpose of American Psychology* (New York: Other Press, 2006), 35.

16. *WHJ Selected Letters*, 47.

17. The second quote is from *Henry James Selected Letters*, ed. Leon Edel (Cambridge, Mass.: Belknap Press of Harvard University Press, 1987), 45; all others from *WHJ Selected Letters*.

18. The brothers use other means of indirection to discuss their digestion, elimination, and career preparation, at key moments switching from English to French, as a more delicate means of expression. In answer to HJ's query about effective treatments for constipation, WJ says the "*douche rectale*" did not work for him. The puns fly back and forth: "You cant expect much *solid* benefit fm. them in less than 2 months" (23 April 1869; *WHJ Selected Letters*, 38), WJ writes. WJ credits HJ's glum letters with his own literary urgency, spurring him to "incontinently sit down & write ye a line" (45). HJ's reply riffs further, referring to his "old enemy no. 2—by which of course I mean *my* unhappy bowels" (48). Cinching the link between writing and excretion, the letter concludes: "Don't let this nasty effusion prey upon your spirits" (51). Both brothers scold the other for withholding writing: "Verily," HJ writes, "it is worthwhile pining for letters for 3 weeks to know the exquisite joy of final relief" (52). To his father HJ writes, much more obliquely, "My malady has done a great deal towards spoiling Florence for me." HJ (again) apologizes for his melancholy letter (he calls it a "dismal effusion") and notes the strain of abandoning his Italian travels: "To be at the very gates of Rome and to turn away requires certainly a strong muscular effort" (26 October 1869; *HJ Selected Letters*, 52).

19. Alice James, *Diary*, 129.

20. Ludwig Wittgenstein, *Culture and Value* (Chicago: University of Chicago Press, 1984), 83e.

21. Strouse, *Alice James: A Biography*, 254.

22. Simon Critchley, *On Humour* (Florence: Routledge, 2002), 3–4, https://doi.org/10.4324/9780203870129.

23. Johan Huizinga, *Homo Ludens: A Study of the Play-Element in Culture* (Kettering, Ohio: Angelico Press, 2016), 122.

24. Duquette, "'A New Claim,'" 719–20.

25. The letter appeared in the *Nation* and was afterward referenced in the London *Daily News* in a short piece published on 29 July 1890. Both the letter and the *Daily News* rendering of it appear in AJ's Diary in an entry dated 24 September 1890.

26. Strouse, *Alice James: A Biography*, 274.

27. Christina Sjödblad, "From Family Notes to Diary: The Development of a Genre," *Eighteenth-Century Studies* 31, no. 4 (Summer 1998): 517–21, 521.

28. Jennifer Sinor, *The Extraordinary Work of Ordinary Writing: Annie Ray's Diary* (Iowa City: University of Iowa Press, 2002), 29.

29. William James, "To Henry James, March 7, 1892," in *WHJ Selected Letters*, 265.

30. Henry James, *Hawthorne* (New York: Harper and Brothers, 1880), 43.

31. Friedrich Nietzsche, *The Birth of Tragedy and Other Writings,* trans. Ronald Speirs (Cambridge: Cambridge University Press, 1999), 40.

32. Herbert Spencer, "The Physiology of Laughter," *Macmillan's Magazine* (March 1860): 395–402, 395.

33. Arthur Schopenhauer, *The World as Will and Idea*, trans. R. B. Haldane and J. Kemp (London: Kegan Paul, Trench, Trubner, 1896), 76.

34. Michael W. Taylor, *The Philosophy of Herbert Spencer* (London: Continuum, 2007), 22, emphasis added.

35. William James, *Psychology: Briefer Course*, in *Writings: 1878–1899*, 141.

36. William James, "What Pragmatism Means" (1904), from a series of eight lectures dedicated to the memory of John Stuart Mill, titled *Pragmatism: A New Name for Some Old Ways of Thinking*, in December 1904; from *William James, Writings 1902–1920*, ed. Bruce Kuklick (New York: Library of America, 1987), 509–10.

37. Critchley, *On Humour*, 90.

38. William James, "To Alice James, July 6, 1891," in *Selected Letters*, ed. Elizabeth Hardwick (New York: Farrar, Straus and Cudahy, 1961), 134.

39. Resisting the pitying gaze of those family members and friends who cast her as an object of sympathy, AJ (argues Haley French) "takes possession of her body's representations"; "The Joke's on You: Invalid as Comic in *The Diary of Alice James*," *Canadian Review of American Studies* 44, no. 1 (2014): 85–101, 88. Lisa M. Koch writes that the Diary allows AJ to "replace her actual sickly body with an imaginative one"; "Bodies as Stage Props: Enacting Hysteria in the Diaries of Charlotte Forten Grimké and Alice James," *Legacy* 15, no. 1 (1998): 59–64, 63. In Kristin Boudreau's terms, AJ's Diary enables "successful detachment from her body"; see "'A Barnum Monstrosity,'" 60. These critics emphasize in particular AJ's savvy resistance to WJ's repeated portrayals of her as an object of suffering.

40. Yeazell, *Death and Letters*, 195.

41. Immanuel Kant, *Critique of the Power of Judgment*, trans. Eric Matthews (Cambridge: Cambridge University Press, 2000), 209.

42. This letter from AJ to WJ was written over a few days and is dated 29–31 January 1889; WJ's original letter to his sister is not archived. It is worth noting that four months later Alice wrote the first entry of her Diary, perhaps inspired by her brother's encouragement.

43. Simon Critchley, "Did You Hear the One About the Philosopher Writing a Book on Humour?" *Richmond Journal of Philosophy* 2 (Autumn 2002): 1–6, 1.

44. Shari Goldberg, "Advanced Pain Studies," *Los Angeles Review of Books* (2 July 2020), http://avidly.lareviewofbooks.org/2020/07/02/advanced-pain-studies/.

45. Cynthia J. Davis, "'The Ache of the Actual': Pain and the Aesthetics of US Literary Realism," *American Literature* 87, no. 3 (September 2015): 547–74.

46. Matthiessen, *The James Family*, 272.

47. Henry James Sr. suffered a terrible burn on his leg as a young man; the threat of gangrene led to the limb being amputated, and he was largely bedridden for three years after. In his *Autobiography* Henry James Sr. writes, "My wound had been very severe, being followed by a morbid process in the bone which ever and anon called for some sharp surgery; and on these occasions I remember—for the use of anaesthetics was still wholly undreamt of—his [father's] sympathy with my sufferings" (quoted in Matthiessen, *The James Family*, 18). WJ and HJ, we have heard, were plagued by stomach and bowel discomfort and existential crises. Wilkie knew firsthand the horrors and wounds of the Civil War battlefield, and HJ described Bob, also a war veteran and addicted to alcohol, as suffering from "the darkness and pain of his stormy life" (Matthiessen, 271). Only Mary Robertson Walsh James and Catherine Walsh (Aunt Kate) seem to have had persistent good health—though they were no strangers to pain, the former having survived five childbirths and the latter having escaped an abusive husband to live with her sister's family.

48. Barbara J. King, "Kindred Spirits," *Aeon* (22 October 2013), https://aeon.co/essays/friends-allies-and-lovers-animal-family-is-complicated.

49. Here, King quotes from Marshall Sahlin's *What Kinship Is—And Is Not* (Chicago: University of Chicago Press, 2013), 21.

50. Yeazell reports that Loring had arranged, in the winter of 1890, for the consul to officiate at the signing of the will, which took place before AJ was diagnosed with breast cancer (46).

51. Robert Anchor, "History and Play: Johan Huizinga and His Critics," *History and Theory* 17, no. 1 (February 1978): 63–93, 91–92.

52. Vanessa Agnew has suggested that the diary conforms to three principles: the "principle of immediacy, by which the diary is closed to hindsight; the autoptic principle of, 'I saw it with my own eyes, therefore it is true'; and the 'reliable witness' principle—he saw it with his own eyes and he is the kind of man to be believed." Quoted in Rachael Langford and Russell West, "Introduction: Diaries and Margins," *Marginal Voices, Marginal Forms: Diaries in European Literature and History* (Amsterdam: Brill, 1999), 15.

53. Thomas Nagel, "The Absurd," *Journal of Philosophy* 68, no. 20 (21 October 1971): 716–27, 720.

54. Henry James, *A Small Boy and Others*, in *Henry James Autobiographies*, ed. Philip Horne (New York: Library of America, 2016), 58.

55. It's amusing to contrast Thackeray's wilting sarcasm—ridiculing a little girl while fingering the fabric of her dress!—with his stated views about the moralizing tenderness of humor: "Besides contributing to our stock of happiness, to our harmless laughter and amusement, to our scorn for falsehood and pretension, to our righteous hatred of hypocrisy [!], to our education in the perception of truth, our love of honesty, our knowledge of life, and shrewd guidance through the world, have not our humorous writers, our gay and kind week-day preachers done much in support of that holy cause . . . of love and charity, the cause of the poor, the weak, and the unhappy; the sweet mission of love and tenderness, and peace and good-will toward men?" William Makepeace Thackeray, "Charity and Humor," *Harper's New Monthly Magazine* (June 1853): 82–88, 82.

56. Ted Cohen, *Jokes: Philosophical Thoughts on Laughing Matters* (Chicago: University of Chicago Press, 1999), 30.

57. The embedded, or better, *en-socketed*, nature of tooth in gum offers a figure for tight-knit friendship, and the pain of separation, that HJ would exploit in *What Maisie Knew* (1895). In a passage at once humorous and horrifying, tooth extraction becomes not just a figure for Maisie's being wrenched out of one household and planted in another but also a metaphor for her relationship with her inadequate governess. The joke, for HJ, is that the adult requires sedation while the ill-used child remains ever stoic; this risible situation is, to use Maisie's term, "screwed-up": "The second parting from Miss Overmore had been bad enough, but this first parting from Mrs. Wix was much worse. The child had lately been to the dentist's and had a term of comparison for the screwed-up intensity of the scene. It was dreadfully silent, as it had been when her tooth was taken out; Mrs. Wix had on that occasion grabbed her hand and they had clung to each other with the frenzy of their determination not to scream. Maisie, at the dentist's, had been heroically still, but just when she felt most anguish had become aware of an audible shriek on the part of her companion, a spasm of stifled sympathy. This was reproduced by the only sound that broke their supreme embrace when, a month later, the 'arrangement,' as her periodical uprootings were called, played the part of the horrible forceps. Embedded in Mrs. Wix's nature as her tooth had been socketed in her gum, the operation of extracting her would really have been a case for chloroform" —(Henry James, *What Maisie Knew* [New York: Viking Penguin, 1985] 51–52).

58. Virginia Woolf, "On Being Ill," in *Selected Essays* (Oxford: Oxford University Press, 2009), 101.

59. Woolf does, however, put her finger on a monumental achievement of the nineteenth century: the development of what was advertised as pain-free dentistry.

60. AJ's signal literary work did not see wide publication until 1934, after Woolf wrote her essay, though four copies of *The Diary of Alice James* were privately printed in 1894. It is nonetheless striking to note the extent to which AJ appears to "answer" Woolf's call for a literature of illness.

61. Charles Baudelaire, *Selected Writings on Art and Artists,* trans. P. E. Charvet (Cambridge: Cambridge University Press, 1981), 148.

62. Critics have noted AJ's tendency to look on her own life with detachment, reading it as a form of dissociation from her circumscribed life or psychological strategy for resisting others' pitying gaze. French, for instance, sees it as a protective "strategy of resistance and self-preservation" ("The Joke's on You," 91). I am making the case for reading the journal as a means of using comedy as a form of philosophizing.

63. Thomas Hobbes, *Leviathan*, ed. Edwin Curley (Indianapolis: Hackett, 1994), 32.

64. Charles Sanders Peirce, "The Architecture of Theories," *Monist* 1, no. 2 (January 1891): 161–76, 175.

65. Charles Sanders Peirce, *Collected Papers of Charles Sanders Peirce, Volume 1, Principles of Philosophy*, ed. Charles Hartshorne and Paul Weiss (Cambridge, Mass.: Harvard University Press, 1931), 175, emphasis added.

66. Charles Sanders Peirce, *The Essential Peirce: Selected Philosophical Writings, Volume 2*, ed. Peirce Edition Project (Bloomington: Indiana University Press, 1998), 177. This passage from Peirce echoes the famous moment from James Boswell's *The Life of Samuel Johnson* in which Johnson famously counters the subjective idealism of Charles Berkeley with a bodily gesture: "After we came out of the church, we stood talking for some time together of Bishop Berkeley's ingenious sophistry to prove the non-existence of matter, and that everything in the universe is merely ideal. I observed, that though we are satisfied his doctrine is not true, it is impossible to refute it. I never shall forget the alacrity with which Johnson answered, striking his foot with mighty force against a large stone, till he rebounded from it, 'I refute it *thus*'" (ed. Christopher Hibbert [New York: Penguin Classics, 1986], 122). Pertinent to my discussion of AJ, the philosophical rebuke comes in the form of not just a bodily action but also a joke.

67. Charles Sanders Peirce, quoted in Robert Stern, "Peirce, Hegel, and the Category of Secondness," *Inquiry* 50, no. 2 (2007): 123–55, 132, 150.

68. Peirce affirms the philosophical importance of the felt experience of resistance, struggle, and realignment. In trying to establish a phenomenology of human experience, Peirce set out to reconcile the realm of perception (Firstness) and the realm of reason (Thirdness). Simply put, the first is too subjective and the second too objective: human beings are neither unencumbered minds floating free of the physical world nor purely rational beings conforming to general rules and concepts. Between perceptions and ideas lies a contact zone where, as Schopenhauer suggests, "this very incongruity of sensuous and abstract knowledge" causes "a very remarkable phenomenon which, like reason itself, is peculiar to human nature, and of which the explanations that have ever anew been attempted, are insufficient: I mean *laughter*" (*The World as Will and Idea*, 76).

69. Thomas Hobbes, *Human Nature and De Corpore Politico,* ed. J. C. A. Gaskin (New York: Oxford University Press, 2008), 54.

70. Sigmund Freud, *Jokes and Their Relation to the Unconscious,* trans. James Strachey (London: Hogarth Press, 1960), 277.

71. Karen Sanchez-Eppler, *Dependent States: The Child's Part in Nineteenth-Century American Culture* (Chicago: University of Chicago Press, 2015), xxiv, xxvii. Allison Samantha Curseen has also traced the significance of what she calls "minor moves"—fugitive moments of child characters that elude the "developmental designs" of U.S. educators and policy makers—in nineteenth-century fiction; see her Ph.D. dissertation, "Minor Moves: Growth, Fugitivity, and Children's Physical Movement" (Duke University, 2014), 17, https://hdl.handle.net/10161/8790.

72. Susan Sontag, "Illness as Metaphor," *New York Review of Books* (26 January 1978), https://www.nybooks.com/articles/1978/01/26/illness-as-metaphor/.

73. Gilles Deleuze and Félix Guattari, *Kafka: Toward a Minor Literature,* trans. Dana Polan (Minneapolis: University of Minnesota Press, 1986).

74. Edel, "Preface to the 1964 Edition," xxix.

75. Ross Posnock, *The Trial of Curiosity: Henry James, William James, and the Challenge of Modernity* (New York: Oxford University Press, 1991), 42.

76. See French, "The Joke's on You," 97. Whereas biographers such as Edel have centered their discussions on AJ's "sickroom world"—Strouse bluntly asserts "her miserable health *was* her career" (*Alice James: A Biography*, 291)—scholars of nineteenth-century American women's writing have shifted the critical terrain. Rather than approaching the journal in documentary terms, as testimony of a thwarted, less-than-valid life, more recent critics have read the journal as a means of self-authorship in which AJ resists stultifying conventions associated with sentimentalism and invalidism. Duquette, for instance, focuses on AJ's deployment of the picturesque as "a critique of sympathetic identification" ("'A New Claim,'" 734), and French sees humor as AJ's way "to resist the self-erasure that accompanies the sentimental exchange" ("The Joke's on You," 93) and "construct[] a barrier against the de-authorizing effects of the sentimental relationship between the invalid and the 'healthy' observer" (95). Boudreau writes, "An ironic voice in a sentimental age, James explodes the fiction of sympathy" ("'A Barnum Monstrosity,'" 63).

77. Gilles Deleuze, *Essays Critical and Clinical*, trans. Daniel W. Smith and Michael A. Greco (Minneapolis: University of Minnesota Press, 1997), 22. Deleuze developed his conception of the body without organs through a reading of Lewis Carroll's *Alice in Wonderland*; I am suggesting that AJ occupies and narrates her eccentric bodily and textual existence. It's as if child Alice has escaped Carroll's story and also slipped away from those who would make her the object of philosophizing.

78. Hobbes, *Human Nature*, 54–55.

79. Baudelaire, *Selected Writings*, 146.

80. Sinor, *Extraordinary Work of Ordinary Writing*, 156.

81. Theorizing the nineteenth-century diary as a genre, Margo Culley has identified two central purposes for women's journal keeping: to reach outward and chronicle events within the family or wider social milieu, and thereby construct a "sense of self as part of the social fabric," or to reach inward and keep an "exclusive focus on her own exquisitely analyzed individual sensibility" (Culley, *A Day at a Time: The Diary Literature of American Women from 1764 to the Present* [New York: Feminist Press, 1995], 7). With regard to the former, Rebecca Steinitz has noted that "nineteenth-century diaries were, to a significant degree, familial texts, intimate rather than private in scope, representing family life and frequently shared among family members" (Steinitz, *Time, Space, and Gender in the Nineteenth-Century British Diary* [New York: Palgrave Macmillan, 2011], 140). Journal keeping served as a way to "maintain kin and community networks," sometimes functioning as "extended letters often actually sent to those left behind" (Culley, 16) when a woman married or moved away. I am suggesting that we can read AJ's experimentations with the diary as an experiential mode of philosophizing.

82. For a fascinating account of AJ's use of the microbe as a figure, see Kym Weed's Ph.D. dissertation, "Our Microbes: Imagining Human Interdependence with Bacteria in American Literature, Science, and Culture, 1880–1920" (University of North Carolina at Chapel Hill, Ann Arbor, 2018).

83. AJ plays for humor the failure of the reflex arc six years before John Dewey described its operation in his reputation-establishing article, "The Reflex Arc Concept in Psychology."

84. Henri Bergson, *Matter and Memory,* trans. Nancy Margaret Paul and W. Scott Palmer (London: George Allen, 1950), xiv.

85. The image of Alice's "amiable" temperament is in another entry explicitly dismissed as a dispiriting habit: "When it has become simply automatic thro' a sense of the expedient—of the grotesque futility of the perverse—it's degrading! And then the dolts praise one for being 'amiable!' just as if one didn't avoid ruffling one's feathers as one avoids plum-pudding or any other indigestible compound!" (64).

86. Daniel Kahneman, *Thinking, Fast and Slow* (New York: Farrar, Straus and Giroux, 2011), 4.

87. Freud, *Jokes and Their Relation,* 227.

88. Helen Dendrinou Kolias, "Empowering the Minor: Translating Woman's Autobiography," *Journal of Modern Greek Studies* 8, no. 2 (October 1990): 213–21, 218; Deleuze and Guattari, "What Is a Minor Literature?" *Mississippi Review* 11, no. 3 (Winter/Spring 1983): 13–33, 17.

89. John Limon, *Stand-Up Comedy in Theory, or, Abjection in America* (Durham: Duke University Press, 2000), 4.

90. Paul Fleming, *The Pleasures of Abandonment: Jean Paul and the Life of Humor* (Würzburg: Königshausen and Neumann, 2006), 51.

91. Elaine Scarry, *The Body in Pain: On the Making and Unmaking of the World* (New York: Oxford University Press, 1985), 32.

92. Kant, *Critique of the Power of Judgment,* 209.

93. Charles Darwin, *The Expression of the Emotions in Man and Animals,* ed. Francis Darwin (Cambridge: Cambridge University Press, 2009), 210.

94. For an outstanding discussion of the metaphysics of tickling, see Aaron Schuster's "A Philosophy of Tickling," *Cabinet Magazine* 50 (Summer 2013), http://cabinetmagazine.org/issues/50/schuster.php.

95. Jocelyn Chua, *In Pursuit of the Good Life: Aspiration and Suicide in Globalizing South India* (Berkeley: University of California Press, 2014), 19.

96. Bergson, *Laughter,* 28.

97. Henry James, "Is There a Life After Death?" in *In After Days: Thoughts on the Future Life* [1910] by W. D. Howells, Henry James, et al. (New York: Arno Press, 1977), 199–233.

98. Wai Chee Dimock, *Through Other Continents: American Literature Across Deep Time* (Princeton: Princeton University Press, 2008), 87. A young woman encountering "imperial" Rome provides the primal scene for Dimock: in *The Portrait of a Lady* Isabel Archer's marital sorrow, in the shadow of the Colosseum, is an event of "despicable size" that becomes "a small entry" to the "large fact" that is the "large Roman record" (88).

99. Henry James, *The Portrait of a Lady* (Oxford: Oxford University Press, 1998), 346.

100. Nagel, "The Absurd," 725.

101. Thomas P. Kasulis, "Ch'an Spirituality," in *Buddhist Spirituality: Later China, Korea, Japan, and the Modern World,* ed. Takeuchi Yoshinori (New York: Crossroad, 1999), 24–32, 30.

102. Katharine Peabody Loring to Frances Rollins Morse, 11 February [1891?], box 12, Henry James Jr. Papers, Houghton Library.

103. Helmuth Plessner, *Laughing and Crying: A Study of the Limits of Human Behavior,* trans. James Spencer Churchill and Marjorie Grene (Evanston, Ill.: Northwestern University Press, 1970), 31.

104. Charles Sanders Peirce, *Collected Papers: Volumes I and II,* ed. Charles Hartshorne and Paul Weiss (Cambridge, Mass.: Belknap Press of Harvard University Press, 1958–1966), 282.

105. The personal diary is distinct from other genres of life writing, such as the spiritual autobiography and the travel journal. The first is distinguished by its theological function: the tracing of an individual's spiritual life, which touches fairly glancingly on worldly matters, interpreting external events through a religious lens. The second, the travel journal, tends to be organized spatially and is focused on the novelty of geographical motion. The personal diary, though containing elements of both, is nonetheless a different thing: the *journal intime* (as it was known) is a secular, subjective, quotidian, and domestic mode of writing. Nancy Armstrong has traced its emergence to the rise of the novel, a mimetic genre similarly organized around the everyday experiences of common persons (see Nancy Armstrong and Leonard Tennenhouse, *The Imaginary Puritan* [Berkeley: University of California Press, 1992]). As with the novel, the personal journal or diary as a European literary practice coincides with the advent of empirical observation in science and philosophy (see Ian Watt, *The Rise of the Novel* [Berkeley: University of California Press, 1971]). Empiricism placed human sense perception at the center of knowledge about the world, knitting the subjective element into epistemological practice along with the modern value of objectivity.

106. Langford and West, "Introduction: Diaries and Margins," 7.

107. *The Letters of William James,* ed. Henry James (Boston: Little, Brown, 1926), 307.

108. Mathilde Blind, "Introduction," *The Journal of Marie Bashkirtseff,* vol. 1, ed. and trans. Mathilde Blind (London: Cassell, 1890), vi, vii.

109. Arthur W. Frank, *The Wounded Storyteller: Body, Illness, Ethics* (Chicago: University of Chicago Press, 1995), 31.

CHAPTER 2

Epigraph: Ralph Waldo Emerson, "Experience," in *The Essential Writings of Ralph Waldo Emerson,* ed. Brooks Atkinson (New York: Random House, 2000), 313.

1. *Ralph Waldo Emerson: Essays and Lectures,* ed. Joel Porte (New York: Library of America, 1983), 261.

2. Edward Waldo Emerson, *The Early Years of the Saturday Club, 1855-1870* (Boston: Houghton Mifflin, 1918), 328. In *House of Wits,* Paul Fisher writes of the James family dinner table, "It was a fast-moving blood sport" (172).

3. Gregory Bateson, *Steps to an Ecology of Mind: Collected Essays in Anthropology, Psychiatry, Evolution, and Epistemology* (Chicago: University of Chicago Press, 2000), 185. Bateson emphasizes the paradox of play, in which some sort of frame (a field, say, or a set of rules) marks off the activity as not-serious, yet also allows the possibility that seriousness can bleed into the frame. There always exists a potential turning of the tables in play: think of a fight erupting between players and the crowd emptying their seats to join the fray. For Bateson (as for HJ, as we shall see) this serious/not-serious paradox is not a problem but a condition of human existence: "Without these paradoxes the evolution of communication would be at an end. Life would then be an endless interchange of stylized ['as if'] messages, a game with rigid rules, unrelieved by change or humor" (193).

4. Johan Huizinga, *Homo Ludens: A Study of the Play-Element in Culture* [1949] (Kettering, Ohio: Angelico Press, 2016), 10–11.

5. Elizabeth Grosz, *The Nick of Time: Politics, Evolution, and the Untimely* (Durham: Duke University Press, 2004), 47.

6. Alice James, *The Diary of Alice James*, ed. Leon Edel (Boston: Northeastern University Press, 1999), 57.

7. George Santayana, *The Middle Span* (New York: Scribner, 1945), 7; quoted in John J. Fisher, "Santayana on James: A Conflict of Views on Philosophy," *American Philosophical Quarterly* 2, no. 1 (January 1965): 67–73, 72. Santayana had an unsavory tendency to align WJ, pejoratively, with groups who are discriminated against: in another comment, he writes that WJ "gave a sincerely respectful hearing to sentimentalists, mystics, spiritualists, wizards, cranks, quacks and imposters—for it is hard to draw the line, and James was not willing to draw it prematurely. He thought, with his usual modesty, that any of these might have something to teach him. The lame, the halt, and the blind, and those speaking with tongues could come to him with the certainty of finding sympathy; and if they were not healed, at least they were comforted, that a famous professor should take them so seriously: and they began to feel that after all to have only one leg, or one hand, or one eye, or to have three, might be in itself no less beauteous than to have just two, like the stolid majority" (qtd. Fisher, 69).

8. William James, *A Pluralistic Universe*, in *Writings: 1902–1910*, ed. Bruce Kuklick (New York: Library of America, 1987), 751.

9. Melvin Konner, *The Evolution of Childhood* (Cambridge, Mass.: Belknap Press of Harvard University Press, 2010), 71.

10. Ernst Haeckel, *The Riddle of the Universe at the Close of the Nineteenth Century* (New York: Harper and Brothers, 1905), 80.

11. Hector Rodriguez, "The Playful and the Serious: An Approximation to Huizinga's *Homo Ludens*," *Game Studies: The International Journal of Computer Game Research* 6, no. 1 (December 2006): http://gamestudies.org/0601/articles/rodriges.

12. Robert D. Richardson, *William James: In the Maelstrom of American Modernism* (Boston: Houghton Mifflin, 2006), 21.

13. Henry James, *A Small Boy and Others*, in *Henry James: Autobiographies*, ed. Philip Horne (New York: Library of America, 2016), 9–10.

14. Paul Fisher, *House of Wits: An Intimate Portrait of the James Family* (New York: Henry Holt, 2008), 500.

15. G. Stanley Hall, "A Century Later: Reflections on 'The Principles of Psychology' by William James and on the Review by G. Stanley Hall," *American Journal of Psychology* 103, no. 44 (December 1991): 539, 585; the original review appeared in the *American Journal of Psychology* 3, no. 4 (1890–91): 578–591.

16. Jacques Barzun, *A Stroll with William James* (Chicago: University of Chicago Press, 1983), 43, 45.

17. Ross Posnock, *The Trial of Curiosity: Henry James, William James, and the Challenge of Modernity* (New York: Oxford University Press, 1991), 171.

18. William James, *Talks to Teachers*, in *Writings: 1878–1899*, ed. Gerald E. Myers (New York: Library of America, 1992), 740.

19. James Mark Baldwin, *Thoughts and Things: A Study of the Development and Meaning of Thought, or Genetic Logic*, vol. III (London: George Allen, 1911), 51.

20. James Mark Baldwin, *Mental Development in the Child and the Race: Methods and Processes* (New York: Macmillan, 1895), 18.

21. Theodora Bosanquet, *Henry James at Work* [1924], ed. Lyall H. Powers (Ann Arbor: University of Michigan Press, 2006), 57.

22. This renowned phrase is drawn from *In Memoriam A.H.H.,* by Alfred, Lord Tennyson (1849). Published a decade before Charles Darwin's *On the Origin of Species*, the poem reflects a pre-Darwinian understanding of the natural world drawn from *Naturphilosophie*, a Romantic scientific movement in Europe. For an account of Tennyson's sources, see Stephen Jay Gould, "The Tooth and Claw Centennial," in *Dinosaur in a Haystack: Reflections in Natural History* (New York: Three Rivers Press, 1995), 71.

23. Philip Stevick, for instance, writes, "Novelists of the nineteenth century learned how to make their characters grow and change; they learned, in James's word, to make them 'emerge'; they learned how to reveal the pressure of the environment." Stevick, *The Theory of the Novel* (New York: Free Press, 1967), 183.

24. The phrase "survival of the fittest" led many in the nineteenth century (and beyond) to construe Darwin's theories as "red in tooth and claw"—both deterministic and tending toward heartless social policies based on "eugenics," in which "unfit" human beings are "weeded out" from the social body. It's worth noting that the phrase "survival of the fittest" was coined by Herbert Spencer and did not appear in the first editions of *On the Origin of Species*. Alfred Russel Wallace, in an 1866 letter to Darwin, urged him to replace the term "natural selection" with Spencer's formulation, arguing that Darwin's preferred term seemed to imply an "intelligent chooser" and was liable to misunderstanding. See *The Correspondence of Charles Darwin*, vol. 14 [1866], ed. Frederick Burkhardt et al., Letter from A. R. Wallace, 2 July 1866 (Cambridge: Cambridge University Press, 2004), 228. Darwin responded to Wallace with characteristic politeness and included the phrase in later editions.

25. Charles Darwin, *On the Origin of Species by Means of Natural Selection* [1859], ed. Joseph Carroll (Peterborough, Ont.: Broadview, 2003), 398, 143.

26. Charles Lyell's magisterial *Principles of Geology* (1830–33) provided the deep time necessary for Charles Darwin's theory of species adaptation and natural selection to operate; Darwin once wrote to a colleague, "I always feel as if my books came half out of Lyell's brains" (Darwin Correspondence Project, Letter no. 771, accessed on 3 July 2020. http://www.darwinproject.ac.uk/letter/DCF-LETT-771.xml). Ironically, the nineteenth-century naturalist Louis Agassiz, who famously argued *against* Darwin's theory of evolution, affirmed that the geological record indicated that a series of sudden catastrophic events (which he attributed to the hand of God) had disrupted the stately, accretive changes that Lyell described and that provided support for Darwin's theory of slow, steady species transmutation. Gould has defended this aspect of Agassiz's work and argued for "punctuated equilibrium," an evolutionary theory accommodated to dramatic shifts in the environment; see his article, written with Niles Eldredge, "Punctuated Equilibria: An Alternative to Phyletic Gradualism," in *Models in Paleobiology*, ed. T. J. M. Schopf (San Francisco: Freeman, Cooper, 1972), 82–115.

27. William James, *Psychology: Briefer Course,* in *Writings: 1878–1899*, 137.

28. Stephen Crane, *Prose and Poetry*, ed. J. C. Levenson (New York: Library of America, 1984), 1249.

29. Alison Gopnik, *The Philosophical Baby: What Children's Minds Tell Us About Truth, Love, and the Meaning of Life* (New York: Picador, 2010), 9.

30. Richard Wrangham, *Freedom Through Fire: How Cooking Made Us Human* (New York: Basic Books, 2007), and Dean Falk, *Finding Our Tongues: Mothers, Infants, and the Origins of Language* (New York: Basic Books, 2009).

31. James Mark Baldwin, *Development and Evolution, Including Psychophysical Evolution* (New York: Macmillan, 1902), 101.

32. John Dewey, "Impulse and Change of Habits," in *Human Nature and Conduct: An Introduction to Social Psychology* (New York: Modern Library, 1922): 95–105, 98.

33. Daniel Dennett, *Consciousness Explained* (London: Allen Lane, 1991), 184.

34. Stephen Jay Gould, "Challenges to Neo- Darwinism and Their Meaning for a Revised View of Human Consciousness," Tanner Lectures on Human Values, delivered 20 April and 1 May, 1984, https://tannerlectures.utah.edu/_documents/a-to-z/g/gould85.pdf.

35. In *Elusive Childhood: Impossible Representations in Modern Fiction* (Columbus: Ohio State University Press, 2005), Susan Honeyman analyzes the "theme of neoteny" (110) in modern children's fiction such as Henry Kuttner's *The Last Mimzy* (2007) and Arthur C. Clarke's *Childhood's End* (1953). Honeyman gives a perceptive account of how these works of fiction offer "empowering constructions of childhood" based on "a neotenous interpretation of evolution" (111). She comes to an oddly dissonant conclusion, however, when she argues that a theory affirming the "prolonged necessity of interdependence and education" is an invidious bid for "adult control" of childhood and a form of "ideological imperialism" (111). To my mind, this false note in Honeyman's otherwise smart and thorough account underscores the analytic weakness of a cultural criticism that reduces scientific theories to ideology rather than evaluates the salience and productivity of their accounts.

36. William James, *Pragmatism: A New Name for an Old Way of Thinking*, in *Writings: 1902–1910*, 514.

37. William James, "Are We Automata?" *Mind* 4, no. 13 (January 1879): 1–2, http://www.informationphilosopher.com/solutions/philosophers/james/are_we_automata.html.

38. William James, *The Principles of Psychology*, vol. I (New York: Henry Holt, 1918), 488.

39. John Dewey, "The Reflex Arc Concept in Psychology," *Psychological Review* 3, no. 4 (July 1896): 357–70, 363.

40. Andy Clark, *Supersizing the Mind: Embodiment, Action, and Cognitive Extension* (New York: Oxford University Press, 2010), 31.

41. Karl Groos, *The Play of Man* [1899], trans. Elizabeth L. Baldwin (New York: D. Appleton, 1919), 10. James Mark Baldwin wrote the preface to Groos's study, and his wife, Elizabeth, served as the translator from the German.

42. Henry James Sr., quoted in F. O. Matthiessen, *The James Family: A Group Biography* (New York: Vintage Books, 1980), 34.

43. John Dewey, *Essays in Experimental Logic* (Chicago: University of Chicago Press, 1916), 14.

44. James Mark Baldwin, *Darwin and the Humanities* (Baltimore: William and Wilkins, 1909), 35, 25, 26.

45. Alison Gopnik, Andrew N. Meltzoff, and Patricia K. Kuhl, *The Scientist in the Crib: Minds, Brains, and How Children Learn* (New York: Harper Perennial, 2001), 126.

46. Bird T. Baldwin, "William James' Contributions to Education," *Journal of Educational Psychology* 2, no. 7 (September 1911): 369–82, 374.

47. See Lee Rust Brown's terrific *The Emerson Museum: Practical Romanticism and the Pursuit of the Whole* (Cambridge, Mass.: Harvard University Press, 1997).

48. Sally Shuttleworth, tracing the emergence of this scientific interest to earlier, Romantic formulations about the significance of childhood, writes, "Perhaps [William] Wordsworth's greatest legacy to the Victorian age was his line 'The Child is father of the Man,' which lay behind the novels of development of the period and became the mantra of the educationists, and child psychologists of the late century"; in *The Mind of the Child: Child Development in Literature, Science, and Medicine, 1840–1900* (Oxford: Oxford University Press, 2010), 7.

49. Charles Darwin, *The Descent of Man* [1871], in *Darwin* (Norton Critical Edition, 2nd edition), ed. Philip Appleman (New York: W. W. Norton, 1979), 132.

50. Louis Agassiz, *An Essay on Classification* (London: Longman, Brown, Green, Longmans, and Roberts, and Trubner, 1859), 205.

51. Louis Agassiz and Elizabeth Cary Abbott Agassiz, *A Journey in Brazil* (Boston: Ticknor and Fields, 1869), 33.

52. William James, "Louis Agassiz," in *Memories and Studies* (New York: Longmans, Green, 1912), 10.

53. Lane Cooper, ed., *Louis Agassiz as a Teacher: Illustrative Extracts on His Method of Instruction* (Ithaca, N.Y.: Comstock, 1945), 82.

54. William Dean Howells, *Criticism and Fiction* (New York: Harper and Brothers, 1891), 10–11.

55. William James, "Louis Agassiz," 11–12.

56. For a brilliant account of the intellectual reciprocity between Emerson and Agassiz, in relation to the design of the Jardin des Plantes in Paris, see Lee Rust Brown, *The Emerson Museum: Practical Romanticism and the Pursuit of the Whole* (Berkeley: University of California Press, 1997), esp. 65–66, 102–3.

57. Quoted in Randall Fuller, *The Book That Changed America: How Darwin's Theory of Evolution Ignited a Nation* (New York: Penguin, 2017), 85.

58. Reprinted in *The Letters of William James: Edited by His Son Henry James* (Boston: Atlantic Monthly Press, 1920), 35; 16 September 1861, addressed to his family.

59. For a terrific discussion of WJ's experience of racial otherness on the expedition, see Nihad M. Farooq, *Undisciplined: Science, Ethnography, and Personhood in the Americas, 1830–1840* (New York: New York University Press, 2016), esp. 86–87.

60. Gregory Phipps argues that "economic motifs" are important to WJ's account of experience, representing "symbolic lines of exchange between the individual's mind and her context"; *Henry James and the Philosophy of Literary Pragmatism* (New York: Palgrave Macmillan, 2016), 97.

61. Louis Menand, discussing the Thayer Expedition in *The Metaphysical Club: A Story of Ideas in America* (New York: Farrar, Straus and Giroux, 2001), describes WJ's perspective as more settled than the letters suggest. Here is Menand: "From the start William James was much more interested in Agassiz than he was in glacial activity—or in any other aspect of natural history, for that matter. And he was perfectly aware of the extent to which the expedition was, in its grander ambitions, a charade" (128–29).

62. William James, "Louis Agassiz," 13.

63. Herbert Spencer, *An Autobiography* (London: Williams and Norgate, 1904), 11.

64. Herbert Spencer, *The Principles of Psychology, Volume. I*, 2nd ed. (London: Williams and Norgate, 1870), 425.

65. Herbert Spencer, *First Principles of a New System of Philosophy* (New York: D. Appleton, 1865), 216, emphasis in original.

66. William James, "How to Make Our Ideas Clear," *Popular Science Monthly*, January 1878; quoted in Menand, *Metaphysical Club*, 357.

67. William James, "Brute and Human Intellect," in *Writings: 1878–1899*, 929.

68. William James, "Remarks on Spencer's Definition of Mind as Correspondence," in *Writings: 1878–1899*, 908.

69. Antonello La Vergata, "Herbert Spencer: Biology, Sociology, and Cosmic Evolution," in *Biology as Society, Society as Biology: Metaphors*, Sociology of the Sciences series, vol. 18, ed. Sabine Maasen, Everett Mendelsohn, and Peter Weingart (Dordrecht: Springer, 1994).

70. Huizinga, *Homo Ludens*, 89.

71. Richard Hofstadter, *Social Darwinism in American Thought* (Philadelphia: University of Pennsylvania Press, 1944), 35.

72. Quoted in Michael P. Lempert, "Pragmatic Constructivism: Revisiting William James's Critique of Herbert Spencer," *Philosophical Inquiry in Education* 11, no. 1 (January 1997): 33–50, 37.

73. Hofstadter, *Social Darwinism*, 129.

74. Quoted in Morton Hunt, *The Story of Psychology* (New York: Anchor Books, 2007), 159–60.

75. William James, *The Principles of Psychology*, vol. I (New York: Henry Holt, 1890), v.

76. Barzun, *A Stroll*, 36.

77. Alice James, *Diary*, 217.

78. William James, letter dated 20 August 1891, *William and Henry James: Selected Letters*, ed. Ignas K. Skrupskelis (Charlottesville: University of Virginia Press, 1997), 258.

79. Shuttleworth, *Mind of the Child*, 270.

80. Richardson, *In the Maelstrom*, 20. For a discussion of the term "zig-zag" to describe WJ's life and philosophy, see "Growing Up Zig-Zag," chapter 12 in Martin Halliwell and Joel D. S. Rasmussen, *William James and the Transatlantic Conversation: Pragmatism, Pluralism, and Philosophy of Religion* (Oxford: Oxford University Press, 2014).

81. Quoted in Richardson, *In the Maelstrom*, 179.

82. Barzun, *A Stroll*, 39.

83. Quoted in Lev Vygotsky, "Consciousness as a Problem in the Psychology of Behavior" [1925]; at *Lev Vygotsky Archive*, https://www.marxists.org/archive/vygotsky/works/1925/consciousness.htm.

84. 17 December 1908 letter from WJ to Helen Keller; at *Helen Keller Archive* at the American Foundation for the Blind, https://www.afb.org/HelenKellerArchive?a=d&d=A-HK01-03-B063-F02-003&e-------en-20--1--txt--------7-7-6-5-3--------------0-1. Richardson describes WJ taking graduate students to meet Helen Keller in 1892, where he presented her with an ostrich feather: "'I thought,' he said, 'you would like the feather, it is soft, light, and caressing'" (321).

85. William James, "Brute and Human Intellect," in *Writings: 1878–1899*, 939.

86. Nicola Twilley, "Seeing with Your Tongue," *New Yorker* (15 May 2017), https://www.newyorker.com/magazine/2017/05/15/seeing-with-your-tongue.

87. Grosz, *The Nick of Time*,18.

88. John Dewey, "Play and Imagination in Relation to Early Education" [1899] in *The Middle Works of John Dewey, 1899-1924*, ed. Jo Anne Boydston (Carbondale: Southern Illinois University Press, 2008), 339.

89. G. Stanley Hall, *Youth: Its Education, Regimen, and Hygiene* (New York: D. Appleton, 1914), 79, https://www.google.com/books/edition/Youth/XcUZAAAAYAAJ?hl=en&gbpv=1.

90. In *Social Darwinism* Hofstadter writes, "Although Hall felt that the childlike character of backward peoples entitled them to tender and sympathetic treatment by their phylogenetic 'elders,' who should be ashamed to make war on children, the condescending approach to primitive culture underlying the recapitulation theory was not calculated to disturb the spokesmen of racial superiority" (193).

91. Groos, *The Play of Man*, 376.

92. Paul Stob, *William James and the Art of Popular Statement* (East Lansing: Michigan State University Press, 2013), 82. Stob reports that the book version of *Talks to Teachers* was popular and lucrative, with over 100,000 sold during his life (75). Stob argues this lecture series helped

WJ's teacher-audience to professionalize by drawing the practice of education under the rubric of science and specialized expertise.

93. "Book List: 1878–2018, *Chautauqua Literary and Scientific Circle*, https://chq.org/phocadownload/LiteraryArts/CLSCBookList.pdf.

94. Huizinga, *Homo Ludens*, 10.

95. Jan Simon, "Narrative, Games, and Theory," *Game Studies: The International Journal of Computer Game Research* 7, no. 1 (2007), http://gamestudies.org/07010701/articles/simons.

96. Adolf Meyer, "The Philosophy of Occupation Therapy," *Archives of Occupational Therapy* 1, no. 1 (October 1921), 5, 6, https://www.aotf.org/Portals/0/Meyers%20full%20article.pdf.

97. William James, *The Will to Believe and Other Essays in Popular Philosophy*, in *Writings: 1878–1899*, 447.

98. Walt Whitman, *Song of Myself* [1855] (New York: Roycrofters, 1904), 69, https://www.google.com/books/edition/Song_of_Myself/drchAAAAMAAJ?hl=en&gbpv=1&kptab=overview.

99. Ralph Barton Perry, *The Thought and Character of William James* (Nashville: Vanderbilt University Press, 1996), 373.

100. Louis Althusser, "Ideology and Ideological State Apparatuses," in *Lenin and Philosophy and Other Essays* (New York: New York University Press, 2001), 118.

101. "Mr. Lincoln and Negro Inequality," *New York Times* (28 December 1860), https://www.nytimes.com/1860/12/28/archives/mr-lincoln-and-negro-equality.html.

102. Scott Black, *Of Essays and Reading in Early Modern Britain* (New York: Palgrave Macmillan, 2006), 3, 6.

103. Charles S. Peirce, "The Logic of Abduction," in *Collected Papers of Charles Sanders Peirce, Volumes 5 and 6: Pragmatism and Pragmaticism and Scientific Metaphysics* (Cambridge, Mass.: Harvard University Press, 1974), 6.524. Subsequent references to the works of Peirce appear in parentheses in the text, with CP indicating the author, followed by the volume and page numbers.

104. Charles S. Peirce, "Deduction, Induction, and Hypothesis," in *Writings of Charles S. Peirce: A Chronological Edition, Volume 3* (Bloomington: Indiana University Press, 1986), 330.

105. Nathan Houser, "Peirce's Post-Jamesian Pragmatism," *European Journal of Pragmatism and American Philosophy* 3, no. 1 (2001), https://journals.openedition.org/ejpap/866.

106. James J. Gibson, *The Senses Considered as Perceptual Systems* (Boston: Houghton Mifflin, 1966), 285.

107. Donald Norman, *The Design of Everyday Things* (New York: Basic Books, 2013), 11.

108. William James, *Talks to Teachers*, in *Writings: 1878–1899*, 739.

109. Quoted in Barzun, *A Stroll*, 29.

110. William James, *Pragmatism: A New Name for Some Old Ways of Thinking*, in *Writings: 1902–1910*, 600.

111. Barzun, *A Stroll*, 289.

112. Stob has aptly noted the "orality" of WJ's explicitly lecture-based books: "Rather than simply pointing his audience to important concepts in pedagogical psychology, James wanted to initiate a discursive confrontation with listeners and readers" (*William James and the Art of Popular Statement*, 94).

113. Black, *Of Essays*, 3.

114. Amanda Anderson, *The Way We Argue Now: A Study in the Cultures of Theory* (Princeton: Princeton University Press, 2006), 118. Certain contemporary proponents of pragmatist

thought—Anderson calls them "strong personalities"—appear, to her eye, oddly "[un]bothered" (130) by "the fractured and contentious nature of our cultural life," which "necessarily condemns us to forms of uncertainty, uneasiness, and anxiety" (128). According to Anderson, Stanley Fish and Barbara Herrnstein Smith in particular demonstrate an inappropriately "relaxed attitude . . . toward contingency" (124) and are troublingly "cheerful[]," even "comic" in their mediations (125). Richard Rorty, Anderson notes with approval, admits that an "exuberant Nietzschean playfulness" is "hard to imagine" in a world governed by "contingency rather than necessity" (126).

115. Henry James, *The Middle Years*, in *Henry James: Autobiographies*, ed. Philip Horne (New York: Library of America, 2016), 577. This is the image of pragmatism, in fact, that appears in Anderson's *The Way We Argue*. Anderson disapproves of the excessively "genial" "projects of postmodernism, pragmatism, and constructivism," arguing that there's dissonance between a "pragmatist worldview" and its accompanying "attitudinal" (118) stance. Contemporary pragmatists, she argues, have an inappropriately nonchalant or "calm relation to an uncontrolled and uncontrollable world" (128): rather than uneasy or doubt-ridden, such thinkers are, Anderson argues, "smug, complacent, cynical, blithe, and dismissive" (116).

116. Mary Reilly, *Play as Exploratory Learning: Studies of Curiosity Behavior* (London: Sage, 1974), 53.

117. William James, *The Varieties of Religious Experience*, in *Writings: 1902–1910*, 136.

118. Ria Cheruvu, "The Neuroscience of Flow" (May 2018), https://www.researchgate.net/publication/325273409_The_Neuroscience_of_Flow.

119. William James, *The Varieties of Religious Experience*, in *Writings: 1902–1910*), 192.

120. Although I take the term "wildness" from James, here I mean to invoke Edwin Hutchins's conception of the term in his *Cognition in the Wild* (Cambridge, Mass.: MIT Press, 1995). Hutchins, a cognitive anthropologist, distinguishes between "the laboratory, where cognition is studied in captivity, and the *everyday world*, where human cognition adapts to its natural surroundings" (xiv, emphasis added). In speaking of "wildness," I am not, for instance, referring to "wild facts" in the sense that James used the term in "The Unclassified Residuum," as strange, mystical, or otherwise extraordinary, uncategorizable experiences.

121. William James, "Bergson and Intellectualism," in *Writings: 1902–1910*, 755.

122. In his review of *Pragmatism* Bertrand Russell famously wrote, "The truth is anything which it pays to believe"; "Transatlantic 'Truth,'" *Albany Review* 2 (1908): 393.

123. Richardson, *In the Maelstrom*, 494.

124. Elizabeth F. Cooke, "Peirce on Musement: The Limits of Purpose and the Importance of Noticing," *European Journal of Pragmatism and American Philosophy* 10, no. 2 (2018), https://journals.openedition.org/ejpap/1370#toctoin1.

125. Robert Burch, "Charles Sanders Peirce: Pragmatism, Pragmaticism, and the Scientific Method," *Stanford Encyclopedia of Philosophy* (November 2014), ed. Edward N. Zalta, https://plato.stanford.edu/entries/peirce/#prag.

126. Joseph Brent, *Charles Sanders Peirce: A Life* (Bloomington: Indiana University Press, 1998), 26.

127. Charles S. Peirce, "A Neglected Argument for the Reality of God" [1908], in *Collected Papers of Charles Sanders Peirce, Volumes 5 and 6: Pragmatism and Pragmaticism and Scientific Metaphysics* (Cambridge: Harvard University Press, 1974), 6.458–59.

128. Brent, *Charles Sanders Peirce*, 130.

129. Quoted in Brent, *Charles Sanders Peirce*, 102–3.

130. Friedrich Schiller, *Æsthetical and Philosophical Essays* (Boston: S. E. Cassino, 1884), 78.

131. Cooke, "Peirce on Musement," https://journals.openedition.org/ejpap/1370#tocto1n1.

132. Houser, "Post-Jamesian Pragmatism," https://journals.openedition.org/ejpap/866.

133. Frank Pajares, "William James: Our Father Who Begat Us," in *Educational Psychology: A Century of Contributions*, ed. Barry J. Zimmerman and Dale H. Schunk (New York: Routledge, 2002), 41.

CHAPTER 3

Epigraph: Ludwig Wittgenstein, *Philosophical Investigations*, 4th ed., trans. and ed. P.M.S. Hacker and Joachim Schulte (Oxford: Wiley-Blackwell, 2009), 224e.

1. *William and Henry James: Selected Letters,* ed. Ignas K. Skrupskelis and Elizabeth M. Berkeley (Charlottesville: University Press of Virginia, 1997), 251.

2. Henry James, letter to Alice James dated 6 June 1890, *Selected Letters*, ed. Leon Edel (Cambridge, Mass.: Harvard University Press, 1987), 234.

3. Henry James, *Guy Domville: Play in Three Acts*, ed. Leon Edel (New York: J. B. Lippincott, 1960), https://archive.org/stream/guydomvilleplayi00jame/guydomvilleplayi00jame_djvu.txt.

4. Walter Benjamin, "The Work of Art in the Age of Mechanical Reproduction," in *Illuminations* (New York: Random House, 1968), 228.

5. Paul Fisher, *House of Wits: An Intimate Portrait of the James Family* (New York: Henry Holt, 2008), 524–25.

6. Virginia Woolf, "Henry James's Ghost Stories," in *Collected Essays of Virginia Woolf, Volume I* (London: Hogarth Press, 1966), 289–90.

7. Sharon Cameron in *Thinking in Henry James* (Chicago: Chicago University Press, 1989) argues that while James recoils from the "vulgar materialism that is the antithesis of consciousness," he nonetheless becomes "intoxicated by his newfound alienation" (3) from consumer culture.

8. Martha Banta, *Henry James and the Occult: The Great Extension* (Bloomington: Indiana University Press, 1972).

9. Kristin Boudreau, "Immensities of Perception and Yearning: The Haunting of Henry James's Heroes," in *Henry James and the Supernatural*, ed. Anna Despotopoulou and Kimberly C. Reed (New York: Palgrave, 2011), 44.

10. Leon Edel, *The Life of Henry James, Volume 2* (Harmondsworth, Middlesex: Penguin, 1977), 149.

11. Henry Popkin, "The Two Theatres of Henry James," *New England Quarterly* 24, no. 1 (March 1951): 69–83, 69.

12. David Kurnick, *Empty Houses: Theatrical Failure and the Novel* (Princeton: Princeton University Press, 2011), 3.

13. Sharon Marcus, "Victorian Theatrics: Response," *Victorian Studies* 54, no. 3 (Spring 2012): 438–50, 439.

14. Thanks to Greg W. Zacharias, who reminded me that HJ, even as he wrote his great late-stage novels, continued to write plays and sought to stage them: "He never abandoned the theater as theater" (message to author, 12 May 2019). See Leon Edel, *The Complete Plays of Henry James* (New York: Oxford University Press, 1990), esp. 519n.

15. Leon Edel sees this turn to the figure of the child in psychobiographical terms: "The jeering audience in St. James's had reduced him to the helplessness of an unappreciated child; it

had cut at the heart of his creativity. It is perhaps no coincidence that the first note he set down after *Guy Domville* was that of a tale of horror, a nightmare story, told to him by the Archbishop at Addington, that become 'The Turn of the Screw'" (Henry James, *Guy Domville*).

16. Critics have long noted how HJ in his fiction engages with both artists and artistic media, with sculpture crucial to *Roderick Hudson*, theater a key venue for *The Tragic Muse*, and painting at the core of *The Wings of the Dove* (to name just a few). Richard Menke has aligned James's realism with the immediacy of the technology of the telegraph, though he suggests that HJ finally diagnoses the new mode of communication as a vehicle for individual fantasies; see Menke's "Telegraphic Realism: Henry James's *In the Cage*," *PMLA* 115, no. 5 (October 2000): 975–90. Some have also argued for James's affinities with cinema: Ellis Hanson's excellent article on *The Turn of the Screw* and its filmic iterations is a prime example; see "Screwing with Children in Henry James," *GLQ: A Journal of Lesbian and Gay Studies* 9, no. 3 (2003): 367–91. See also Boosung Kim, "Shock and Astonishment: The Rise of Cinema Spectatorship and *What Maisie Knew*," *Henry James Review* 40, no. 1 (2019): 1–17.

17. Jennifer L. Fleissner's terrific article "Henry James's Art of Eating" examines the compatibilities between bodily sensations, aesthetics, and communal experience in James's *In the Cage*. She urges that the story succeeds in "imagining a truly embodied subjectivity," *English Literary History* 75, no. 1 (Spring 2008): 32. Fleissner's description of "savoring"—an activity "in which necessity and extravagance, animal need and human desire, are literally rendered inseparable from one another" (51) is reminiscent of play.

18. Herbert Spencer, "The Physiology of Laughter," *Macmillan's Magazine* 5 (March 1860): 395–402, 395.

19. Henri Bergson, *Laughter: An Essay on the Meaning of the Comic* [1900] (Mineola, N.Y.: Dover, 2005), 19.

20. Given the centrality of the hat for humor, the absence of a hat is the other side of the coin: a good shibboleth for humor's dark twin, horror. This helps to explain, in *The Turn of the Screw*, the significance of the governess's odd detail about the man she saw on the tower at Bly, that he "was wearing no hat" (16). Thanks to Heath Sledge for calling my attention to this detail.

21. Bergson, *Laughter*, 19.

22. Henry James, "Daisy Miller: A Study," in *Tales of Henry James*, ed. Christof Wegelin (New York: Norton, 1984).

23. William James, *Talks to Teachers*, in *Writings: 1878–1899*, ed. Gerald E. Myers (New York: Library of America, 1992), 747.

24. James Wood, "Cult of the Master," *Atlantic* (1 April 2003), https://www.theatlantic.com/magazine/archive/2003/04/cult-of-the-master/302716/.

25. David Lodge, *Author, Author!* (New York: Viking Press, 2004).

26. Edel, *The Life of Henry James, Volume 2*, 150–51.

27. Benjamin, "The Work of Art," 229.

28. James Mark Baldwin, *Thought and Things: A Study of the Development and Meaning of Thought, or Genetic Logic* (New York: Macmillan, 1906), 126.

29. Bruce McConachie, "An Evolutionary Perspective on Play, Performance, and Ritual," *The Drama Review* n55, no. 4 (Winter 2011): 33–50, 40.

30. Mark Turner, in *The Literary Mind* (New York: Oxford University Press, 1997), explains: "Conceptual blending is a fundamental instrument of the everyday mind, used in our basic construal of all our realities, from the social to the scientific" (93).

31. Baldwin, *Thought and Things*, 111.

32. For my reading of Huck's naïve response to a circus trick, see *Affecting Fictions: Mind, Body, and Emotion in American Literary Realism* (Cambridge, Mass.: Harvard University Press, 2007), 44–51.

33. George Dumont, in *A History of Personality Psychology: Theory, Science and Research from Hellenism to the Twenty-First Century* (New York: Cambridge University Press, 2010), writes that Winnicott "gave importance to the relational aspect of human function" over and above a Freudian emphasis on "the libidinal. If one grants that humans are driven, they are driven more by their need for meaningful relationships than by the search for pleasure" (72).

34. D. W. Winnicott, *Playing and Reality* (New York: Basic Books, 1971).

35. Henry James, *The Complete Notebooks of Henry* James, ed. Leon Edel and Lyall H. Powers (New York: Oxford University Press, 1987), 248.

36. Henry James, *Notebooks*, 198–99.

37. Johan Huizinga, *Homo Ludens: A Study of the Play-Element in Culture* (Boston: Routledge, 1949), 7.

38. Paul Armstrong, "Art and the Construction of Community in 'The Death of the Lion,'" *Henry James Review* 17, no. 2 (Spring 1996): 99–106, 103. Armstrong is analyzing a different tale, but his point about communal seeing is apt for my discussion: "Recognizing that the uncertainty of knowing requires other readers and prevents final agreement can thereby give rise to a reciprocal exchange of interpretations that would constitute a different form of community than the conflict between rival wills" (103).

39. Terry Castle, "Phantasmagoria: Spectral Technology and the Metaphorics of Modern Reverie," *Critical Inquiry* 15, no. 1 (Autumn 1988): 26–61, 58.

40. Stephen Nachmanovitch, "This Is Play," *New Literary History* 40, no. 1 (Winter 2009): 1–24, 7.

41. "If Compton's maximum in the country is £100 (gross-receipts) a night it ought to be taken (always assuming, of course, the play to be successful) as his *average* in a London theatre, where prices are higher—twice as high—and seats, above all, stalls, more numerous. Therefore with weekly matinees my ten per cent would certainly bring me upwards of £80 a week" (Henry James, *Selected Letters*, 235).

42. Kurnick, *Empty Houses*, 1. There is much to admire in Kurnick's discussion of how the theater haunts the modern novel, an idea that he stages through readings of a range of "novels of interiority" (10) as well as Henry James. At one point Kurnick suggestively writes, "Most radically, James prompts his readership to reconstitute itself as a ghostly theatrical public, a collective body made over in the image of the permissive coterie he depicts in *The Awkward Age*" (112). Given the compatibility of our arguments, I was surprised that Kurnick didn't address James's ghost stories, nor does he explore James's experimentation with film and filmic audiences in the late fiction.

43. Hugo Münsterberg, *The Film: A Psychological Study* (Mineola, N.Y.: Dover, 2004), 2.

44. Henry James, *What Maisie Knew* [1895] (New York: Viking Penguin, 1985), 117–18.

45. Paul Clee, *Before Hollywood: From Shadow Play to the Silver Screen* (New York: Clarion Books, 2005), 45.

46. Castle, "Phantasmagoria: Spectral Technology," 26–61.

47. In *The Shock of the Real: Romanticism and Visual Culture, 1760–1860* (New York: Palgrave Macmillan, 2001), Gillen D'Arcy Wood argues that new technologies of projection (phantasmagoria, magic lantern shows, panoramas) commandeer viewers' imaginative agency. HJ, as I discuss, forges an alignment, exploring the new affordances that come along with new devices such as the thaumatrope.

48. Athanasius Kircher (1601–80) published *Ars magna lucis et umbrae* in 1646; the Dutch astronomer Christiaan Huygens (1629–95) is credited with inventing the projecting lantern, which equipped the camera obscura with lenses to correct the flipping of the image inside the box and added a mirror to intensify the candle light source.

49. Henry James, *Notebooks*, 162.

50. Nancy Bentley, *Frantic Panoramas: American Literature and Mass Culture, 1870–1920* (Philadelphia: University of Pennsylvania Press, 2009).

51. Clee, *Before Hollywood*, 47.

52. Christina Britzolakis, "Technologies of Vision in Henry James's *What Maisie Knew*," *Novel* 34, no. 3 (2001): 369–90, 374.

53. Omri Moses, *Out of Character: Modernism, Vitalism, Psychic Life* (Palo Alto: Stanford University Press, 2014), 79. Our arguments are deeply compatible, especially in describing the provisional nature of "relational being" (88). Moses, however, is more concerned with the problem of ethical judgment that arises from a lack of predetermined norms, interests, values, and beliefs (what usually counts as "character"). Turning the interpretive lens just a click, to think in terms of play rather than vitalist psychology, makes clear how (for the Jameses) negotiation over different positions within a shared field of play creates the care and salience that allow for meaningful (and less coercive) judgments in the first place. And for those who lose the spirit of play, or spoil the magic circle, the remonstrance of the joke is a less punitive means to recruit them back into the comic relationality that constitutes sociality in the first place. For more on this see AJ and Bergson on laughter, Chapter 1.

54. One of adults' primary deficits, for HJ, is that they are usually unaware of their own rigidity and are largely blind to the cognitive flexibility and ethical complexity of the young people who seek to enlist them in relations of care and compassion.

55. John Dewey, *Democracy and Education* [1916], excerpted in *Pragmatism: A Reader*, ed. Louis Menand (New York: Vintage, 1997), 210.

56. Charles Hughes Johnston, "Mental Conservation of the Child," *Journal of the Michigan Schoolmaster's Club* 45 (1910): 15–27, https://books.google.com/books?id=tLsVAAAAIAAJ&dq=%22mental+conservation+of+the+child%22&source=gbs_navlinks_s.

57. Brad Evans, *Ephemeral Bibelots: How an International Fad Buried American Modernism* (Baltimore: Johns Hopkins University Press, 2019), 94. Evans's sparkling prose captures the sense of play, making him an especially perspicacious reader of *Maisie*: "What she knows is quite often a delicious surprise for us, both in those moments when what she knows is not as much as what we think she ought to know, but even more so in those moments when she comes out with something in excess of what we know" and thus "send[s] our heads spinning" (94).

58. *What Maisie Knew* marks HJ's transition away from the Victorian stage and into the age of mechanical reproduction, in another sense. Partway through composing the novel, a hand injury prompted him to hire a secretary, who typed the second half of *Maisie*.

59. Pamela Thurschwell has convincingly argued for the eighteen-year-old Nanda's status as an adolescent, a new category defined by G. Stanley Hall; Pamela Thurschwell, "Bringing Nanda Forward, or Acting Your Age in *The Awkward Age*," *Critical Quarterly* 58, no. 2 (2016): 72–90.

60. Henry James, *The Turn of the Screw* (Norton Critical Edition), ed. Deborah Esch and Jonathan Warren (New York: W. W. Norton, 1999), 63.

61. In *The School and Society and The Child and the Curriculum* (Chicago: University of Chicago Press, 1990, 7), Dewey approvingly quotes these words of Horace Mann, who advocated for public schooling in the first half of the nineteenth century..

62. Henry James, *The Awkward Age* (New York: Penguin, 1966), 10.

63. Quoted in Mary Poovey, *Uneven Developments: The Ideological Work of Gender in Mid-Victorian England* (Chicago: University of Chicago Press, 1988), 130.

64. Jean Piaget, *The Construction of Reality in the Child* (London: Routledge, 1999).

65. Maria Edgeworth and Richard Lovell Edgeworth, *Practical Education* (London, 1798), 22; quoted in Teresa Michals, "Experiments Before Breakfast: Toys, Education, and Middle Class Childhood," in *The Nineteenth-Century Child and Consumer Culture*, ed. Denis Denisoff (New York: Routledge, 2014), 39.

66. Edgeworth, *Practical Education*, 2, quoted in Michals, "Experiments Before Breakfast," 39.

67. Henry James, *The Art of the Novel: Critical Prefaces*, ed. Richard P. Blackmur (New York: Scribner, 1962), 154.

68. Lexico, *Online Oxford English Dictionary*, https://www.lexico.com/en/definition/toy.

69. Steven Beschloss, "Object of Interest: Rube Goldberg Machines," *New Yorker*, July 2013, https://www.newyorker.com/tech/annals-of-technology/object-of-interest-rube-goldberg-machines.

70. Katherine Camp Mayhew and Anna Camp Edwards, *The Dewey School: The Laboratory School of the University of Chicago, 1896–1903* (New Brunswick, N.J.: Transaction, 1966), 34; L. S. Vygotsky, *Mind in Society: The Development of Higher Psychological Processes* (Cambridge, Mass.: Harvard University Press, 1978), 126.

71. Adam Phillips, "On Interest," *London Review of Books*, 20 June 1996, 12–14.

72. Shoshana Felman, "Turning the Screw of Interpretation," *Yale French Studies* 55–56 (1977): 94–207, 94.

73. In echoing the governess's insistence that "it is a game" and "it is a joke," Felman's dazzling reading picks up on so much that is resonant about the story's playfulness; moreover, her observation that the text's "twists and whirls" offer a "functional metaphor, the figure of dynamic functioning" (179) seems to me to be just right. The false move, to my mind, is Felman's suggestion that reading is an "enterprise of fixity and closure" (178) or of "stopping" (172) the play of signification. The intellectual vivacity and sustained generativity make her reading the *beau idéal* of spin-offs.

74. Robin Bernstein, *Racial Innocence: Performing American Childhood from Slavery to Civil Rights* (New York: New York University Press, 2011): "I use the term *script* as a theatrical practitioner might: to denote an evocative primary substance from which actors, directors, and designers build complex, variable performances that occupy real time and space" (12).

75. Hanson, "Screwing with Children," 369.

76. Elena Bodrova and Deborah J. Leong, "Vygotskian and Post-Vygotskian View on Children's Play," *American Journal of Play* 7, no. 3 (Spring 2015): 371–88, 373.

77. Henry James, *Art of the Novel*, 341–42.

78. Walter Benn Michaels, "Writers Reading: James and Eliot," *Modern Language Notes* 91, no. 5 (October 1976): 827–49, 833.

79. Nicholas J. Wade, "Philosophical Instruments and Toys: Optical Devices Extending the Art of Seeing," *Journal of the History of the Neurosciences* 13, no. 1 (2004): 102–24, 102.

80. Charles Wheatstone, quoted in Wade, "Philosophical Instruments and Toys," 108.

81. Wade, "Philosophical Instruments and Toys," 102–24.

82. John Ayrton Paris, *Philosophy in Sport Made Science in Earnest! Being an Attempt to Illustrate the First Principles of Natural Philosophy* (London: Sherwood, Gilbert, and Piper, 1833), 12.

83. Daniel Brown, *The Poetry of Victorian Scientists: Style, Science and Nonsense* (New York: Cambridge University Press, 2013), 33.

84. In *Chromographia: American Literature and the Modernization of Color* (Minneapolis: University of Minnesota Press, 2018), Nicholas Gaskill describes how a "color wheel"—a device created by Milton Bradley—was adopted by the first psychology labs in the United States: "William James and Hugo Münsterberg stocked them at Harvard, where Gertrude Stein, then a student at Radcliffe, adjusted the spinning colored disks to test the perception of color saturation" (3).

85. Impressionist painters in the 1890s were exploring how colors change depending on ambient lighting; readers today may recall the "blue/gold dress optical illusion" from 2015, in which gold stripes appeared black when bathed in yellow light. See *Wikipedia*, s.v. "The dress," last modified 15 July 2020, 22:56, https://en.wikipedia.org/wiki/The_dress.

86. Edward Fine et al., "Alice in Wonderland Syndrome: A History," *Neurology* 84, no. 14 (Supplement; 6 April 2015), https://n.neurology.org/content/84/14_Supplement/P6.337.

87. Henry James, *Art of the Novel*, 169.

88. Don Anderson, "'A Fury of Intention': The Scandal of Henry James' *The Turn of the Screw*," *Sydney Studies in English* 15 (1989): 140–52, 145.

89. William James, *The Principles of Psychology, Volume I* [1890] (New York: Henry Holt, 1918), 244.

90. Daniel M. Albert and David M. Gamm, "Blind Spot," *Encyclopedia Britannica Online*, last modified 21 January 2020, https://www.britannica.com/science/blind-spot.

91. Henry James, *Art of the Novel*, 170.

92. Henry James, letter to F. W. Myers dated 19 December 1898, *Henry James: A Life in Letters*, ed. Philip Horne (New York: Penguin Books, 2000), 314.

93. Clee, *Before Hollywood*, 46.

94. Henry James, *Art of the Novel*, 171.

95. Henry James, *Art of the Novel*, 172.

96. The Norton Critical Edition provides a footnote explaining that an "amusette" is "a piece of child's play" (*Screw*, 125).

97. Scott G. Eberle, "The Elements of Play: Toward a Philosophy and a Definition of Play," *American Journal of Play* 6, no. 2 (Winter 2014): 214–33, 227.

98. Huizinga, *Homo Ludens*, 11, 43.

99. Linda Martisiute, "Ten Terrifying Toys from the Past," Listverse.com, https://listverse.com/2016/08/23/10-terrifying-toys-from-the-past/. Accessed 2 August 2020.

100. The timeline is fairly efficiently and precisely rendered. The story begins on Christmas Eve (24 December); Douglas the next day sends for the "album" (25 December); it "reached him on the third of these days" (27 December); "he began to read to our hushed little circle on the night of the fourth" (28 December), and the reading itself "took indeed more nights than one" (30 or 31 December).

101. Felman, "Turning the Screw of Interpretation," 123.

102. Ryan Walsh describes ekphrasis as fundamentally about translating images into words: "Many scholars make use of James Heffernan's general conception of ekphrasis as "'the verbal representation of visual representation.'" Walsh goes on to describe W. J. T. Mitchell's description of "ekphrastic fear": "Mitchell writes, 'This is the moment of resistance or counterdesire that occurs when we sense that the difference between "the verbal and the visual representation might collapse and the figurative, imaginary desire of ekphrasis might be realized literally and actually"'";

see Walsh's entry in the University of Chicago *Theories of Media Keywords Glossary* (Winter 2007), http://csmt.uchicago.edu/glossary2004/ekphrasis.htm.

103. Henry James, *Art of the Novel*, 172, 173.

104. J. L. Austin, *How to Do Things with Words* (Cambridge, Mass.: Harvard University Press, 1975): "When I say, before the registrar or altar, &c., 'I do,' I am not reporting on a marriage: I am indulging in it" (6).

105. Henry James, *The Novels and Tales of Henry James*, vol. 12 (New York: Scribner, 1908), vi.

106. Graham Good, *The Observing Self: Rediscovering the Essay* (New York: Routledge, 2014), 103.

107. Hershel Parker notes that while many scholars of James's work have applauded the prefaces as works of criticism in their own right, they nonetheless bemoan the editorial changes that James brought to bear on the works themselves: "Aesthetic blindness and bullheaded denial were part of his day-to-day life during the preparation of the New York Edition. In the prefaces he displayed great joy in his memories of writing some of the very fictions he had just been coarsening in his revisions" ("Deconstructing *The Art of the Novel* and Liberating James's Prefaces," *Henry James Review* 14, no. 3 [Fall 1993]: 284–307, 292).

108. Henry James, *Art of the Novel*, 160.

109. Henry James, *The Aspern Papers and The Turn of the Screw* (New York: Penguin Books, 1987), x.

110. Wittgenstein, *Philosophical Investigations*, 224e.

111. Jonathan Crary, *Techniques of the Observer: On Vision and Modernity in the Nineteenth Century* (Cambridge, Mass.: MIT Press, 1992), 14.

112. Tom Gunning, "Hand and Eye: Excavating a New Technology of the Image in the Victorian Era," *Victorian Studies* 54, no. 3 (2012): 495–516.

113. Charles Babbage, *Passages from the Life of a Philosopher* (London: Longman, 1864), 189.

114. Walter Benn Michaels described the either/or critical debate in succinct terms: "What people want to know still seems to be, is it a ghost story or a psychological thriller, and critics are still aligning themselves either on what Martha Banta calls the 'Far Left, anti-ghost, pro-Freudian' position or the 'Far Right, pro-ghost, pro-religious' position"; "Writers Reading: James and Eliot," 831.

115. Edmund Wilson, *The Triple Thinkers: Twelve Essays on Literary Subjects* (New York: Farrar, Straus and Giroux, 1976), 170–73.

116. Daniel Kahneman, *Thinking, Fast and Slow* (New York: Farrar, Straus and Giroux, 2011), 11.

117. Donna Haraway, "SF: Science Fiction, Speculative Fabulation, String Figures, So Far," *ADA: A Journal of Gender, Technology, and New Media* 3 (2013), https://adanewmedia.org/2013/11/issue3-haraway/.

118. John Ayrton Paris, *Science in Sport Made Philosophy in Earnest: Being an Attempt to Illustrate Some Elementary Principles of Physical Knowledge by Means of Toys and Pastimes*, ed. Robert Routledge (New York, 1877), 12–13, emphasis added.

119. Stephen R. Mitroff et al., "Reversing How to Think About Ambiguous Figure Reversals: Spontaneous Alternating by Uninformed Observers," *Journal of Vision* 6, no. 52 (June 2006): 1–6, 2, http://alisongopnik.com/Papers_Alison/MitroffSobelGopnik.pdf.

120. Michael Bérubé, "A Theory of Theory of Mind," *American Scientist* 101, no. 2 (March–April 2013): 148, https://www.americanscientist.org/article/a-theory-of-theory-of-mind.

121. Jörgen L. Pind, "Looking Back: Figure and Ground at 100," *The Psychologist* 25 (January 2012): 90–91, 90.

122. William James, *Writings: 1902–1910*, 217.

123. Pericles Lewis, "'The Reality of the Unseen': Shared Fictions and Religious Experience in the Ghost Stories of Henry James," *Arizona Quarterly*, 61 no. 2 (Summer 2005): 33–66, 33.

124. Huizinga, *Homo Ludens*, 15.

125. Crary, *Techniques of the Observer*, 127.

126. Stephen Best and Sharon Marcus, "Surface Reading: An Introduction," *Representations* 108, no. 1 (Fall 2009): 1–21.

127. Henry James, "The Jolly Corner," in *Tales of Henry James*, 313.

128. William James, *Psychology: Briefer Course* [1892], in *Writings: 1878–1899*, 159.

129. Henri Bergson, *An Introduction to Metaphysics* (New York: G. P. Putnam's Sons, 1912), 11.

130. William James, *Psychology: Briefer Course*, 154.

131. Henri Bergson, *Creative Evolution* (New York: H. Holt, 1911), 308.

132. "Infinitesmal calculus," *Encyclopedia of Mathematics*, last revised 5 June 2020, https://encyclopediaofmath.org/wiki/Infinitesimal_calculus.

133. Gregory Flaxman, "Cinema Year Zero," in *The Brain Is the Screen: Deleuze and the Philosophy of Cinema*, ed. Gregory Flaxman (Minneapolis: University of Minnesota Press, 2000), 87–108, 88.

134. Henry James, *The American Scene* (New York: Harper and Brothers, 1907), 4.

135. Notably, there is a lack of clarity in the meaning of the term "clear": it could signify "easy to perceive," and it could also mean "unmarked" (or in reference to a coin, unembossed). The meanings and distinctions easily oscillate, coalesce, overlap, fall apart—as with a thaumatrope, one can (almost) endlessly play with the different sides of the simplest-seeming term.

136. Mark Schiebe, "Stereo Rivalry in 'The Jolly Corner,'" *American Literary Realism* 50, no. 1 (Fall 2017): 49–62, 50.

137. Münsterberg, *The Film: A Psychological Study*, 20.

138. Corners were prime real estate for New York City's movie palaces. The early locations for viewing movies were vaudeville theaters; in 1886 "The Corner" opened at the intersection of Twenty-third Street and Sixth Avenue. "Koster and Bial's Music Hall," *Experience NoMad* (25 September 2015), accessed 21 May 2019, https://experiencenomad.com/koster-and-bials-music-hall/.

139. Luke Thurston, in *Literary Ghosts from the Victorians to Modernism: The Haunting Interval* (New York: Routledge, 2012), reads the relationship between Brydon and Alice as a *folie à deux*: "It is a conversation between Norman Bates and his mother. Within a penumbral private world locked away from the harsh 'masculine' light of the city outside, an imaginary twin is granted existence as both Spencer's rival and his naughty self" (84). I am suggesting quite the opposite: that the mutual seeing affirms the public space (problematically) figured by the rise of moving picture palaces. Thurston makes the connection to *Guy Domville* but arrives at conclusions very different from the argument I make in this chapter.

CONCLUSION

1. Johan Huizinga, *Homo Ludens: A Study of the Play-Element in Culture* (Kettering, Ohio: Angelico Press, 2016), 75.

2. The chapters in this book are presented in the sequence in which the siblings died. This telescoping order—from shortest to longest lived—acknowledges that the writings of the

surviving siblings continued the familial conversation and indeed responded to the loss of each in turn. Alice James died before William and Henry, in 1892; WJ passed away in 1910; and HJ lived until 1916. Strikingly, it was not until forty-two years after AJ's death that a heavily edited version of her Diary was published, under the title *Alice James ~ Her Brothers ~ Her Journal* (ed. Anna Robeson Burr [Cornwall, N.Y.: Dodd, Mead, 1934]).

3. Alice James, *The Diary of Alice James*, ed. Leon Edel (Boston: Northeastern University Press, 1999), 127.

4. William James, *The Varieties of Religious Experience*, in *Writings: 1902–1910,* ed. Bruce Kuklick (New York: Library of America, 1987), 345.

5. Henry James, *The Art of the Novel: Critical Prefaces*, ed. Richard P. Blackmur (New York: Scribner, 1962), 345.

6. Brian Sutton-Smith, "Play Theory: A Personal Journal and New Thoughts," *American Journal of Play* 1, no. 1 (Summer 2008): 82–128, 97.

INDEX

ACKNOWLEDGMENTS

As with so many second projects, this one had a long gestation. In the fifteen years since book number one, my husband and I raised two lovely daughters and lost three beloved parents; I cofounded a health humanities lab and grieved the death of the friend who inspired it; I became depressed and recovered my equilibrium through a potent combination of people, pharmaceuticals, and play. Exhilarated and a bit stunned at this project's completion, I am eager to thank everyone who helped coax *Philosophical Siblings* into existence.

First, my thanks to Jerry Singerman of Penn Press. Jerry is the most tolerant and erudite editor a writer could ask for; he made me look forward to MLA, where his patience, high expectations, and restaurant recommendations gave me the sustenance to carry on. It was a joy, too, to work with Noreen O'Connor-Abel.

Thanks to my colleagues at UNC, whose intellectual energy fueled my thinking and animates these pages: Danielle Christmas, Pam Cooper, Tyler Curtain, Eric Downing, Jordynn Jack, Joy Kasson, John McGowan, Michelle Robinson, and Matthew Taylor. Kym Weed—who has moved from student to colleague and friend—has been a steadfast ally throughout. Writing alongside Eliza Richards, with her sympathy and insight, kept me on course during an especially rocky summer. I am indebted to friends in other fields who fertilized my thinking: Sue Coppola, Laurie Maffly-Kipp, Cherie Rosemond, Michele Rivkin-Fish, and Raj Telhan. Talented research assistants Elisabeth McClanahan Harris and Kylan Rice helped with every aspect of the manuscript, from obtaining images to making astute edits. My department chair, Mary Floyd-Wilson, approved a research leave at a critical moment, giving me space to bring the project to a close. Jennifer Washington, office manager extraordinaire, has ushered me through all the logistical hurdles along the way—with a dazzling smile!

I have been lucky to work with wonderful graduate students (now professors) with whom I first tested out ideas about childhood, play, and the Jameses: warm thanks to Kelly Bezio, Nathaniel Cadle, Graham Culbertson, Allison

Curseen, Josh Doty, Jen McDaneld, Jit Pruttipurk, and Ashley Reed. Nicholas Gaskill has been a fabulous sounding board from start to finish. In 2019, I had the pleasure of hashing out these ideas with students in my James Family class: Brendan Chambers, Emily Long, Elisabeth McClanahan Harris, Sally Greene, Theodore Nollert, Ian Sawyer, and Jordan Williamson. I am grateful to Grant Glass, for his electronic wizardry; and to Heath Sledge, who gracefully moved from student to teacher with her careful edits of the Introduction.

A writing retreat on Bald Head Island with Joy Goodwin and Jan Koelb helped spark the book into being. Priscilla Wald's early enthusiasm for the project gave me the confidence to forge ahead. Participants in the Wildbrook Institute for Second Projects provided savvy advice and hilarity: big thanks to WISPers Elizabeth Duquette, Jennie Kassanoff (who suggested the title), and Stacey Margolis. Joining me in the Berkshires, Scott Black and Lauren Shohet witnessed as I pieced together an early draft in strips of paper on the floor. I am sincerely grateful to Hitomi Nabae, Katsunori Takeushi, Megan Marshall, and the many Americanists I met during a 2017 lecture tour in Japan, where I shared early versions of these chapters.

I am indebted to colleagues who gave wise suggestions for revisions. Penn Press enlisted gifted scholars to review the manuscript: a heartfelt "thank you for the surgery" to Paul Gilmore and Jennifer Fleissner. Randall Knoper has been a good friend and colleague; I relish our Amherst conversations and value his critical eye. For their generosity as readers, interlocutors, and role models, I am grateful to Cynthia Davis, Brad Evans, Shari Goldberg, Ross Posnock, Karen Sanchez-Eppler, and Greg Zacharias.

Jeanne Follansbee and Ann Keniston have been fellow travelers in the land of academia for twenty-five years; it's hard to imagine accomplishing anything without their sparkling minds and beautiful friendship.

In the final year of writing, I had ongoing back-and-forths with a fantastic group of tennis players, including Stacy Brehm, Lynn Farber, Melissa Fitzpatrick, Brook Holton Sheehan, Amy Strong, Anna Tomkins, and many others: thank you for tolerating my questions and musings in between games!

To the dear friends who have offered advice, sipped martinis, and buoyed my spirits over the years it took to write this book, thank you! Thinking of you, Ada Adimora, Jane Anderson, Mimi Chapman, Faulkner Fox, Karen Kemp, Julia Knerr, Alex Lightfoot, Jenni Owen, Jane Satter, Courtney Van Houtven, Bill Wofford, and Ginger Young. Friends from farther afield have been stalwart champions over the years, which have mysteriously morphed into decades: my love and gratitude to Ruthanne Deutsch, Jon Kranes, Carmen MacDougall, and Ira Paneth.

Thanks to my extended family: my own philosophical siblings, David Thrailkill and Elsbeth Miller; my soul sisters, Carol Fawcett, BJ Thrailkill, Alice Truax & Betsy Tanner, and Susanna Wenniger; and everyone at Fernside, where I put the book to bed. My remarkable mother-in-law, Elizabeth Kramer, was the first to read a full draft and among the last to help whittle it down; her cheering words gave me the buoyancy to finish.

And to my lifelong playmates Hawley, Naomi, and Olivia Truax: you are my inspiration! Here's to many more decades of love and fun.